ZENESCOPE ENTERTAINMENT PRESENTS

Grimm Fairy Tales

UNLEASHED

Volume One

zenescope

Grimm Fairy Tales UNLEASHED

Volume One

GRIMM FAIRY TALES CREATED BY
JOE BRUSHA AND RALPH TEDESCO

STORY
**PAT SHAND
RAVEN GREGORY
JOE BRUSHA
RALPH TEDESCO**

WRITER
PAT SHAND

ART DIRECTOR
ANTHONY SPAY

TRADE DESIGN
CHRISTOPHER COTE

EDITOR
RALPH TEDESCO

ASSISTANT EDITORS
**MATT ROGERS
HANNAH GORFINKEL**

THIS VOLUME REPRINTS THE
COMIC SERIES GRIMM FAIRY TALES
UNLEASHED ISSUES #0-3 AND
"A SHADOW FALLS" FROM BEST
OF ZENESCOPE SPECIAL EDITION
PUBLISHED BY ZENESCOPE
ENTERTAINMENT.

WWW.ZENESCOPE.COM

FIRST EDITION, JULY 2013
ISBN: 978-1-939683-01-4

ZENESCOPE ENTERTAINMENT, INC.

Joe Brusha • President & Chief Creative Officer
Ralph Tedesco • Editor-in-Chief
Jennifer Bermel • Director of Licensing & Business Development
Raven Gregory • Executive Editor
Anthony Spay • Art Director
Christopher Cote • Senior Designer/Production Manager
Dave Franchini • Direct Market Sales & Customer Service
Stephen Haberman • Marketing Manager

zenescope
WWW.ZENESCOPE.COM
FACEBOOK.COM/ZENESCOPE

GRIMM UNIVERSE

Grimm Fairy Tales

UNLEASHED

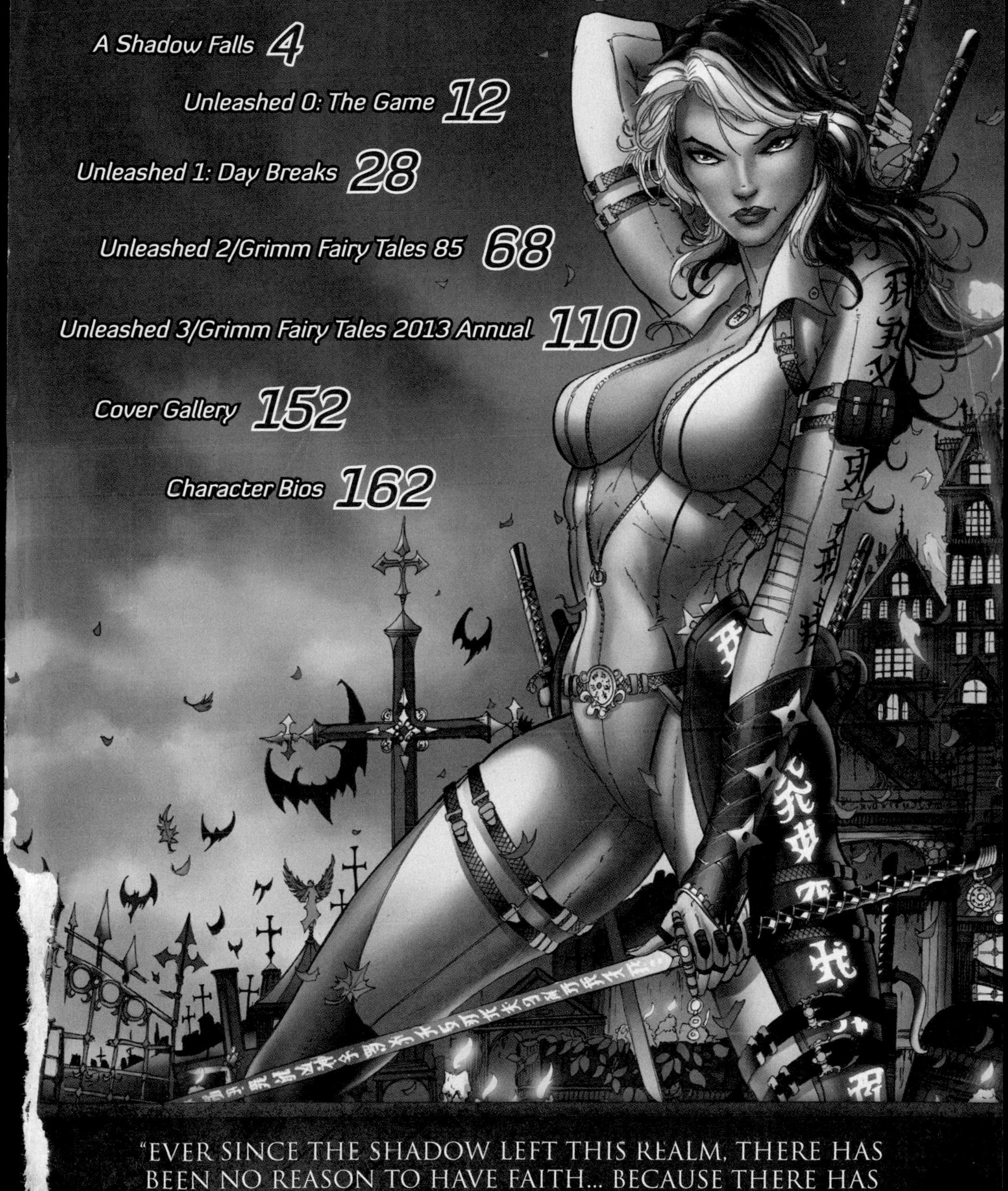

"EVER SINCE THE SHADOW LEFT THIS REALM, THERE HAS BEEN NO REASON TO HAVE FAITH... BECAUSE THERE HAS BEEN NOTHING TO BE TRULY AFRAID OF."

—THE BEING

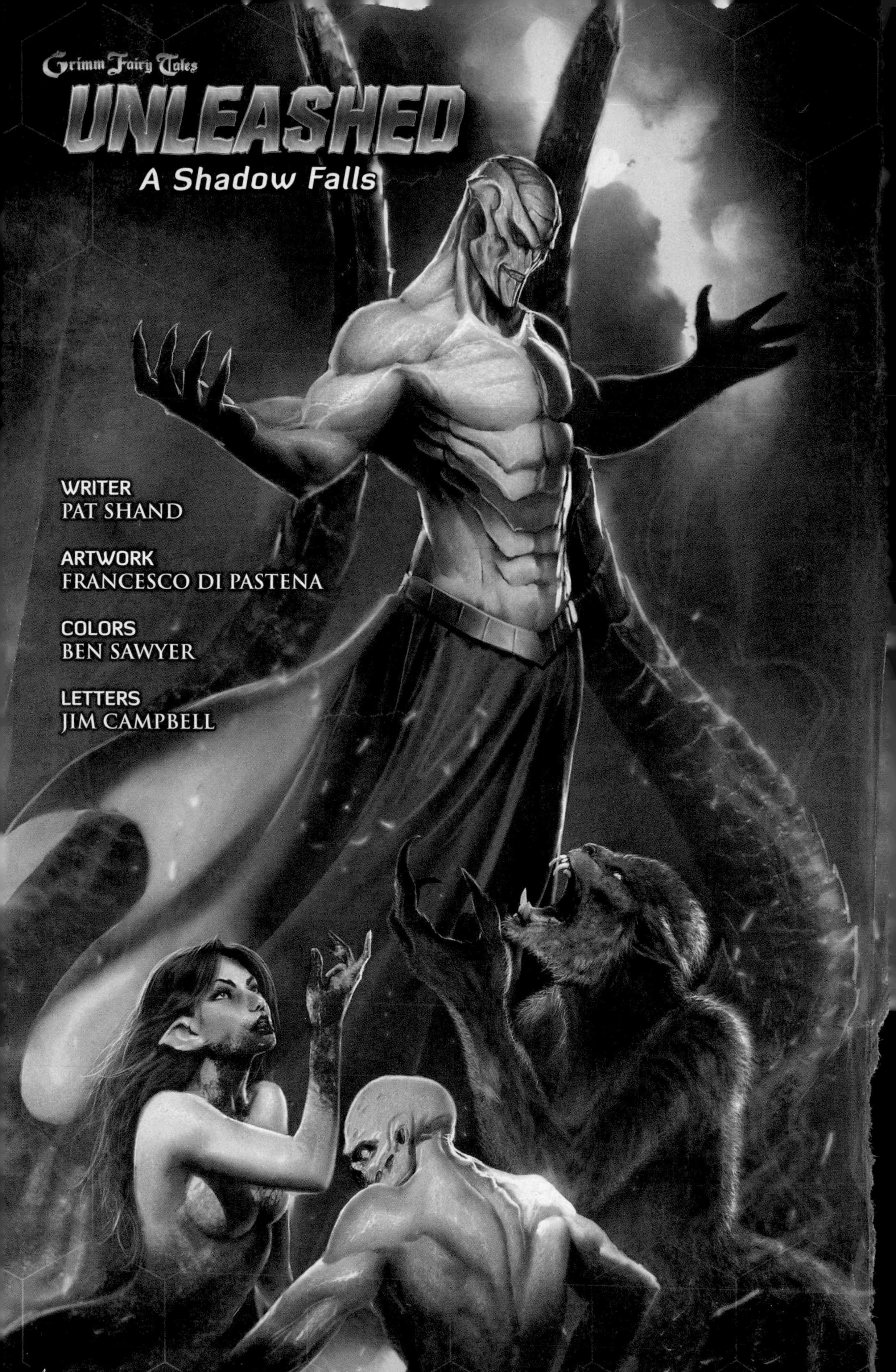
Grimm Fairy Tales
UNLEASHED
A Shadow Falls
WRITER
PAT SHAND
ARTWORK
FRANCESCO DI PASTENA
COLORS
BEN SAWYER
LETTERS
JIM CAMPBELL

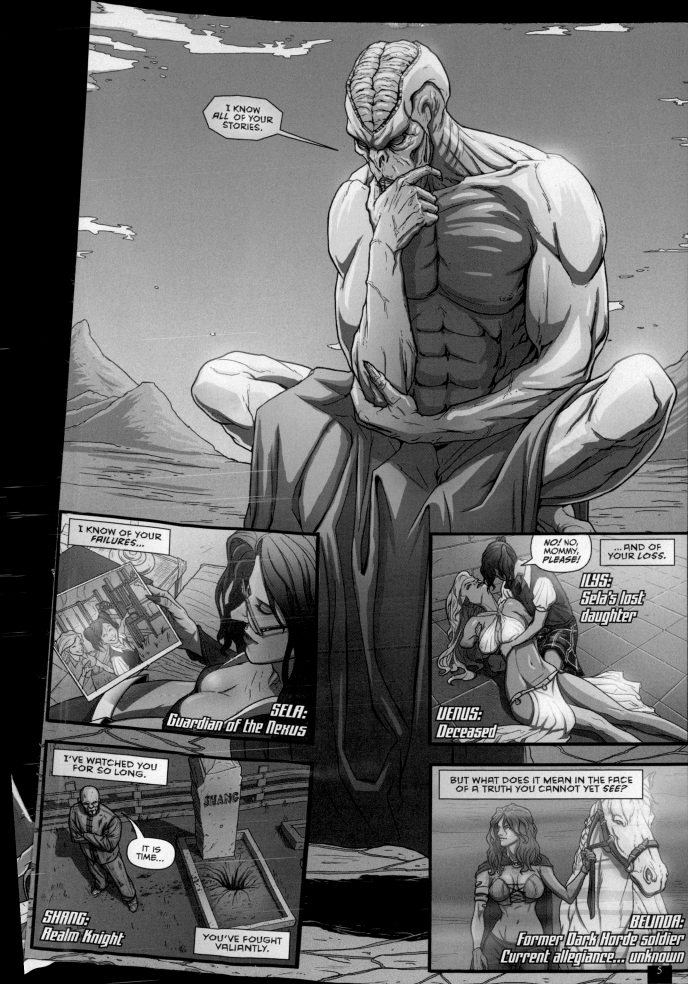

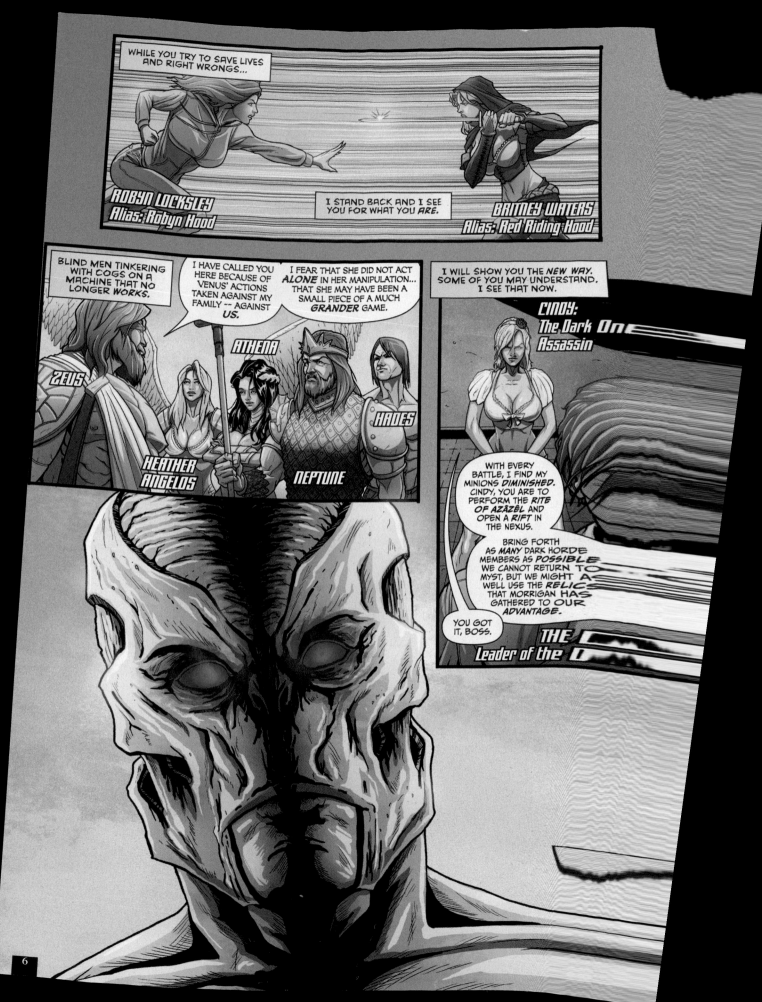

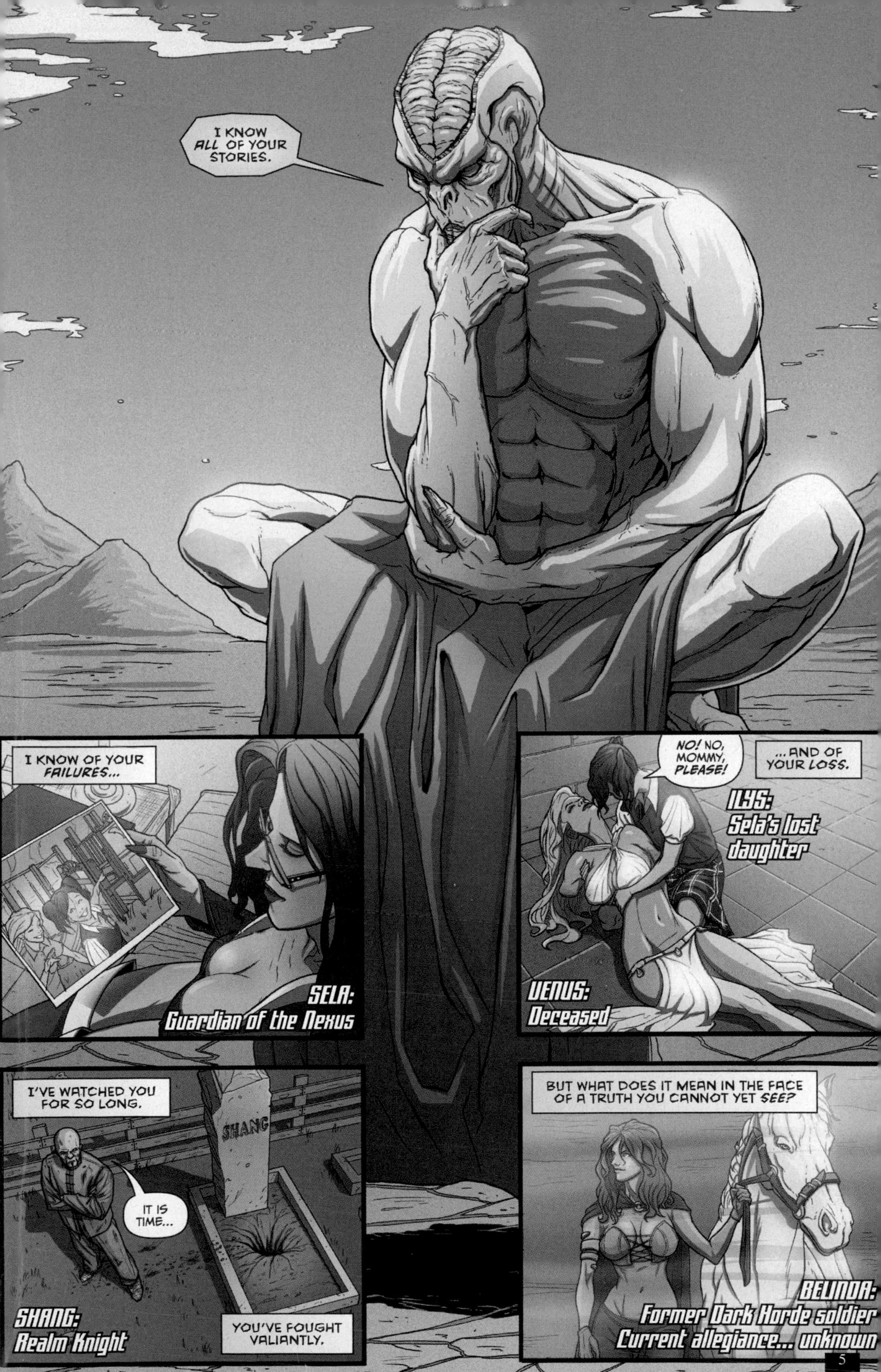
I KNOW ALL OF YOUR STORIES.
I KNOW OF YOUR FAILURES...
SELA: Guardian of the Nexus
NO! NO, MOMMY, PLEASE!
...AND OF YOUR LOSS.
ILYS: Sela's lost daughter
VENUS: Deceased
I'VE WATCHED YOU FOR SO LONG.
SHANG
IT IS TIME...
SHANG: Realm Knight
YOU'VE FOUGHT VALIANTLY.
BUT WHAT DOES IT MEAN IN THE FACE OF A TRUTH YOU CANNOT YET SEE?
BELINDA: Former Dark Horde soldier
Current allegiance... unknown

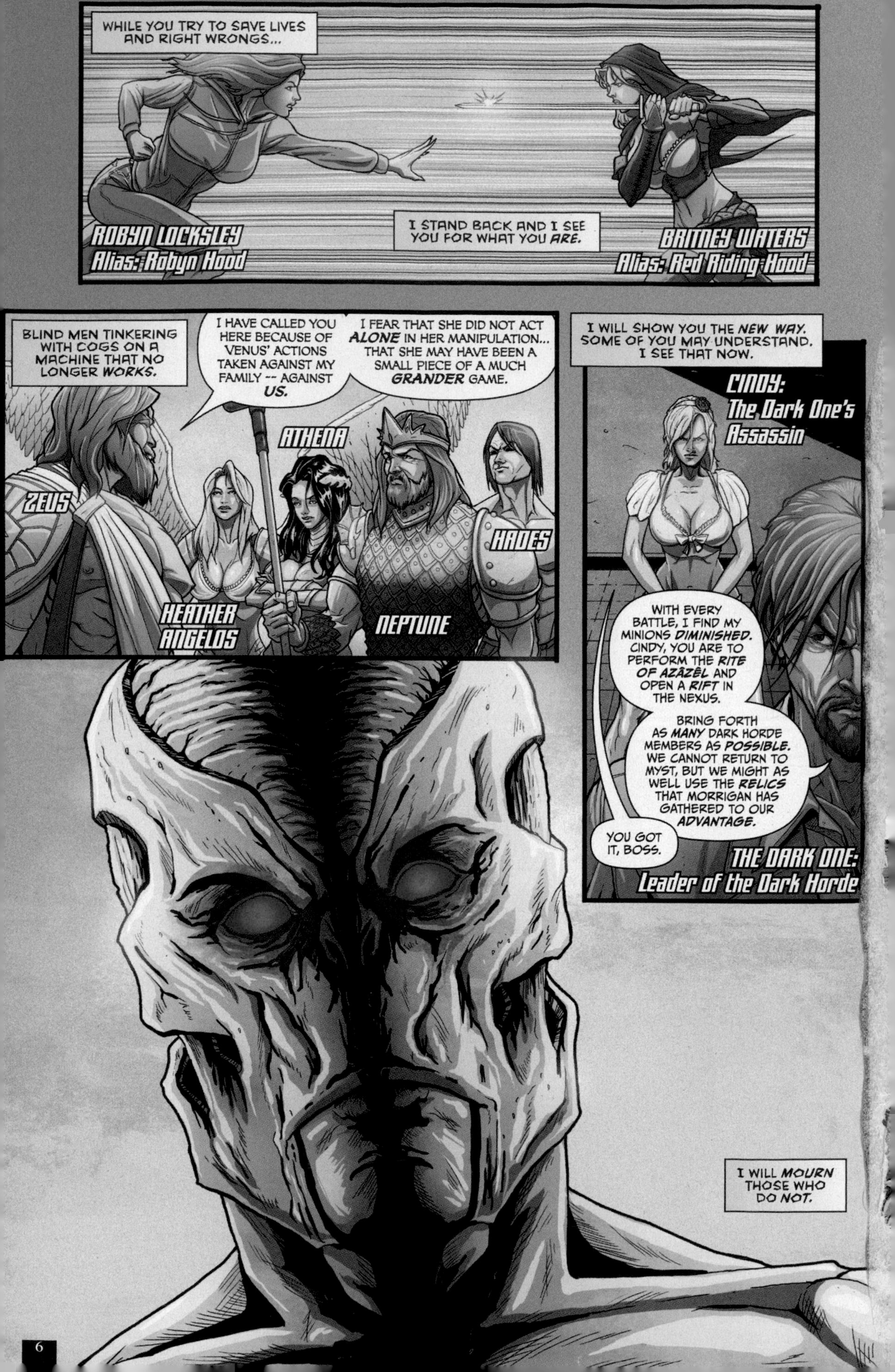

WHILE YOU TRY TO SAVE LIVES AND RIGHT WRONGS...
ROBYN LOCKSLEY Alias: Robyn Hood
I STAND BACK AND I SEE YOU FOR WHAT YOU ARE.
BRITNEY WATERS Alias: Red Riding Hood
BLIND MEN TINKERING WITH COGS ON A MACHINE THAT NO LONGER WORKS.
I HAVE CALLED YOU HERE BECAUSE OF VENUS' ACTIONS TAKEN AGAINST MY FAMILY -- AGAINST US.
I FEAR THAT SHE DID NOT ACT ALONE IN HER MANIPULATION... THAT SHE MAY HAVE BEEN A SMALL PIECE OF A MUCH GRANDER GAME.
ATHENA
ZEUS
HADES
HEATHER ANGELOS
NEPTUNE
I WILL SHOW YOU THE NEW WAY. SOME OF YOU MAY UNDERSTAND. I SEE THAT NOW.
CINDY: The Dark One's Assassin
WITH EVERY BATTLE, I FIND MY MINIONS DIMINISHED. CINDY, YOU ARE TO PERFORM THE RITE OF AZÂZÊL AND OPEN A RIFT IN THE NEXUS.
BRING FORTH AS MANY DARK HORDE MEMBERS AS POSSIBLE. WE CANNOT RETURN TO MYST, BUT WE MIGHT AS WELL USE THE RELICS THAT MORRIGAN HAS GATHERED TO OUR ADVANTAGE.
YOU GOT IT, BOSS.
THE DARK ONE: Leader of the Dark Horde
I WILL MOURN THOSE WHO DO NOT.

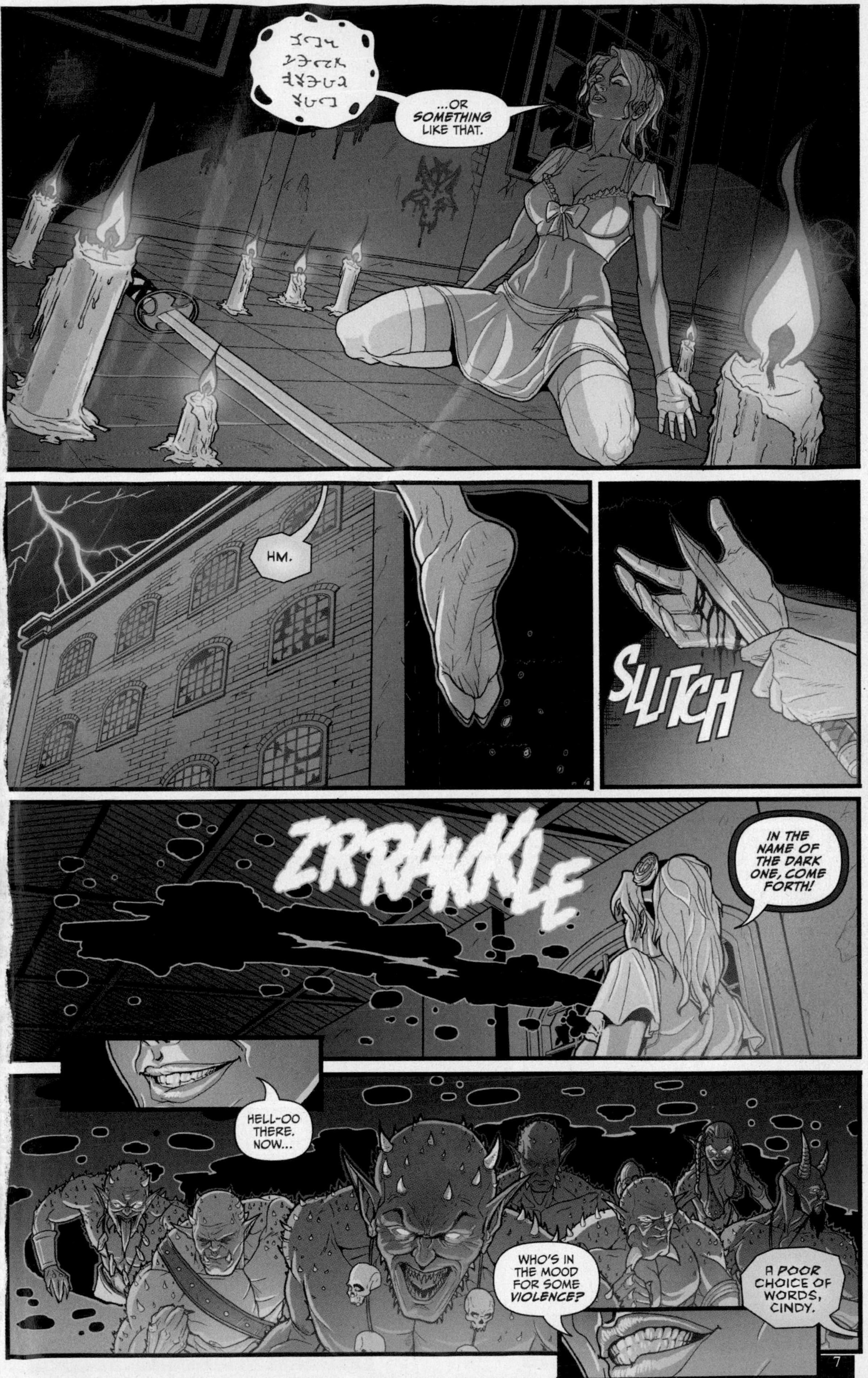

...OR SOMETHING LIKE THAT.
HM.
SLUTCH
ZRRAKKLE
IN THE NAME OF THE DARK ONE, COME FORTH!
HELL-OO THERE. NOW...
WHO'S IN THE MOOD FOR SOME VIOLENCE?
A POOR CHOICE OF WORDS, CINDY.

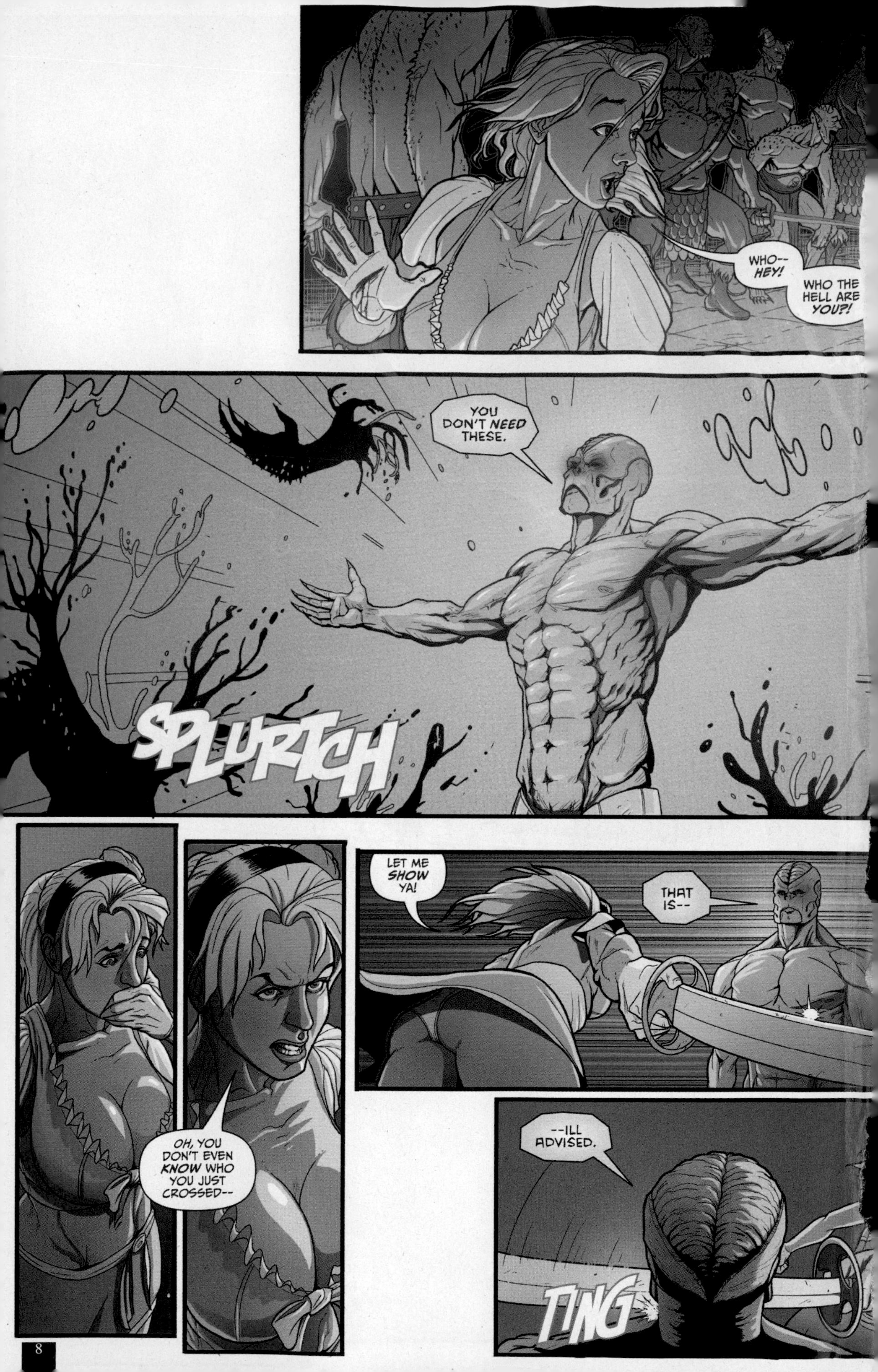
WHO-- HEY!
WHO THE HELL ARE YOU?!
YOU DON'T NEED THESE.
SPLURTCH
OH, YOU DON'T EVEN KNOW WHO YOU JUST CROSSED--
LET ME SHOW YA!
THAT IS--
--ILL ADVISED.
TING

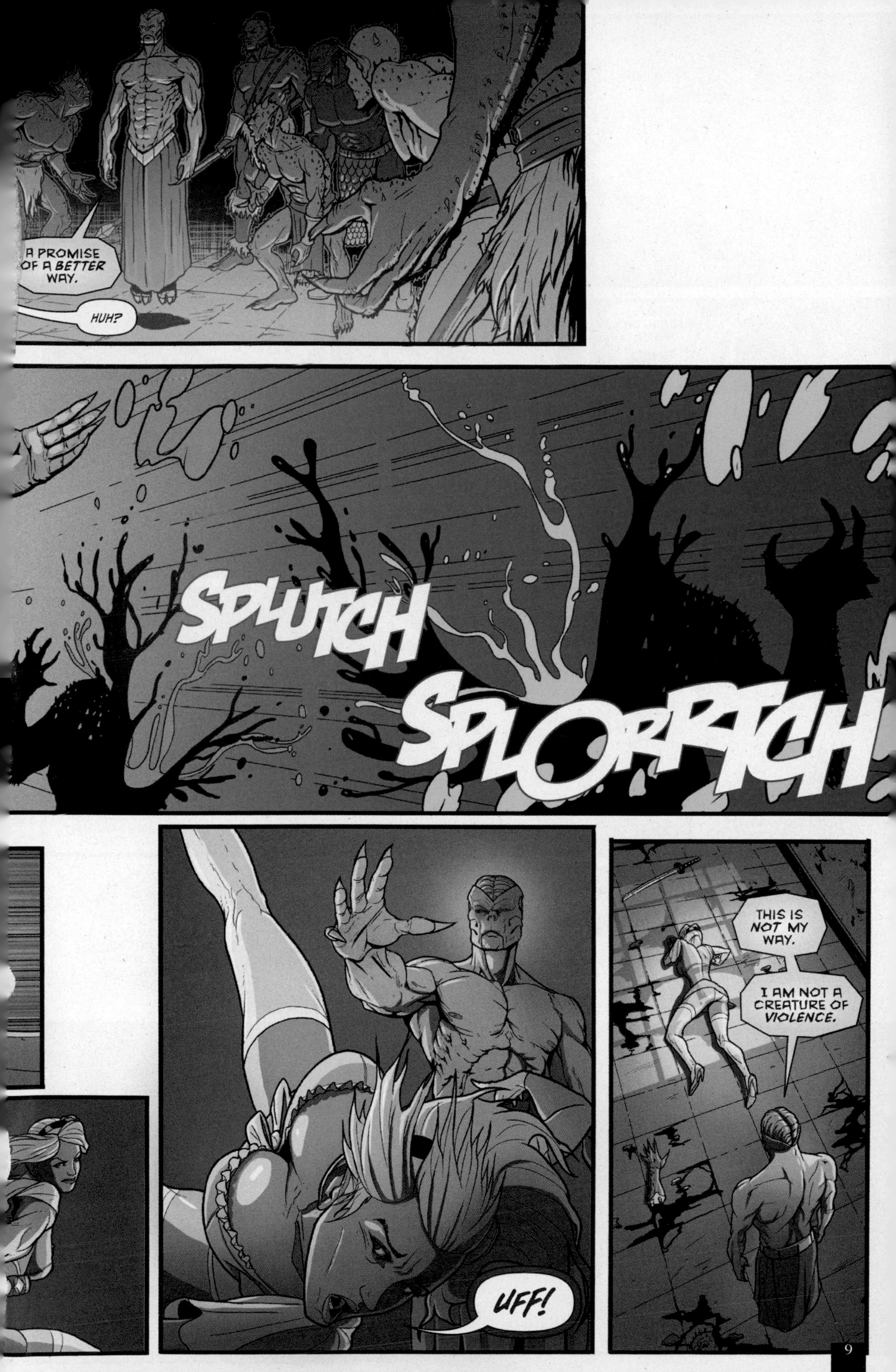
A PROMISE OF A BETTER WAY.
HUH?
SPLUTCH
SPLORRTCH
UFF!
THIS IS NOT MY WAY.
I AM NOT A CREATURE OF VIOLENCE.

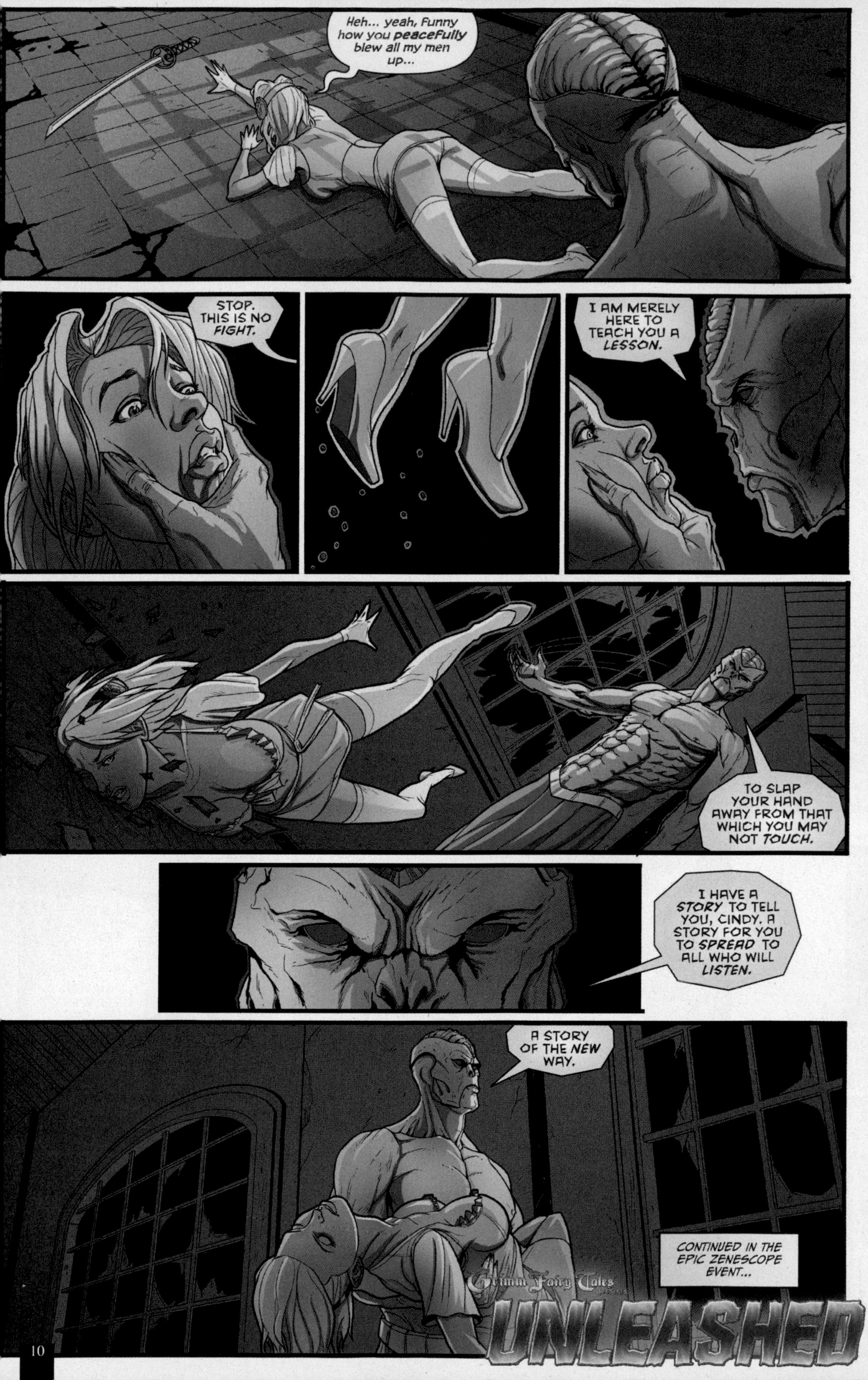
Heh... yeah, funny how you peacefully blew all my men up...
STOP. THIS IS NO FIGHT.
I AM MERELY HERE TO TEACH YOU A LESSON.
TO SLAP YOUR HAND AWAY FROM THAT WHICH YOU MAY NOT TOUCH.
I HAVE A STORY TO TELL YOU, CINDY. A STORY FOR YOU TO SPREAD TO ALL WHO WILL LISTEN.
A STORY OF THE NEW WAY.
CONTINUED IN THE EPIC ZENESCOPE EVENT...
Grimm Fairy Tales
UNLEASHED

Grimm Fairy Tales

UNLEASHED

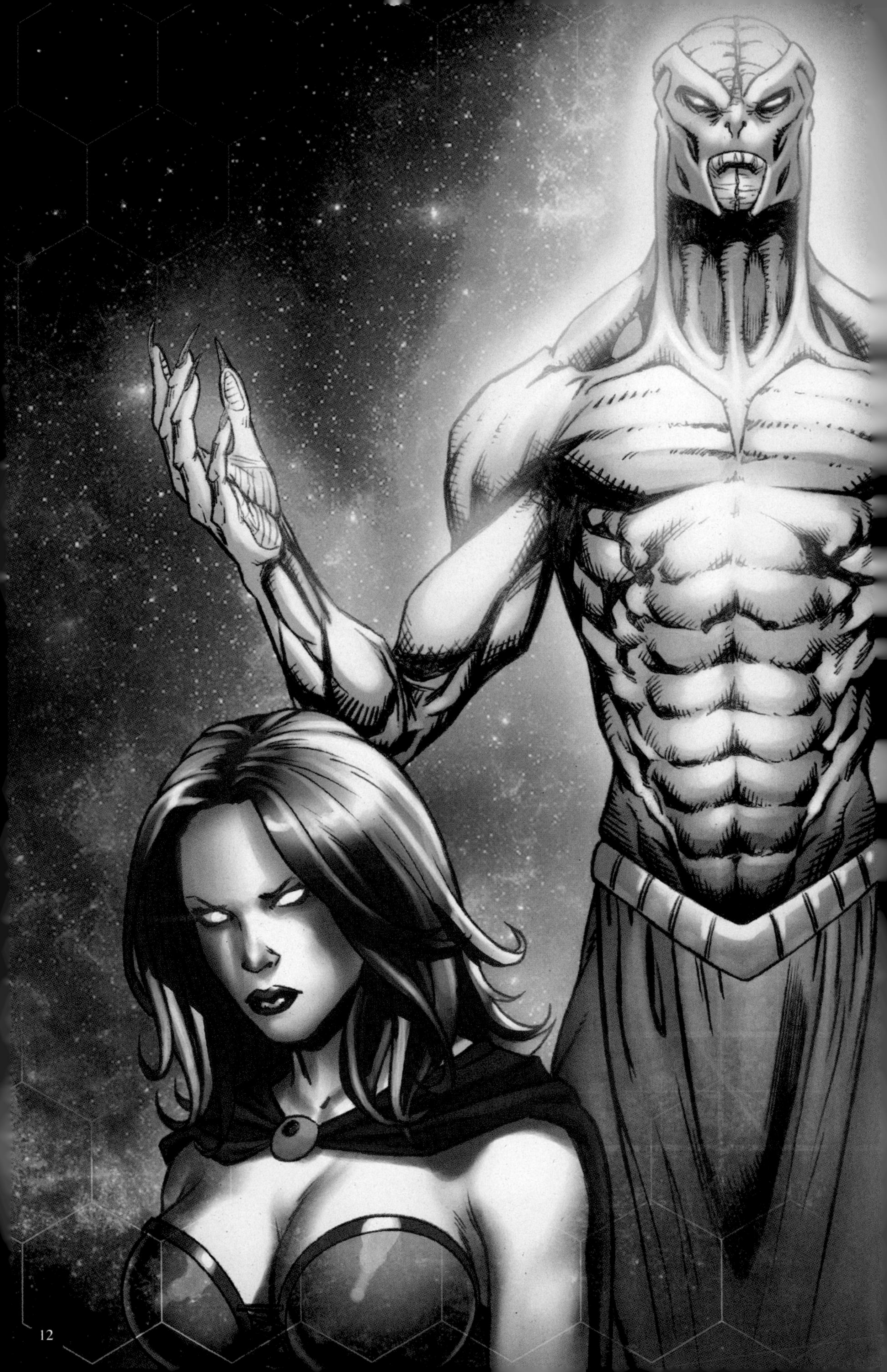

Grimm Fairy Tales

UNLEASHED

Part 0: The Game

WRITER
PAT SHAND

ARTWORK
NEI RUFFINO

LETTERS
JIM CAMPBELL

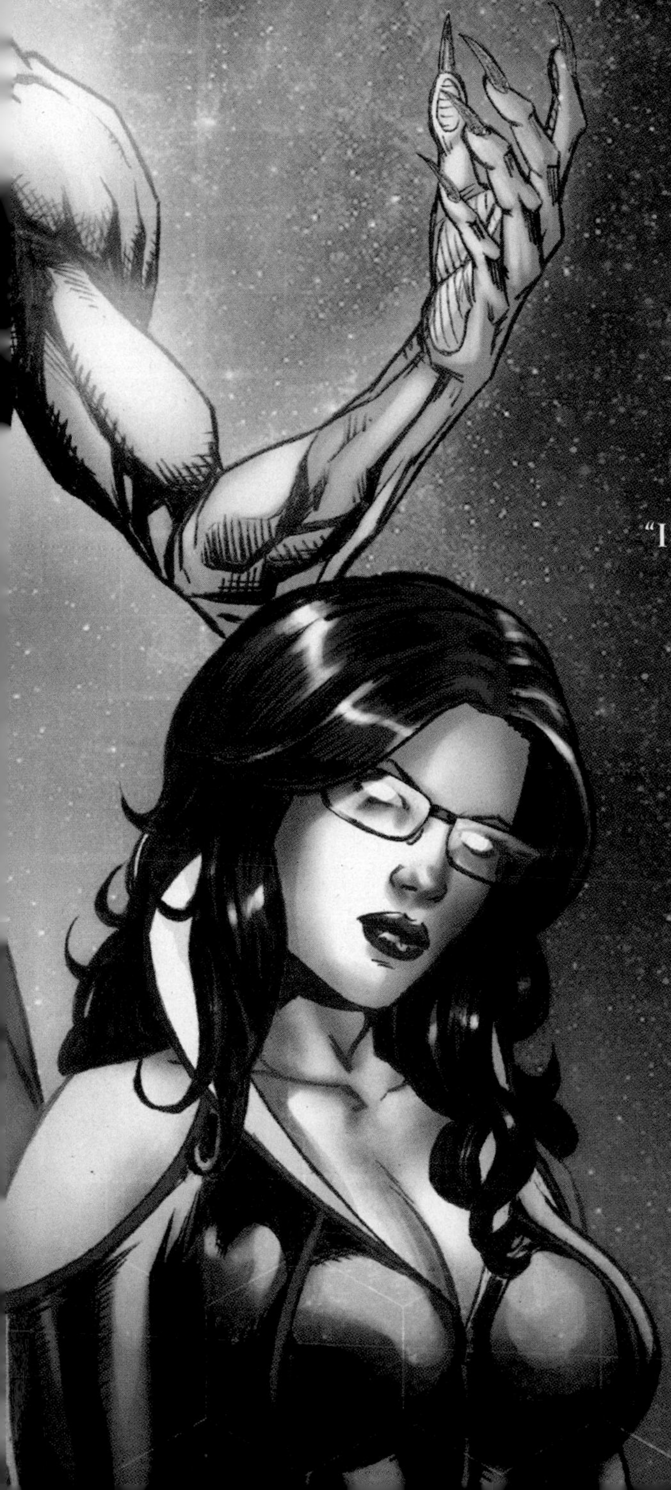

"I AM NOT A CREATURE OF *VIOLENCE*."
—THE BEING

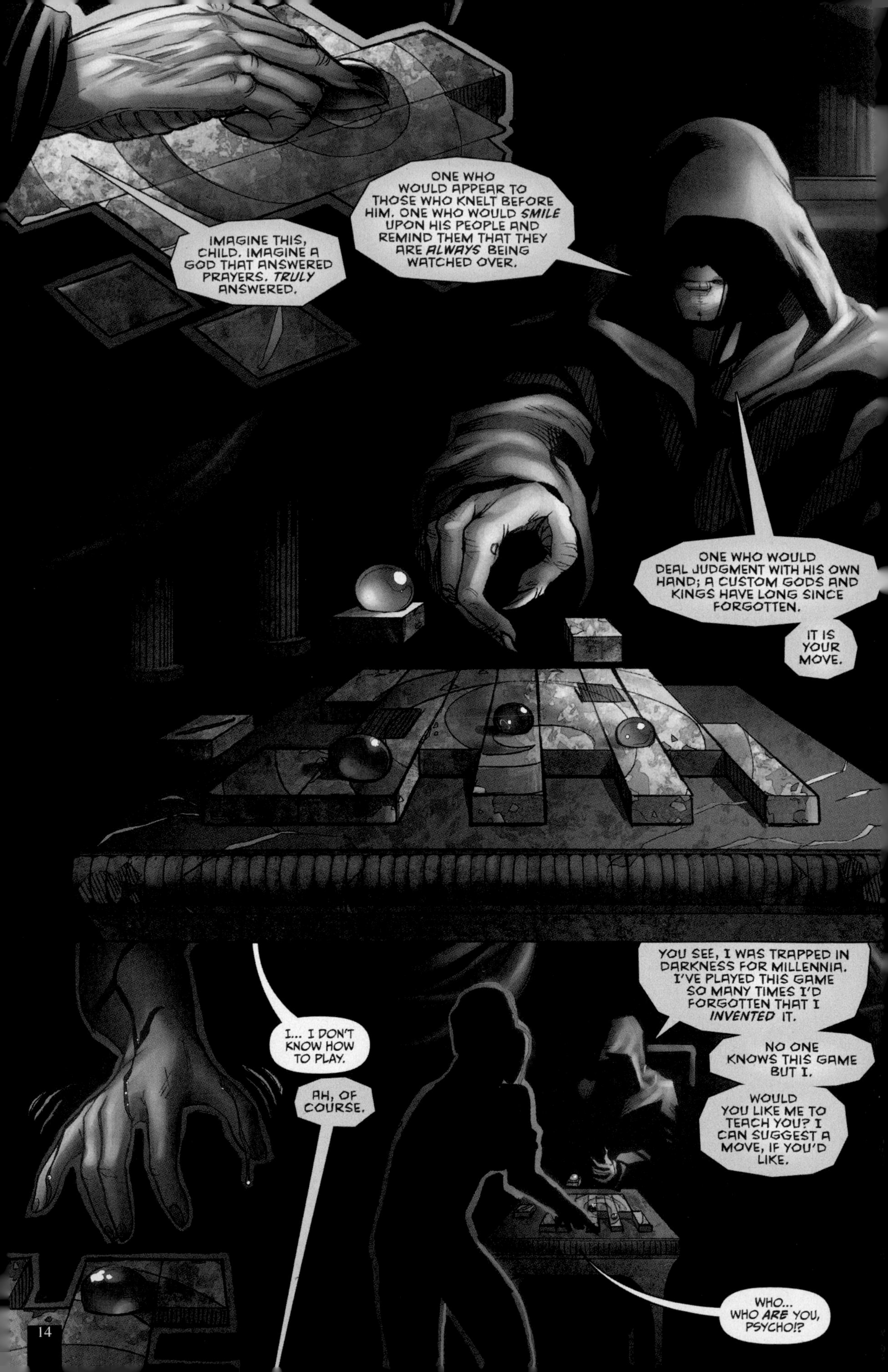
IMAGINE THIS, CHILD. IMAGINE A GOD THAT ANSWERED PRAYERS. TRULY ANSWERED.
ONE WHO WOULD APPEAR TO THOSE WHO KNELT BEFORE HIM. ONE WHO WOULD SMILE UPON HIS PEOPLE AND REMIND THEM THAT THEY ARE ALWAYS BEING WATCHED OVER.
ONE WHO WOULD DEAL JUDGMENT WITH HIS OWN HAND; A CUSTOM GODS AND KINGS HAVE LONG SINCE FORGOTTEN.
IT IS YOUR MOVE.
I... I DON'T KNOW HOW TO PLAY.
AH, OF COURSE.
YOU SEE, I WAS TRAPPED IN DARKNESS FOR MILLENNIA. I'VE PLAYED THIS GAME SO MANY TIMES I'D FORGOTTEN THAT I INVENTED IT.
NO ONE KNOWS THIS GAME BUT I.
WOULD YOU LIKE ME TO TEACH YOU? I CAN SUGGEST A MOVE, IF YOU'D LIKE.
WHO... WHO ARE YOU, PSYCHO!?

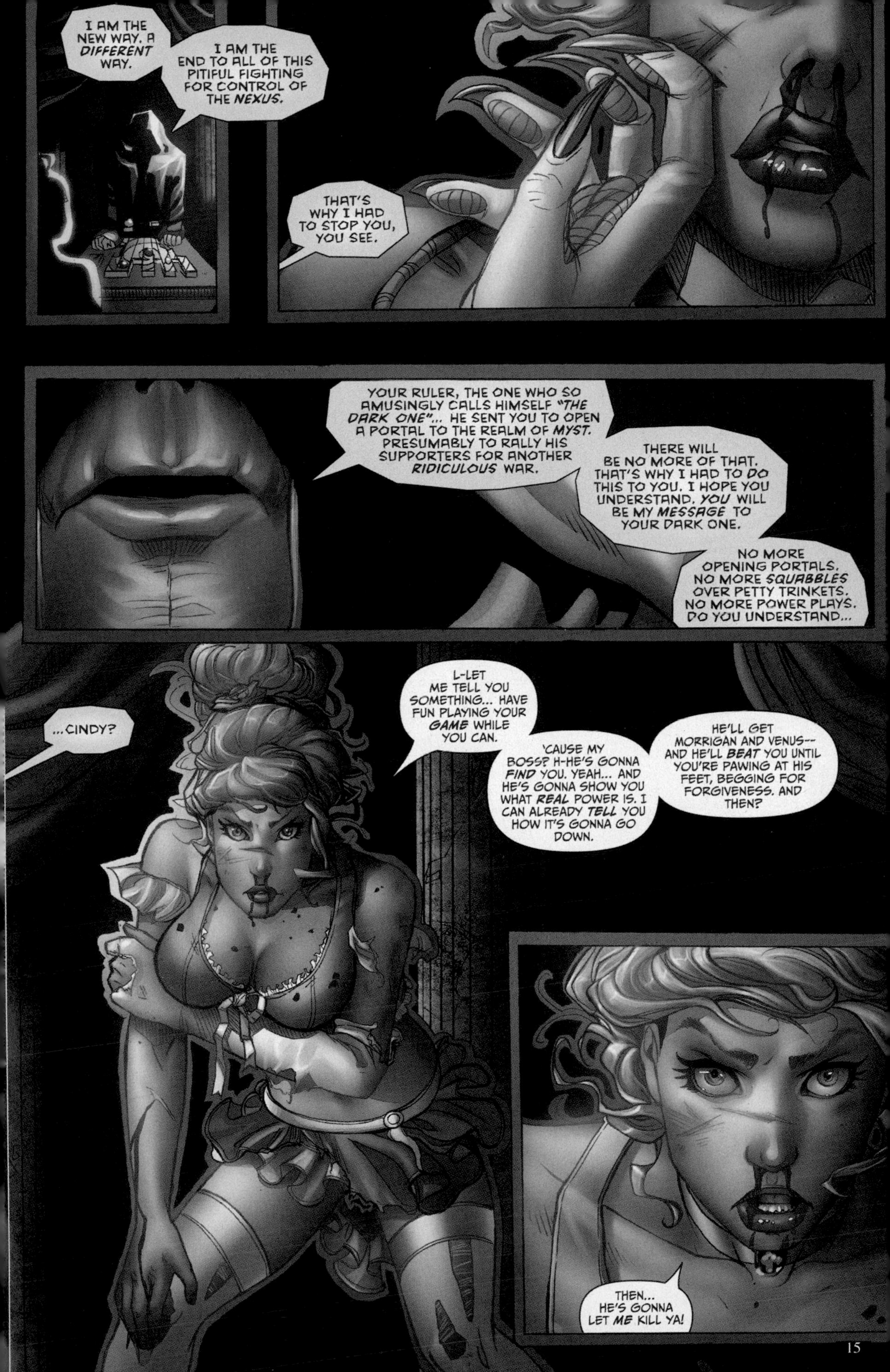
I AM THE NEW WAY. A DIFFERENT WAY.
I AM THE END TO ALL OF THIS PITIFUL FIGHTING FOR CONTROL OF THE NEXUS.
THAT'S WHY I HAD TO STOP YOU, YOU SEE.
YOUR RULER, THE ONE WHO SO AMUSINGLY CALLS HIMSELF "THE DARK ONE"... HE SENT YOU TO OPEN A PORTAL TO THE REALM OF MYST. PRESUMABLY TO RALLY HIS SUPPORTERS FOR ANOTHER RIDICULOUS WAR.
THERE WILL BE NO MORE OF THAT. THAT'S WHY I HAD TO DO THIS TO YOU. I HOPE YOU UNDERSTAND. YOU WILL BE MY MESSAGE TO YOUR DARK ONE.
NO MORE OPENING PORTALS. NO MORE SQUABBLES OVER PETTY TRINKETS. NO MORE POWER PLAYS. DO YOU UNDERSTAND...
...CINDY?
L-LET ME TELL YOU SOMETHING... HAVE FUN PLAYING YOUR GAME WHILE YOU CAN.
'CAUSE MY BOSS? H-HE'S GONNA FIND YOU. YEAH... AND HE'S GONNA SHOW YOU WHAT REAL POWER IS. I CAN ALREADY TELL YOU HOW IT'S GONNA GO DOWN.
HE'LL GET MORRIGAN AND VENUS-- AND HE'LL BEAT YOU UNTIL YOU'RE PAWING AT HIS FEET, BEGGING FOR FORGIVENESS. AND THEN?
THEN... HE'S GONNA LET ME KILL YA!

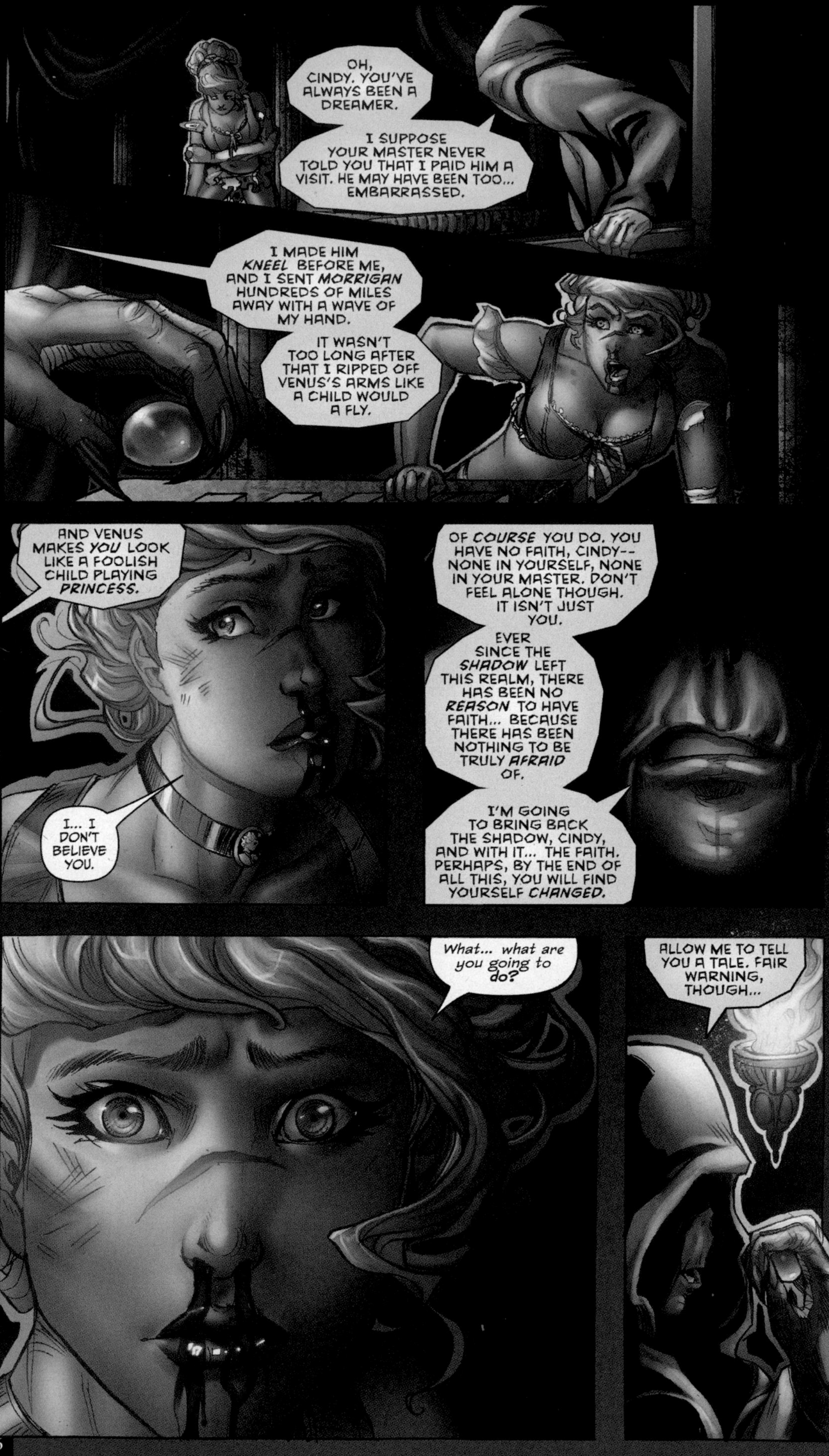
OH, CINDY. YOU'VE ALWAYS BEEN A DREAMER.
I SUPPOSE YOUR MASTER NEVER TOLD YOU THAT I PAID HIM A VISIT. HE MAY HAVE BEEN TOO... EMBARRASSED.
I MADE HIM KNEEL BEFORE ME, AND I SENT MORRIGAN HUNDREDS OF MILES AWAY WITH A WAVE OF MY HAND.
IT WASN'T TOO LONG AFTER THAT I RIPPED OFF VENUS'S ARMS LIKE A CHILD WOULD A FLY.
AND VENUS MAKES YOU LOOK LIKE A FOOLISH CHILD PLAYING PRINCESS.
I... I DON'T BELIEVE YOU.
OF COURSE YOU DO. YOU HAVE NO FAITH, CINDY-- NONE IN YOURSELF, NONE IN YOUR MASTER. DON'T FEEL ALONE THOUGH. IT ISN'T JUST YOU.
EVER SINCE THE SHADOW LEFT THIS REALM, THERE HAS BEEN NO REASON TO HAVE FAITH... BECAUSE THERE HAS BEEN NOTHING TO BE TRULY AFRAID OF.
I'M GOING TO BRING BACK THE SHADOW, CINDY, AND WITH IT... THE FAITH. PERHAPS, BY THE END OF ALL THIS, YOU WILL FIND YOURSELF CHANGED.
What... what are you going to do?
ALLOW ME TO TELL YOU A TALE. FAIR WARNING, THOUGH...

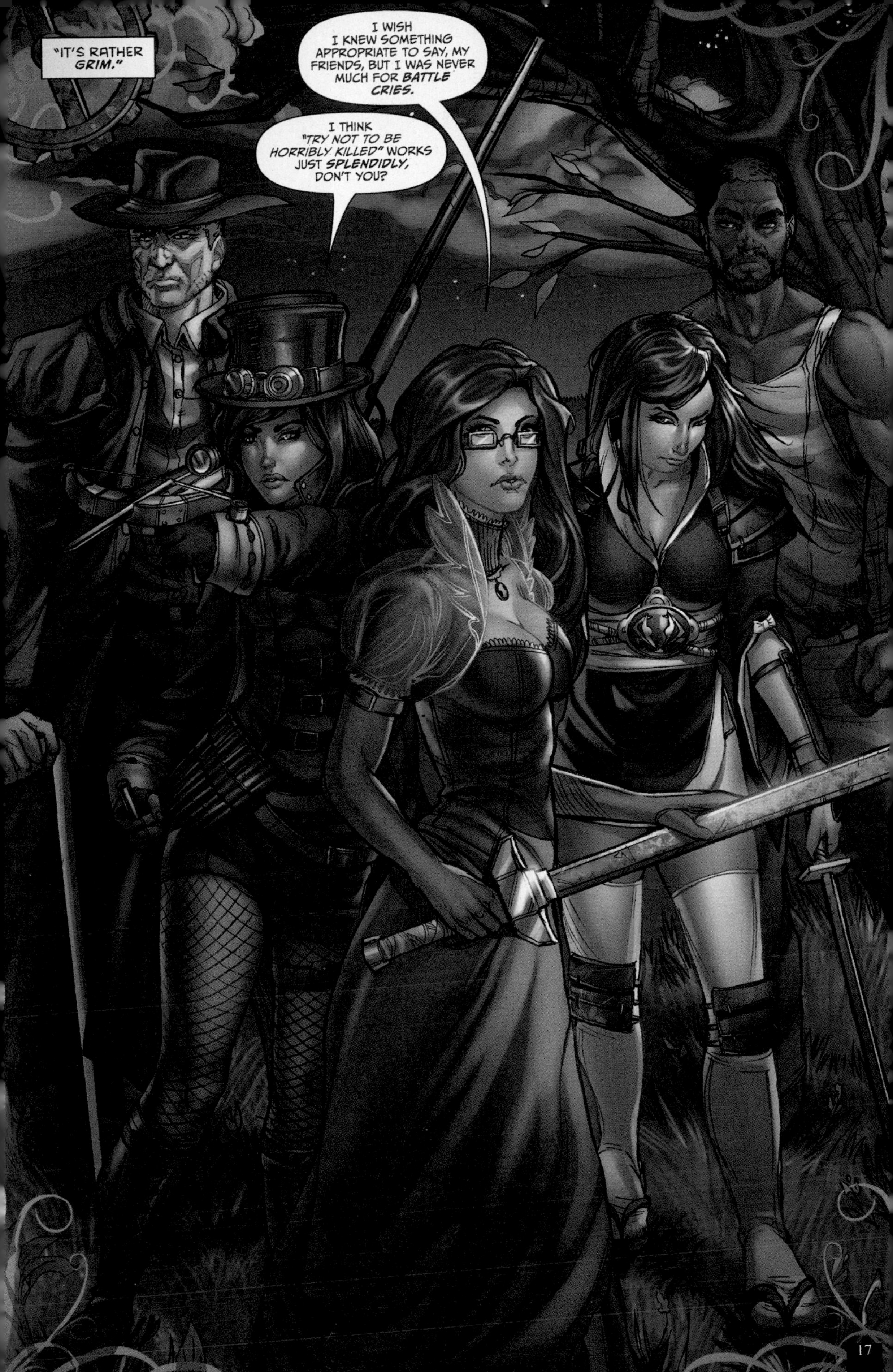
"IT'S RATHER GRIM."
I WISH I KNEW SOMETHING APPROPRIATE TO SAY, MY FRIENDS, BUT I WAS NEVER MUCH FOR BATTLE CRIES.
I THINK "TRY NOT TO BE HORRIBLY KILLED" WORKS JUST SPLENDIDLY, DON'T YOU?

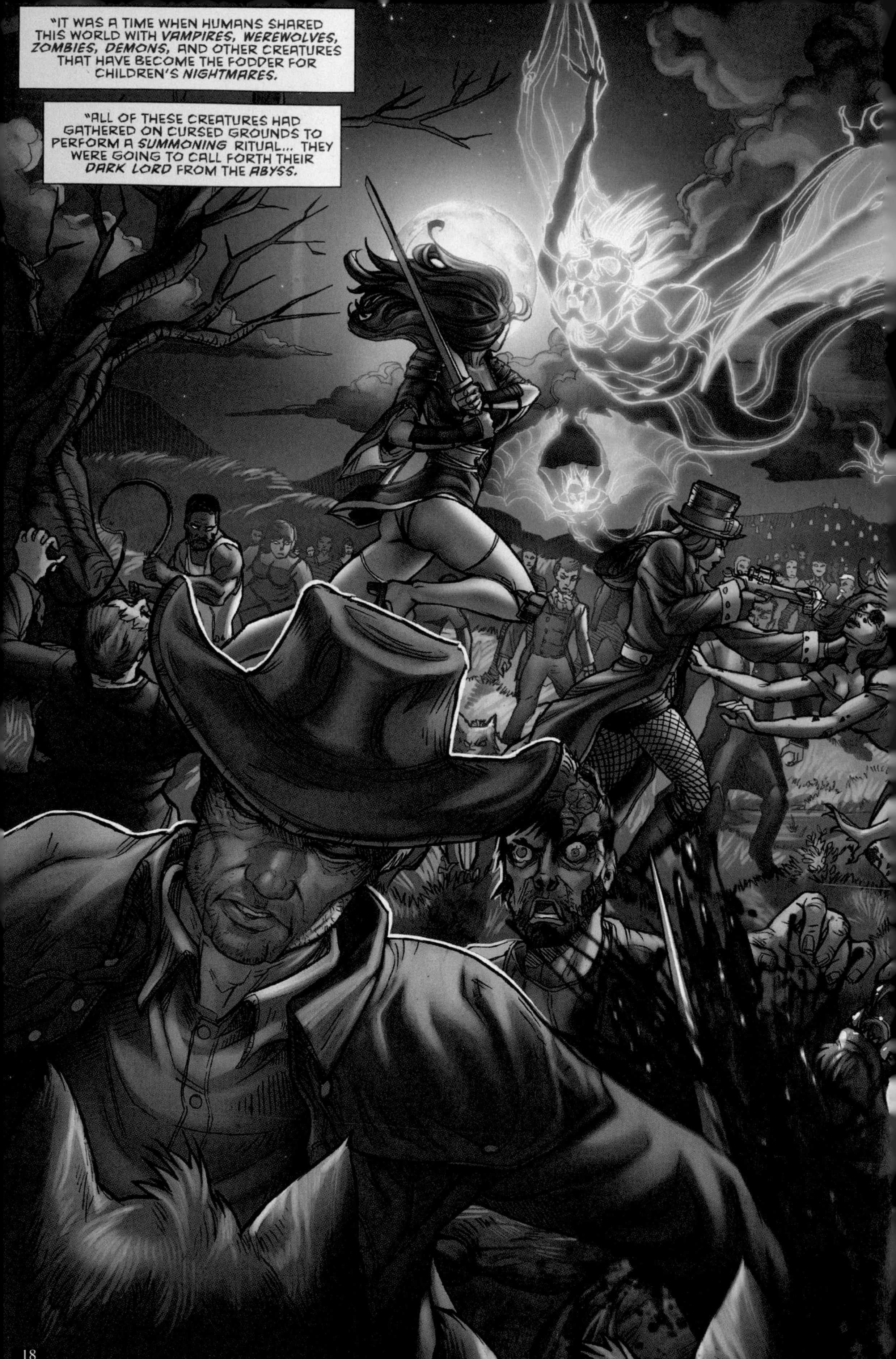
"IT WAS A TIME WHEN HUMANS SHARED THIS WORLD WITH VAMPIRES, WEREWOLVES, ZOMBIES, DEMONS, AND OTHER CREATURES THAT HAVE BECOME THE FODDER FOR CHILDREN'S NIGHTMARES.
"ALL OF THESE CREATURES HAD GATHERED ON CURSED GROUNDS TO PERFORM A SUMMONING RITUAL... THEY WERE GOING TO CALL FORTH THEIR DARK LORD FROM THE ABYSS.

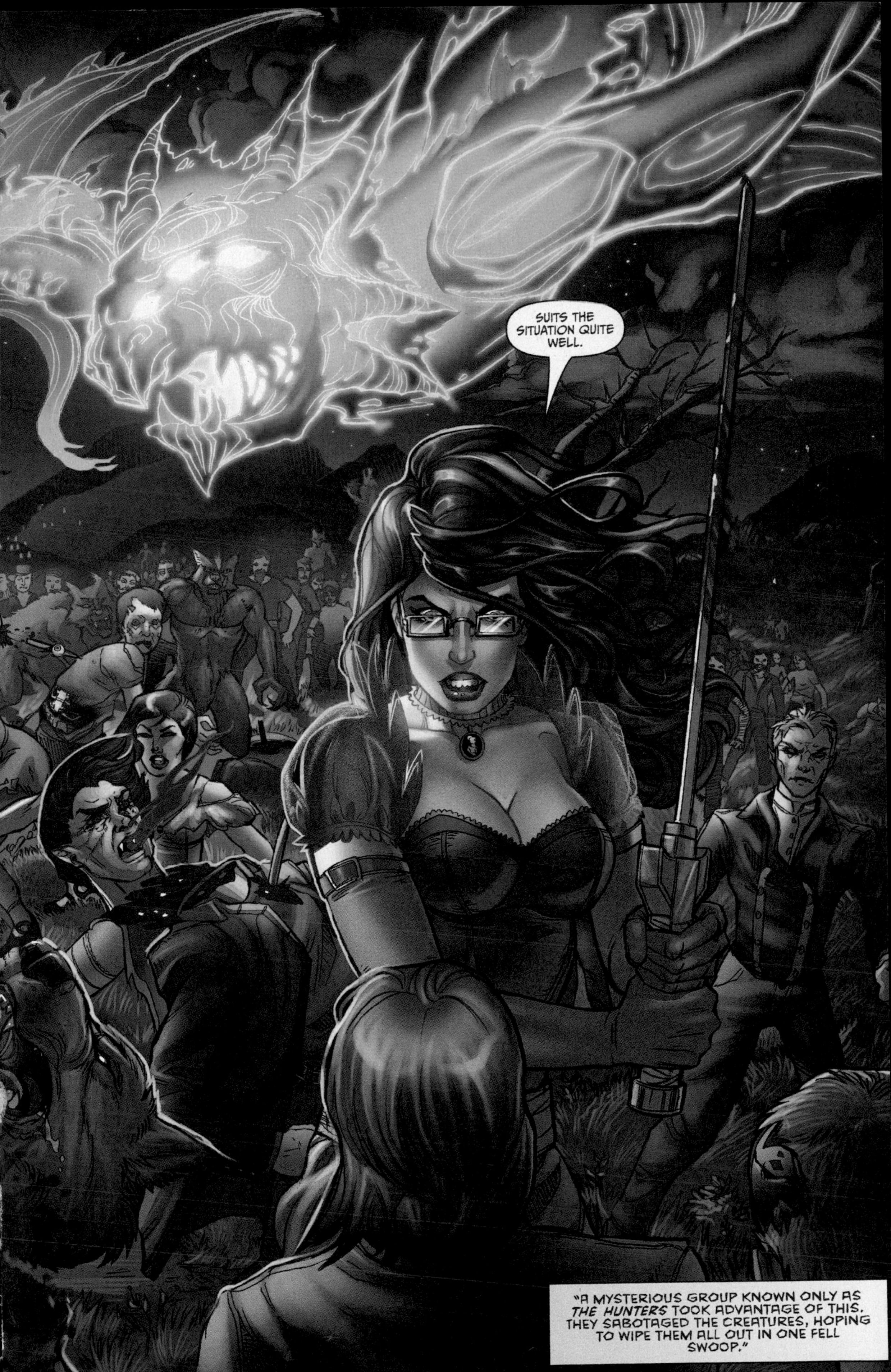
SUITS THE SITUATION QUITE WELL.
"A MYSTERIOUS GROUP KNOWN ONLY AS *THE HUNTERS* TOOK ADVANTAGE OF THIS. THEY SABOTAGED THE CREATURES, HOPING TO WIPE THEM ALL OUT IN ONE FELL SWOOP."

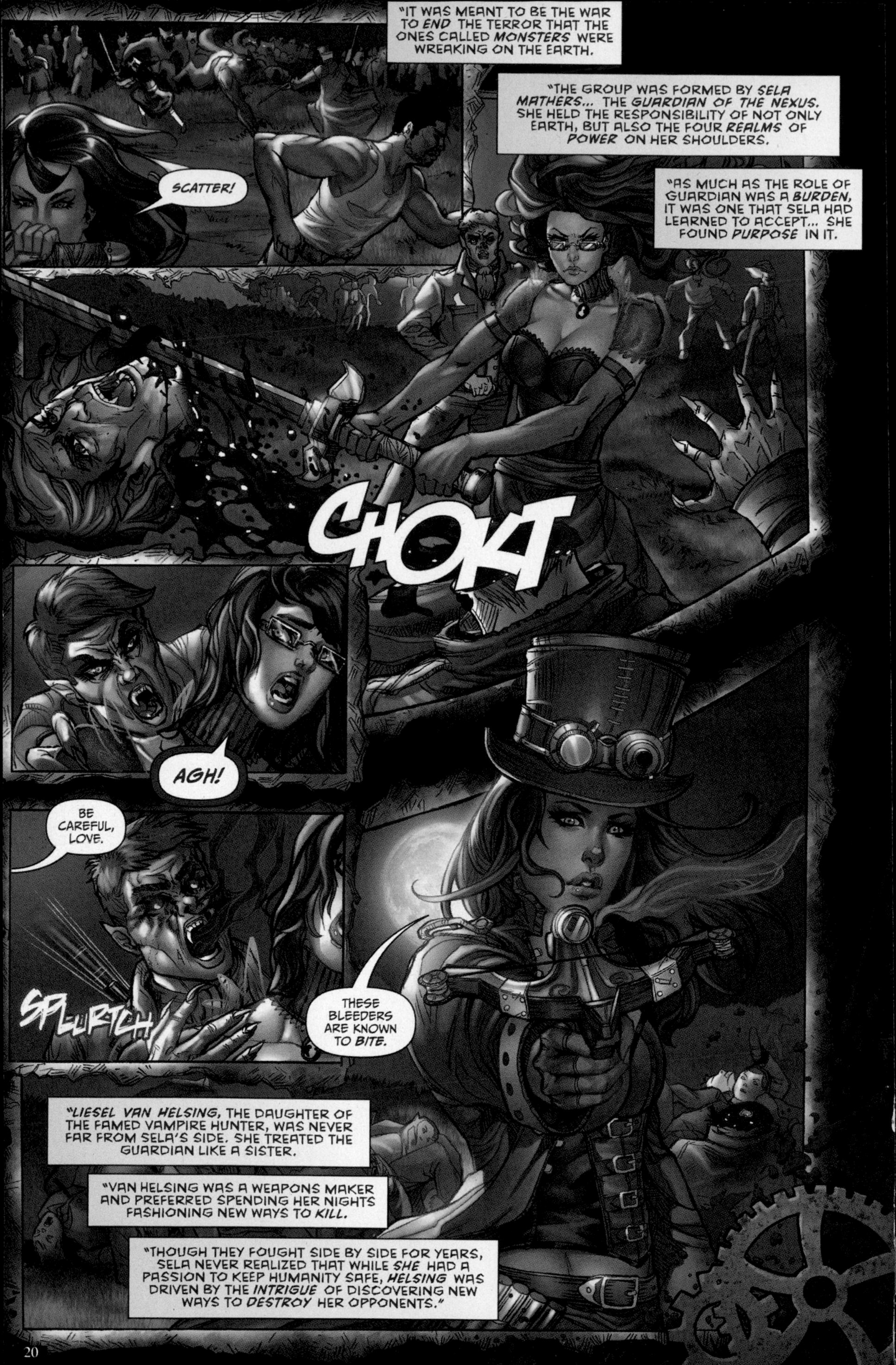
"IT WAS MEANT TO BE THE WAR TO END THE TERROR THAT THE ONES CALLED MONSTERS WERE WREAKING ON THE EARTH.
SCATTER!
"THE GROUP WAS FORMED BY SELA MATHERS... THE GUARDIAN OF THE NEXUS. SHE HELD THE RESPONSIBILITY OF NOT ONLY EARTH, BUT ALSO THE FOUR REALMS OF POWER ON HER SHOULDERS.
"AS MUCH AS THE ROLE OF GUARDIAN WAS A BURDEN, IT WAS ONE THAT SELA HAD LEARNED TO ACCEPT... SHE FOUND PURPOSE IN IT.
CHOK!
AGH!
BE CAREFUL, LOVE.
SPLURTCH
THESE BLEEDERS ARE KNOWN TO BITE.
"LIESEL VAN HELSING, THE DAUGHTER OF THE FAMED VAMPIRE HUNTER, WAS NEVER FAR FROM SELA'S SIDE. SHE TREATED THE GUARDIAN LIKE A SISTER.
"VAN HELSING WAS A WEAPONS MAKER AND PREFERRED SPENDING HER NIGHTS FASHIONING NEW WAYS TO KILL.
"THOUGH THEY FOUGHT SIDE BY SIDE FOR YEARS, SELA NEVER REALIZED THAT WHILE SHE HAD A PASSION TO KEEP HUMANITY SAFE, HELSING WAS DRIVEN BY THE INTRIGUE OF DISCOVERING NEW WAYS TO DESTROY HER OPPONENTS."

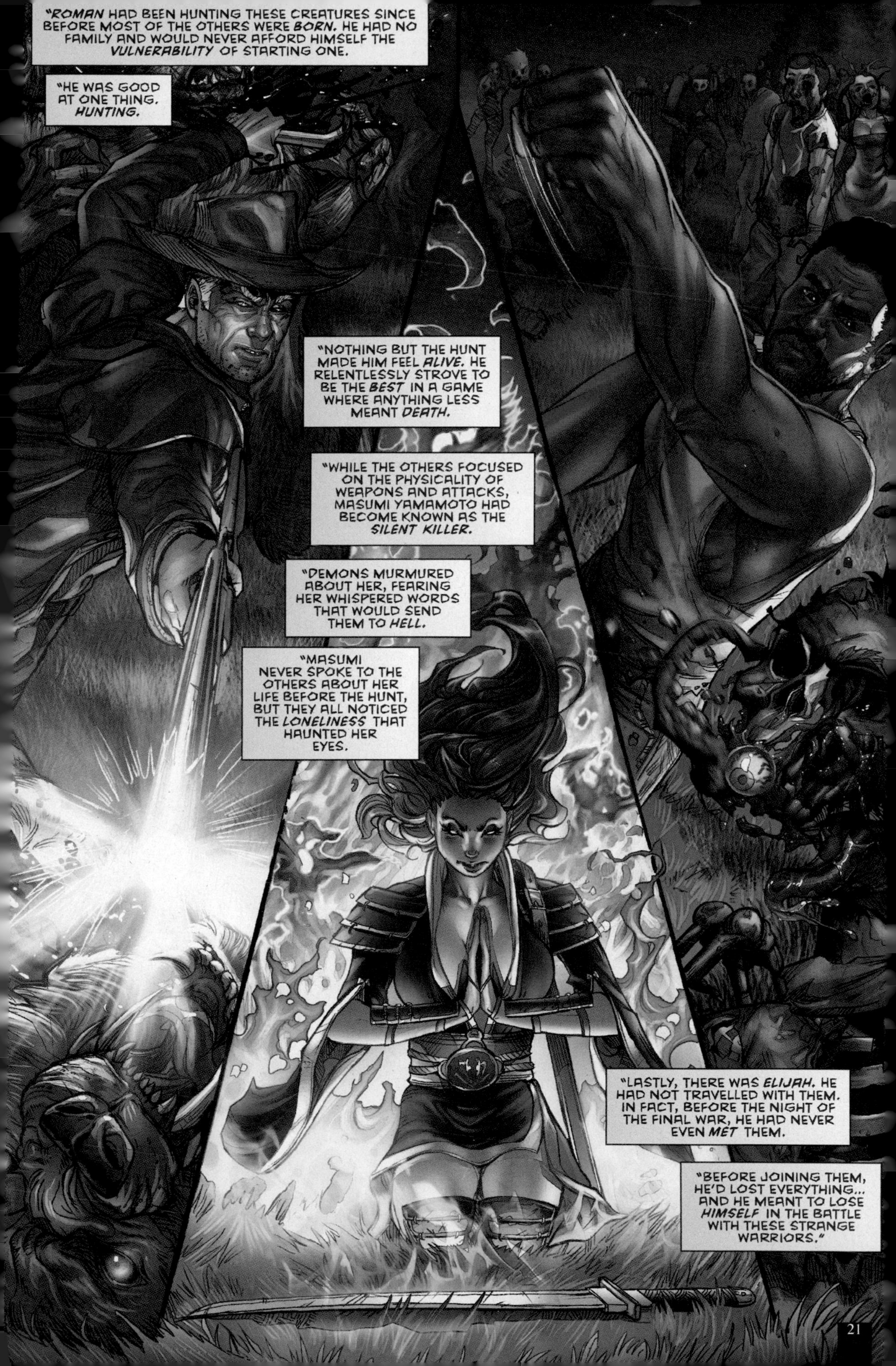
"ROMAN HAD BEEN HUNTING THESE CREATURES SINCE BEFORE MOST OF THE OTHERS WERE BORN. HE HAD NO FAMILY AND WOULD NEVER AFFORD HIMSELF THE VULNERABILITY OF STARTING ONE.
"HE WAS GOOD AT ONE THING. HUNTING.
"NOTHING BUT THE HUNT MADE HIM FEEL ALIVE. HE RELENTLESSLY STROVE TO BE THE BEST IN A GAME WHERE ANYTHING LESS MEANT DEATH.
"WHILE THE OTHERS FOCUSED ON THE PHYSICALITY OF WEAPONS AND ATTACKS, MASUMI YAMAMOTO HAD BECOME KNOWN AS THE SILENT KILLER.
"DEMONS MURMURED ABOUT HER, FEARING HER WHISPERED WORDS THAT WOULD SEND THEM TO HELL.
"MASUMI NEVER SPOKE TO THE OTHERS ABOUT HER LIFE BEFORE THE HUNT, BUT THEY ALL NOTICED THE LONELINESS THAT HAUNTED HER EYES.
"LASTLY, THERE WAS ELIJAH. HE HAD NOT TRAVELLED WITH THEM. IN FACT, BEFORE THE NIGHT OF THE FINAL WAR, HE HAD NEVER EVEN MET THEM.
"BEFORE JOINING THEM, HE'D LOST EVERYTHING... AND HE MEANT TO LOSE HIMSELF IN THE BATTLE WITH THESE STRANGE WARRIORS."

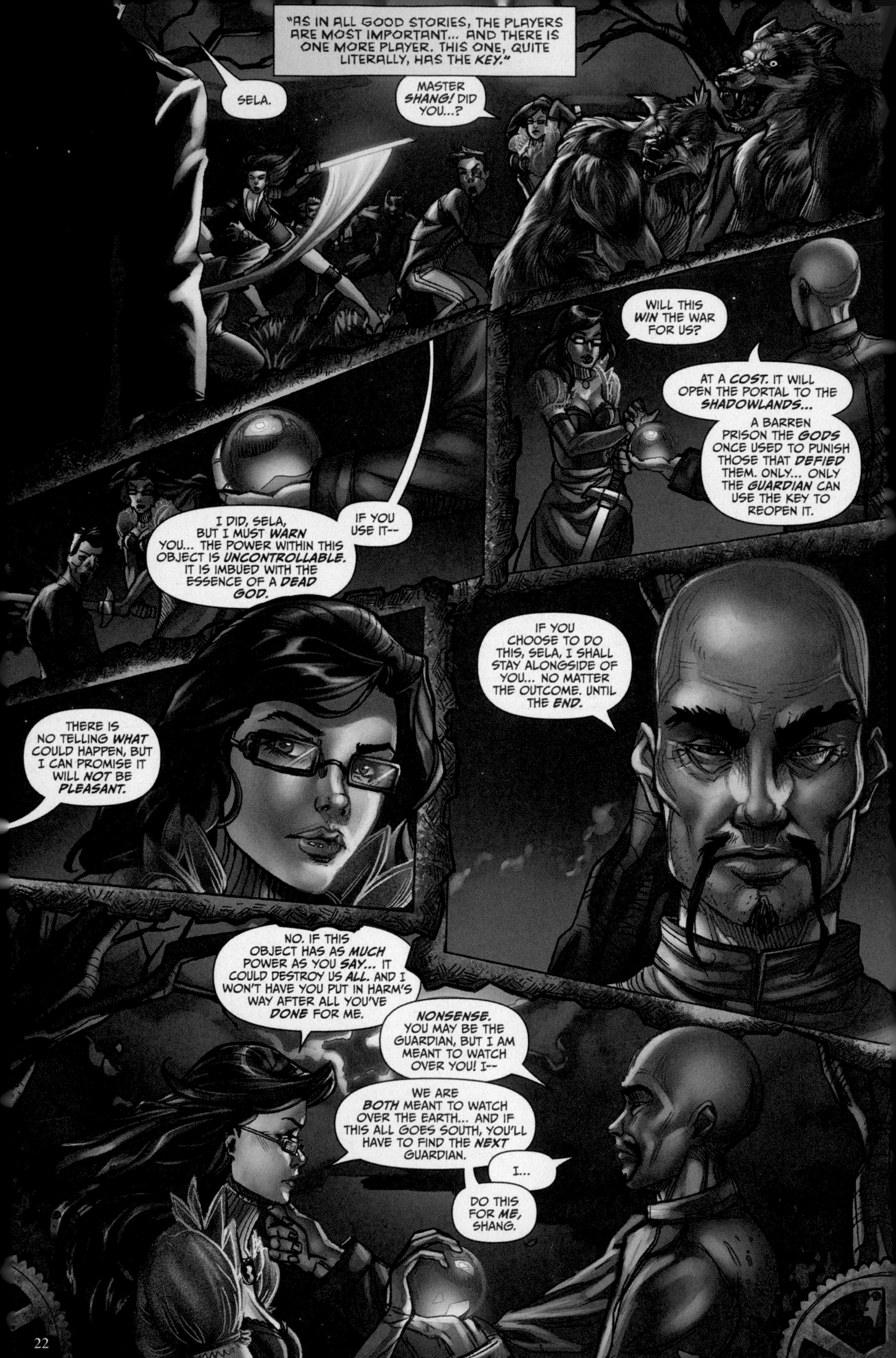
"AS IN ALL GOOD STORIES, THE PLAYERS ARE MOST IMPORTANT... AND THERE IS ONE MORE PLAYER. THIS ONE, QUITE LITERALLY, HAS THE KEY."
SELA.
MASTER SHANG! DID YOU...?
I DID, SELA, BUT I MUST WARN YOU... THE POWER WITHIN THIS OBJECT IS UNCONTROLLABLE. IT IS IMBUED WITH THE ESSENCE OF A DEAD GOD.
IF YOU USE IT--
WILL THIS WIN THE WAR FOR US?
AT A COST. IT WILL OPEN THE PORTAL TO THE SHADOWLANDS...
A BARREN PRISON THE GODS ONCE USED TO PUNISH THOSE THAT DEFIED THEM. ONLY... ONLY THE GUARDIAN CAN USE THE KEY TO REOPEN IT.
THERE IS NO TELLING WHAT COULD HAPPEN, BUT I CAN PROMISE IT WILL NOT BE PLEASANT.
IF YOU CHOOSE TO DO THIS, SELA, I SHALL STAY ALONGSIDE OF YOU... NO MATTER THE OUTCOME. UNTIL THE END.
NO. IF THIS OBJECT HAS AS MUCH POWER AS YOU SAY... IT COULD DESTROY US ALL. AND I WON'T HAVE YOU PUT IN HARM'S WAY AFTER ALL YOU'VE DONE FOR ME.
NONSENSE. YOU MAY BE THE GUARDIAN, BUT I AM MEANT TO WATCH OVER YOU! I--
WE ARE BOTH MEANT TO WATCH OVER THE EARTH... AND IF THIS ALL GOES SOUTH, YOU'LL HAVE TO FIND THE NEXT GUARDIAN.
I...
DO THIS FOR ME, SHANG.

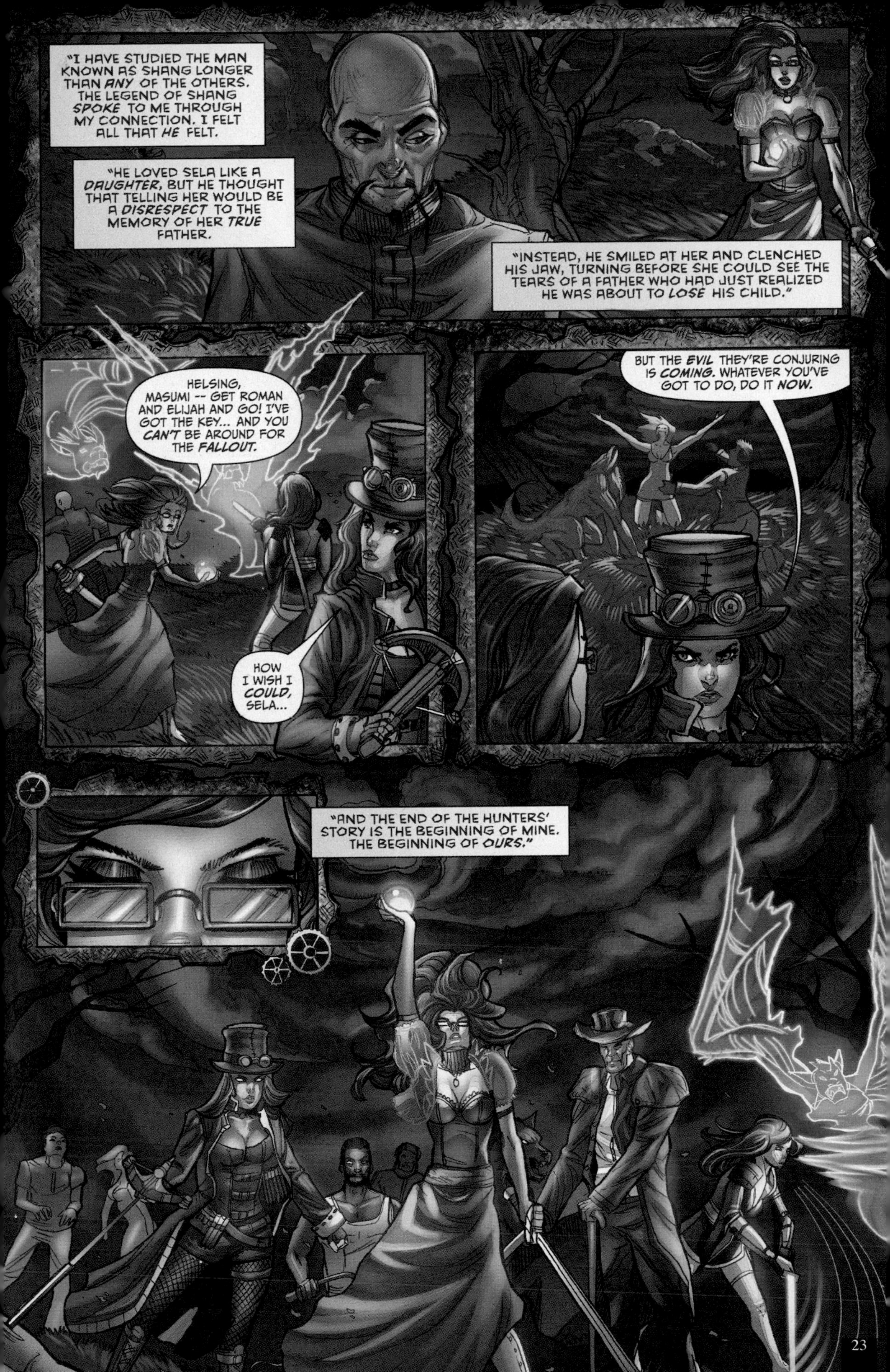
"I HAVE STUDIED THE MAN KNOWN AS SHANG LONGER THAN ANY OF THE OTHERS. THE LEGEND OF SHANG SPOKE TO ME THROUGH MY CONNECTION. I FELT ALL THAT HE FELT.
"HE LOVED SELA LIKE A DAUGHTER, BUT HE THOUGHT THAT TELLING HER WOULD BE A DISRESPECT TO THE MEMORY OF HER TRUE FATHER.
"INSTEAD, HE SMILED AT HER AND CLENCHED HIS JAW, TURNING BEFORE SHE COULD SEE THE TEARS OF A FATHER WHO HAD JUST REALIZED HE WAS ABOUT TO LOSE HIS CHILD."
HELSING, MASUMI -- GET ROMAN AND ELIJAH AND GO! I'VE GOT THE KEY... AND YOU CAN'T BE AROUND FOR THE FALLOUT.
HOW I WISH I COULD, SELA...
BUT THE EVIL THEY'RE CONJURING IS COMING. WHATEVER YOU'VE GOT TO DO, DO IT NOW.
"AND THE END OF THE HUNTERS' STORY IS THE BEGINNING OF MINE. THE BEGINNING OF OURS."

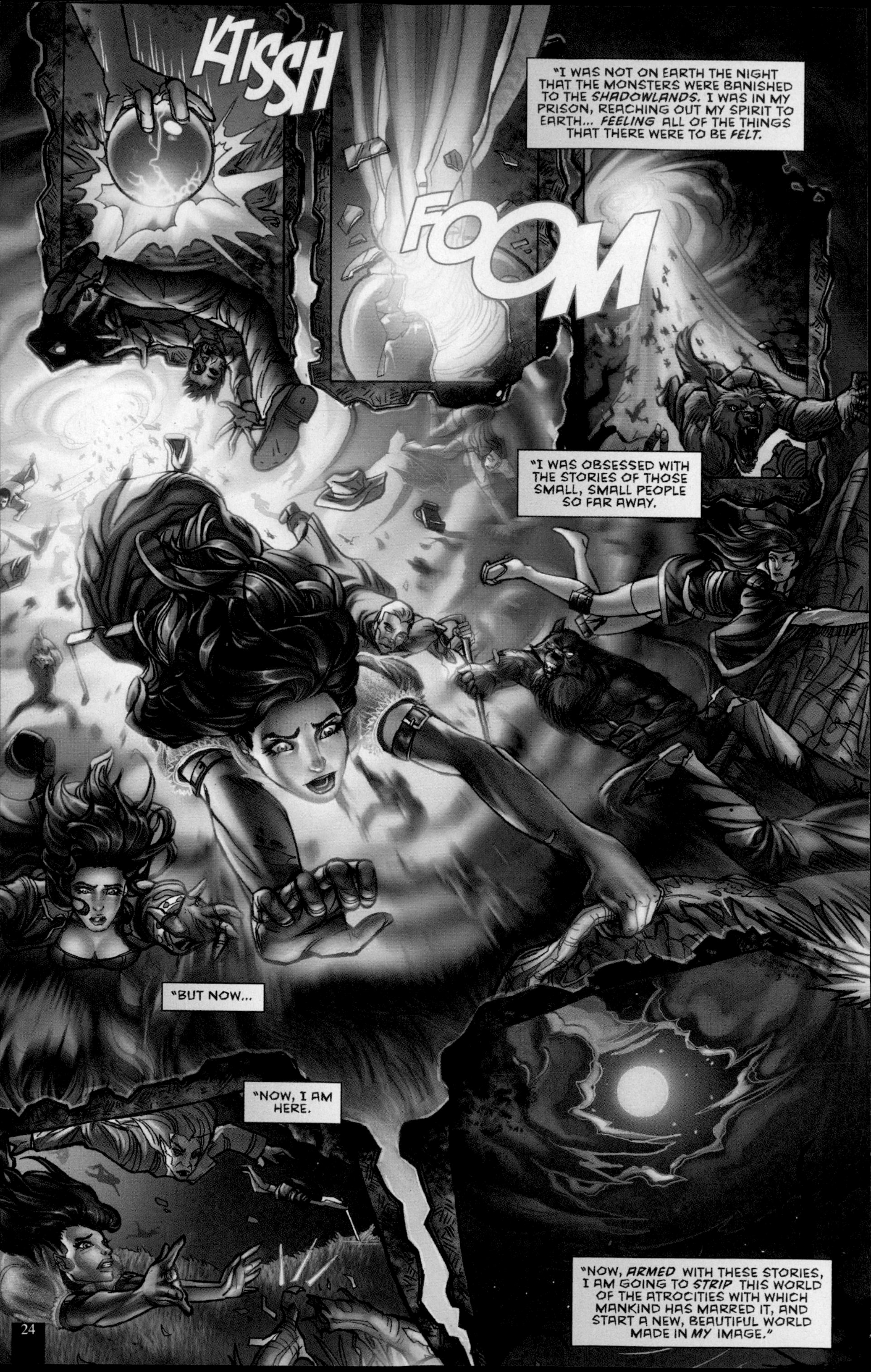
KTISSH
"I WAS NOT ON EARTH THE NIGHT THAT THE MONSTERS WERE BANISHED TO THE SHADOWLANDS. I WAS IN MY PRISON, REACHING OUT MY SPIRIT TO EARTH... FEELING ALL OF THE THINGS THAT THERE WERE TO BE FELT.
FOOM
"I WAS OBSESSED WITH THE STORIES OF THOSE SMALL, SMALL PEOPLE SO FAR AWAY.
"BUT NOW...
"NOW, I AM HERE.
"NOW, ARMED WITH THESE STORIES, I AM GOING TO STRIP THIS WORLD OF THE ATROCITIES WITH WHICH MANKIND HAS MARRED IT, AND START A NEW, BEAUTIFUL WORLD MADE IN MY IMAGE."

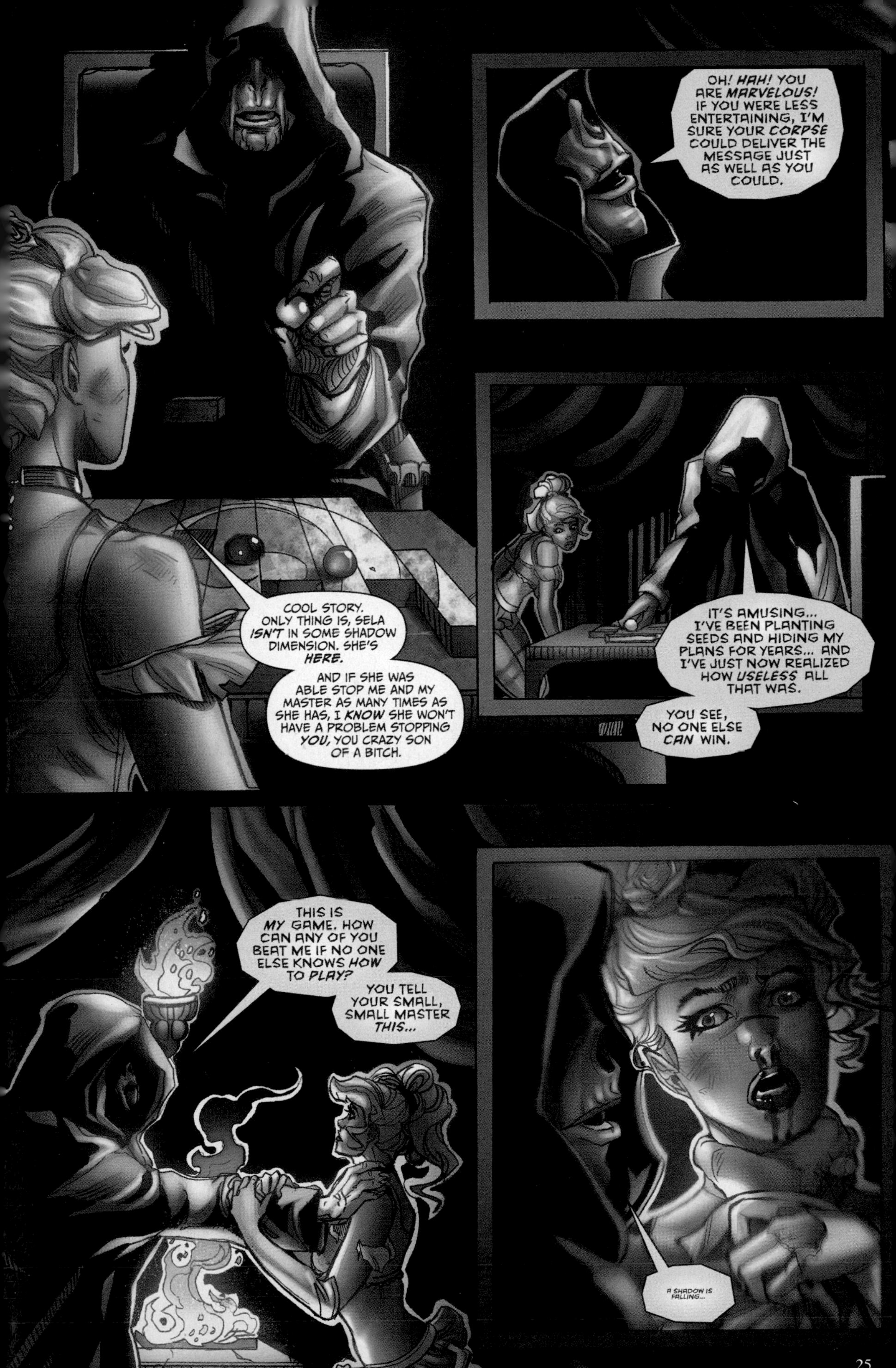
OH! HAH! YOU ARE MARVELOUS! IF YOU WERE LESS ENTERTAINING, I'M SURE YOUR CORPSE COULD DELIVER THE MESSAGE JUST AS WELL AS YOU COULD.
COOL STORY. ONLY THING IS, SELA ISN'T IN SOME SHADOW DIMENSION. SHE'S HERE.
AND IF SHE WAS ABLE STOP ME AND MY MASTER AS MANY TIMES AS SHE HAS, I KNOW SHE WON'T HAVE A PROBLEM STOPPING YOU, YOU CRAZY SON OF A BITCH.
IT'S AMUSING... I'VE BEEN PLANTING SEEDS AND HIDING MY PLANS FOR YEARS... AND I'VE JUST NOW REALIZED HOW USELESS ALL THAT WAS.
YOU SEE, NO ONE ELSE CAN WIN.
THIS IS MY GAME. HOW CAN ANY OF YOU BEAT ME IF NO ONE ELSE KNOWS HOW TO PLAY?
YOU TELL YOUR SMALL, SMALL MASTER THIS...
A SHADOW IS FALLING...

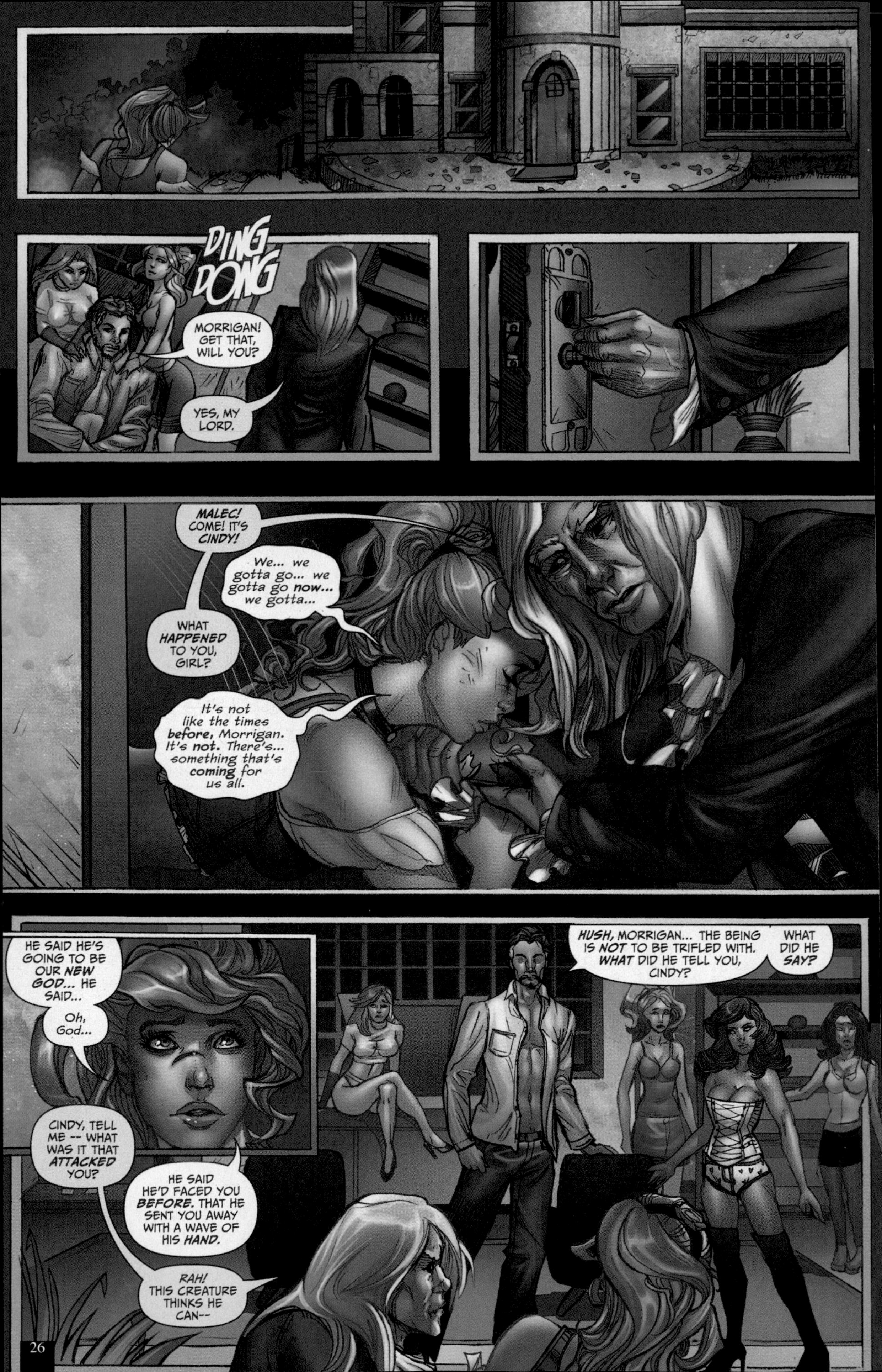
DING DONG
MORRIGAN! GET THAT, WILL YOU?
YES, MY LORD.
MALEC! COME! IT'S CINDY!
We... we gotta go... we gotta go now... we gotta...
WHAT HAPPENED TO YOU, GIRL?
It's not like the times before, Morrigan. It's not. There's... something that's coming for us all.
HE SAID HE'S GOING TO BE OUR NEW GOD... HE SAID...
Oh, God...
HUSH, MORRIGAN... THE BEING IS NOT TO BE TRIFLED WITH. WHAT DID HE TELL YOU, CINDY?
WHAT DID HE SAY?
CINDY, TELL ME -- WHAT WAS IT THAT ATTACKED YOU?
HE SAID HE'D FACED YOU BEFORE. THAT HE SENT YOU AWAY WITH A WAVE OF HIS HAND.
RAH! THIS CREATURE THINKS HE CAN--

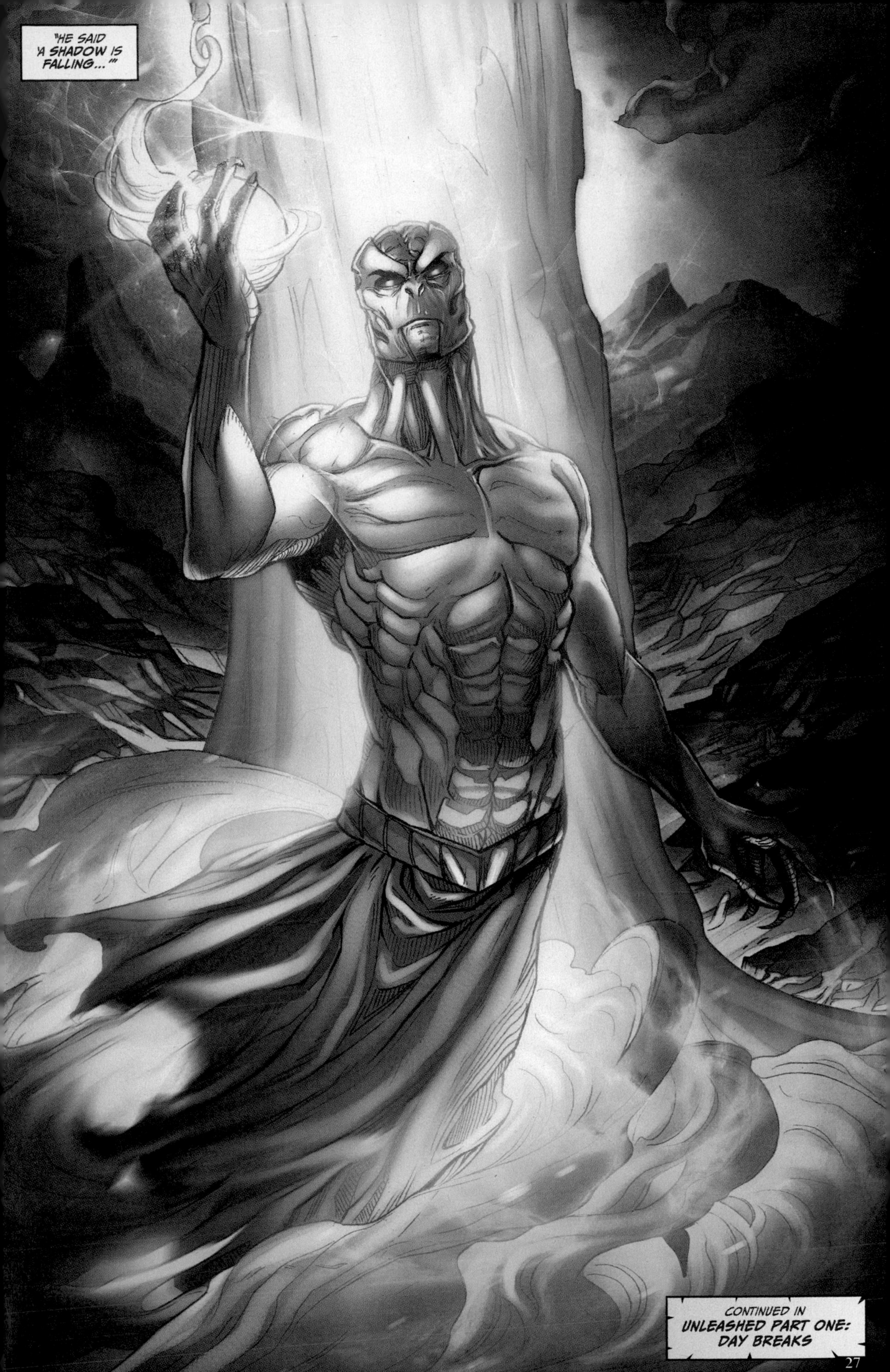
"HE SAID 'A SHADOW IS FALLING...'"
CONTINUED IN UNLEASHED PART ONE: DAY BREAKS

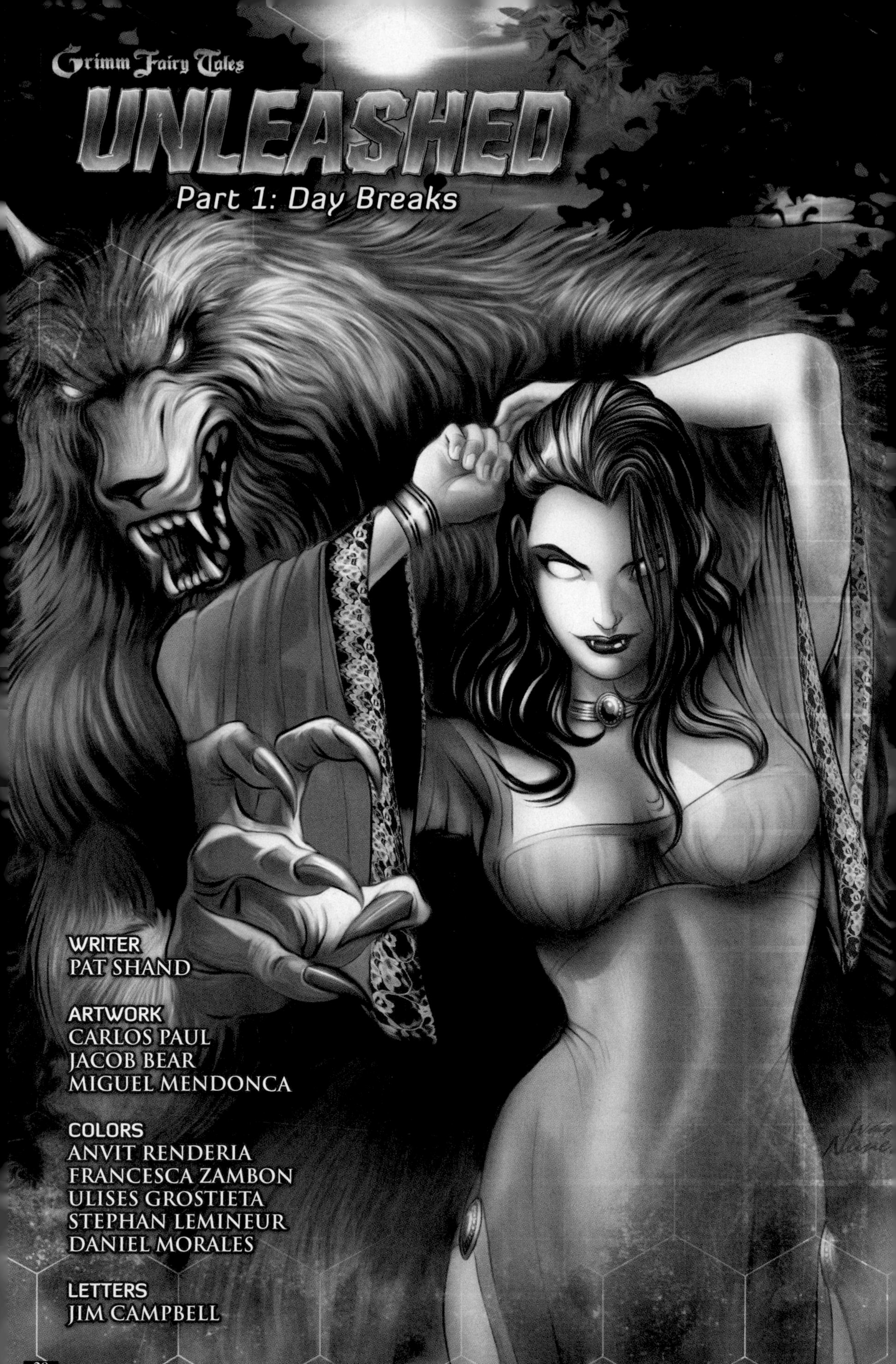
Grimm Fairy Tales
UNLEASHED
Part 1: Day Breaks
WRITER
PAT SHAND
ARTWORK
CARLOS PAUL
JACOB BEAR
MIGUEL MENDONCA
COLORS
ANVIT RENDERIA
FRANCESCA ZAMBON
ULISES GROSTIETA
STEPHAN LEMINEUR
DANIEL MORALES
LETTERS
JIM CAMPBELL

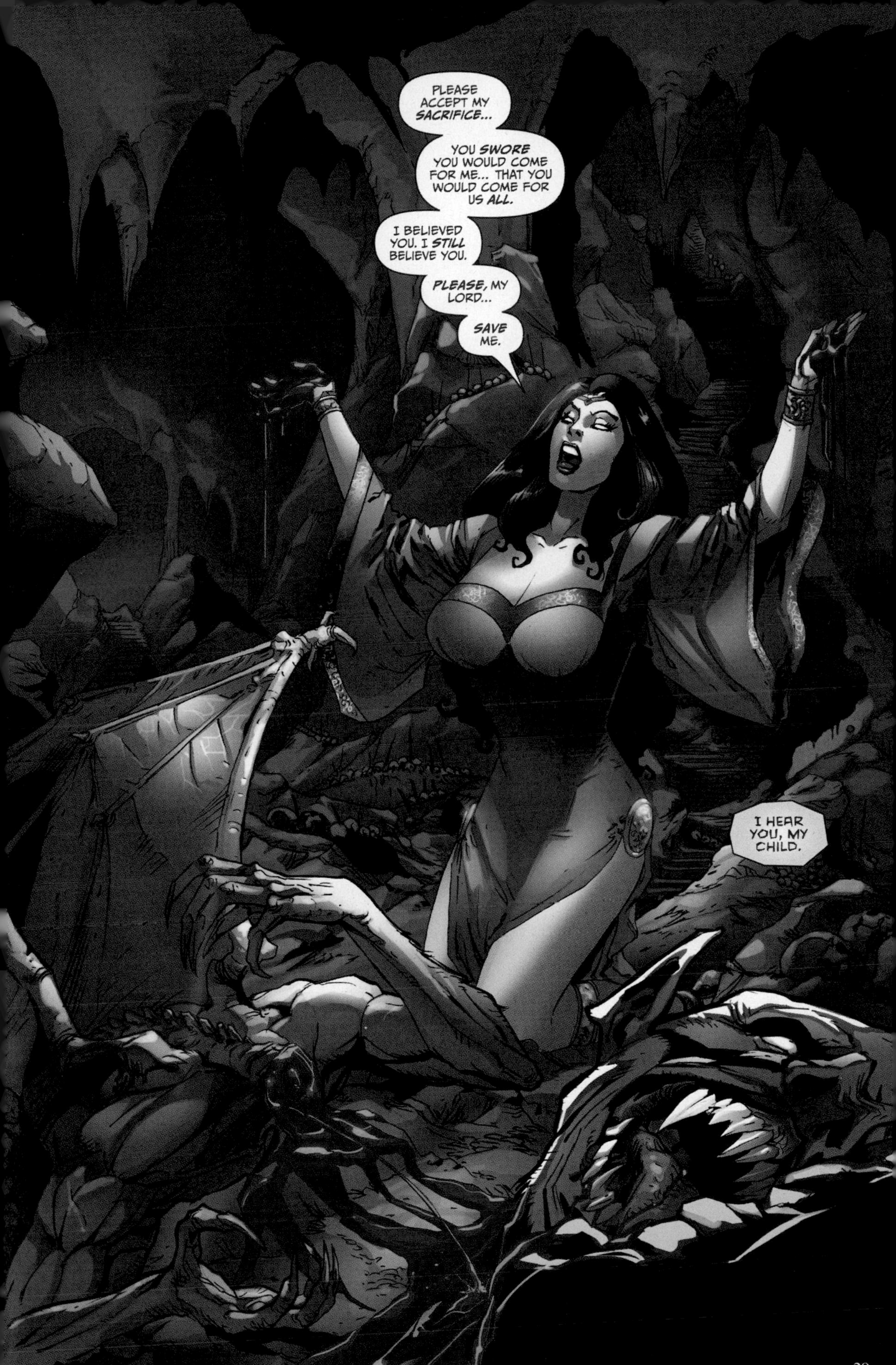
PLEASE ACCEPT MY SACRIFICE...
YOU SWORE YOU WOULD COME FOR ME... THAT YOU WOULD COME FOR US ALL.
I BELIEVED YOU. I STILL BELIEVE YOU.
PLEASE, MY LORD...
SAVE ME.
I HEAR YOU, MY CHILD.

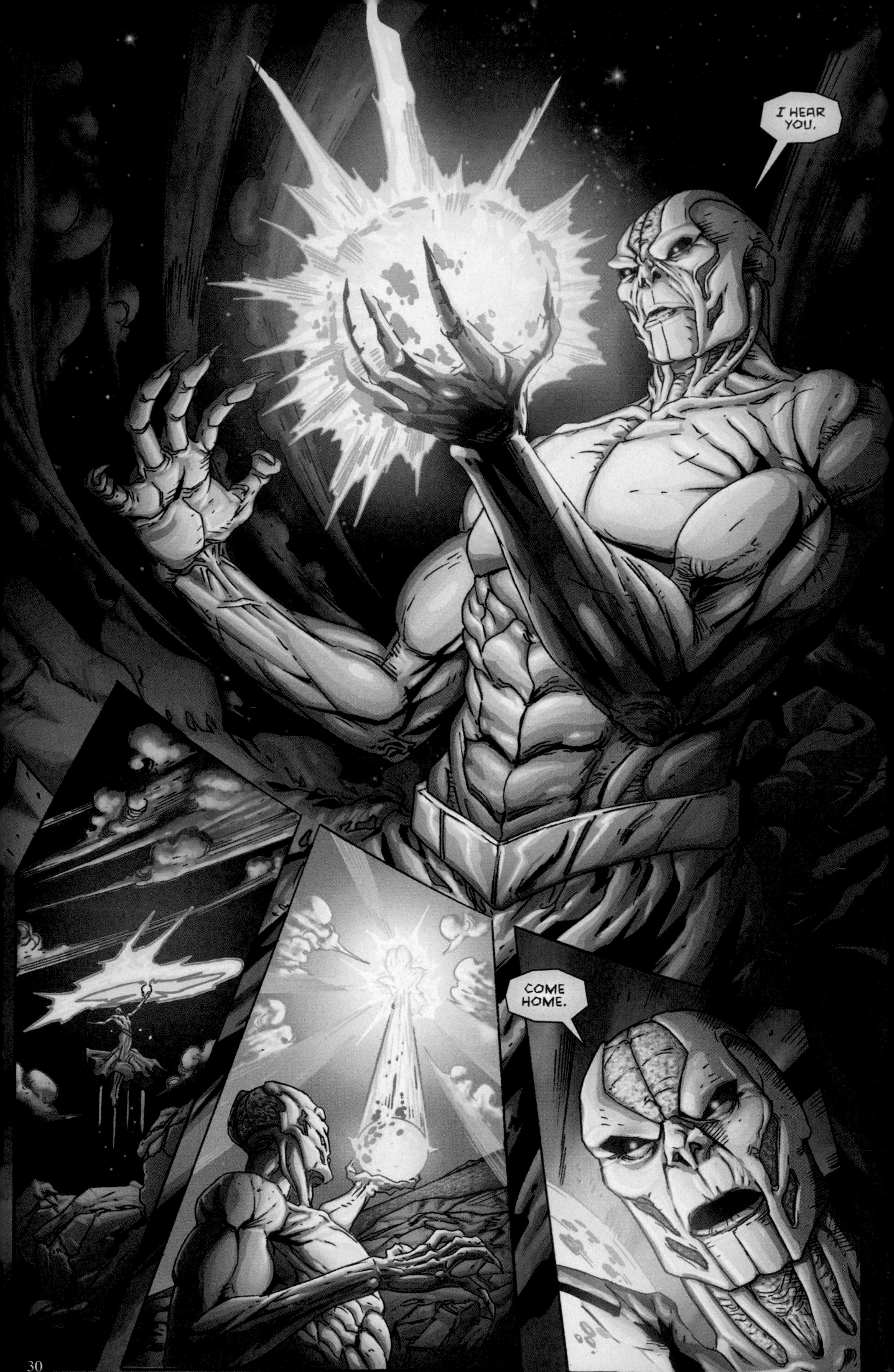
I HEAR YOU.
COME HOME.

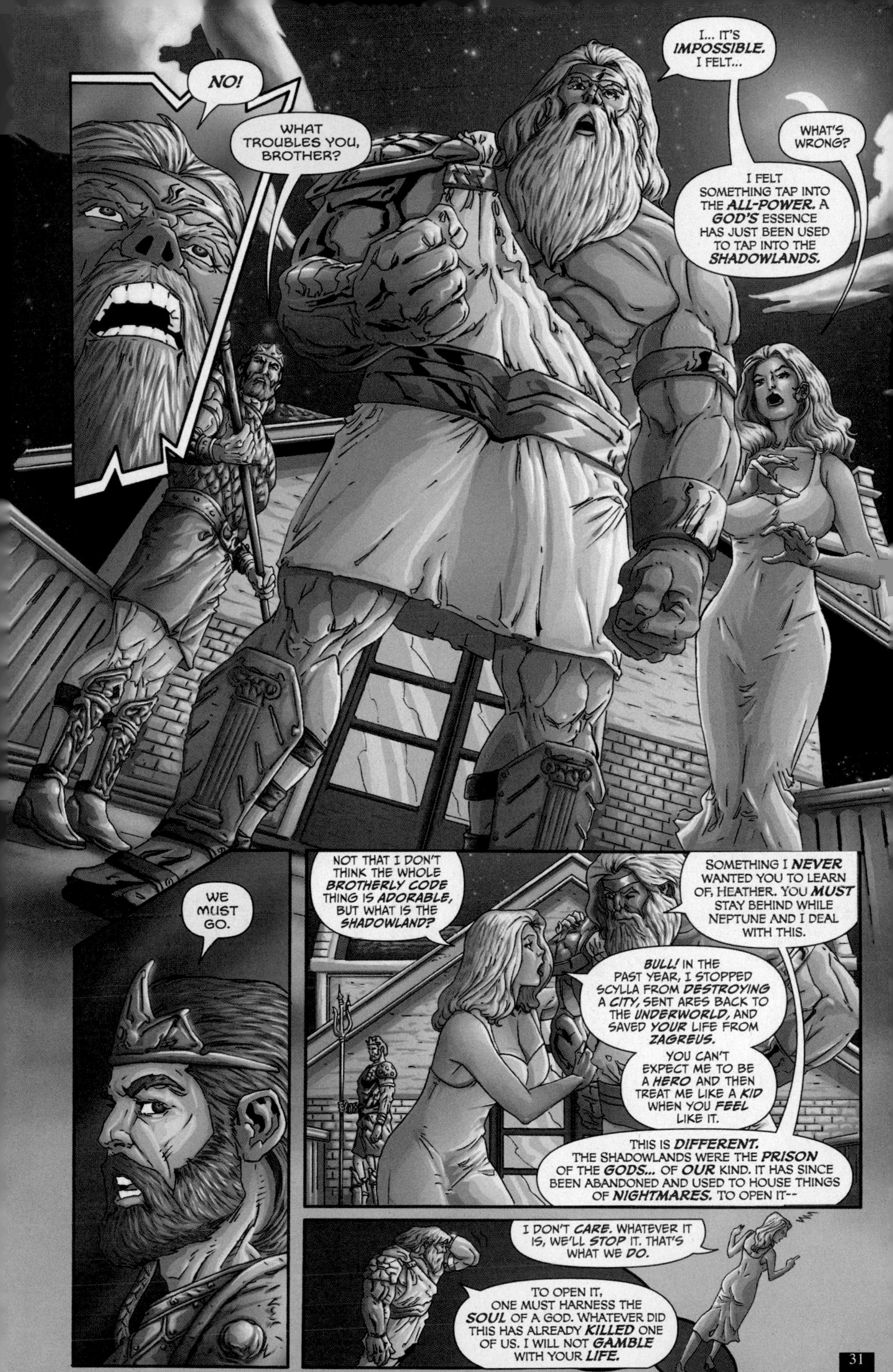

NO!
WHAT TROUBLES YOU, BROTHER?
I... IT'S IMPOSSIBLE. I FELT...
I FELT SOMETHING TAP INTO THE ALL-POWER. A GOD'S ESSENCE HAS JUST BEEN USED TO TAP INTO THE SHADOWLANDS.
WHAT'S WRONG?
WE MUST GO.
NOT THAT I DON'T THINK THE WHOLE BROTHERLY CODE THING IS ADORABLE, BUT WHAT IS THE SHADOWLAND?
SOMETHING I NEVER WANTED YOU TO LEARN OF, HEATHER. YOU MUST STAY BEHIND WHILE NEPTUNE AND I DEAL WITH THIS.
BULL! IN THE PAST YEAR, I STOPPED SCYLLA FROM DESTROYING A CITY, SENT ARES BACK TO THE UNDERWORLD, AND SAVED YOUR LIFE FROM ZAGREUS.
YOU CAN'T EXPECT ME TO BE A HERO AND THEN TREAT ME LIKE A KID WHEN YOU FEEL LIKE IT.
THIS IS DIFFERENT. THE SHADOWLANDS WERE THE PRISON OF THE GODS... OF OUR KIND. IT HAS SINCE BEEN ABANDONED AND USED TO HOUSE THINGS OF NIGHTMARES. TO OPEN IT--
I DON'T CARE. WHATEVER IT IS, WE'LL STOP IT. THAT'S WHAT WE DO.
TO OPEN IT, ONE MUST HARNESS THE SOUL OF A GOD. WHATEVER DID THIS HAS ALREADY KILLED ONE OF US. I WILL NOT GAMBLE WITH YOUR LIFE.

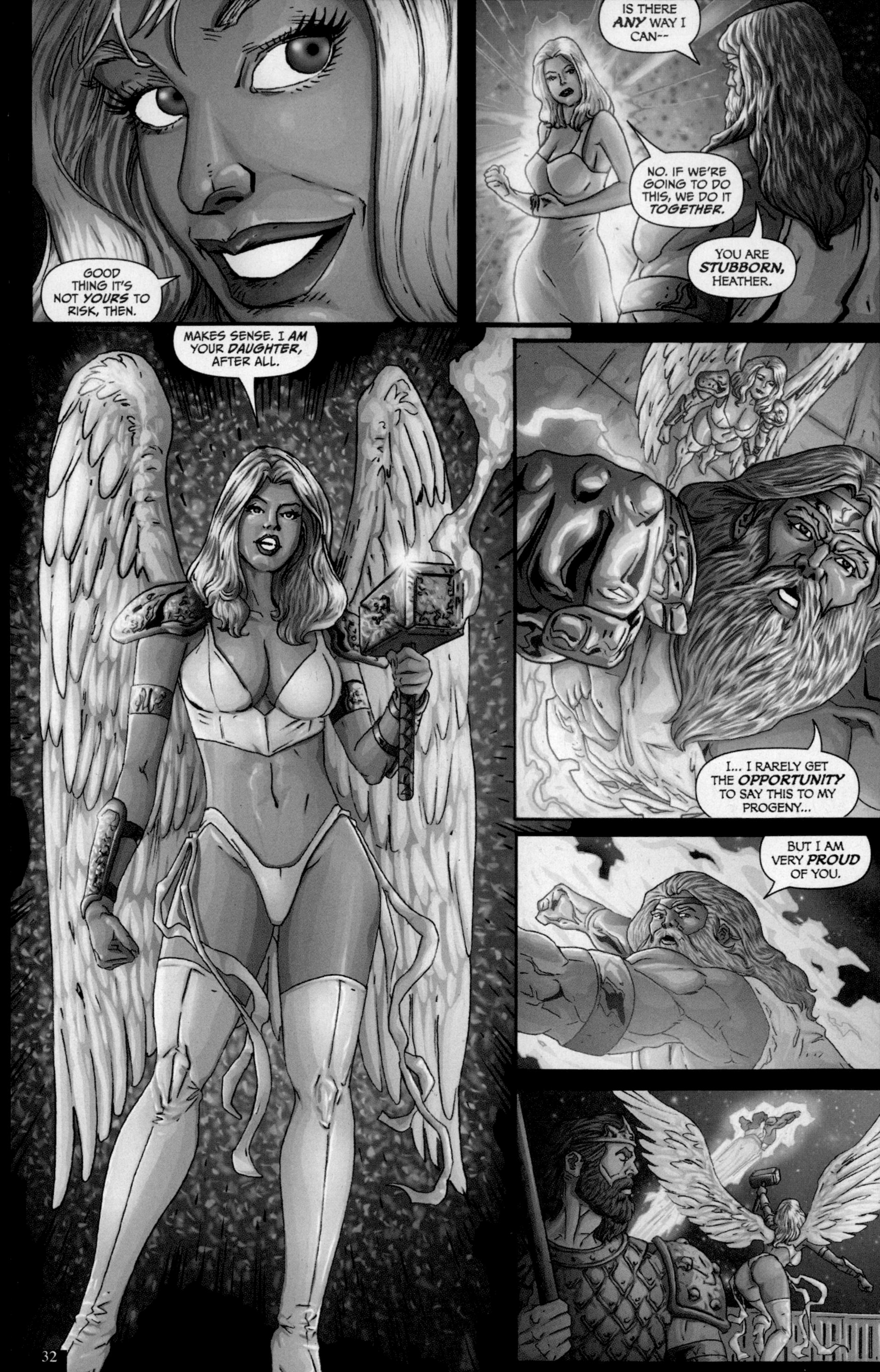
GOOD THING IT'S NOT YOURS TO RISK, THEN.
IS THERE ANY WAY I CAN--
NO. IF WE'RE GOING TO DO THIS, WE DO IT TOGETHER.
YOU ARE STUBBORN, HEATHER.
MAKES SENSE. I AM YOUR DAUGHTER, AFTER ALL.
I... I RARELY GET THE OPPORTUNITY TO SAY THIS TO MY PROGENY...
BUT I AM VERY PROUD OF YOU.

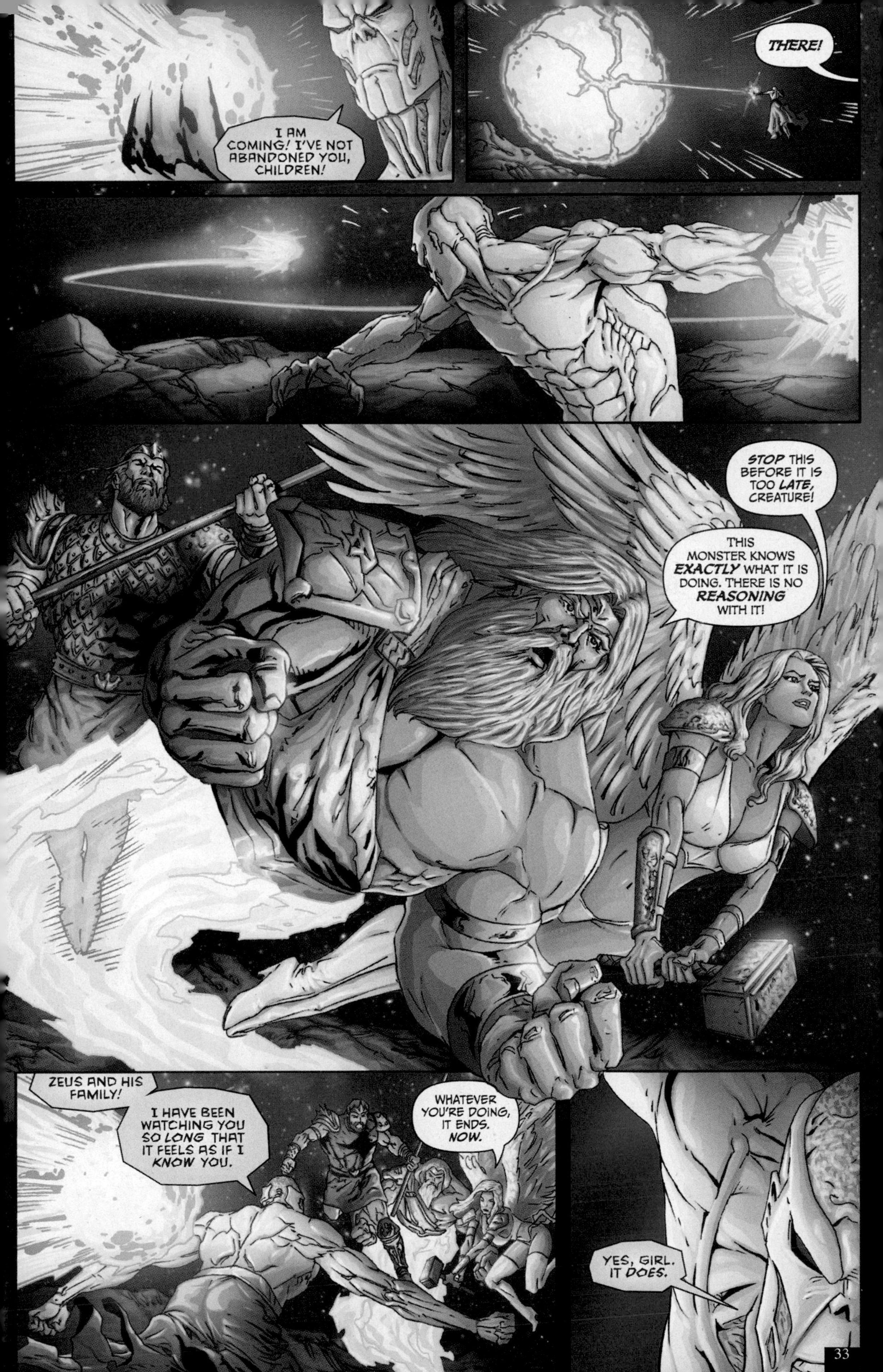
I AM COMING! I'VE NOT ABANDONED YOU, CHILDREN!
THERE!
STOP THIS BEFORE IT IS TOO LATE, CREATURE!
THIS MONSTER KNOWS EXACTLY WHAT IT IS DOING. THERE IS NO REASONING WITH IT!
ZEUS AND HIS FAMILY!
I HAVE BEEN WATCHING YOU SO LONG THAT IT FEELS AS IF I KNOW YOU.
WHATEVER YOU'RE DOING, IT ENDS. NOW.
YES, GIRL. IT DOES.

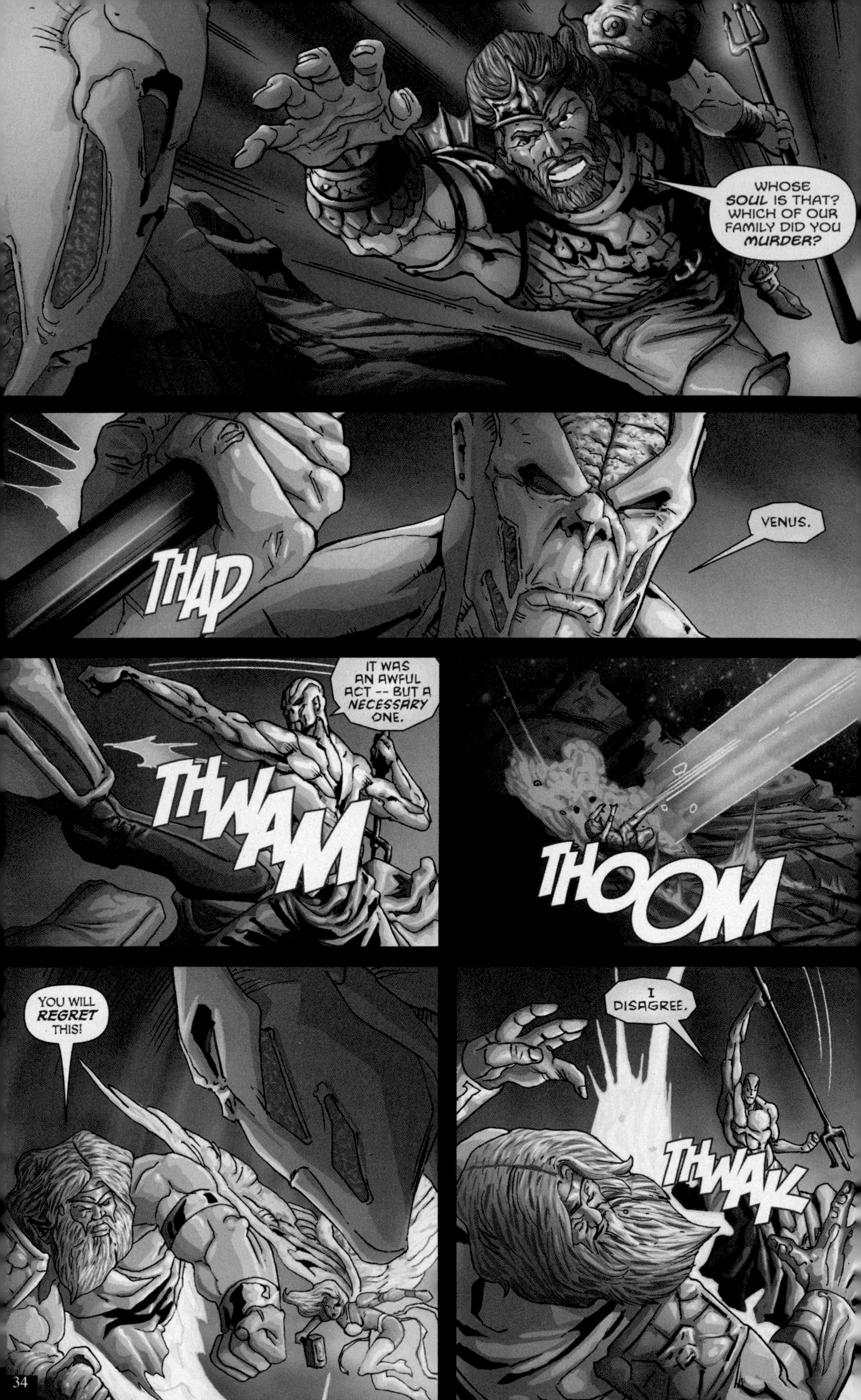
WHOSE SOUL IS THAT? WHICH OF OUR FAMILY DID YOU MURDER?
THAD
VENUS.
IT WAS AN AWFUL ACT -- BUT A NECESSARY ONE.
THWAM
THOOM
YOU WILL REGRET THIS!
I DISAGREE.
THWAK

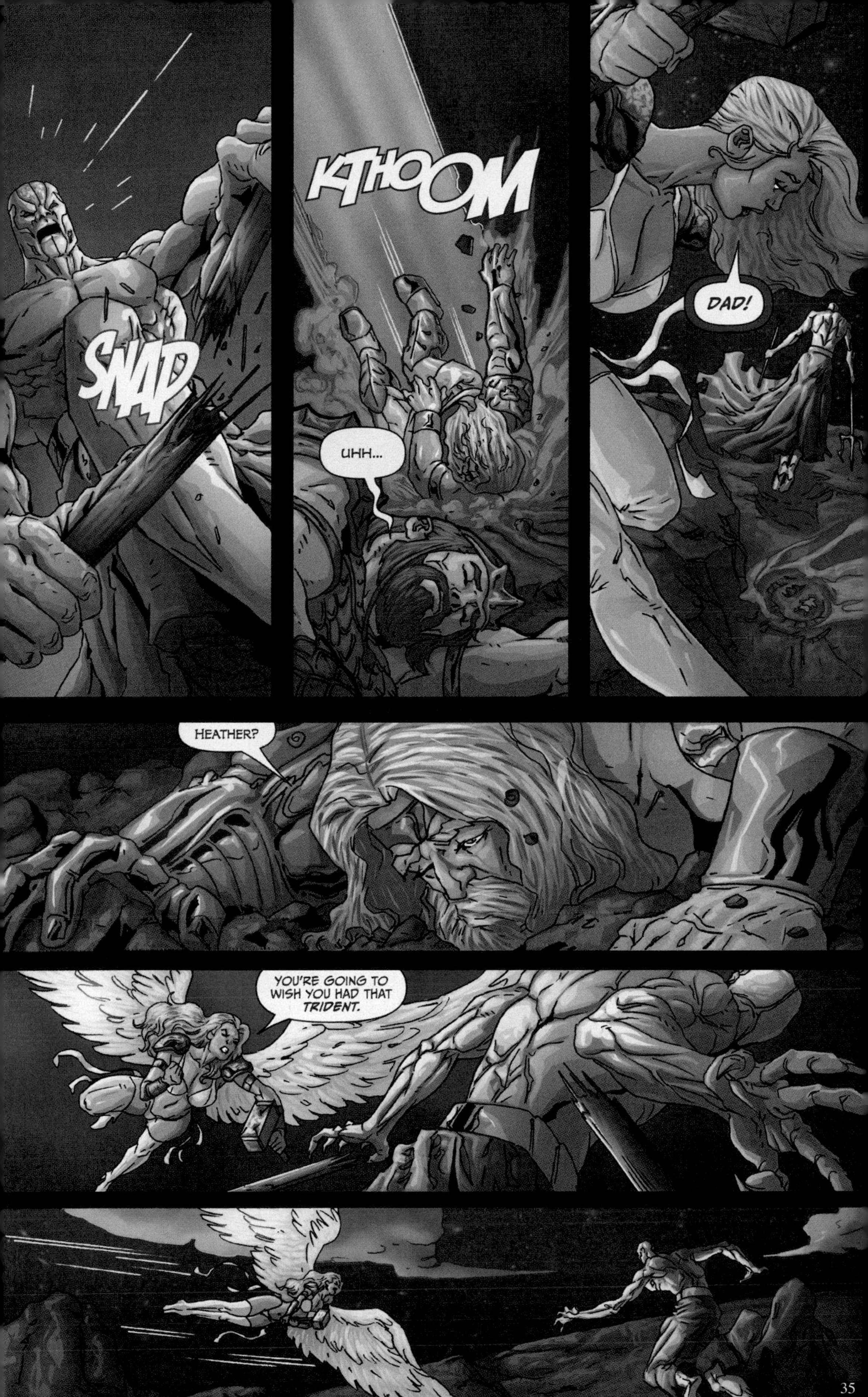
SNAP
KTHOOM
UHH...
DAD!
HEATHER?
YOU'RE GOING TO WISH YOU HAD THAT *TRIDENT.*

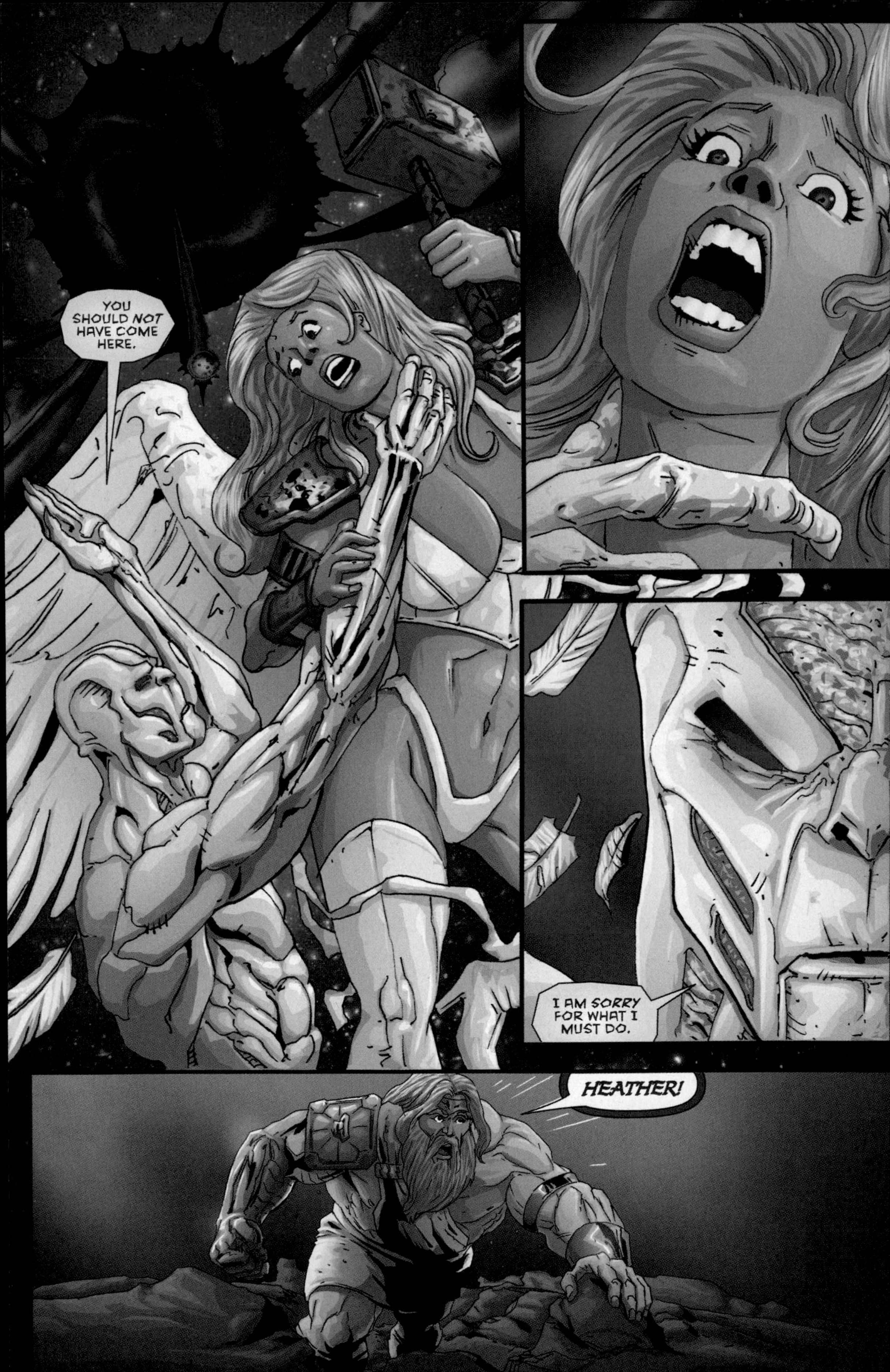
YOU SHOULD NOT HAVE COME HERE.
I AM SORRY FOR WHAT I MUST DO.
HEATHER!

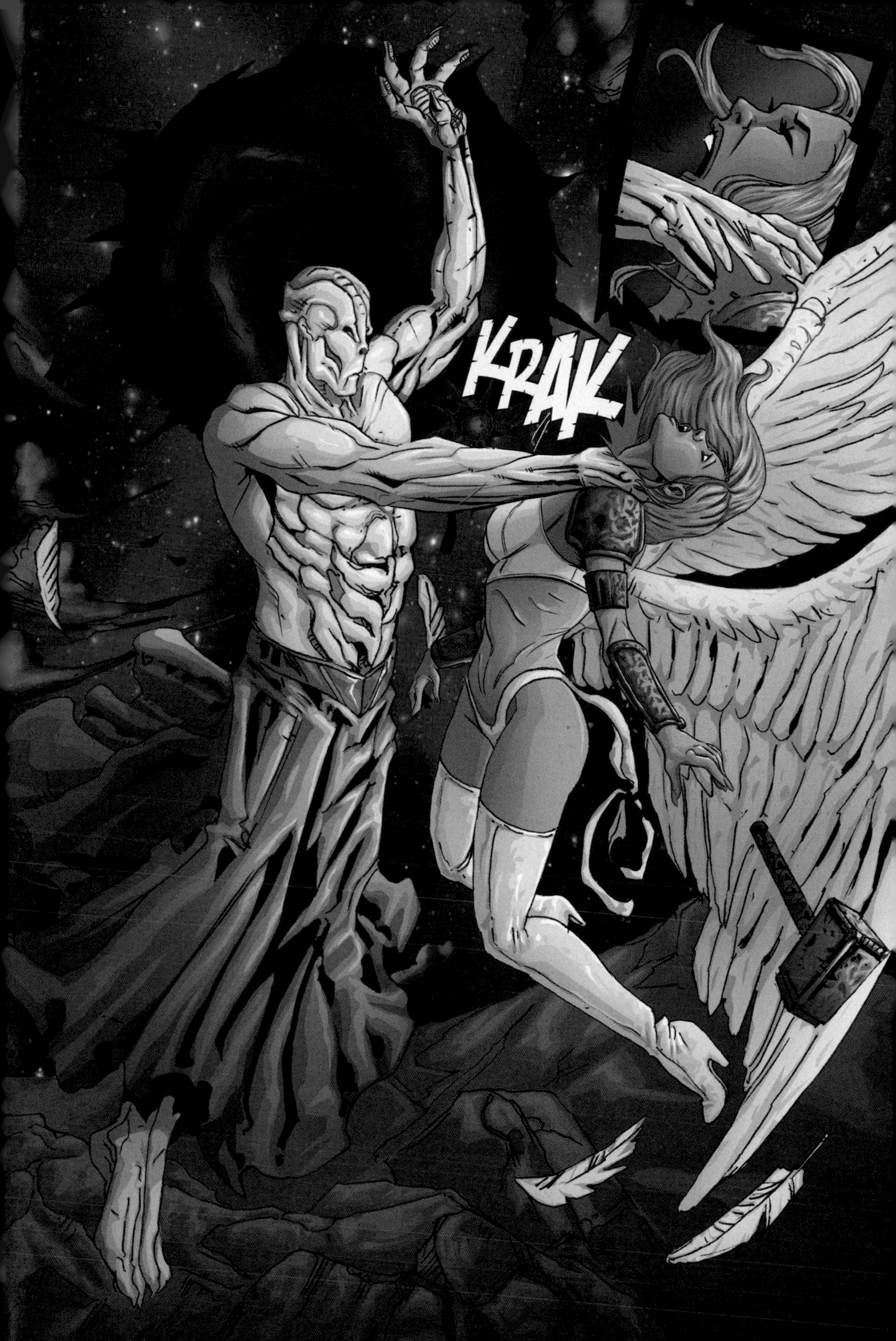
KRAK

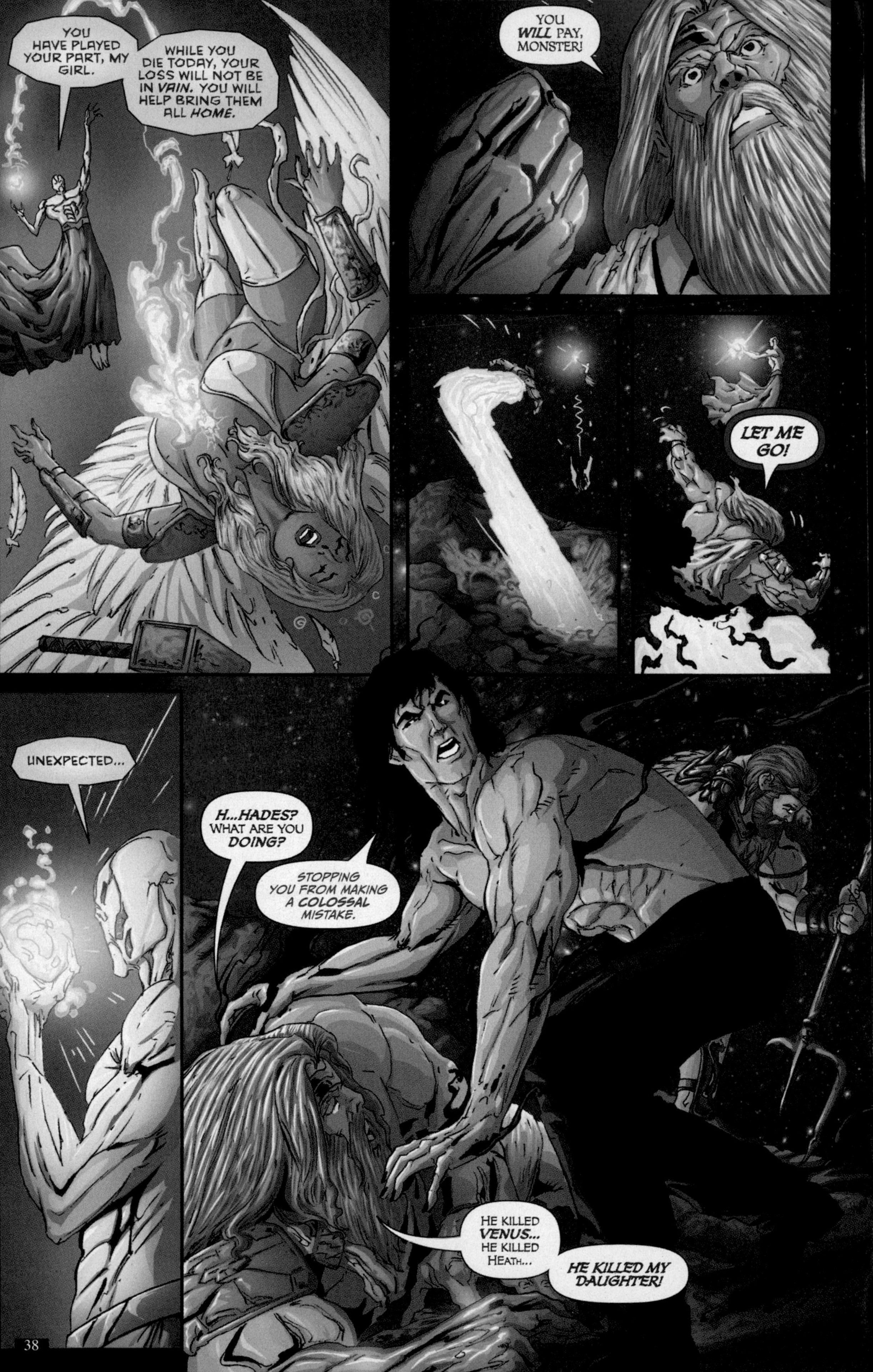
YOU HAVE PLAYED YOUR PART, MY GIRL.
WHILE YOU DIE TODAY, YOUR LOSS WILL NOT BE IN VAIN. YOU WILL HELP BRING THEM ALL HOME.
YOU WILL PAY, MONSTER!
LET ME GO!
UNEXPECTED...
H...HADES? WHAT ARE YOU DOING?
STOPPING YOU FROM MAKING A COLOSSAL MISTAKE.
HE KILLED VENUS... HE KILLED HEATH...
HE KILLED MY DAUGHTER!

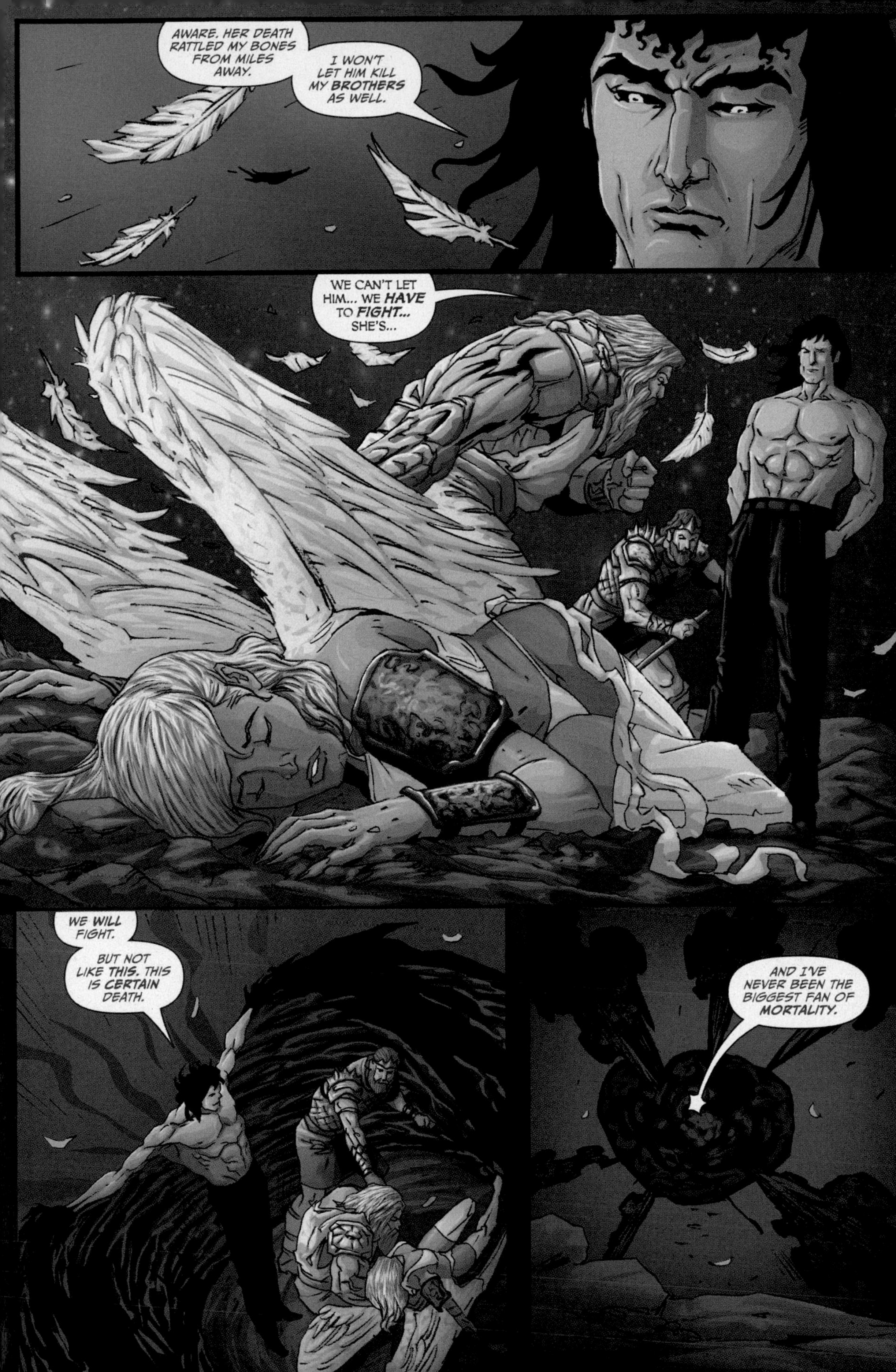
AWARE. HER DEATH RATTLED MY BONES FROM MILES AWAY.
I WON'T LET HIM KILL MY BROTHERS AS WELL.
WE CAN'T LET HIM... WE HAVE TO FIGHT... SHE'S...
WE WILL FIGHT.
BUT NOT LIKE THIS. THIS IS CERTAIN DEATH.
AND I'VE NEVER BEEN THE BIGGEST FAN OF MORTALITY.

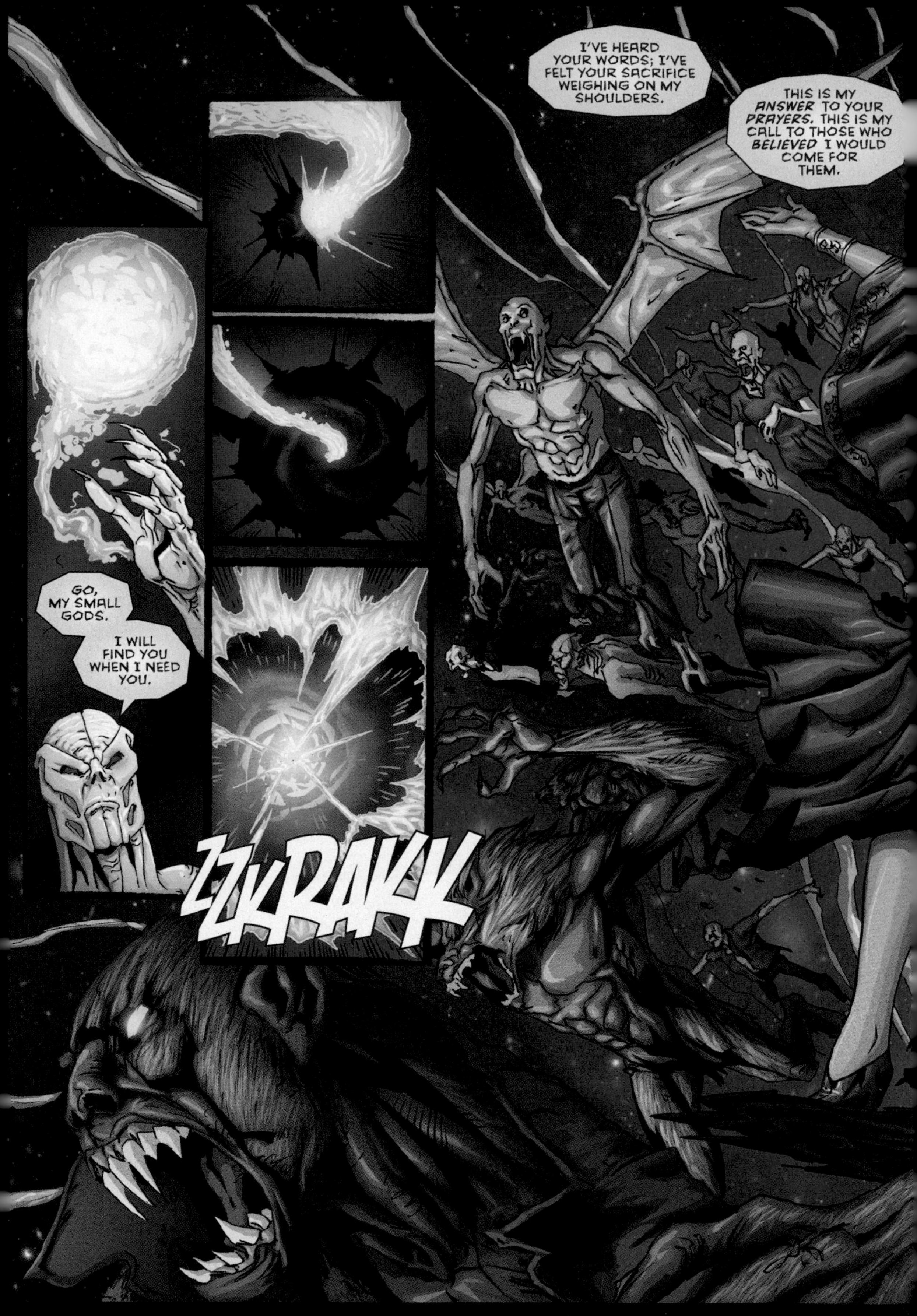
I'VE HEARD YOUR WORDS; I'VE FELT YOUR SACRIFICE WEIGHING ON MY SHOULDERS.
THIS IS MY ANSWER TO YOUR PRAYERS. THIS IS MY CALL TO THOSE WHO BELIEVED I WOULD COME FOR THEM.
GO, MY SMALL GODS.
I WILL FIND YOU WHEN I NEED YOU.
ZZKRAKK

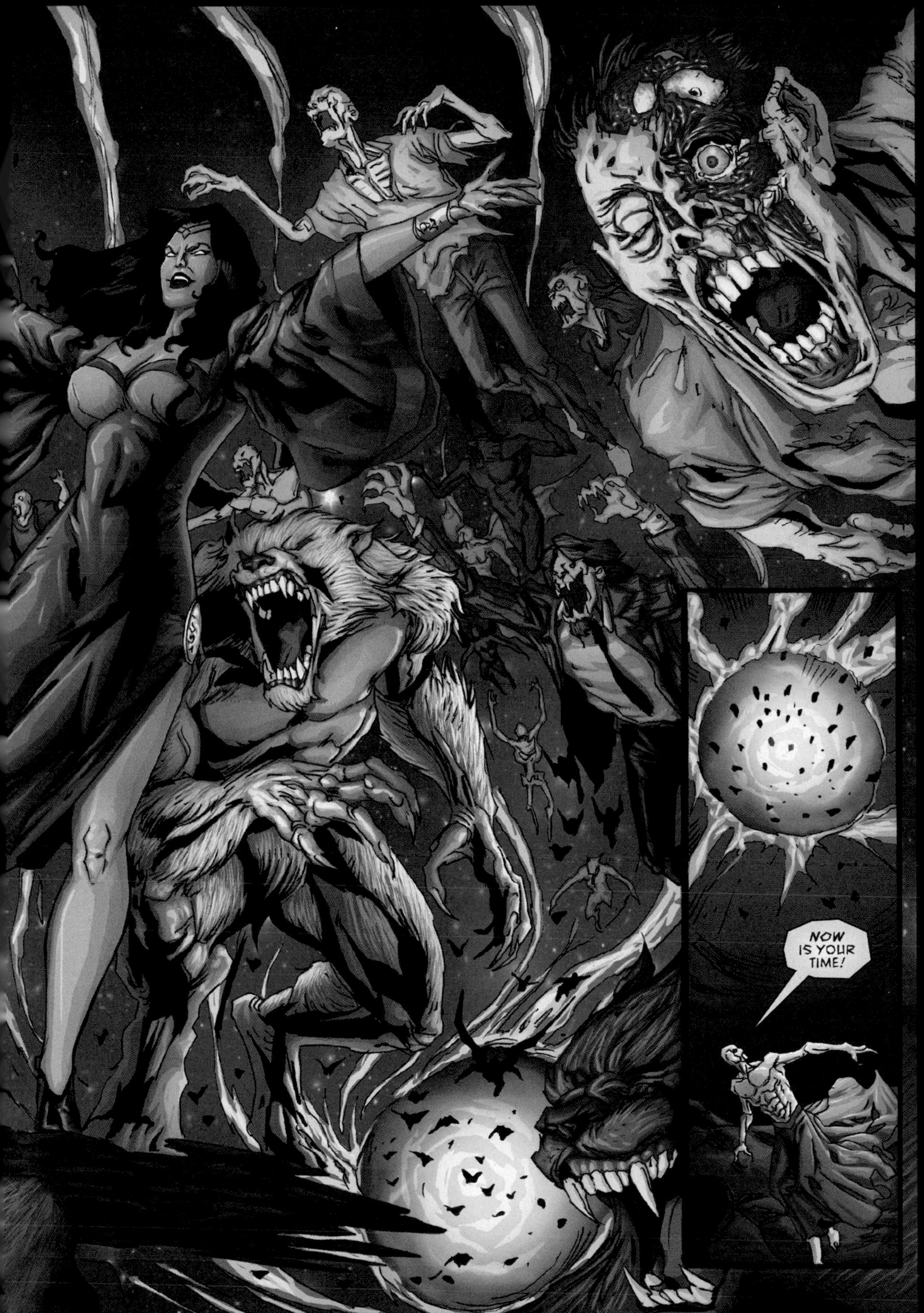
NOW IS YOUR TIME!

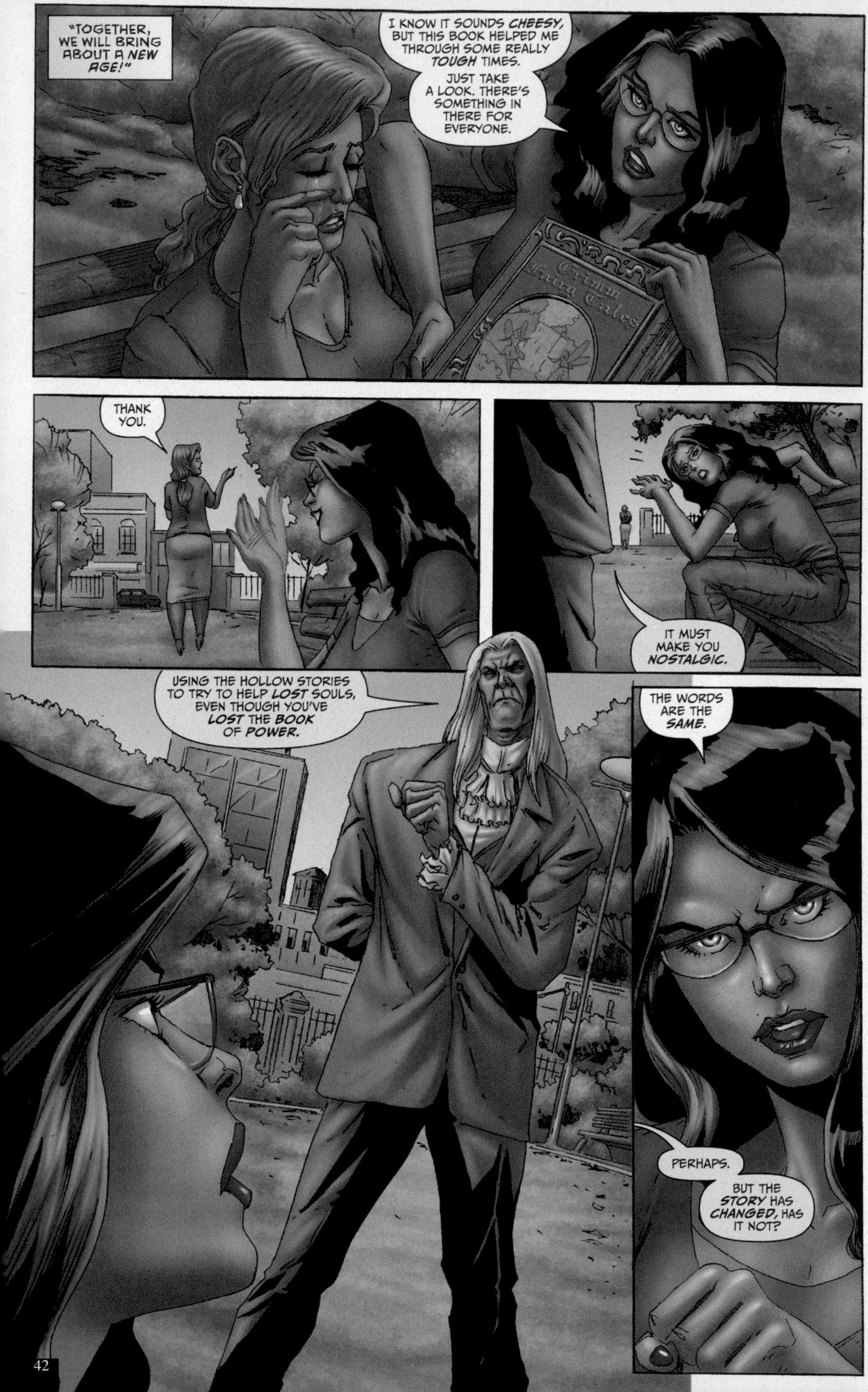
"TOGETHER, WE WILL BRING ABOUT A NEW AGE!"
I KNOW IT SOUNDS CHEESY, BUT THIS BOOK HELPED ME THROUGH SOME REALLY TOUGH TIMES.
JUST TAKE A LOOK. THERE'S SOMETHING IN THERE FOR EVERYONE.
Grimm Fairy Tales
THANK YOU.
IT MUST MAKE YOU NOSTALGIC.
USING THE HOLLOW STORIES TO TRY TO HELP LOST SOULS, EVEN THOUGH YOU'VE LOST THE BOOK OF POWER.
THE WORDS ARE THE SAME.
PERHAPS.
BUT THE STORY HAS CHANGED, HAS IT NOT?

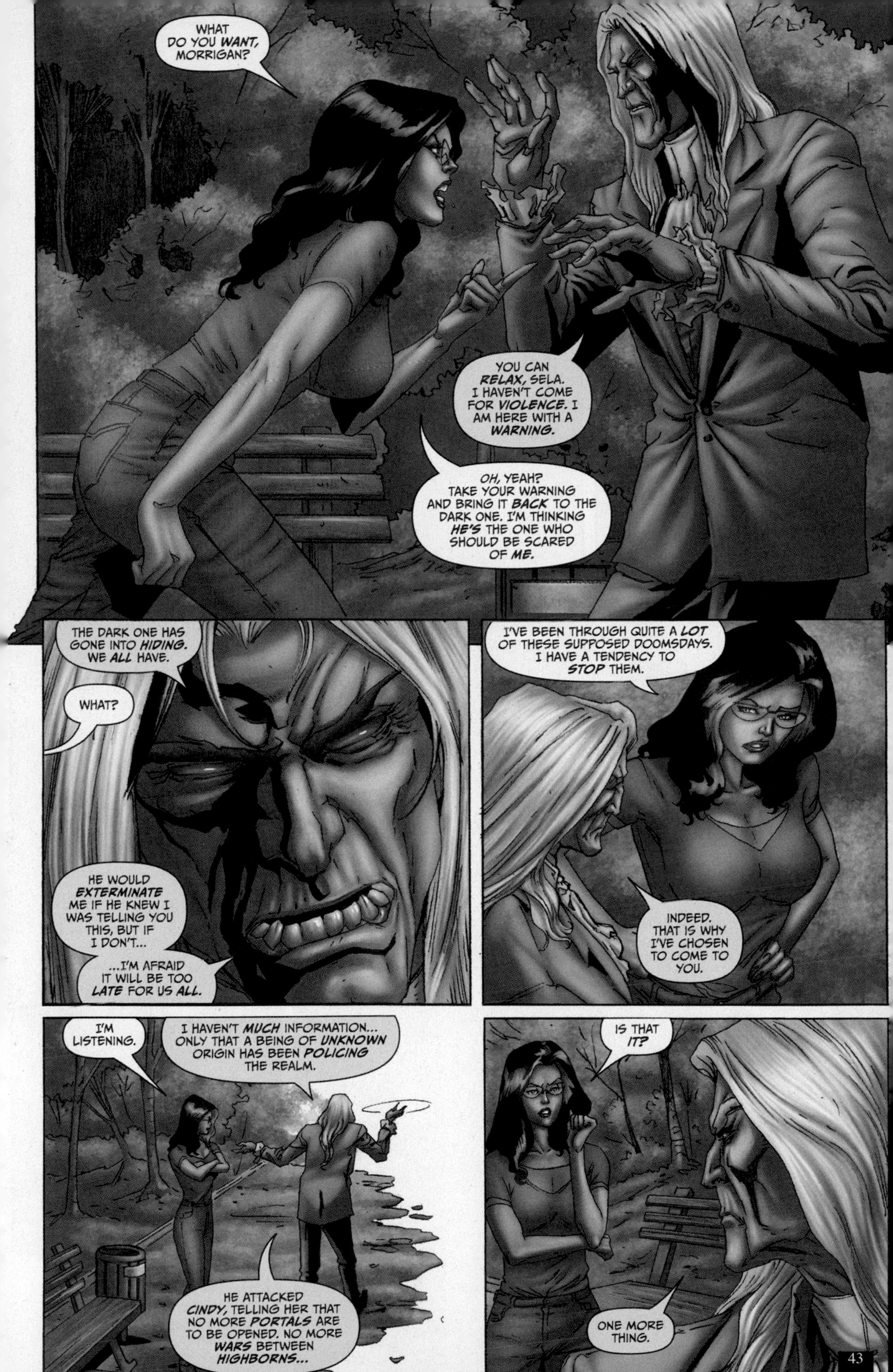
WHAT DO YOU WANT, MORRIGAN?
YOU CAN RELAX, SELA. I HAVEN'T COME FOR VIOLENCE. I AM HERE WITH A WARNING.
OH, YEAH? TAKE YOUR WARNING AND BRING IT BACK TO THE DARK ONE. I'M THINKING HE'S THE ONE WHO SHOULD BE SCARED OF ME.
THE DARK ONE HAS GONE INTO HIDING. WE ALL HAVE.
WHAT?
HE WOULD EXTERMINATE ME IF HE KNEW I WAS TELLING YOU THIS, BUT IF I DON'T...
...I'M AFRAID IT WILL BE TOO LATE FOR US ALL.
I'VE BEEN THROUGH QUITE A LOT OF THESE SUPPOSED DOOMSDAYS. I HAVE A TENDENCY TO STOP THEM.
INDEED. THAT IS WHY I'VE CHOSEN TO COME TO YOU.
I'M LISTENING.
I HAVEN'T MUCH INFORMATION... ONLY THAT A BEING OF UNKNOWN ORIGIN HAS BEEN POLICING THE REALM.
HE ATTACKED CINDY, TELLING HER THAT NO MORE PORTALS ARE TO BE OPENED. NO MORE WARS BETWEEN HIGHBORNS...
IS THAT IT?
ONE MORE THING.

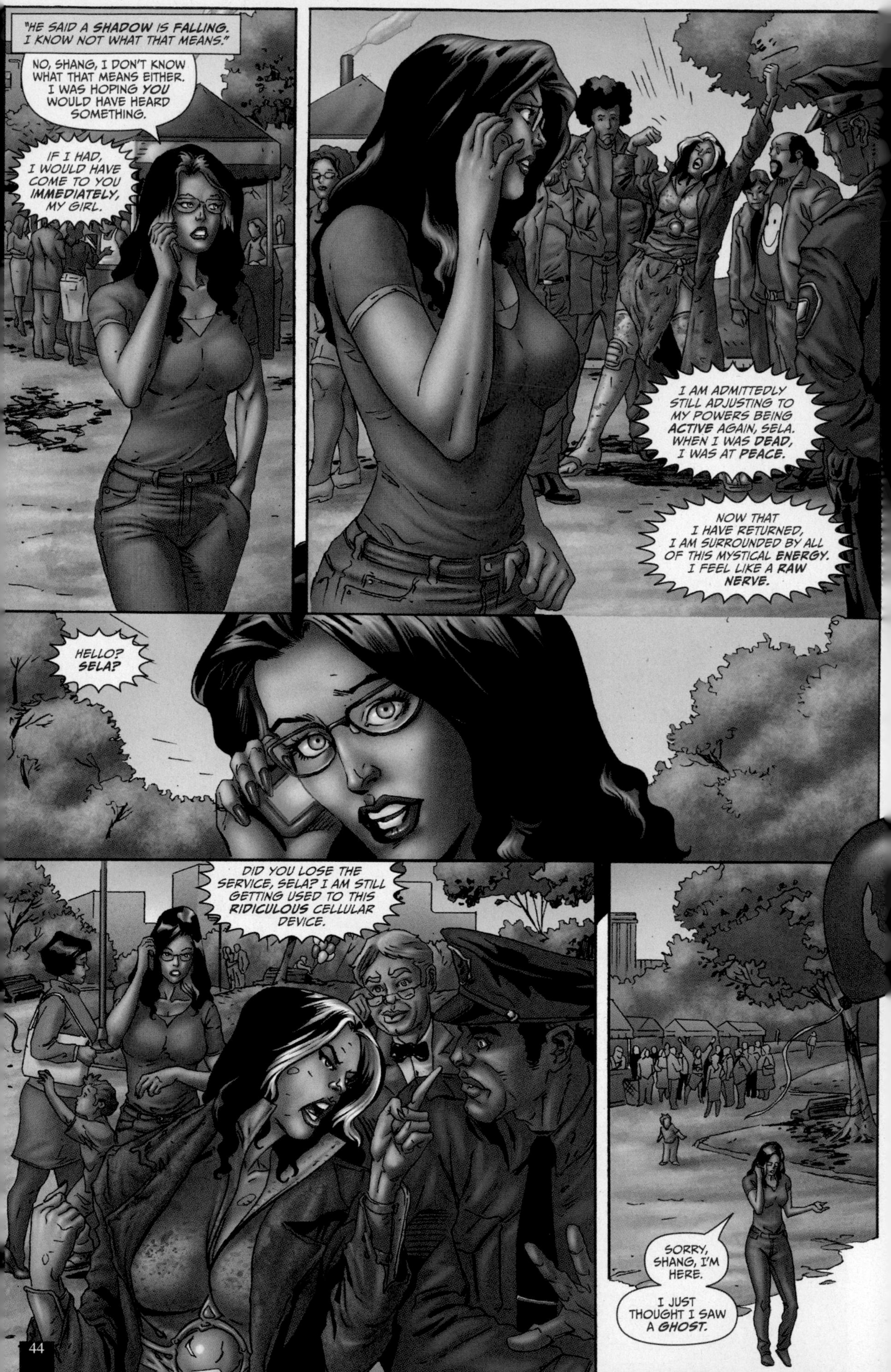

"HE SAID A SHADOW IS FALLING. I KNOW NOT WHAT THAT MEANS."
NO, SHANG, I DON'T KNOW WHAT THAT MEANS EITHER. I WAS HOPING YOU WOULD HAVE HEARD SOMETHING.
IF I HAD, I WOULD HAVE COME TO YOU IMMEDIATELY, MY GIRL.
I AM ADMITTEDLY STILL ADJUSTING TO MY POWERS BEING ACTIVE AGAIN, SELA. WHEN I WAS DEAD, I WAS AT PEACE.
NOW THAT I HAVE RETURNED, I AM SURROUNDED BY ALL OF THIS MYSTICAL ENERGY. I FEEL LIKE A RAW NERVE.
HELLO? SELA?
DID YOU LOSE THE SERVICE, SELA? I AM STILL GETTING USED TO THIS RIDICULOUS CELLULAR DEVICE.
SORRY, SHANG, I'M HERE.
I JUST THOUGHT I SAW A GHOST.

I'M NOT USED TO THE *SUN* RISING... HAVING TO HIDE AWAY DURING DAYLIGHT.

IN THE *SHADOWLANDS*, THE *SUNS* DIDN'T HARM VAMPIRES. I WONDER HOW MANY OF MY BRETHREN ARE *FRYING* THIS MORNING.

DO YOU WISH TO RETURN?

NEVER.

GOOD. I HAVE BEEN WORKING ON SOMETHING FOR YOU, SAMIRA. A... *GIFT* OF SORTS.

I THINK YOU WILL *ENJOY* IT.

HOW *LONG* BEFORE THE PORTAL *FULLY* OPENS?

IN DUE TIME.

THE PEOPLE WHO *BANISHED* US THERE ARE GOING TO *ESCAPE* TOO, AREN'T THEY?

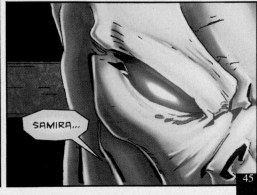

SAMIRA...

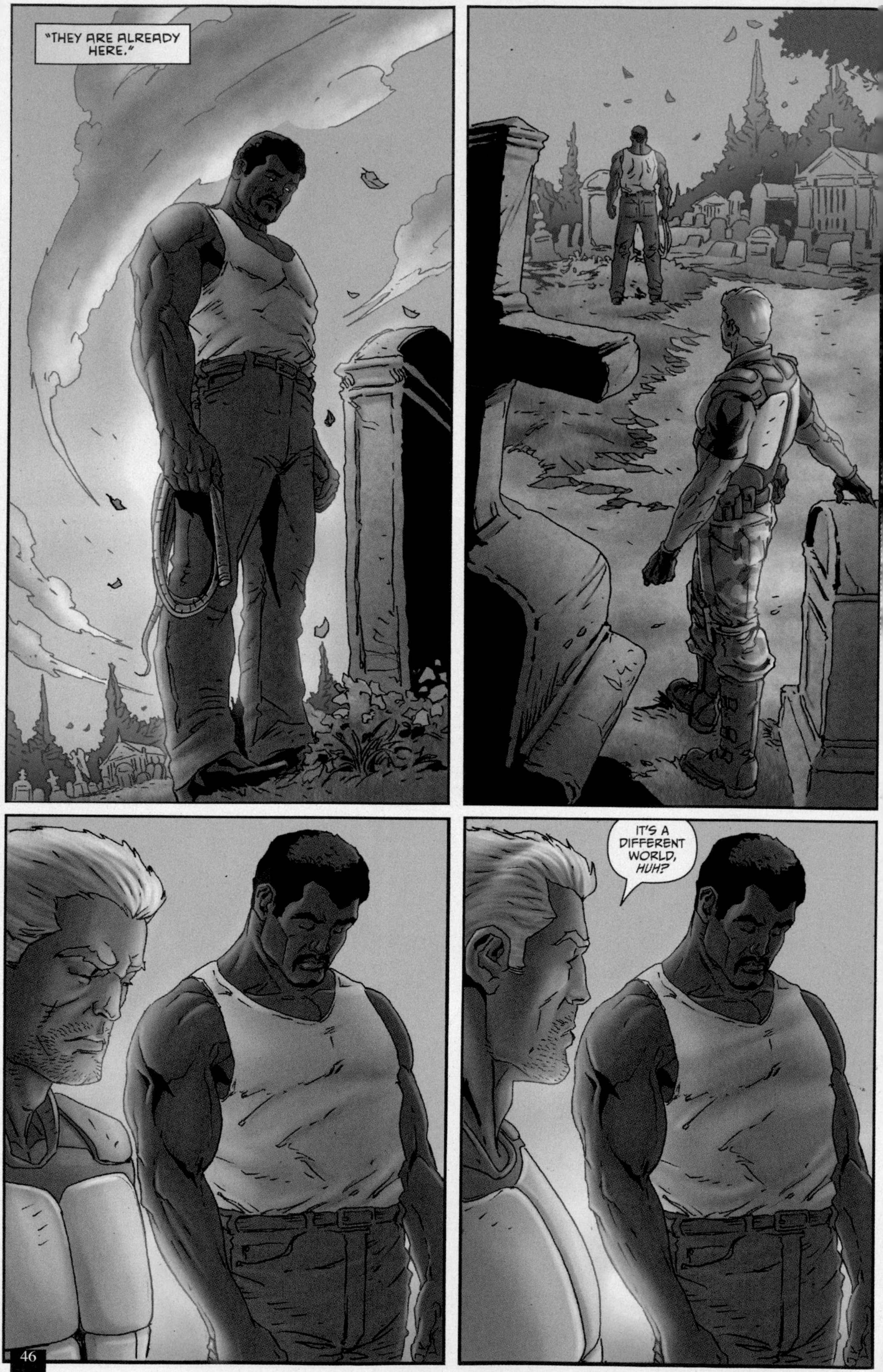
"THEY ARE ALREADY HERE."
IT'S A DIFFERENT WORLD, HUH?

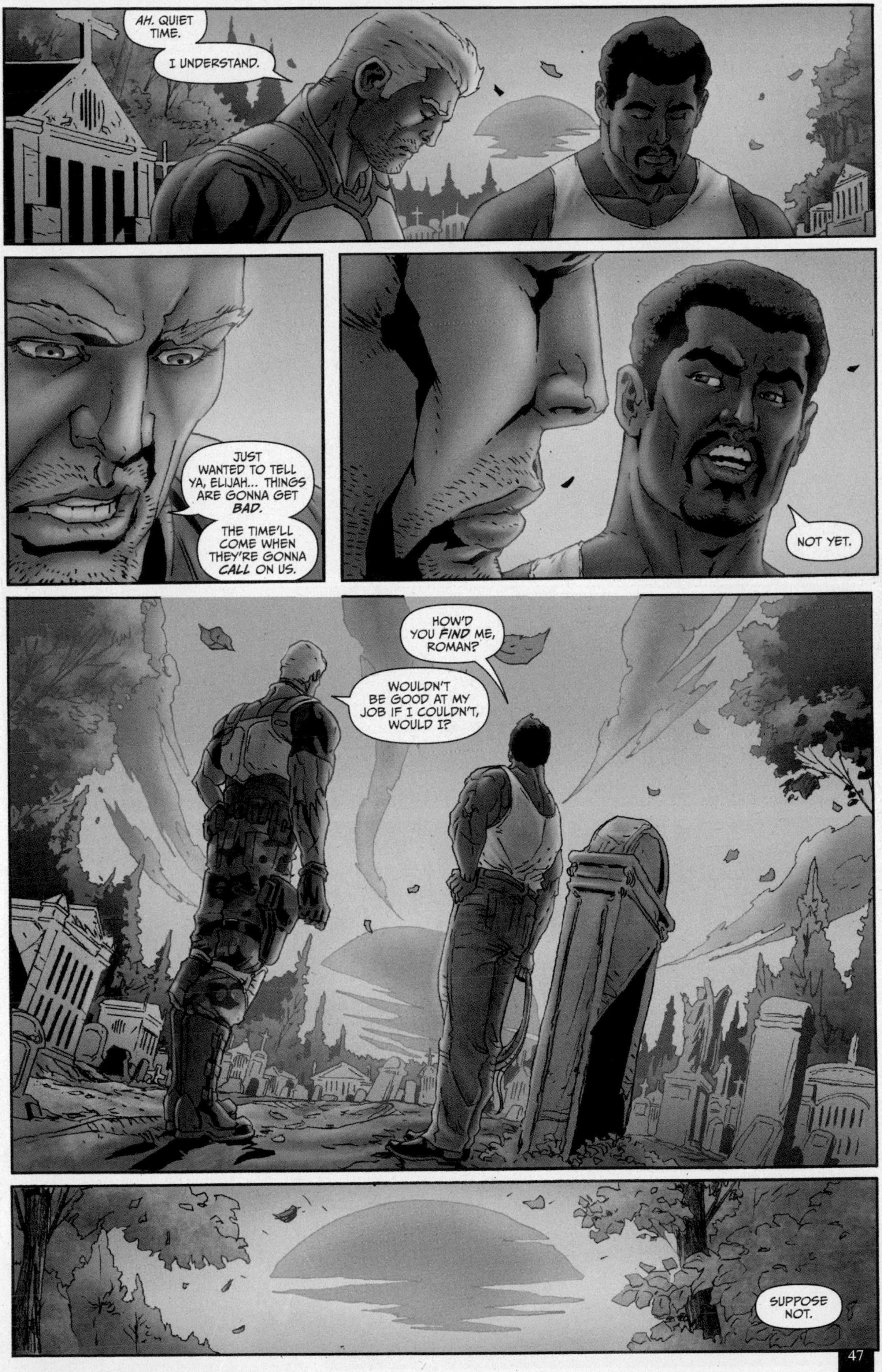
AH. QUIET TIME.
I UNDERSTAND.
JUST WANTED TO TELL YA, ELIJAH... THINGS ARE GONNA GET BAD.
THE TIME'LL COME WHEN THEY'RE GONNA CALL ON US.
NOT YET.
HOW'D YOU FIND ME, ROMAN?
WOULDN'T BE GOOD AT MY JOB IF I COULDN'T, WOULD I?
SUPPOSE NOT.

LATER--

THIS DOES **NOT** LOOK **GOOD**, SHANG.

WE CANNOT JUMP TO **CONCLUSIONS**, SELA.

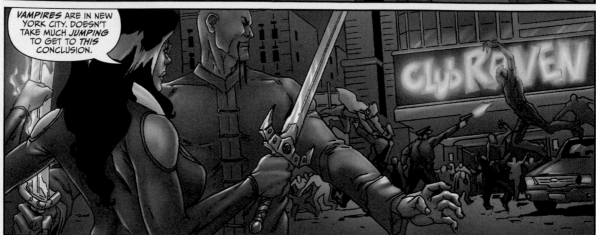

VAMPIRES ARE IN NEW YORK CITY. DOESN'T TAKE MUCH **JUMPING** TO GET TO **THIS** CONCLUSION.

CLUB RAVEN

SHANG, TAKE CARE OF THESE OUT HERE-- I'M GOING IN.

SHRAAK

TH'WOK

SLAM

IMPOSSIBLE.

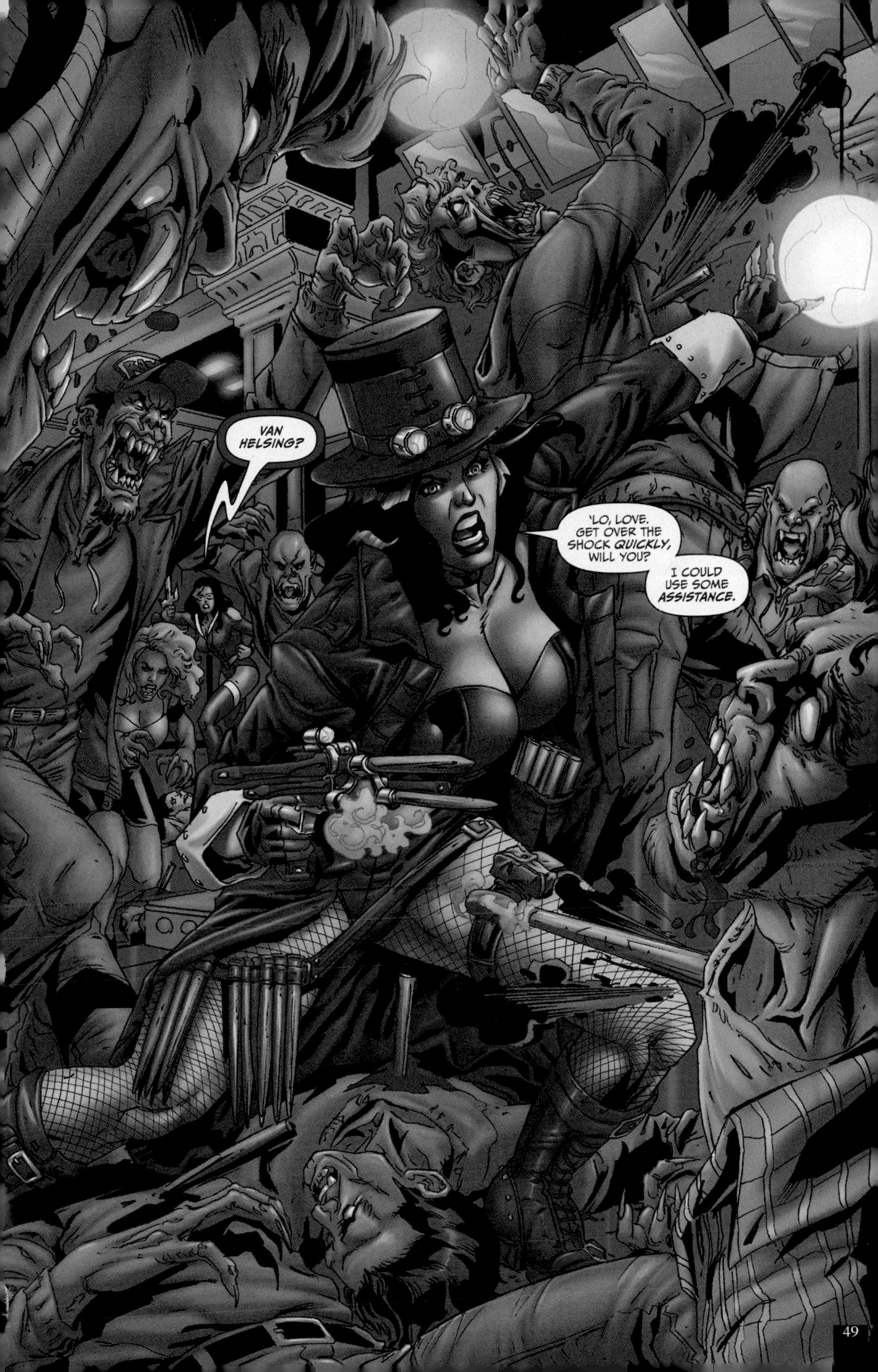
VAN HELSING?
'LO, LOVE. GET OVER THE SHOCK QUICKLY, WILL YOU?
I COULD USE SOME ASSISTANCE.

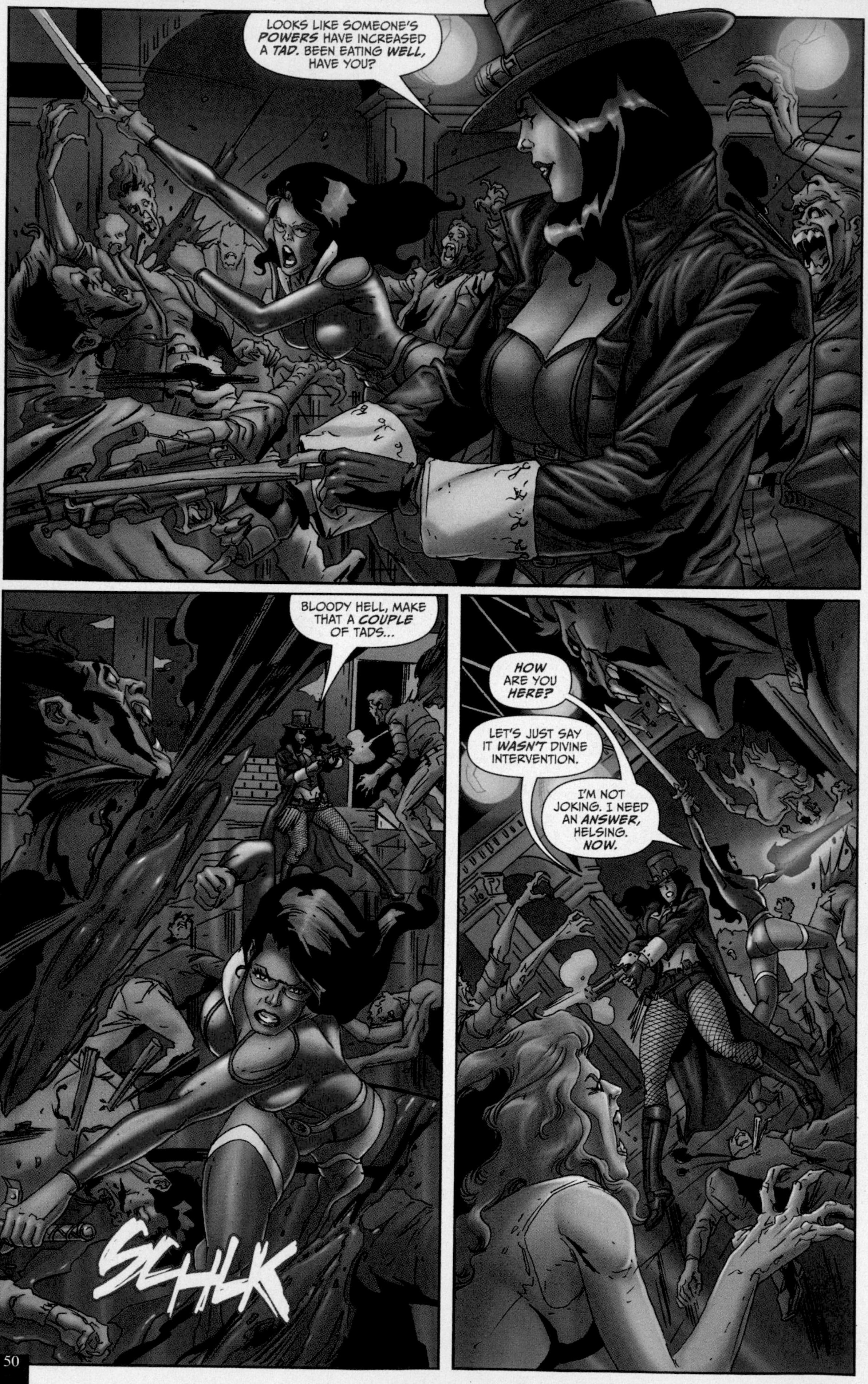
LOOKS LIKE SOMEONE'S POWERS HAVE INCREASED A TAD. BEEN EATING WELL, HAVE YOU?
BLOODY HELL, MAKE THAT A COUPLE OF TADS...
SCHLK
HOW ARE YOU HERE?
LET'S JUST SAY IT WASN'T DIVINE INTERVENTION.
I'M NOT JOKING. I NEED AN ANSWER, HELSING. NOW.

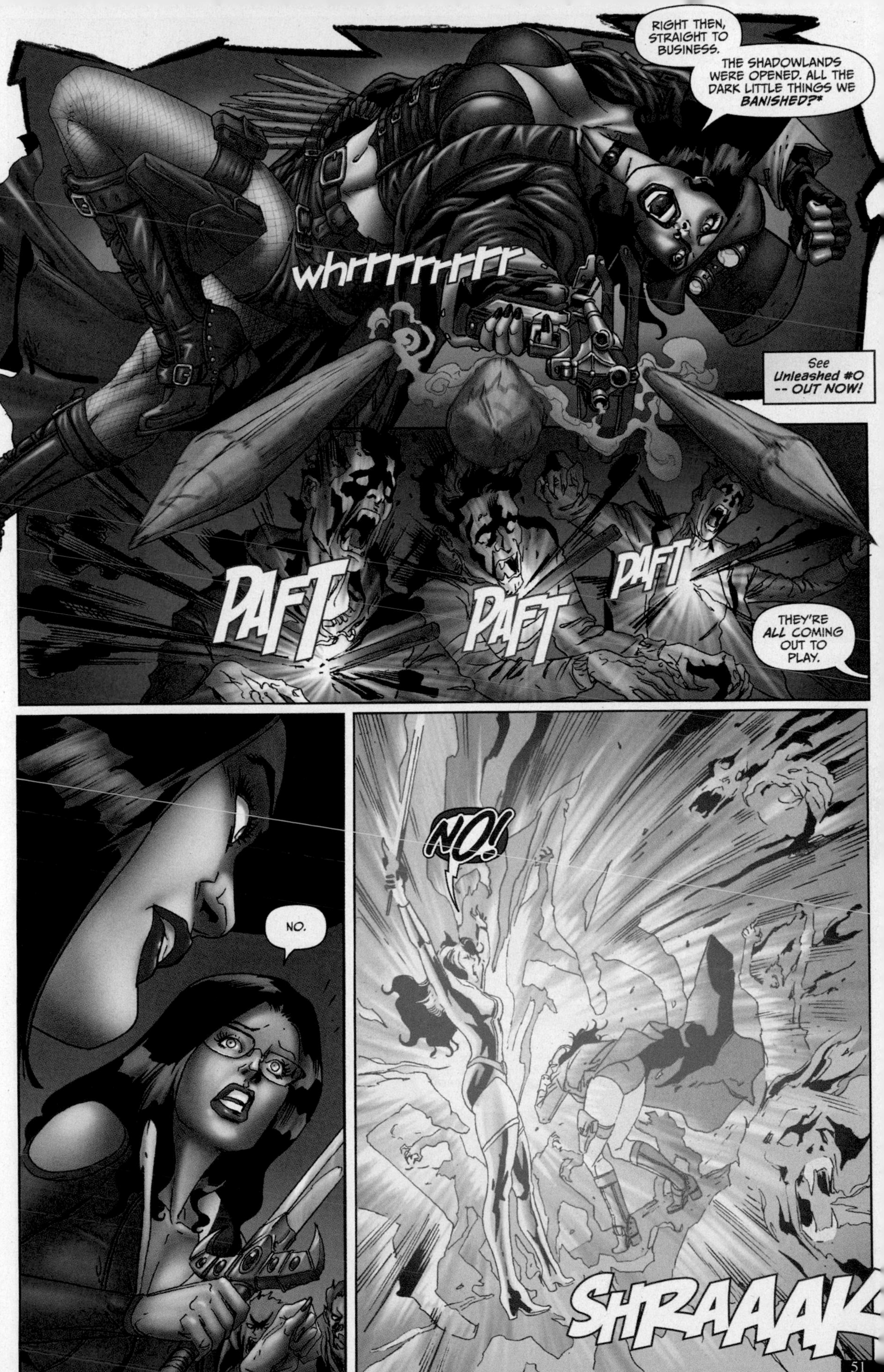
RIGHT THEN, STRAIGHT TO BUSINESS.
THE SHADOWLANDS WERE OPENED. ALL THE DARK LITTLE THINGS WE BANISHED?*
whrrrrrrrr
See Unleashed #0 -- OUT NOW!
PAFT
PAFT
PAFT
THEY'RE ALL COMING OUT TO PLAY.
NO.
NO!
SHRAAAK

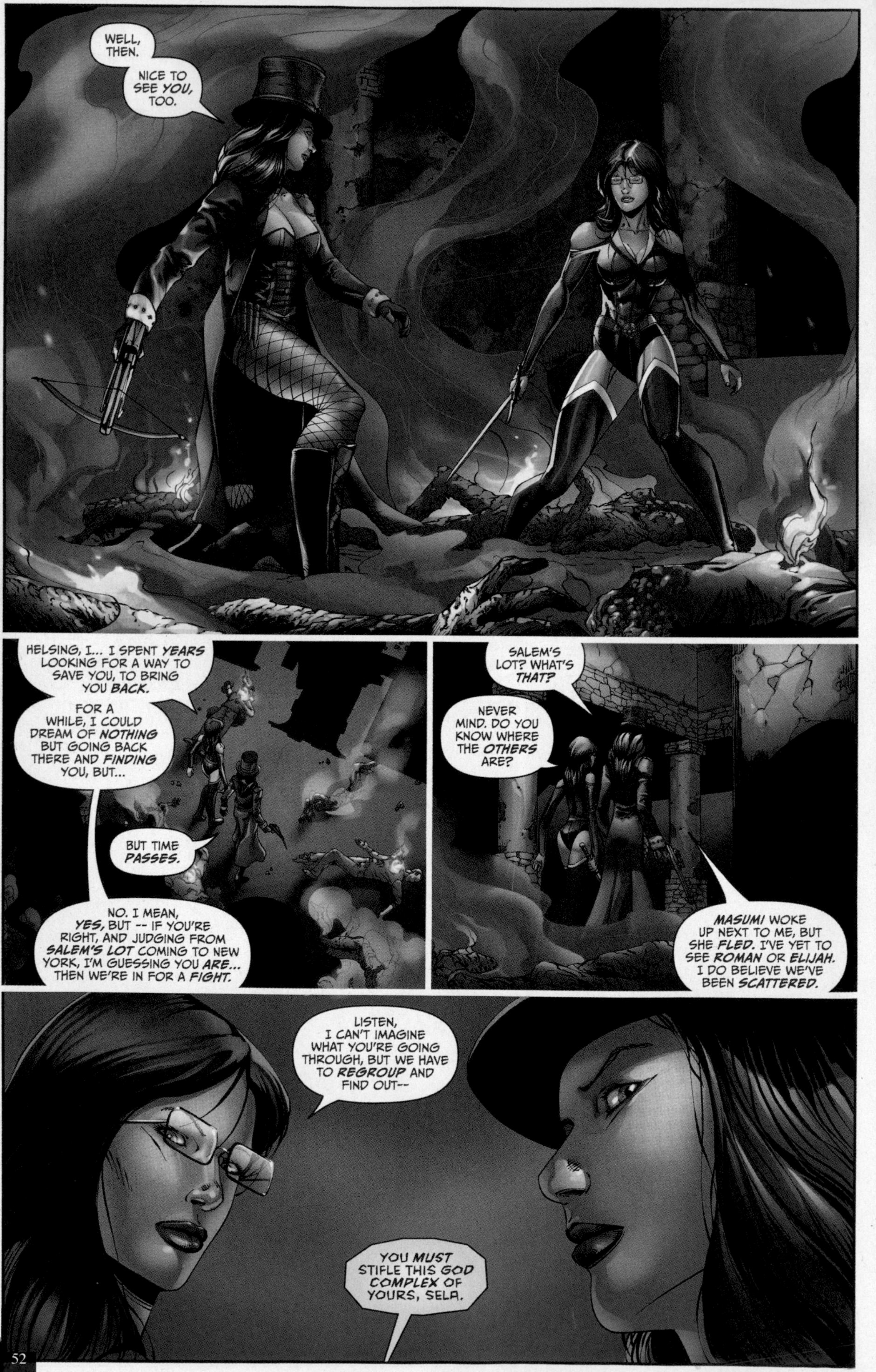
WELL, THEN.
NICE TO SEE YOU, TOO.
HELSING, I... I SPENT YEARS LOOKING FOR A WAY TO SAVE YOU, TO BRING YOU BACK.
FOR A WHILE, I COULD DREAM OF NOTHING BUT GOING BACK THERE AND FINDING YOU, BUT...
BUT TIME PASSES.
NO. I MEAN, YES, BUT -- IF YOU'RE RIGHT, AND JUDGING FROM SALEM'S LOT COMING TO NEW YORK, I'M GUESSING YOU ARE... THEN WE'RE IN FOR A FIGHT.
SALEM'S LOT? WHAT'S THAT?
NEVER MIND. DO YOU KNOW WHERE THE OTHERS ARE?
MASUMI WOKE UP NEXT TO ME, BUT SHE FLED. I'VE YET TO SEE ROMAN OR ELIJAH. I DO BELIEVE WE'VE BEEN SCATTERED.
LISTEN, I CAN'T IMAGINE WHAT YOU'RE GOING THROUGH, BUT WE HAVE TO REGROUP AND FIND OUT--
YOU MUST STIFLE THIS GOD COMPLEX OF YOURS, SELA.

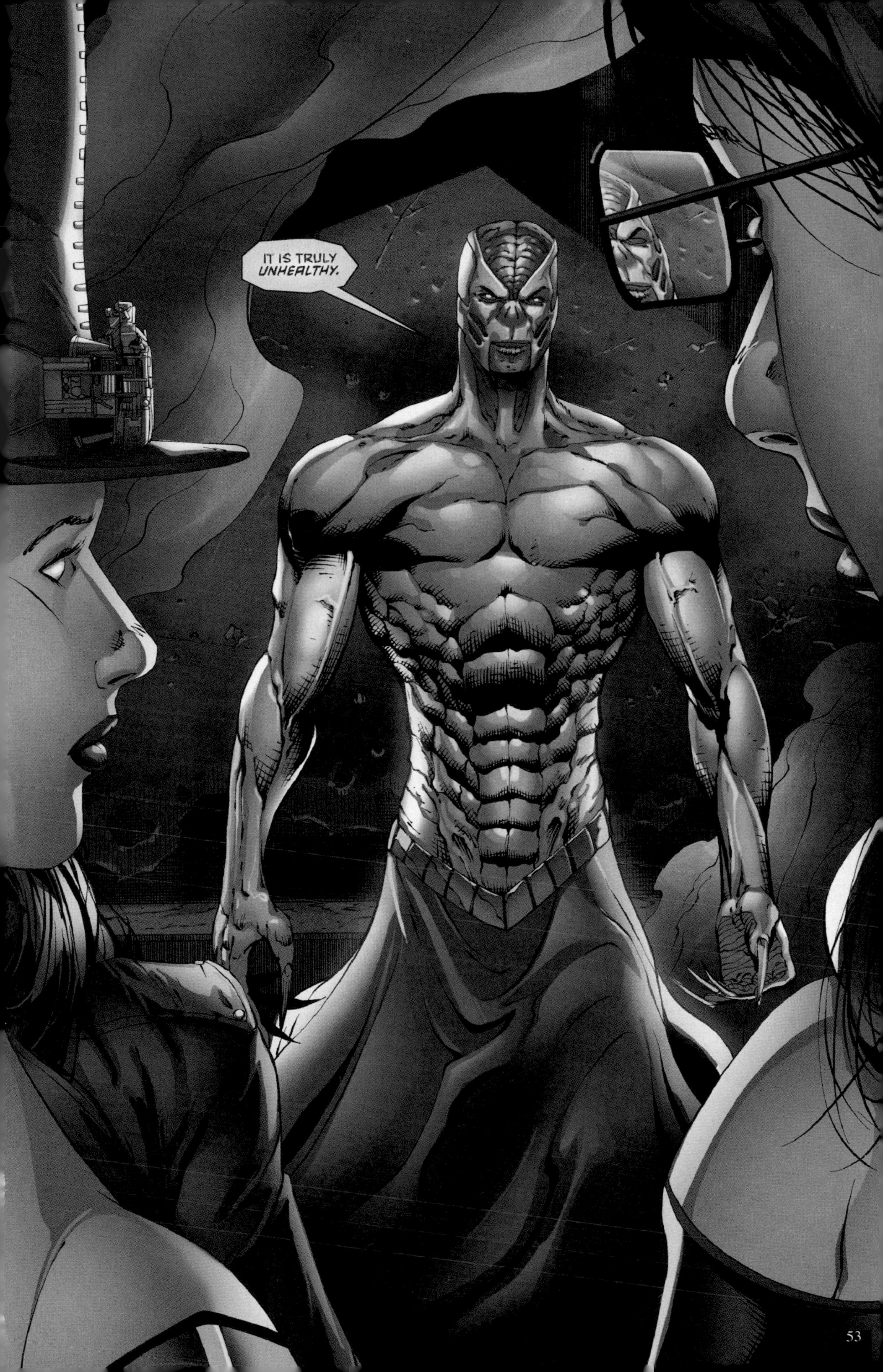
IT IS TRULY UNHEALTHY.

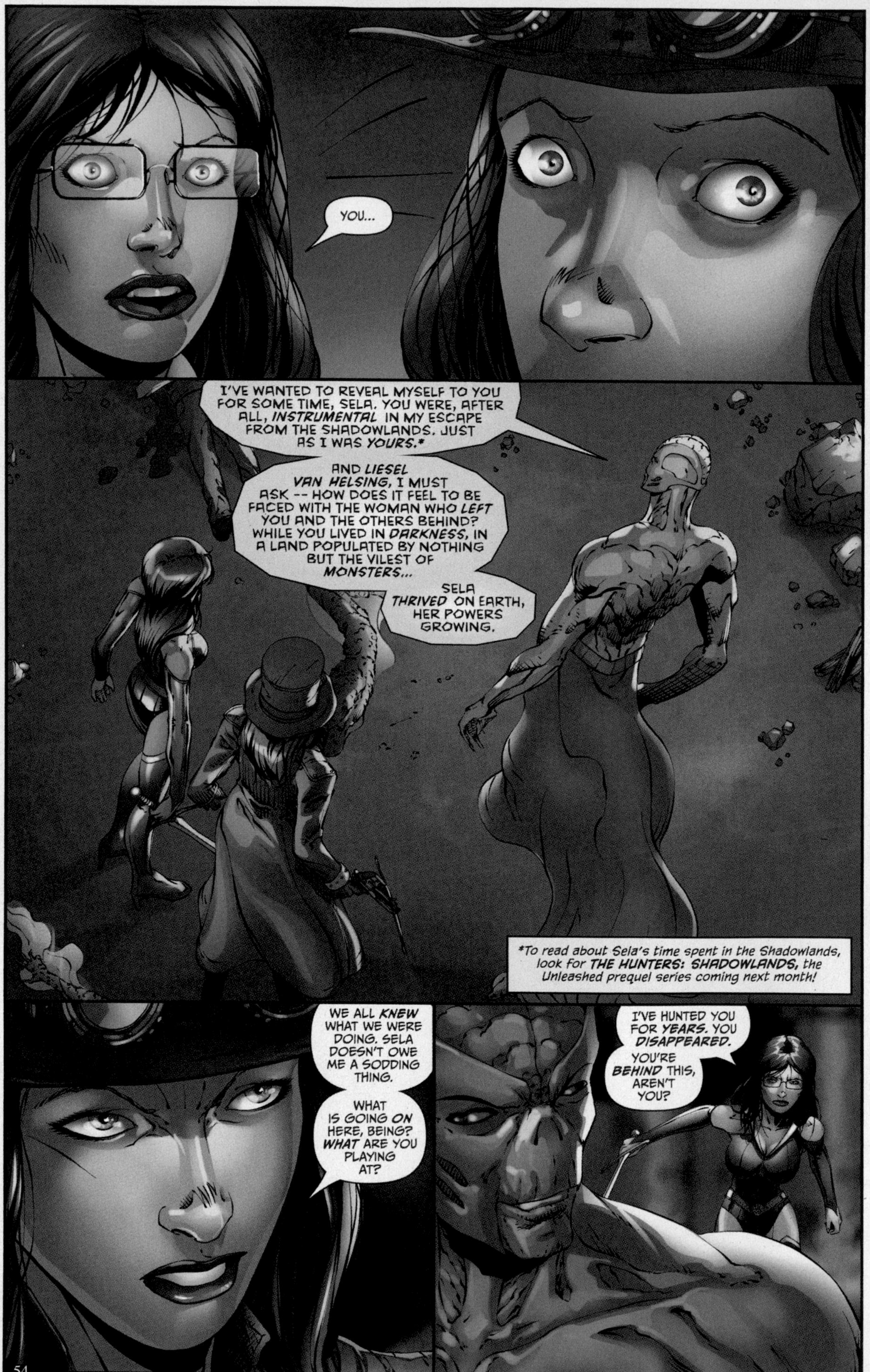

YOU...
I'VE WANTED TO REVEAL MYSELF TO YOU FOR SOME TIME, SELA. YOU WERE, AFTER ALL, INSTRUMENTAL IN MY ESCAPE FROM THE SHADOWLANDS. JUST AS I WAS YOURS.*
AND LIESEL VAN HELSING, I MUST ASK -- HOW DOES IT FEEL TO BE FACED WITH THE WOMAN WHO LEFT YOU AND THE OTHERS BEHIND? WHILE YOU LIVED IN DARKNESS, IN A LAND POPULATED BY NOTHING BUT THE VILEST OF MONSTERS...
SELA THRIVED ON EARTH, HER POWERS GROWING.
*To read about Sela's time spent in the Shadowlands, look for THE HUNTERS: SHADOWLANDS, the Unleashed prequel series coming next month!
WE ALL KNEW WHAT WE WERE DOING. SELA DOESN'T OWE ME A SODDING THING.
WHAT IS GOING ON HERE, BEING? WHAT ARE YOU PLAYING AT?
I'VE HUNTED YOU FOR YEARS. YOU DISAPPEARED.
YOU'RE BEHIND THIS, AREN'T YOU?

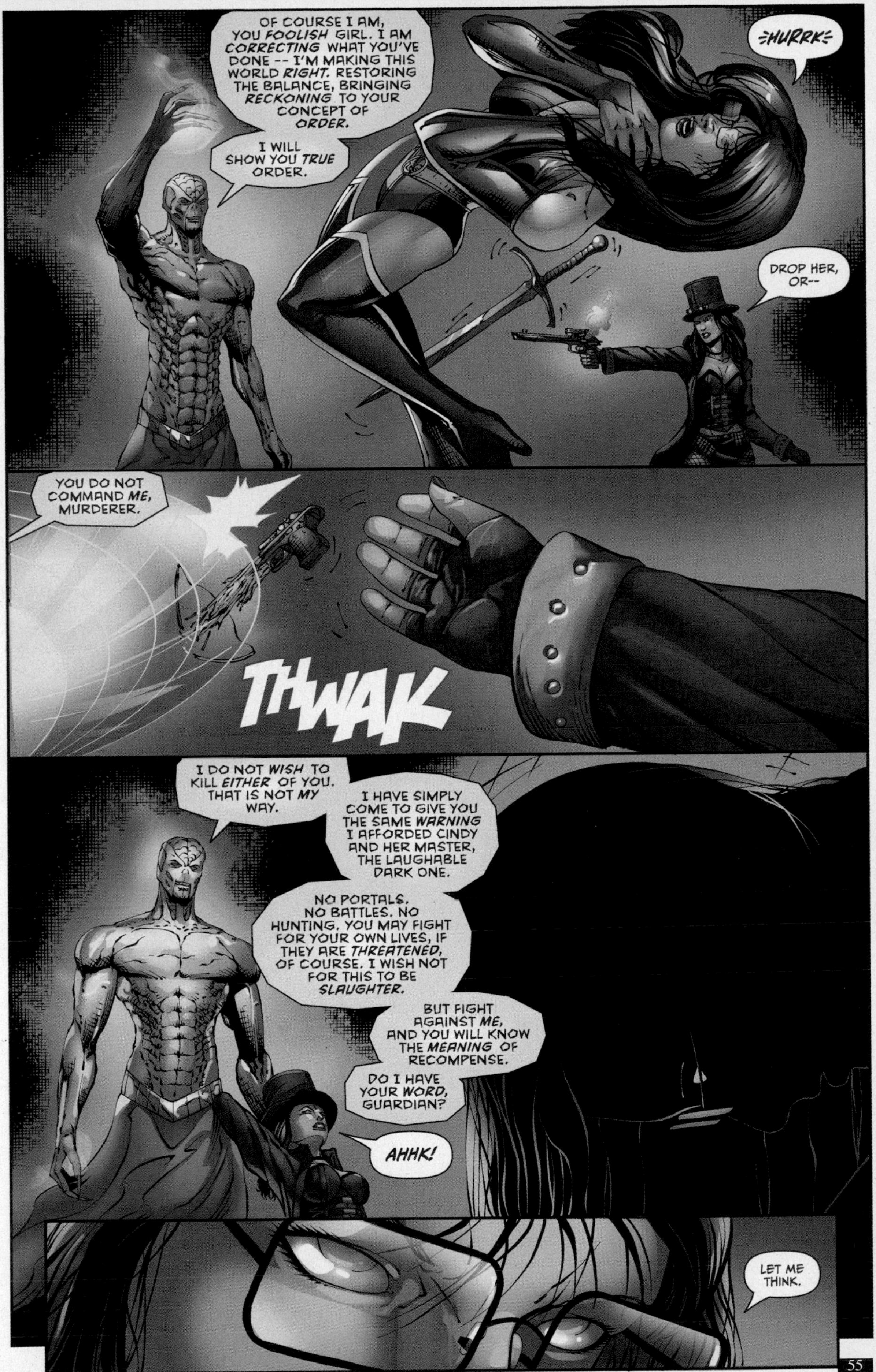
OF COURSE I AM, YOU FOOLISH GIRL. I AM CORRECTING WHAT YOU'VE DONE -- I'M MAKING THIS WORLD RIGHT. RESTORING THE BALANCE, BRINGING RECKONING TO YOUR CONCEPT OF ORDER.
I WILL SHOW YOU TRUE ORDER.
HURRK
DROP HER, OR--
YOU DO NOT COMMAND ME, MURDERER.
THWAK
I DO NOT WISH TO KILL EITHER OF YOU. THAT IS NOT MY WAY.
I HAVE SIMPLY COME TO GIVE YOU THE SAME WARNING I AFFORDED CINDY AND HER MASTER, THE LAUGHABLE DARK ONE.
NO PORTALS. NO BATTLES. NO HUNTING. YOU MAY FIGHT FOR YOUR OWN LIVES, IF THEY ARE THREATENED, OF COURSE. I WISH NOT FOR THIS TO BE SLAUGHTER.
BUT FIGHT AGAINST ME, AND YOU WILL KNOW THE MEANING OF RECOMPENSE.
DO I HAVE YOUR WORD, GUARDIAN?
AHHK!
LET ME THINK.

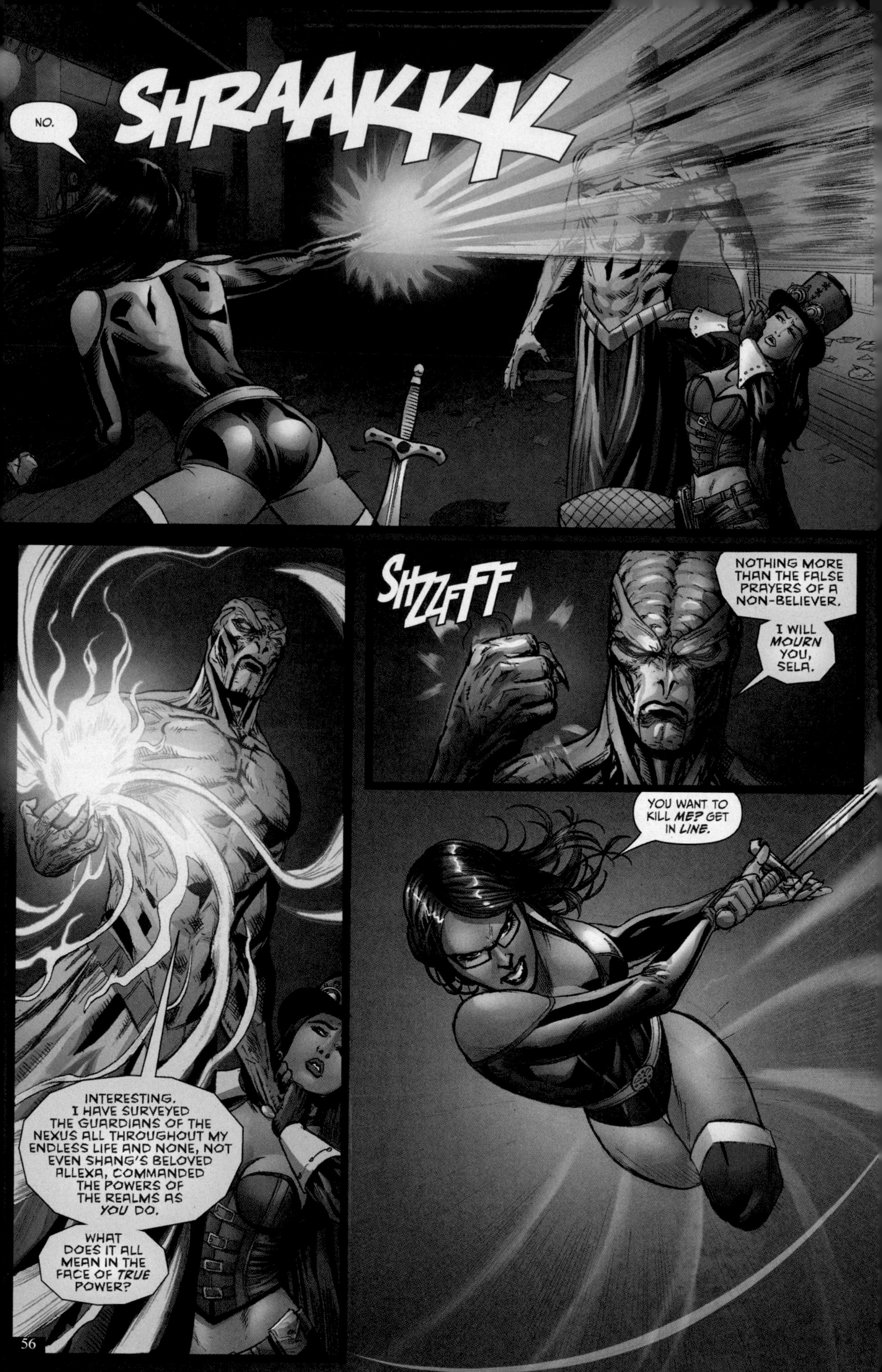
NO.
SHRAAKKK
INTERESTING. I HAVE SURVEYED THE GUARDIANS OF THE NEXUS ALL THROUGHOUT MY ENDLESS LIFE AND NONE, NOT EVEN SHANG'S BELOVED ALLEXA, COMMANDED THE POWERS OF THE REALMS AS YOU DO.
WHAT DOES IT ALL MEAN IN THE FACE OF TRUE POWER?
SHZZFFF
NOTHING MORE THAN THE FALSE PRAYERS OF A NON-BELIEVER.
I WILL MOURN YOU, SELA.
YOU WANT TO KILL ME? GET IN LINE.

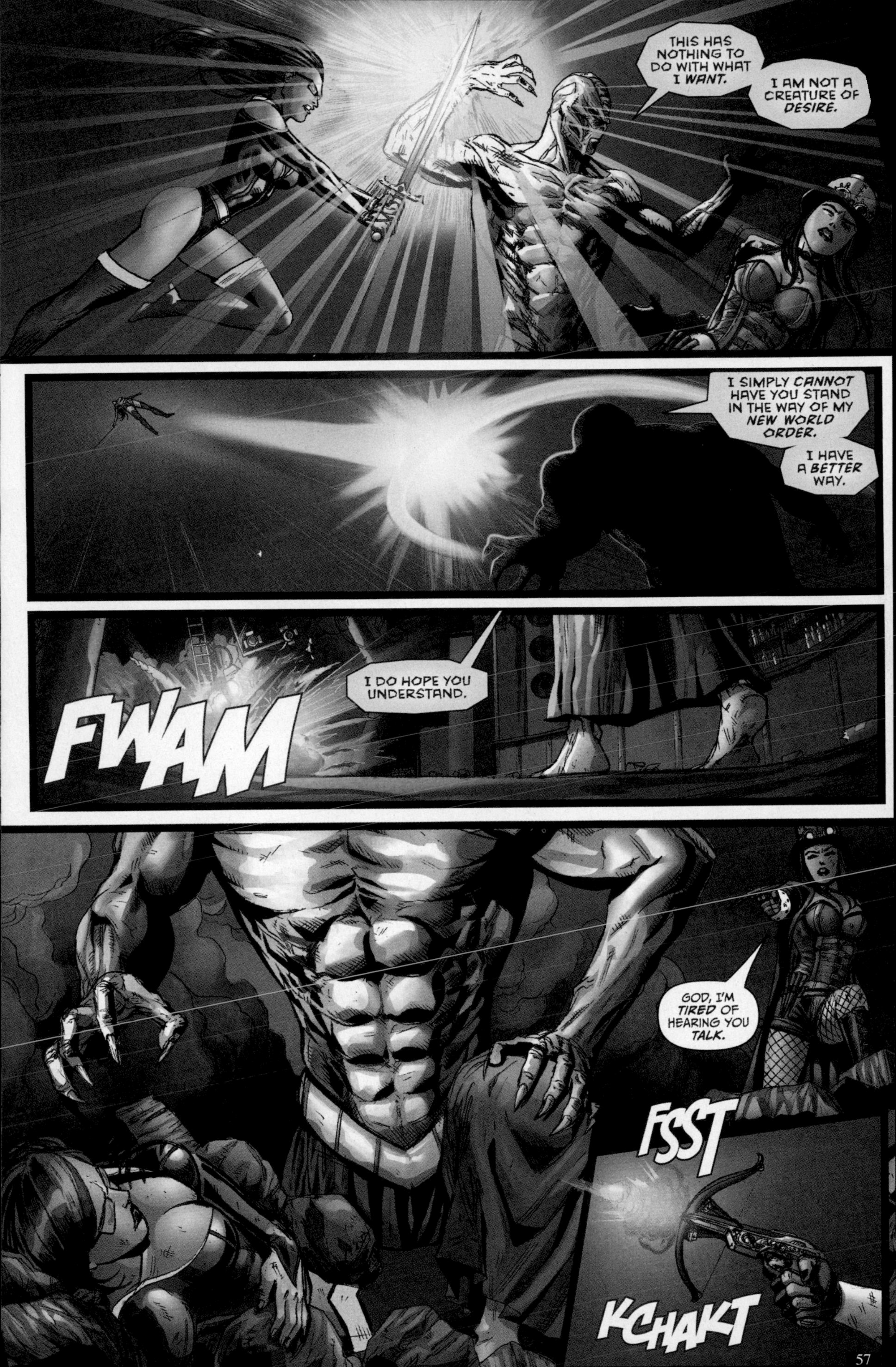
THIS HAS NOTHING TO DO WITH WHAT I WANT.
I AM NOT A CREATURE OF DESIRE.
I SIMPLY CANNOT HAVE YOU STAND IN THE WAY OF MY NEW WORLD ORDER.
I HAVE A BETTER WAY.
I DO HOPE YOU UNDERSTAND.
FWAM
GOD, I'M TIRED OF HEARING YOU TALK.
FSST
KCHAKT

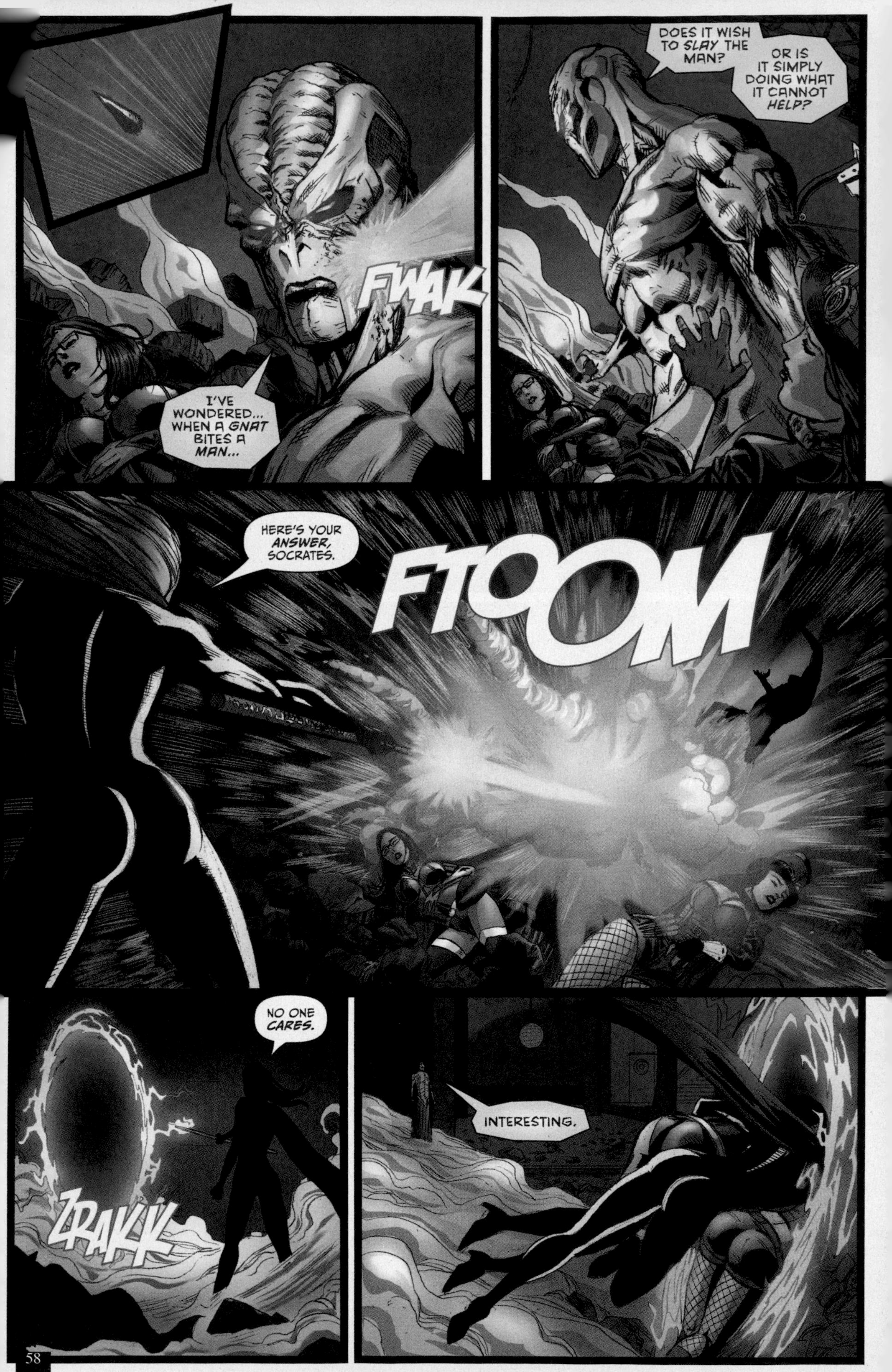
FWAK
I'VE WONDERED... WHEN A GNAT BITES A MAN...
DOES IT WISH TO SLAY THE MAN?
OR IS IT SIMPLY DOING WHAT IT CANNOT HELP?
HERE'S YOUR ANSWER, SOCRATES.
FTOOOM
NO ONE CARES.
ZRAKK
INTERESTING.

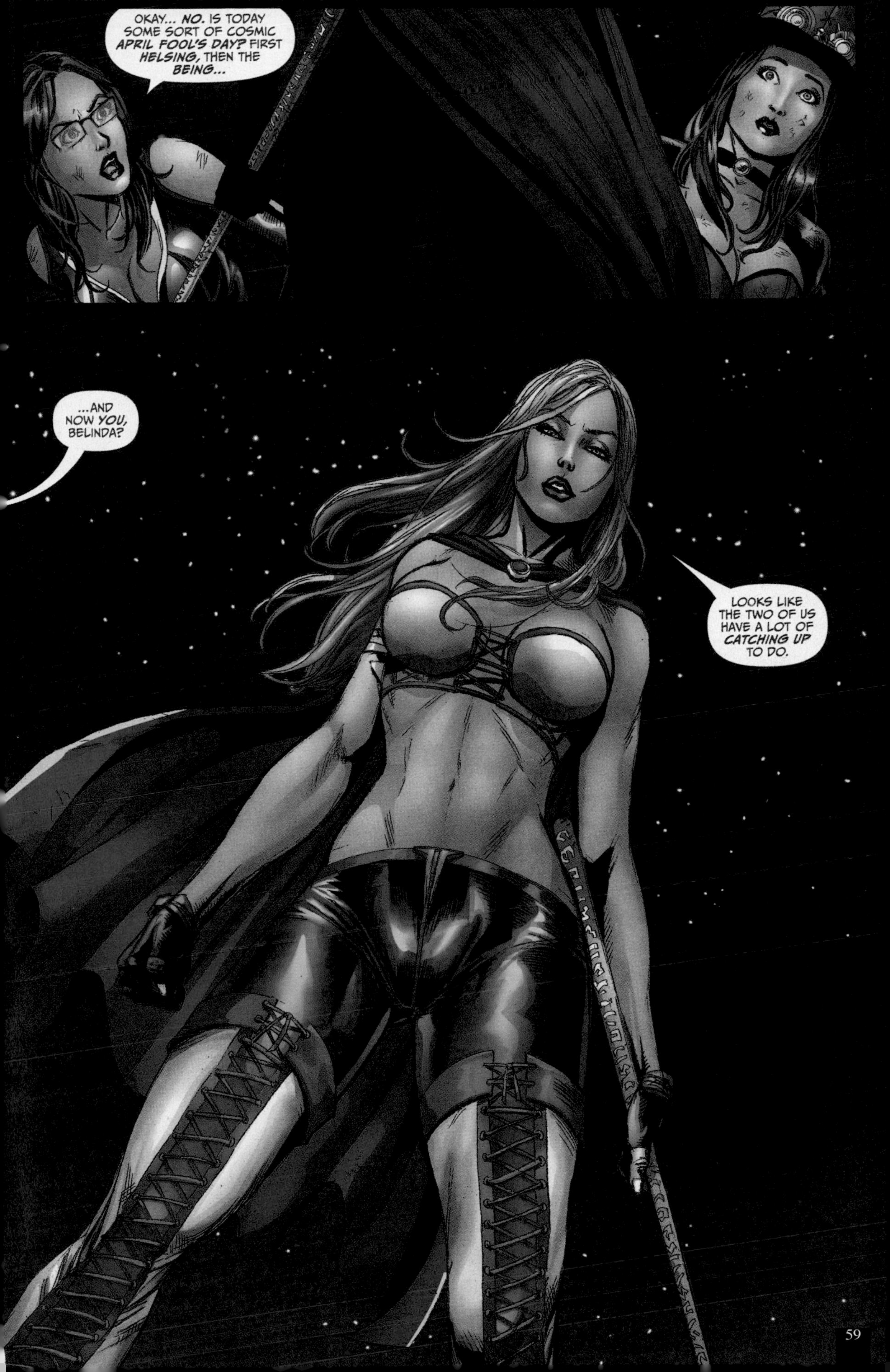
OKAY... NO. IS TODAY SOME SORT OF COSMIC APRIL FOOL'S DAY? FIRST HELSING, THEN THE BEING...
...AND NOW YOU, BELINDA?
LOOKS LIKE THE TWO OF US HAVE A LOT OF CATCHING UP TO DO.

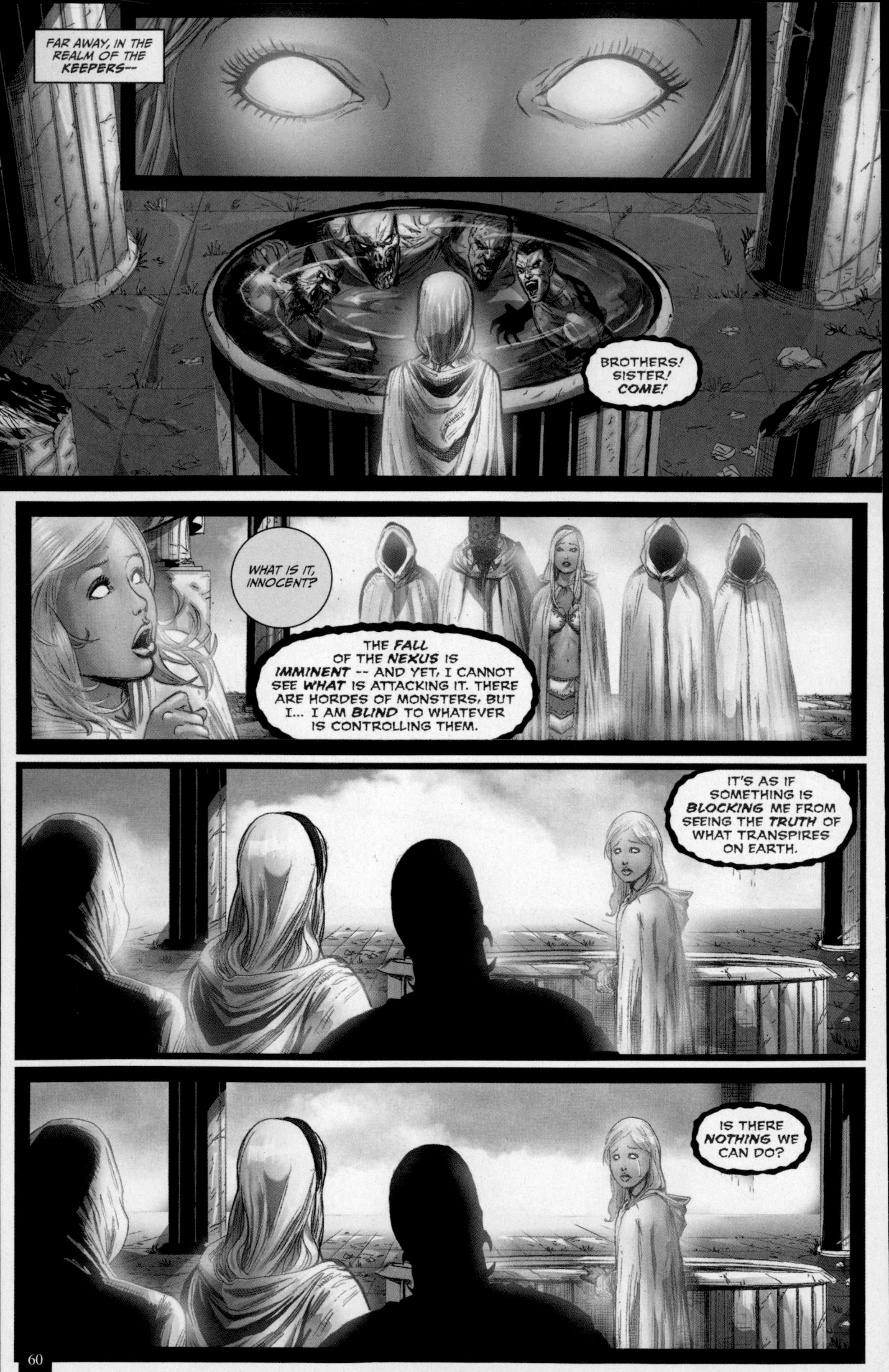
FAR AWAY, IN THE REALM OF THE KEEPERS--
BROTHERS! SISTER! COME!
WHAT IS IT, INNOCENT?
THE FALL OF THE NEXUS IS IMMINENT -- AND YET, I CANNOT SEE WHAT IS ATTACKING IT. THERE ARE HORDES OF MONSTERS, BUT I... I AM BLIND TO WHATEVER IS CONTROLLING THEM.
IT'S AS IF SOMETHING IS BLOCKING ME FROM SEEING THE TRUTH OF WHAT TRANSPIRES ON EARTH.
IS THERE NOTHING WE CAN DO?

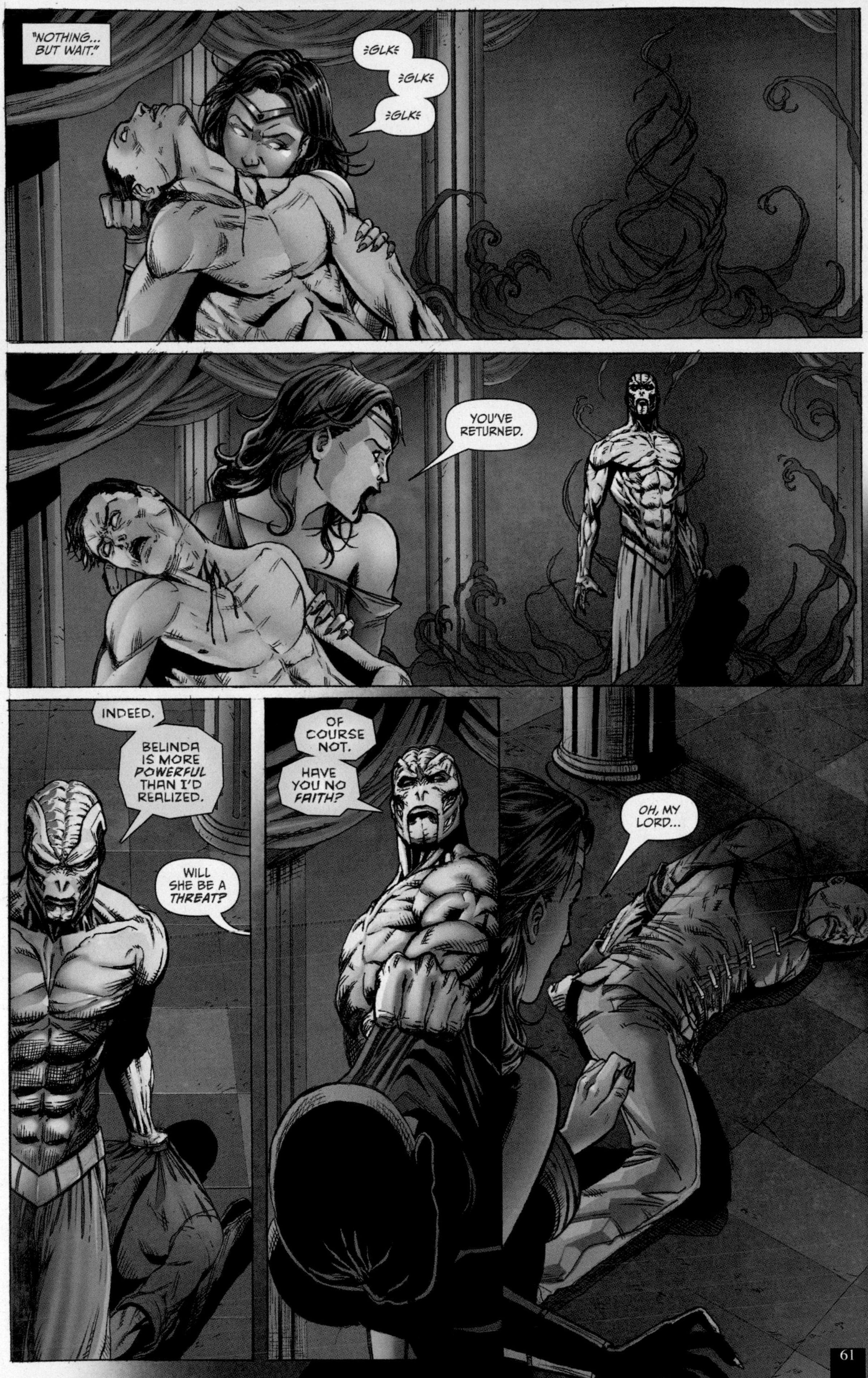
"NOTHING... BUT WAIT."
GLK
GLK
GLK
YOU'VE RETURNED.
INDEED.
BELINDA IS MORE POWERFUL THAN I'D REALIZED.
WILL SHE BE A THREAT?
OF COURSE NOT.
HAVE YOU NO FAITH?
OH, MY LORD...

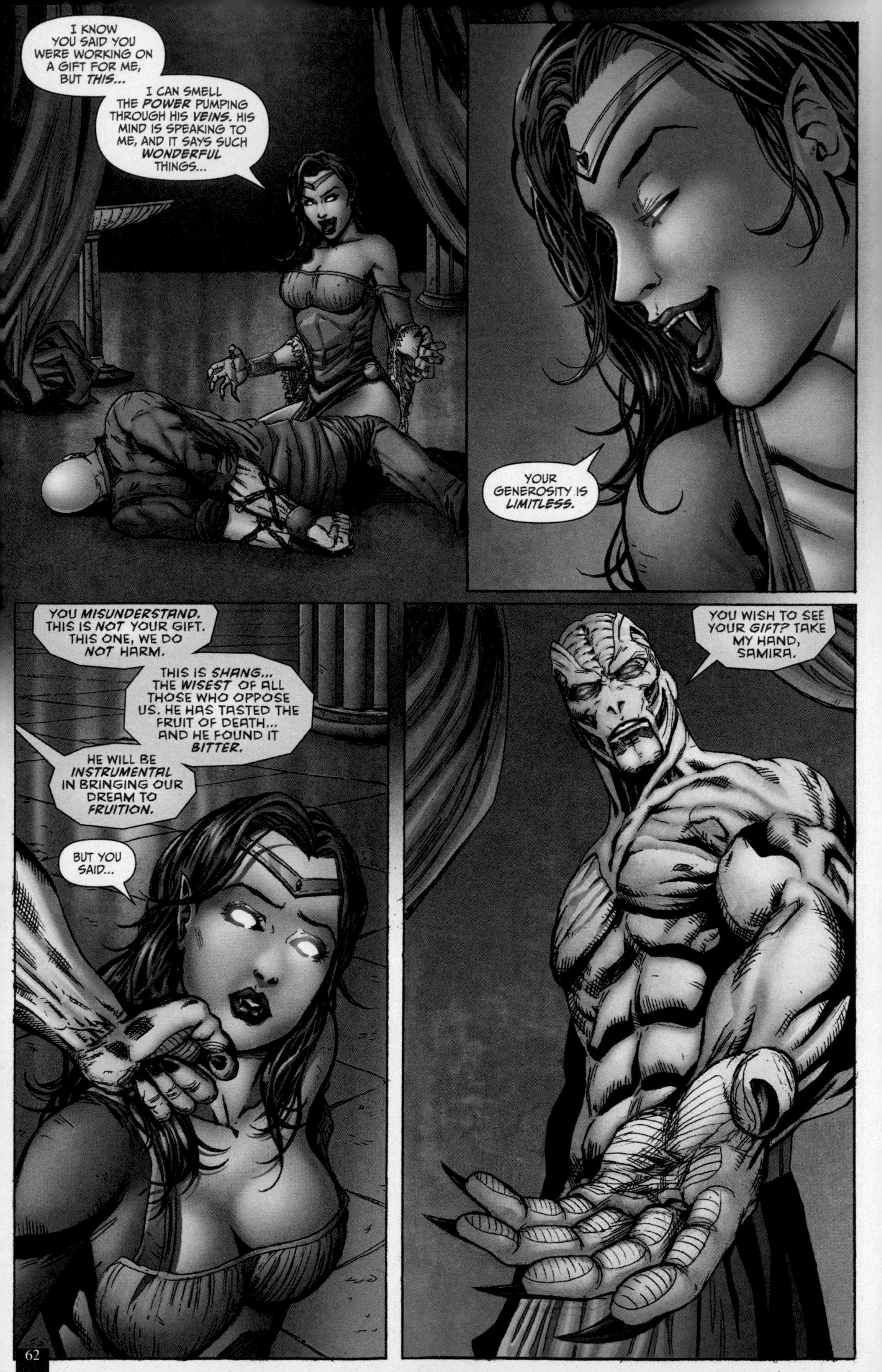
I KNOW YOU SAID YOU WERE WORKING ON A GIFT FOR ME, BUT THIS...
I CAN SMELL THE POWER PUMPING THROUGH HIS VEINS. HIS MIND IS SPEAKING TO ME, AND IT SAYS SUCH WONDERFUL THINGS...
YOUR GENEROSITY IS LIMITLESS.
YOU MISUNDERSTAND. THIS IS NOT YOUR GIFT. THIS ONE, WE DO NOT HARM.
THIS IS SHANG... THE WISEST OF ALL THOSE WHO OPPOSE US. HE HAS TASTED THE FRUIT OF DEATH... AND HE FOUND IT BITTER.
HE WILL BE INSTRUMENTAL IN BRINGING OUR DREAM TO FRUITION.
BUT YOU SAID...
YOU WISH TO SEE YOUR GIFT? TAKE MY HAND, SAMIRA.

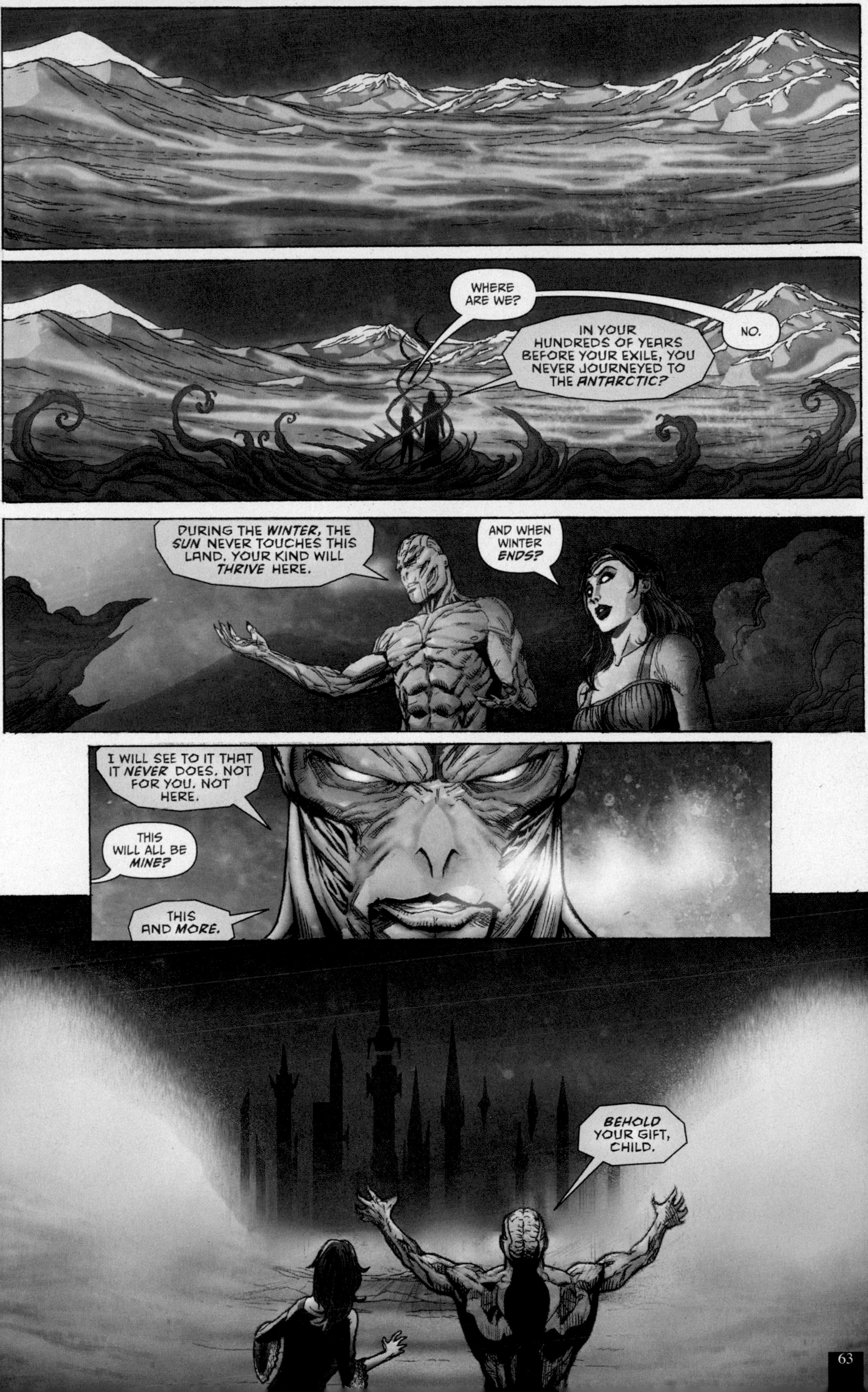
WHERE ARE WE?
IN YOUR HUNDREDS OF YEARS BEFORE YOUR EXILE, YOU NEVER JOURNEYED TO THE ANTARCTIC?
NO.
DURING THE WINTER, THE SUN NEVER TOUCHES THIS LAND. YOUR KIND WILL THRIVE HERE.
AND WHEN WINTER ENDS?
I WILL SEE TO IT THAT IT NEVER DOES. NOT FOR YOU. NOT HERE.
THIS WILL ALL BE MINE?
THIS AND MORE.
BEHOLD YOUR GIFT, CHILD.

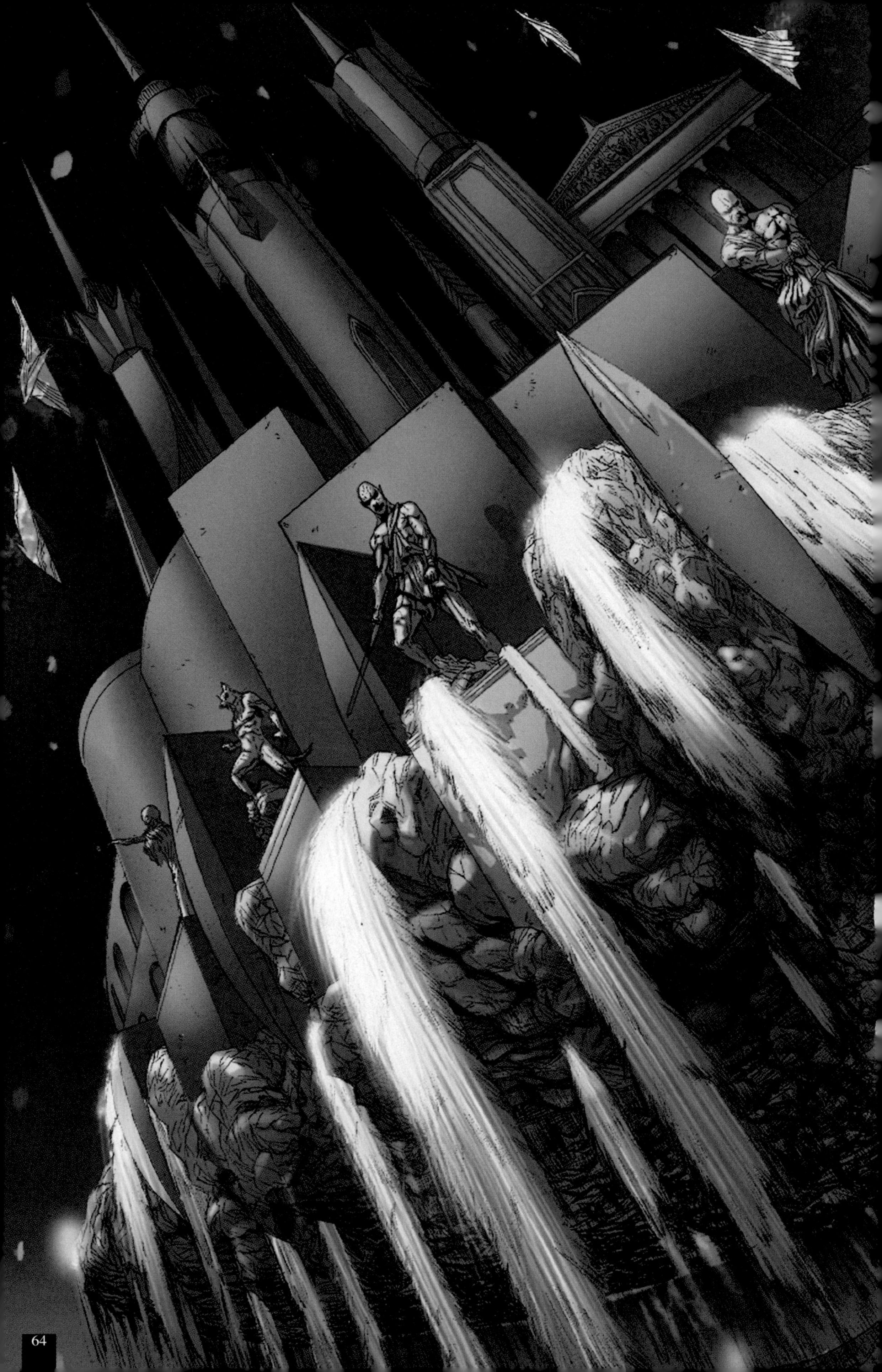

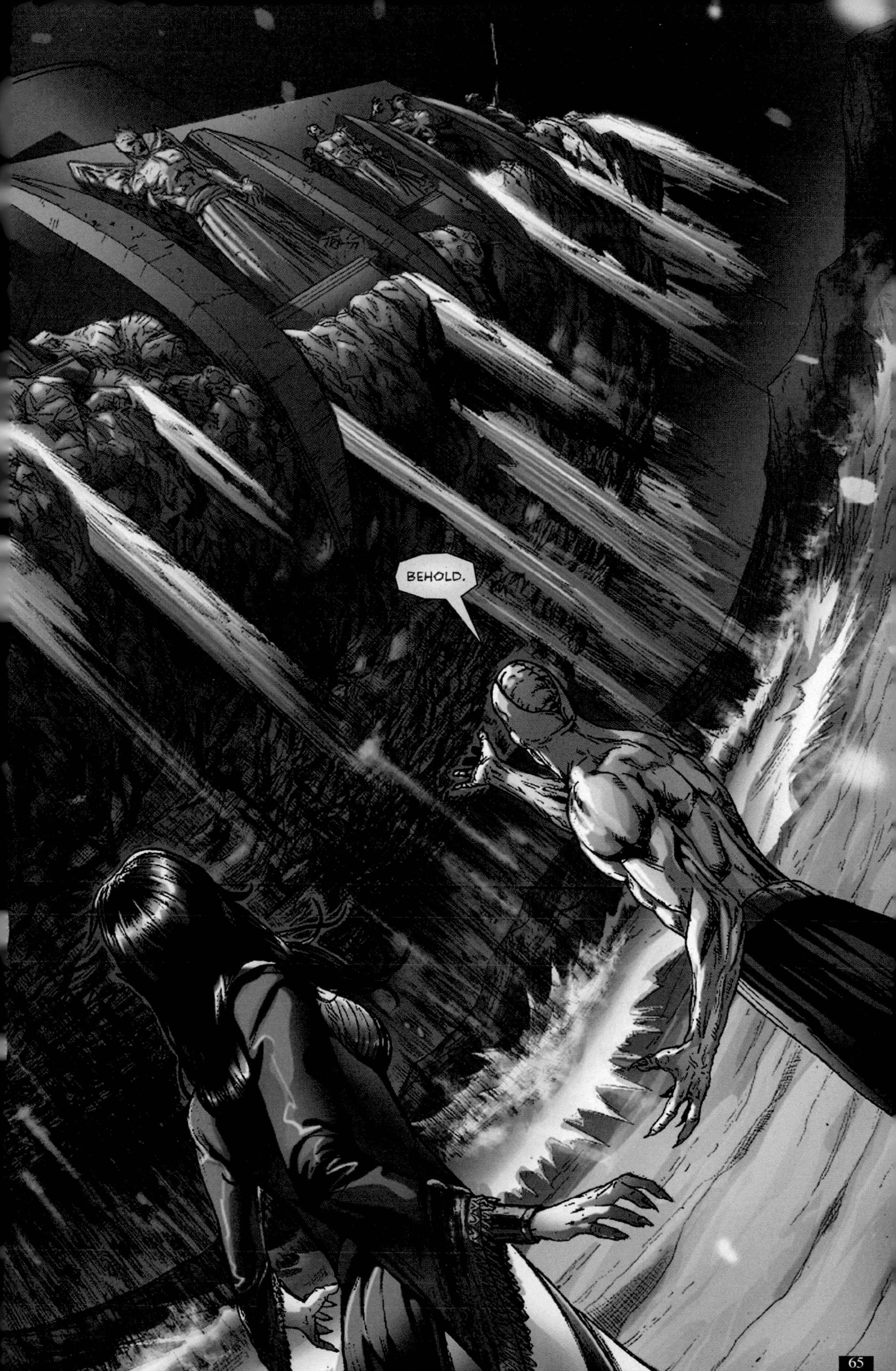
BEHOLD.

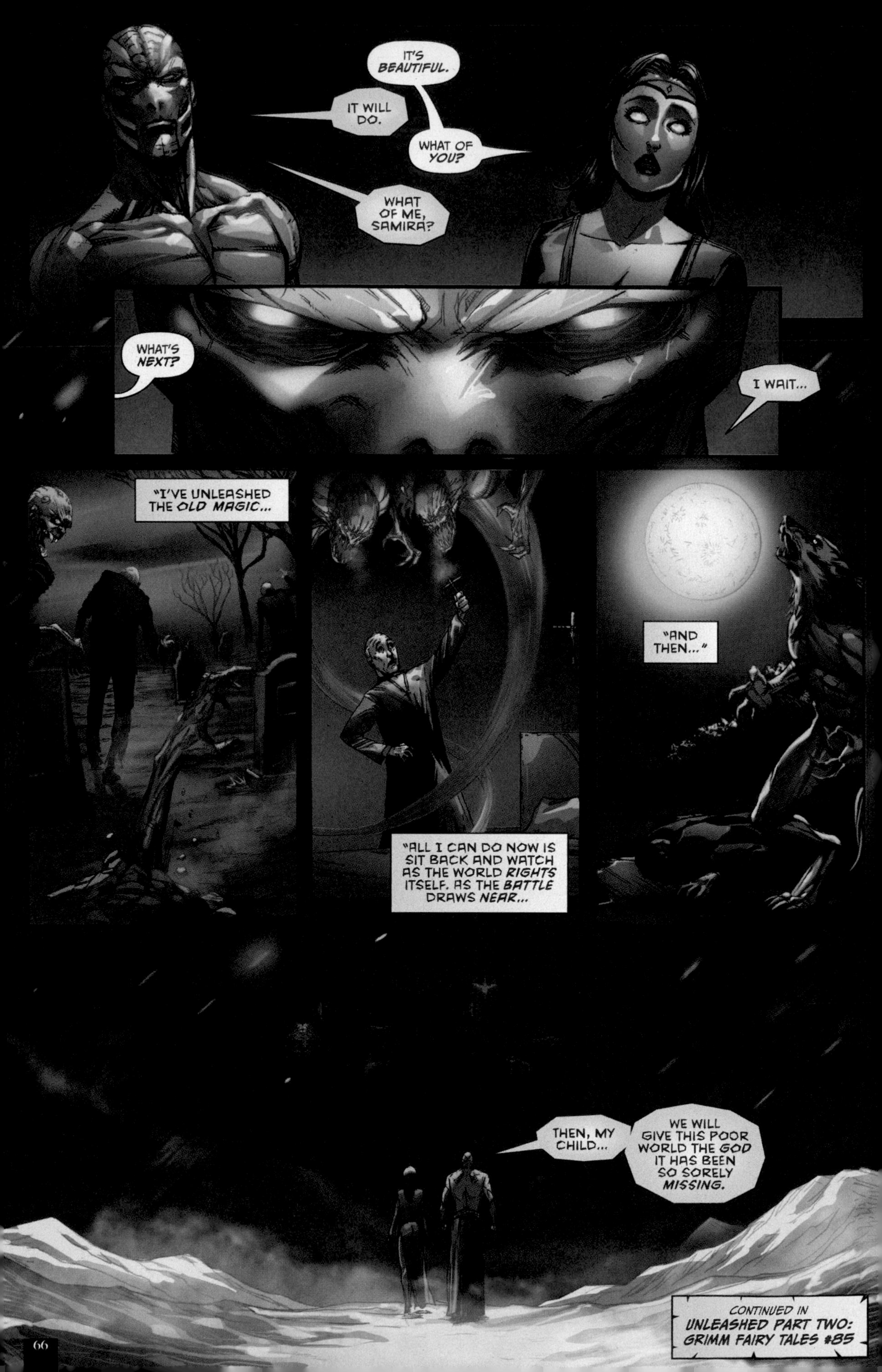

IT'S BEAUTIFUL.
IT WILL DO.
WHAT OF YOU?
WHAT OF ME, SAMIRA?
WHAT'S NEXT?
I WAIT...
"I'VE UNLEASHED THE OLD MAGIC...
"AND THEN..."
"ALL I CAN DO NOW IS SIT BACK AND WATCH AS THE WORLD RIGHTS ITSELF. AS THE BATTLE DRAWS NEAR...
THEN, MY CHILD...
WE WILL GIVE THIS POOR WORLD THE GOD IT HAS BEEN SO SORELY MISSING.
CONTINUED IN UNLEASHED PART TWO: GRIMM FAIRY TALES #85

Grimm Fairy Tales
UNLEASHED

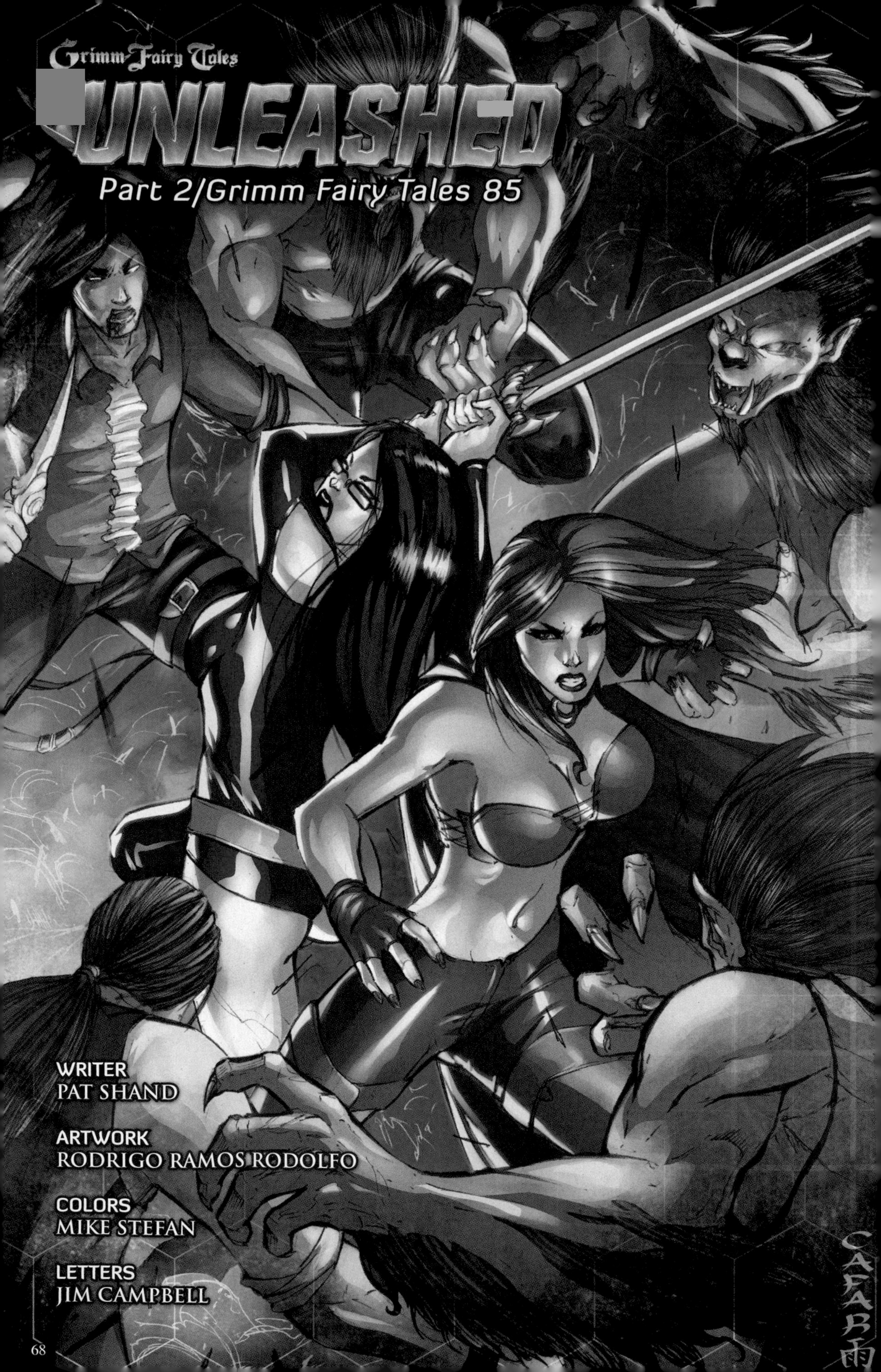
Grimm Fairy Tales
UNLEASHED
Part 2/Grimm Fairy Tales 85
WRITER
PAT SHAND
ARTWORK
RODRIGO RAMOS RODOLFO
COLORS
MIKE STEFAN
LETTERS
JIM CAMPBELL

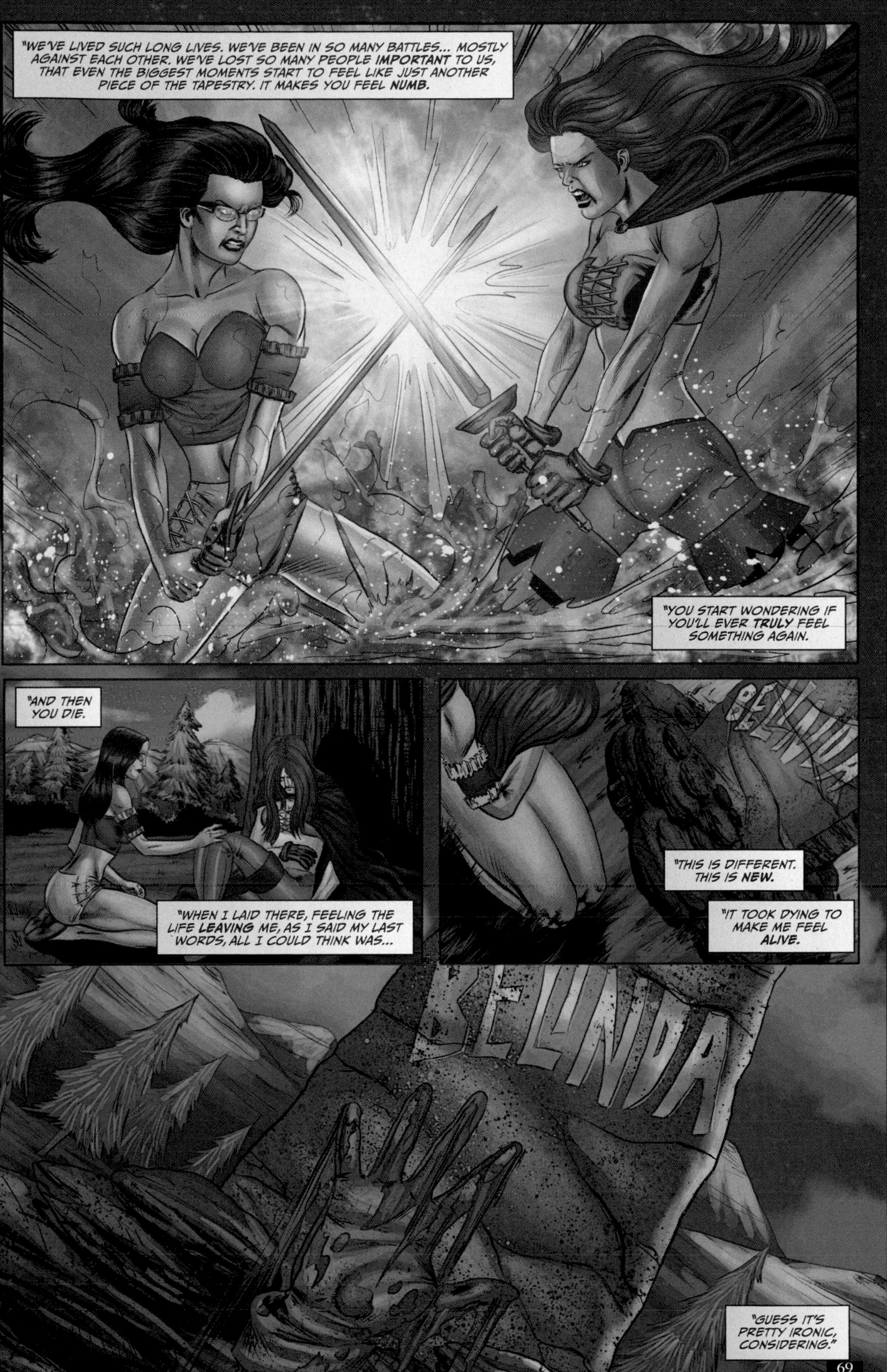
"WE'VE LIVED SUCH LONG LIVES. WE'VE BEEN IN SO MANY BATTLES... MOSTLY AGAINST EACH OTHER. WE'VE LOST SO MANY PEOPLE IMPORTANT TO US, THAT EVEN THE BIGGEST MOMENTS START TO FEEL LIKE JUST ANOTHER PIECE OF THE TAPESTRY. IT MAKES YOU FEEL NUMB.
"YOU START WONDERING IF YOU'LL EVER TRULY FEEL SOMETHING AGAIN.
"AND THEN YOU DIE.
"WHEN I LAID THERE, FEELING THE LIFE LEAVING ME, AS I SAID MY LAST WORDS, ALL I COULD THINK WAS...
"THIS IS DIFFERENT. THIS IS NEW.
"IT TOOK DYING TO MAKE ME FEEL ALIVE.
"GUESS IT'S PRETTY IRONIC, CONSIDERING."

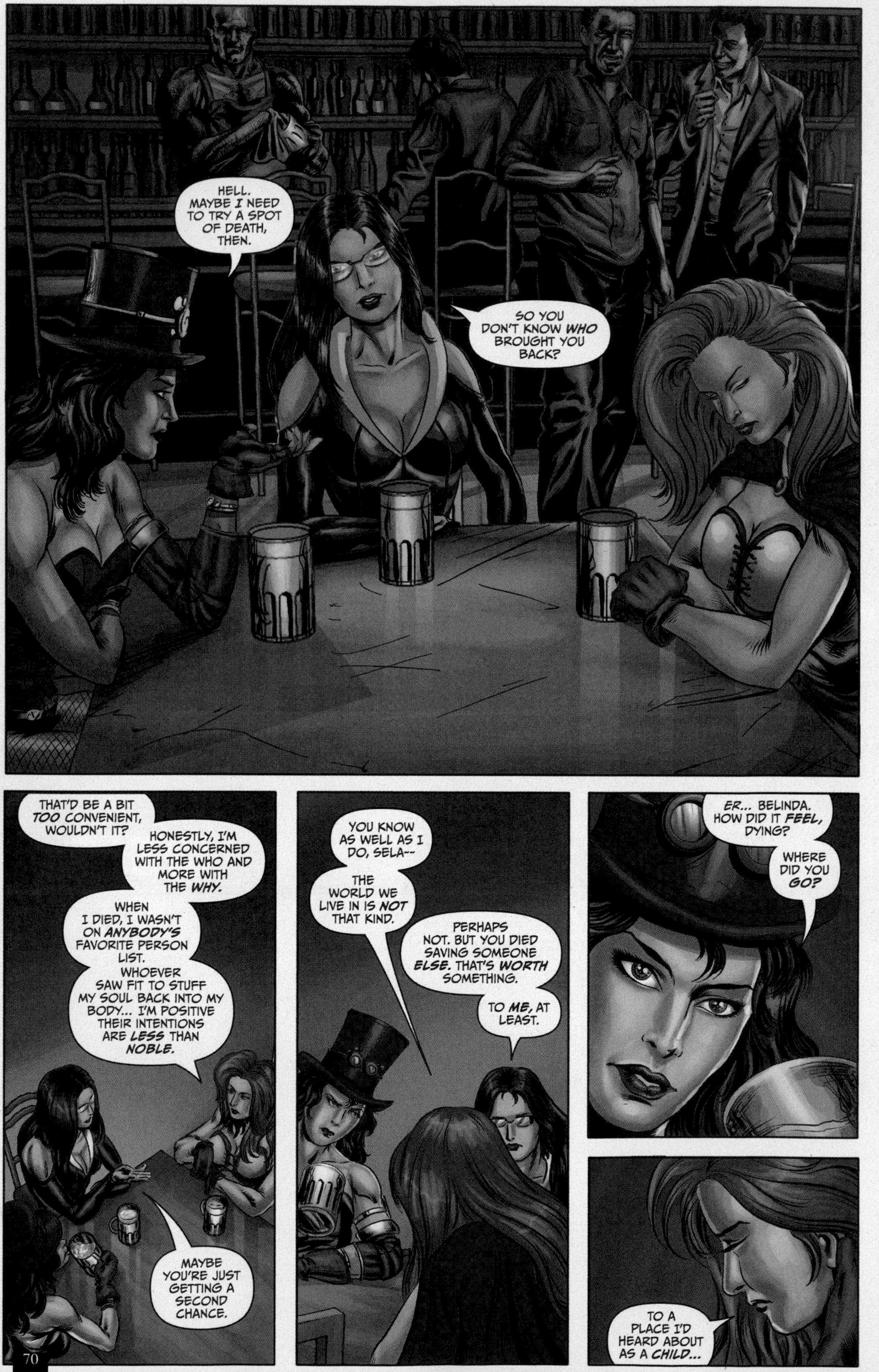
HELL. MAYBE I NEED TO TRY A SPOT OF DEATH, THEN.
SO YOU DON'T KNOW WHO BROUGHT YOU BACK?
THAT'D BE A BIT TOO CONVENIENT, WOULDN'T IT?
HONESTLY, I'M LESS CONCERNED WITH THE WHO AND MORE WITH THE WHY.
WHEN I DIED, I WASN'T ON ANYBODY'S FAVORITE PERSON LIST.
WHOEVER SAW FIT TO STUFF MY SOUL BACK INTO MY BODY... I'M POSITIVE THEIR INTENTIONS ARE LESS THAN NOBLE.
MAYBE YOU'RE JUST GETTING A SECOND CHANCE.
YOU KNOW AS WELL AS I DO, SELA--
THE WORLD WE LIVE IN IS NOT THAT KIND.
PERHAPS NOT. BUT YOU DIED SAVING SOMEONE ELSE. THAT'S WORTH SOMETHING.
TO ME, AT LEAST.
ER... BELINDA. HOW DID IT FEEL, DYING?
WHERE DID YOU GO?
TO A PLACE I'D HEARD ABOUT AS A CHILD...

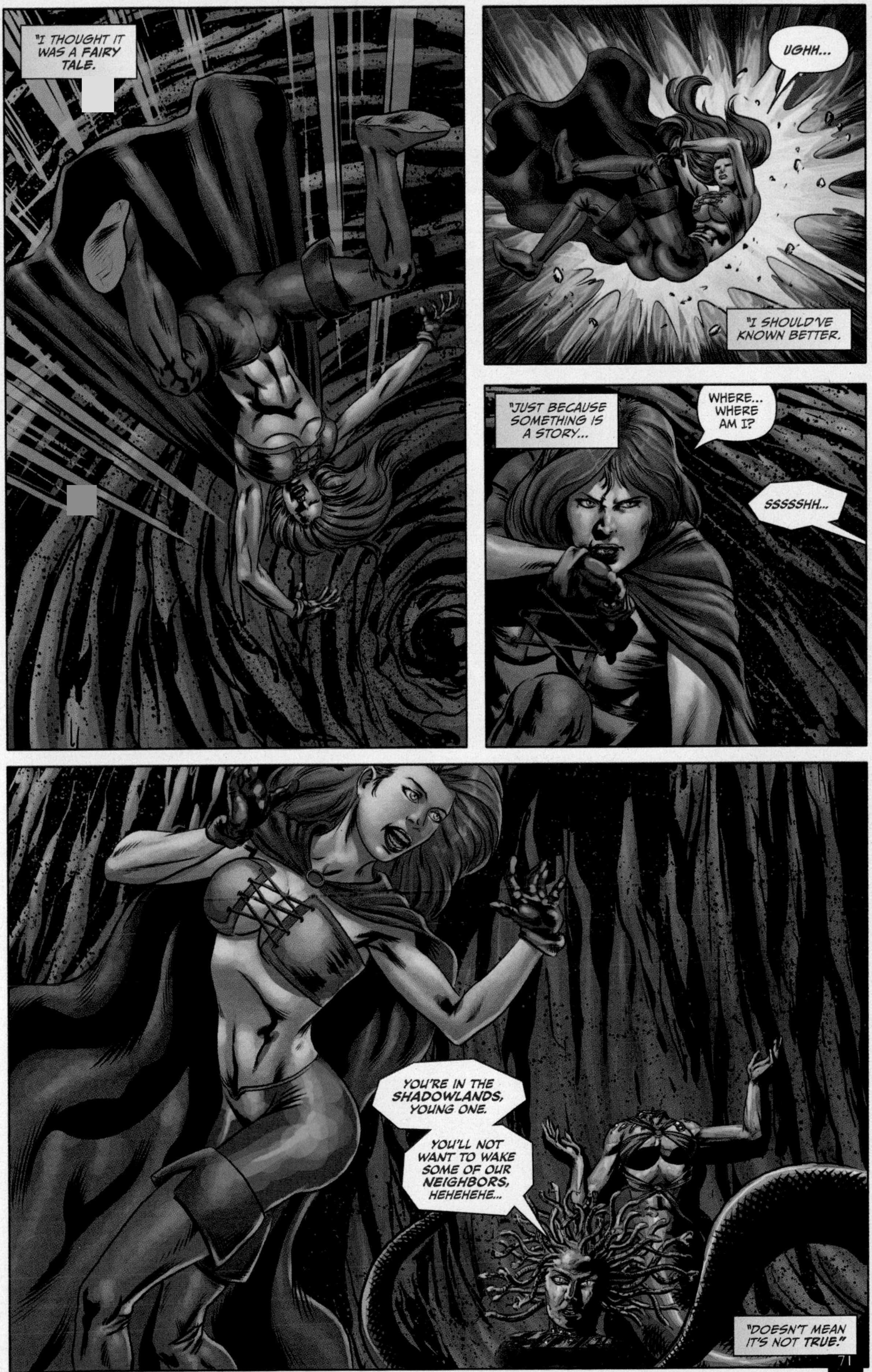
"I THOUGHT IT WAS A FAIRY TALE.
UGHH...
"I SHOULD'VE KNOWN BETTER.
"JUST BECAUSE SOMETHING IS A STORY...
WHERE... WHERE AM I?
SSSSSHH...
YOU'RE IN THE SHADOWLANDS, YOUNG ONE.
YOU'LL NOT WANT TO WAKE SOME OF OUR NEIGHBORS, HEHEHEHE...
"DOESN'T MEAN IT'S NOT TRUE."

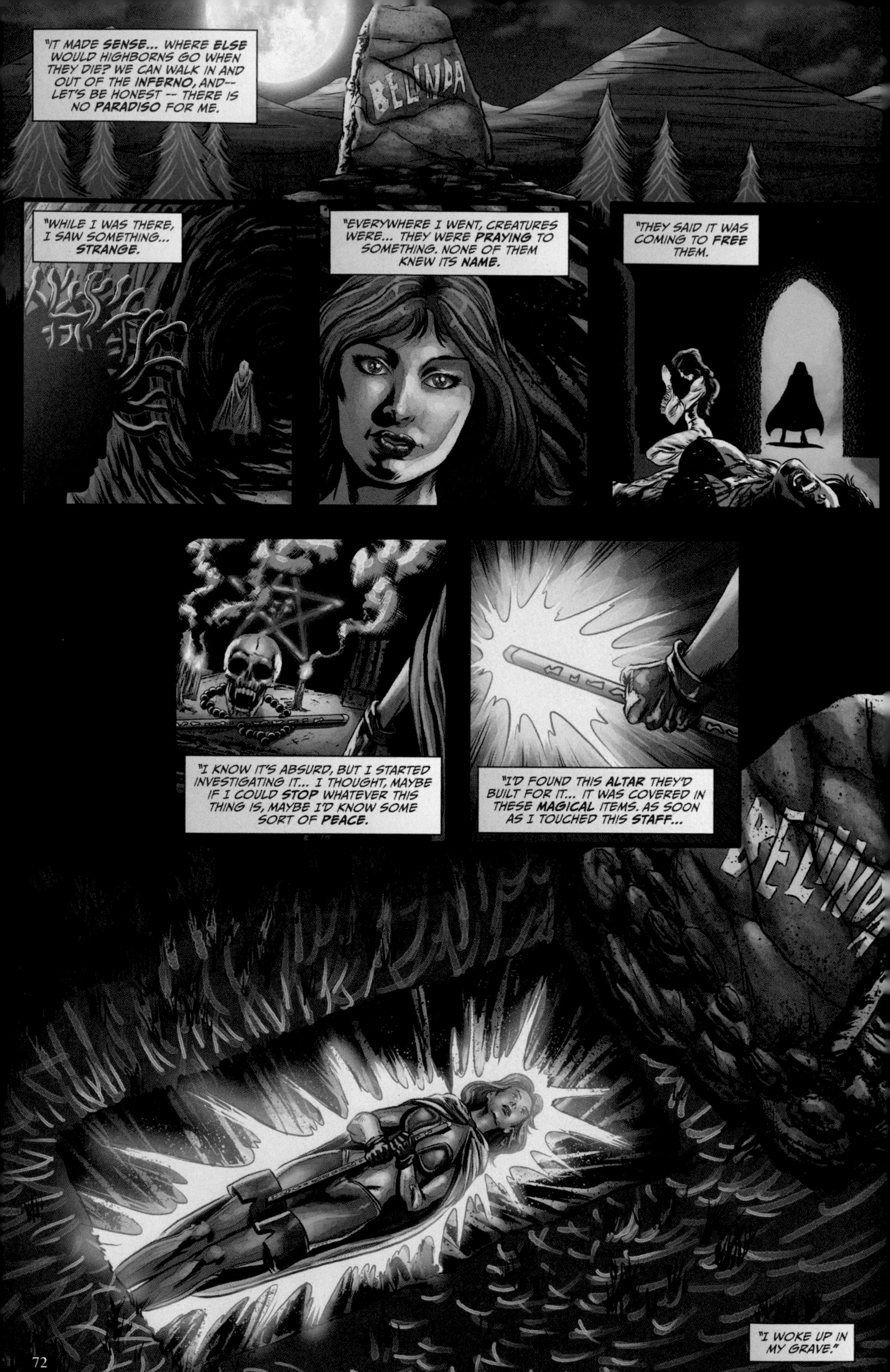

"IT MADE SENSE... WHERE ELSE WOULD HIGHBORNS GO WHEN THEY DIE? WE CAN WALK IN AND OUT OF THE INFERNO, AND-- LET'S BE HONEST -- THERE IS NO PARADISO FOR ME.
BELINDA
"WHILE I WAS THERE, I SAW SOMETHING... STRANGE.
"EVERYWHERE I WENT, CREATURES WERE... THEY WERE PRAYING TO SOMETHING. NONE OF THEM KNEW ITS NAME.
"THEY SAID IT WAS COMING TO FREE THEM.
"I KNOW IT'S ABSURD, BUT I STARTED INVESTIGATING IT... I THOUGHT, MAYBE IF I COULD STOP WHATEVER THIS THING IS, MAYBE I'D KNOW SOME SORT OF PEACE.
"I'D FOUND THIS ALTAR THEY'D BUILT FOR IT... IT WAS COVERED IN THESE MAGICAL ITEMS. AS SOON AS I TOUCHED THIS STAFF...
BELINDA
"I WOKE UP IN MY GRAVE."

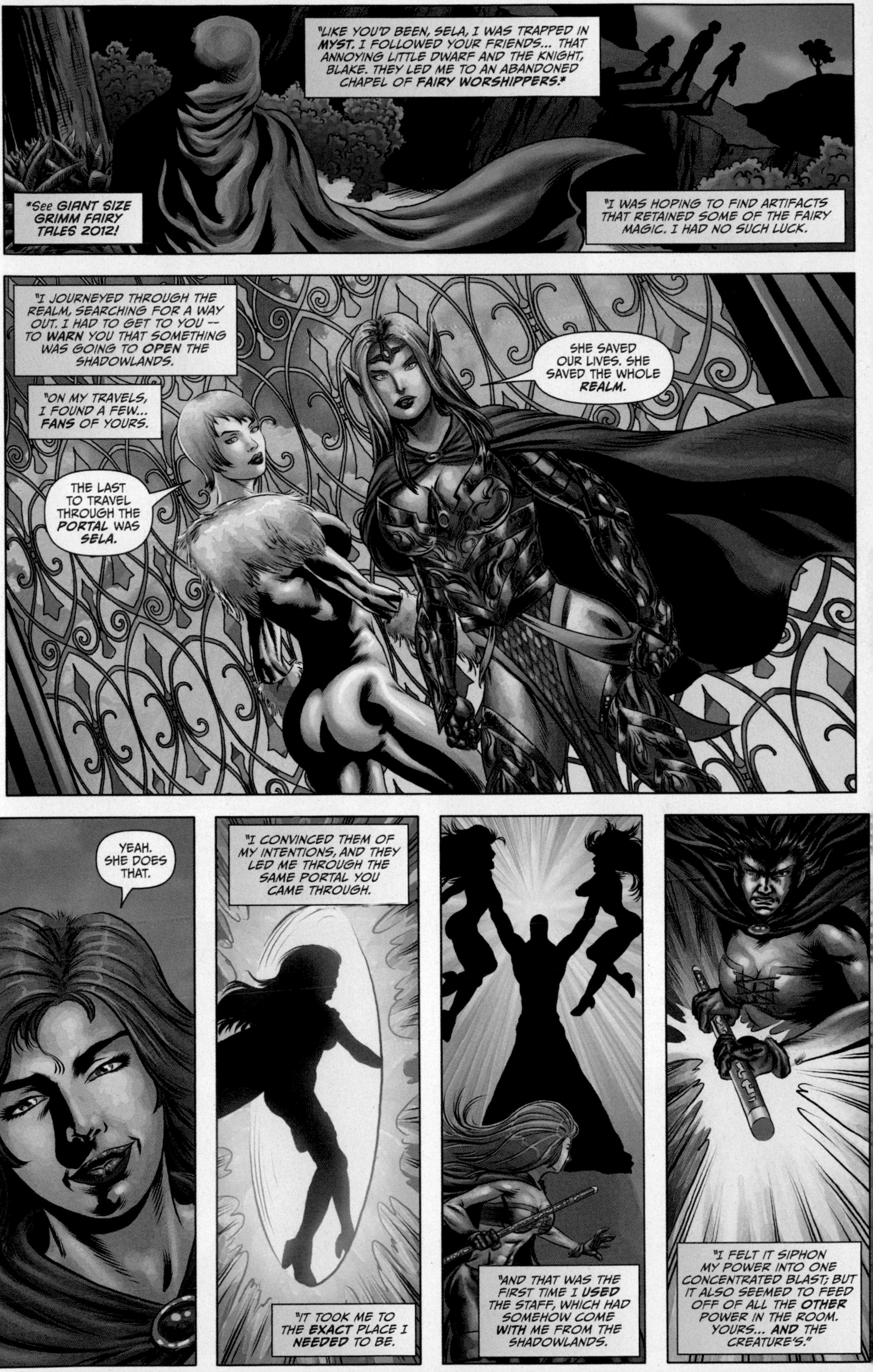
"LIKE YOU'D BEEN, SELA, I WAS TRAPPED IN MYST. I FOLLOWED YOUR FRIENDS... THAT ANNOYING LITTLE DWARF AND THE KNIGHT, BLAKE. THEY LED ME TO AN ABANDONED CHAPEL OF FAIRY WORSHIPPERS.*
*See GIANT SIZE GRIMM FAIRY TALES 2012!
"I WAS HOPING TO FIND ARTIFACTS THAT RETAINED SOME OF THE FAIRY MAGIC. I HAD NO SUCH LUCK.
"I JOURNEYED THROUGH THE REALM, SEARCHING FOR A WAY OUT. I HAD TO GET TO YOU -- TO WARN YOU THAT SOMETHING WAS GOING TO OPEN THE SHADOWLANDS.
SHE SAVED OUR LIVES. SHE SAVED THE WHOLE REALM.
"ON MY TRAVELS, I FOUND A FEW... FANS OF YOURS.
THE LAST TO TRAVEL THROUGH THE PORTAL WAS SELA.
YEAH. SHE DOES THAT.
"I CONVINCED THEM OF MY INTENTIONS, AND THEY LED ME THROUGH THE SAME PORTAL YOU CAME THROUGH.
"IT TOOK ME TO THE EXACT PLACE I NEEDED TO BE.
"AND THAT WAS THE FIRST TIME I USED THE STAFF, WHICH HAD SOMEHOW COME WITH ME FROM THE SHADOWLANDS.
"I FELT IT SIPHON MY POWER INTO ONE CONCENTRATED BLAST; BUT IT ALSO SEEMED TO FEED OFF OF ALL THE OTHER POWER IN THE ROOM. YOURS... AND THE CREATURE'S."

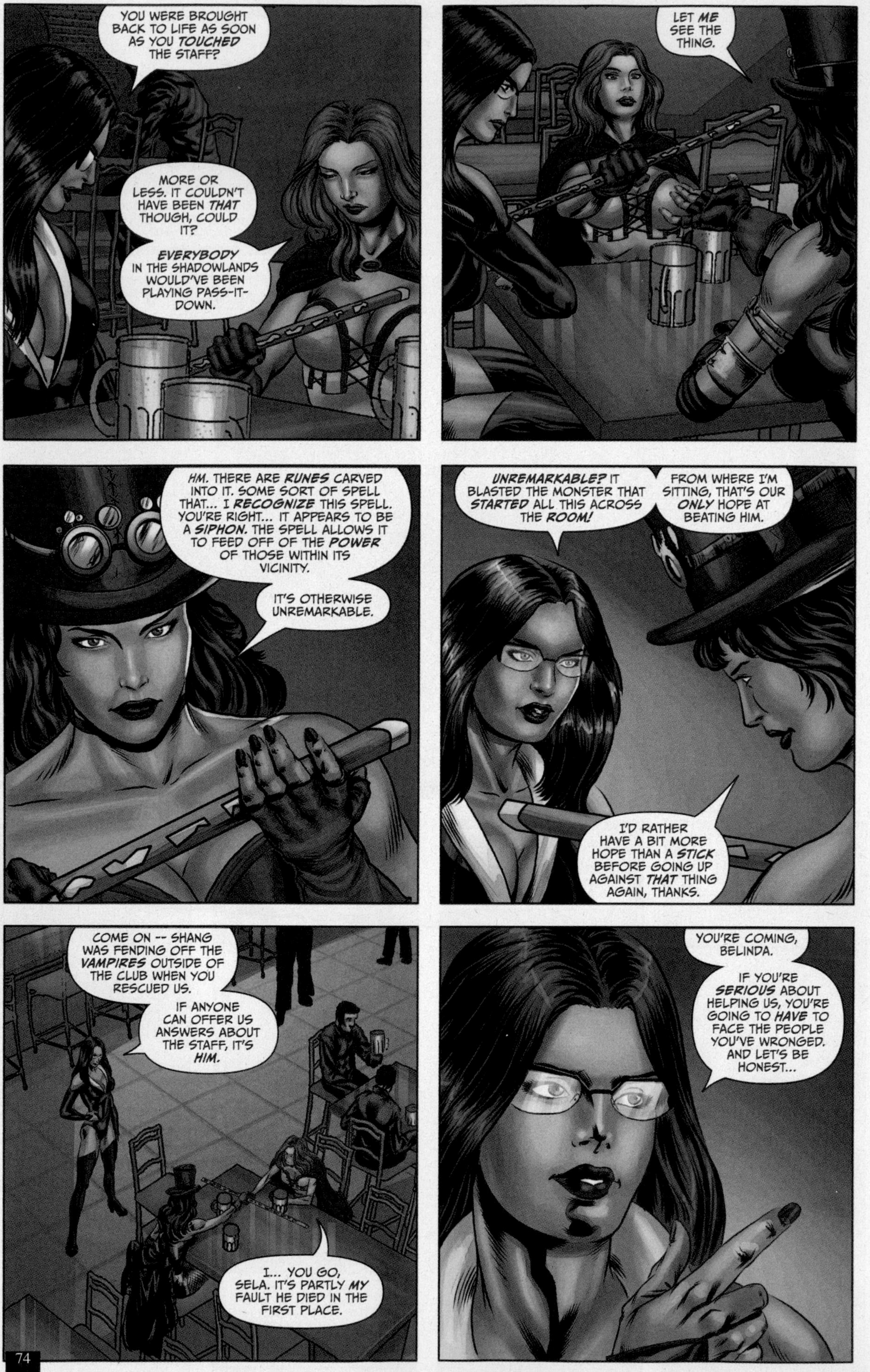
YOU WERE BROUGHT BACK TO LIFE AS SOON AS YOU *TOUCHED* THE STAFF?
MORE OR LESS. IT COULDN'T HAVE BEEN *THAT* THOUGH, COULD IT?
EVERYBODY IN THE SHADOWLANDS WOULD'VE BEEN PLAYING PASS-IT-DOWN.
LET *ME* SEE THE THING.
HM. THERE ARE *RUNES* CARVED INTO IT. SOME SORT OF SPELL THAT... I *RECOGNIZE* THIS SPELL. YOU'RE RIGHT... IT APPEARS TO BE A *SIPHON.* THE SPELL ALLOWS IT TO FEED OFF OF THE *POWER* OF THOSE WITHIN ITS VICINITY.
IT'S OTHERWISE UNREMARKABLE.
UNREMARKABLE? IT BLASTED THE MONSTER THAT *STARTED* ALL THIS ACROSS THE *ROOM!*
FROM WHERE I'M SITTING, THAT'S OUR *ONLY* HOPE AT BEATING HIM.
I'D RATHER HAVE A BIT MORE HOPE THAN A *STICK* BEFORE GOING UP AGAINST *THAT* THING AGAIN, THANKS.
COME ON -- SHANG WAS FENDING OFF THE *VAMPIRES* OUTSIDE OF THE CLUB WHEN YOU RESCUED US.
IF ANYONE CAN OFFER US ANSWERS ABOUT THE STAFF, IT'S *HIM.*
I... YOU GO, SELA. IT'S PARTLY *MY* FAULT HE DIED IN THE FIRST PLACE.
YOU'RE COMING, BELINDA.
IF YOU'RE *SERIOUS* ABOUT HELPING US, YOU'RE GOING TO *HAVE* TO FACE THE PEOPLE YOU'VE WRONGED. AND LET'S BE HONEST...

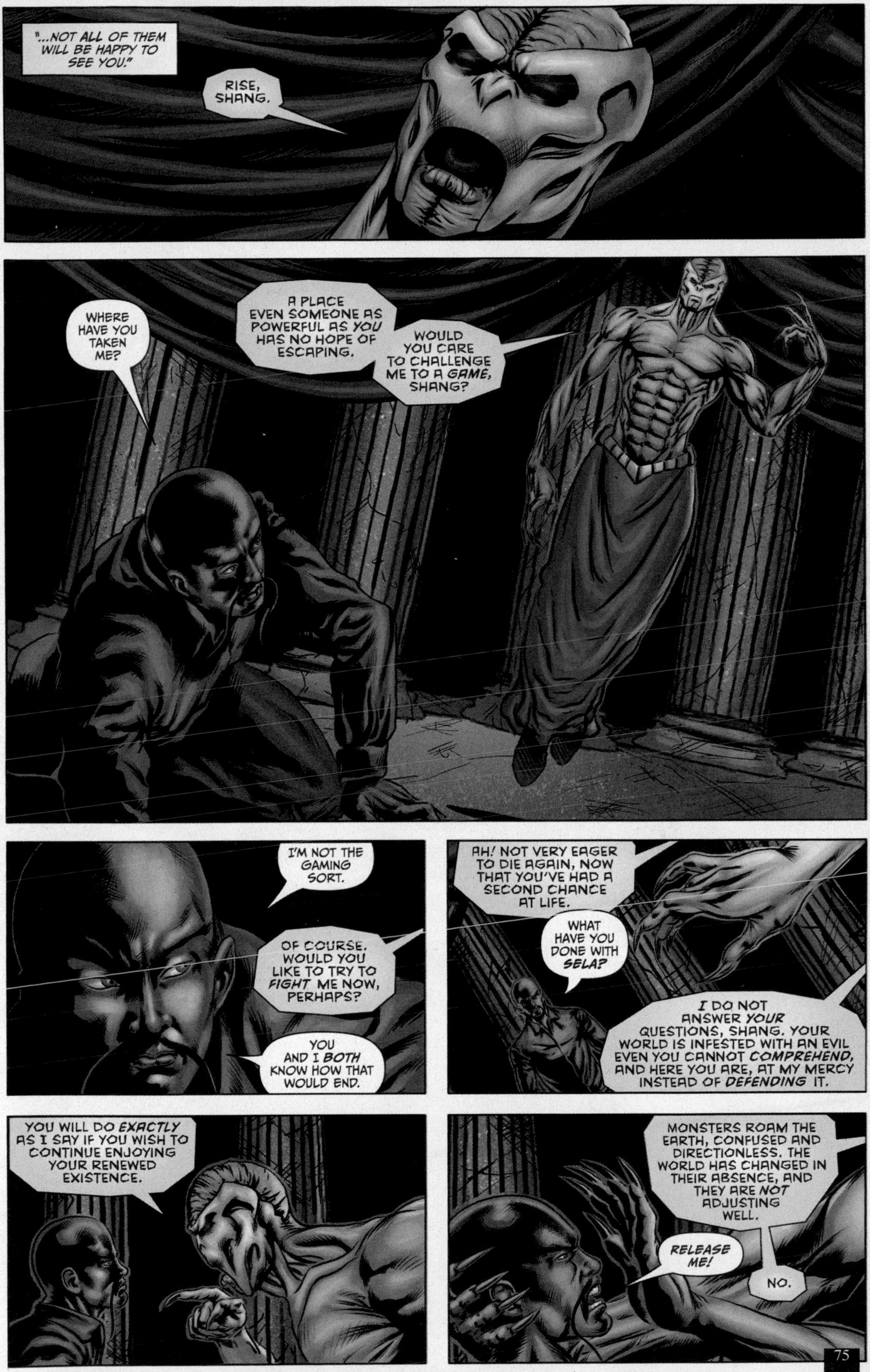
"...NOT ALL OF THEM WILL BE HAPPY TO SEE YOU."
RISE, SHANG.
WHERE HAVE YOU TAKEN ME?
A PLACE EVEN SOMEONE AS POWERFUL AS YOU HAS NO HOPE OF ESCAPING.
WOULD YOU CARE TO CHALLENGE ME TO A GAME, SHANG?
I'M NOT THE GAMING SORT.
OF COURSE. WOULD YOU LIKE TO TRY TO FIGHT ME NOW, PERHAPS?
YOU AND I BOTH KNOW HOW THAT WOULD END.
AH! NOT VERY EAGER TO DIE AGAIN, NOW THAT YOU'VE HAD A SECOND CHANCE AT LIFE.
WHAT HAVE YOU DONE WITH SELA?
I DO NOT ANSWER YOUR QUESTIONS, SHANG. YOUR WORLD IS INFESTED WITH AN EVIL EVEN YOU CANNOT COMPREHEND, AND HERE YOU ARE, AT MY MERCY INSTEAD OF DEFENDING IT.
YOU WILL DO EXACTLY AS I SAY IF YOU WISH TO CONTINUE ENJOYING YOUR RENEWED EXISTENCE.
MONSTERS ROAM THE EARTH, CONFUSED AND DIRECTIONLESS. THE WORLD HAS CHANGED IN THEIR ABSENCE, AND THEY ARE NOT ADJUSTING WELL.
RELEASE ME!
NO.

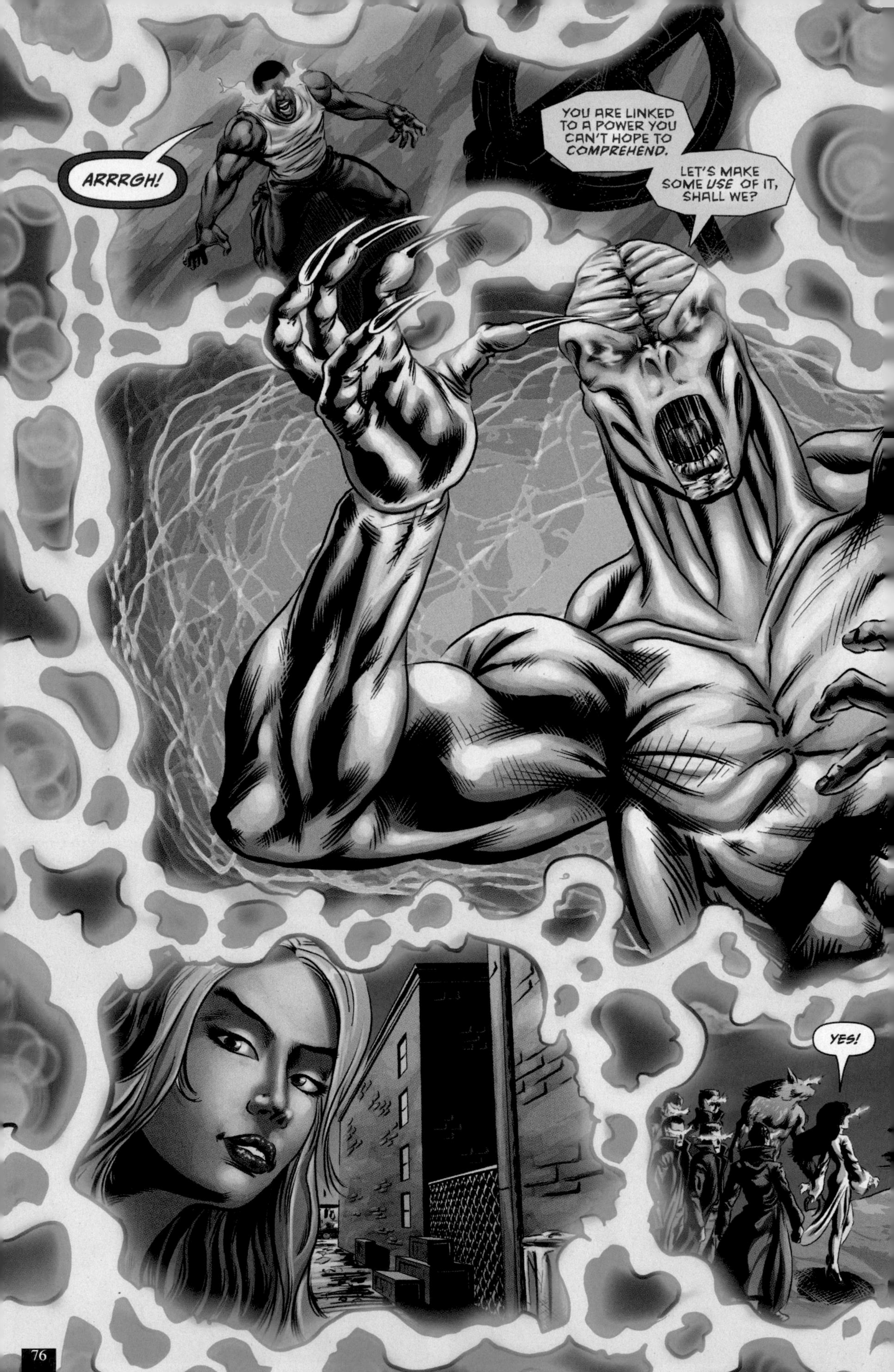
ARRRGH!
YOU ARE LINKED TO A POWER YOU CAN'T HOPE TO COMPREHEND.
LET'S MAKE SOME USE OF IT, SHALL WE?
YES!

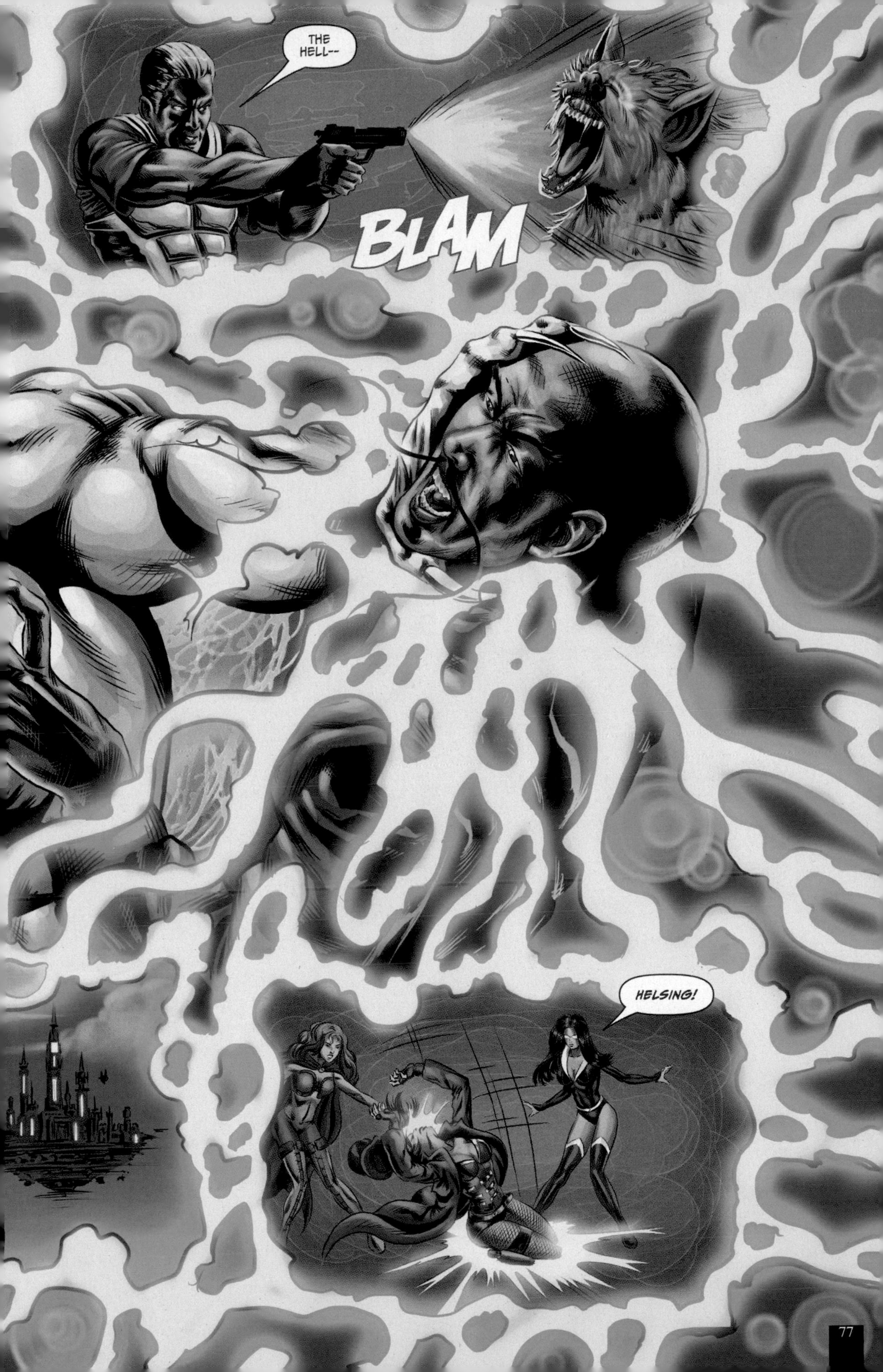
THE HELL--
BLAM
HELSING!

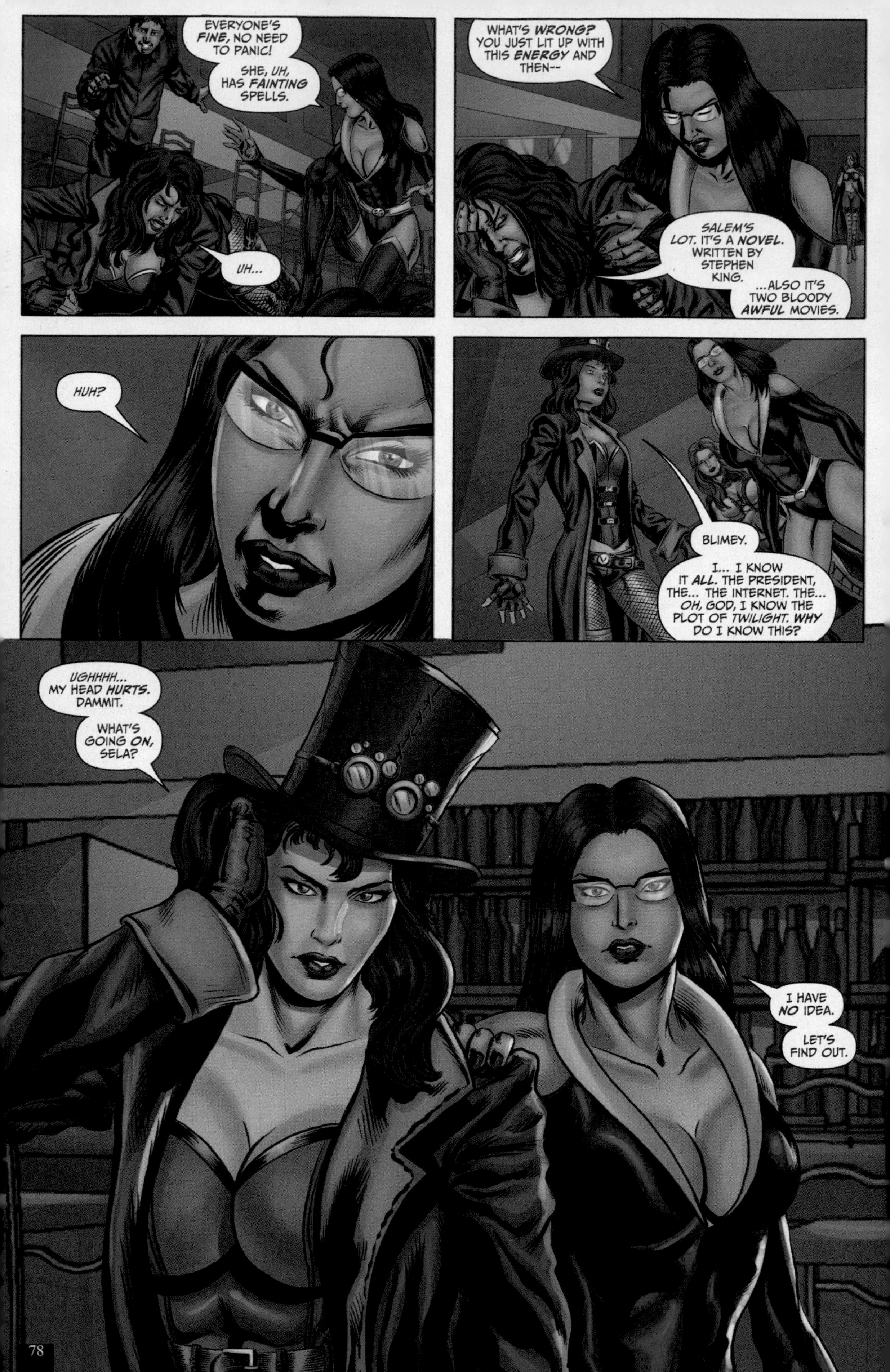
EVERYONE'S FINE, NO NEED TO PANIC!
SHE, UH, HAS FAINTING SPELLS.
UH...
WHAT'S WRONG? YOU JUST LIT UP WITH THIS ENERGY AND THEN--
SALEM'S LOT. IT'S A NOVEL. WRITTEN BY STEPHEN KING.
...ALSO IT'S TWO BLOODY AWFUL MOVIES.
HUH?
BLIMEY.
I... I KNOW IT ALL. THE PRESIDENT, THE... THE INTERNET. THE... OH, GOD, I KNOW THE PLOT OF TWILIGHT. WHY DO I KNOW THIS?
UGHHHH... MY HEAD HURTS. DAMMIT.
WHAT'S GOING ON, SELA?
I HAVE NO IDEA.
LET'S FIND OUT.

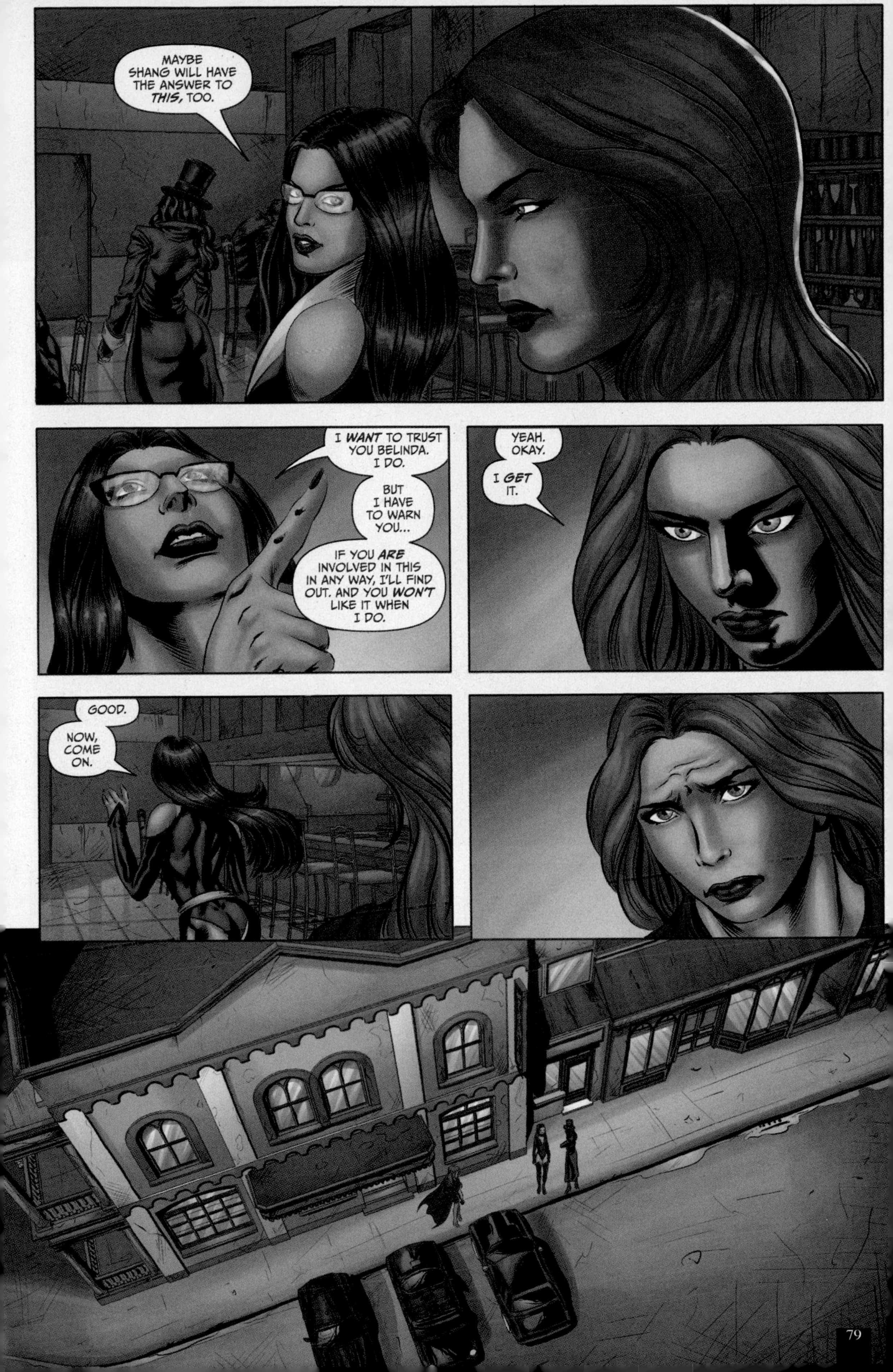
MAYBE SHANG WILL HAVE THE ANSWER TO *THIS,* TOO.
I *WANT* TO TRUST YOU BELINDA. I DO.
BUT I HAVE TO WARN YOU...
IF YOU *ARE* INVOLVED IN THIS IN ANY WAY, I'LL FIND OUT. AND YOU *WON'T* LIKE IT WHEN I DO.
YEAH. OKAY.
I *GET* IT.
GOOD.
NOW, COME ON.

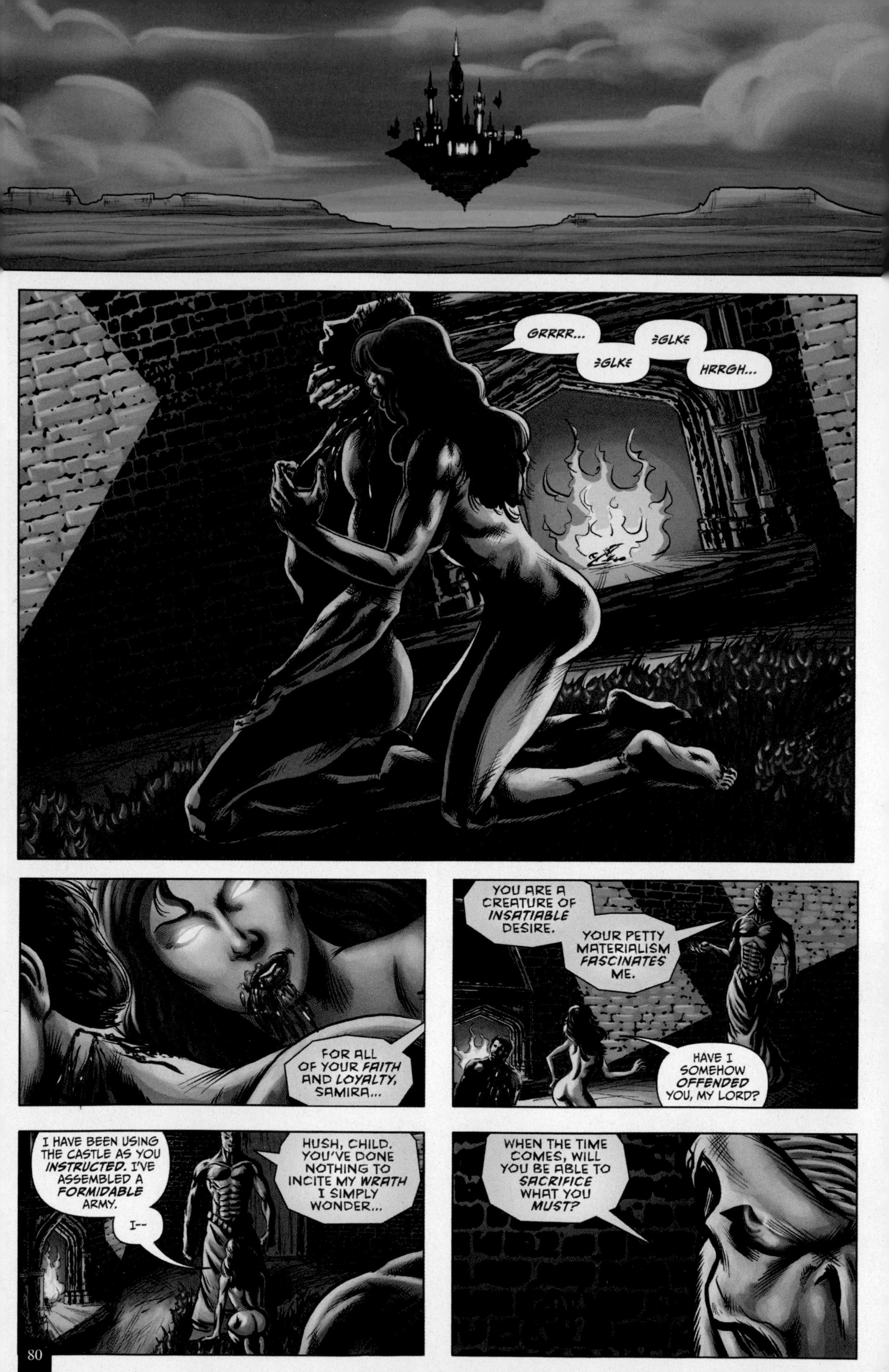
GRRRR...
≥GLK≤
≥GLK≤
HRRGH...
FOR ALL OF YOUR *FAITH* AND *LOYALTY*, SAMIRA...
YOU ARE A CREATURE OF *INSATIABLE* DESIRE.
YOUR PETTY MATERIALISM *FASCINATES* ME.
HAVE I SOMEHOW *OFFENDED* YOU, MY LORD?
I HAVE BEEN USING THE CASTLE AS YOU *INSTRUCTED*. I'VE ASSEMBLED A *FORMIDABLE* ARMY.
I--
HUSH, CHILD. YOU'VE DONE NOTHING TO INCITE MY *WRATH*. I SIMPLY WONDER...
WHEN THE TIME COMES, WILL YOU BE ABLE TO *SACRIFICE* WHAT YOU *MUST*?

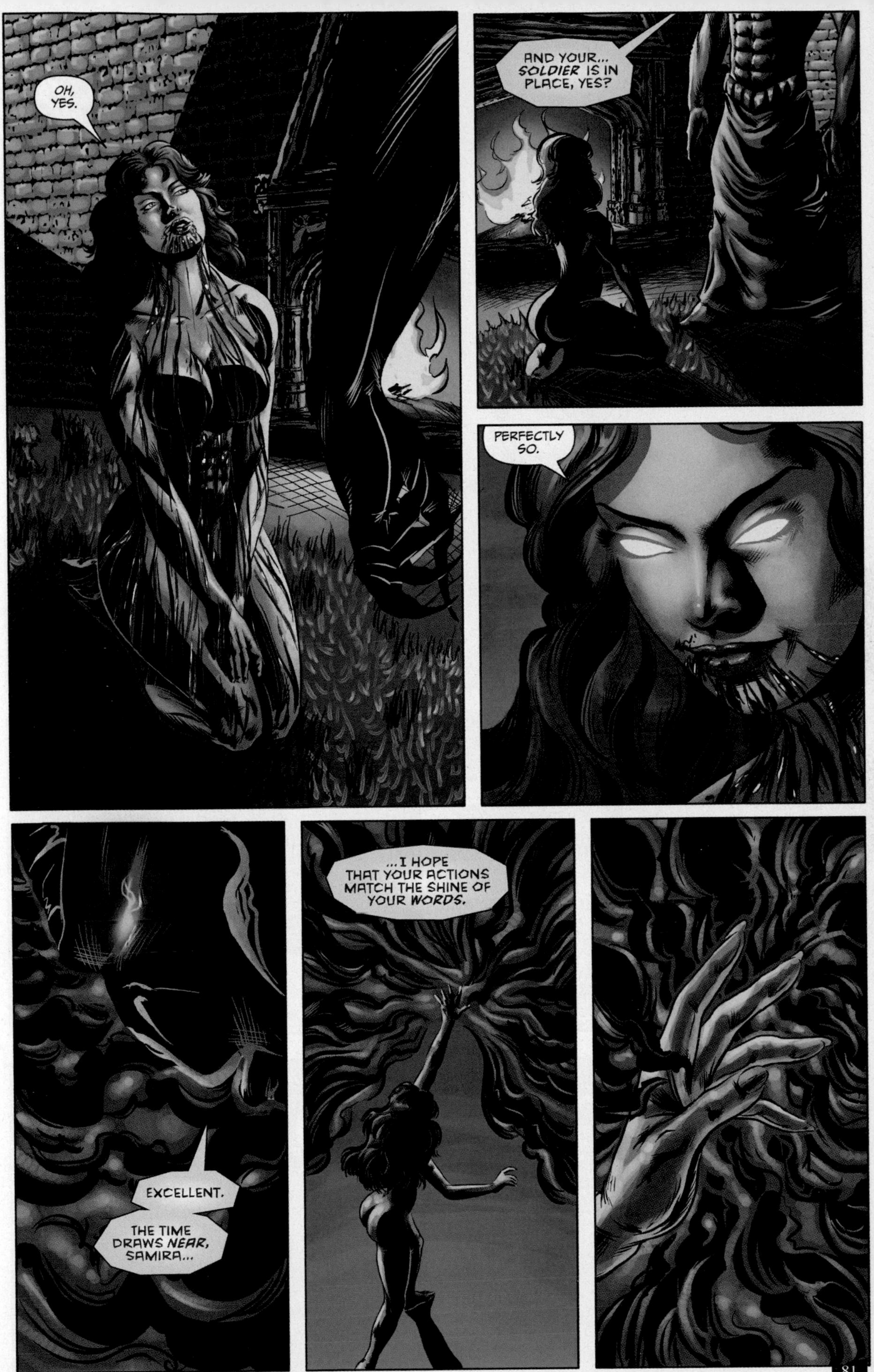
OH, YES.
AND YOUR... SOLDIER IS IN PLACE, YES?
PERFECTLY SO.
EXCELLENT.
THE TIME DRAWS NEAR, SAMIRA...
...I HOPE THAT YOUR ACTIONS MATCH THE SHINE OF YOUR WORDS.

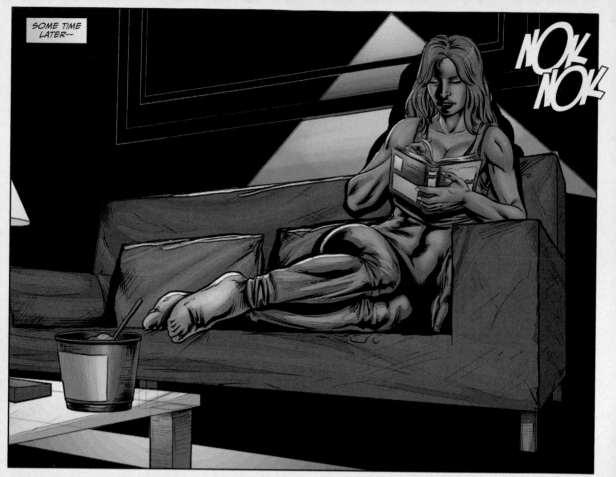

SOME TIME
LATER--

NOK
NOK

SAMANTHA,
I *KNOW* YOU'RE
IN THERE.

IT'S ABOUT
SHANG.

HAVEN'T
SEEN YOU IN
A WHILE,
SAM.

WHAT'S
GOING ON?
IS SHANG
OKAY?

NO. HE'S
MISSING.

WE'VE
BEEN LOOKING
FOR HIM FOR
WEEKS.

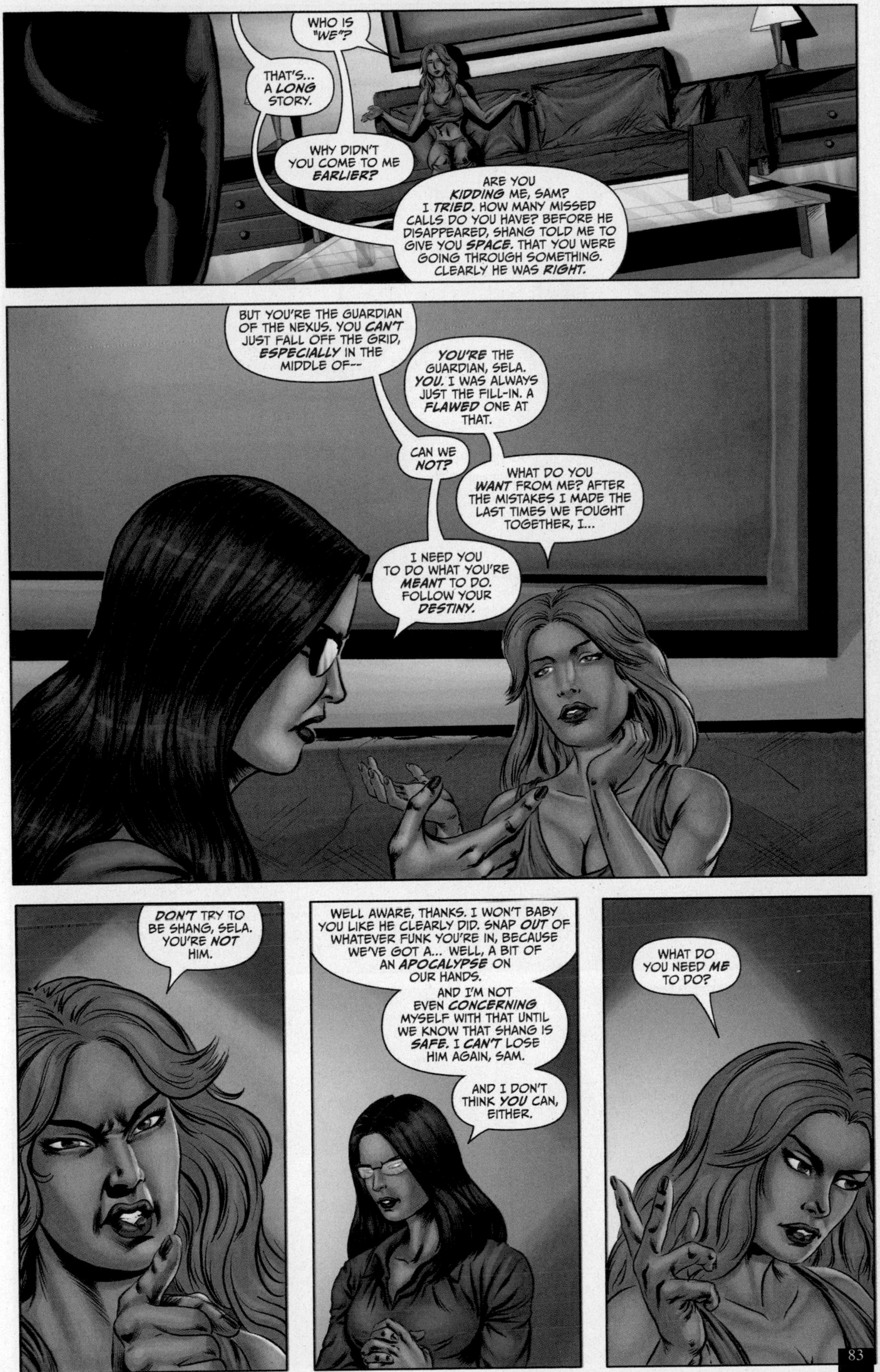
WHO IS "WE"?
THAT'S... A LONG STORY.
WHY DIDN'T YOU COME TO ME EARLIER?
ARE YOU KIDDING ME, SAM? I TRIED. HOW MANY MISSED CALLS DO YOU HAVE? BEFORE HE DISAPPEARED, SHANG TOLD ME TO GIVE YOU SPACE. THAT YOU WERE GOING THROUGH SOMETHING. CLEARLY HE WAS RIGHT.
BUT YOU'RE THE GUARDIAN OF THE NEXUS. YOU CAN'T JUST FALL OFF THE GRID, ESPECIALLY IN THE MIDDLE OF--
YOU'RE THE GUARDIAN, SELA. YOU. I WAS ALWAYS JUST THE FILL-IN. A FLAWED ONE AT THAT.
CAN WE NOT?
WHAT DO YOU WANT FROM ME? AFTER THE MISTAKES I MADE THE LAST TIMES WE FOUGHT TOGETHER, I...
I NEED YOU TO DO WHAT YOU'RE MEANT TO DO. FOLLOW YOUR DESTINY.
DON'T TRY TO BE SHANG, SELA. YOU'RE NOT HIM.
WELL AWARE, THANKS. I WON'T BABY YOU LIKE HE CLEARLY DID. SNAP OUT OF WHATEVER FUNK YOU'RE IN, BECAUSE WE'VE GOT A... WELL, A BIT OF AN APOCALYPSE ON OUR HANDS.
AND I'M NOT EVEN CONCERNING MYSELF WITH THAT UNTIL WE KNOW THAT SHANG IS SAFE. I CAN'T LOSE HIM AGAIN, SAM.
AND I DON'T THINK YOU CAN, EITHER.
WHAT DO YOU NEED ME TO DO?

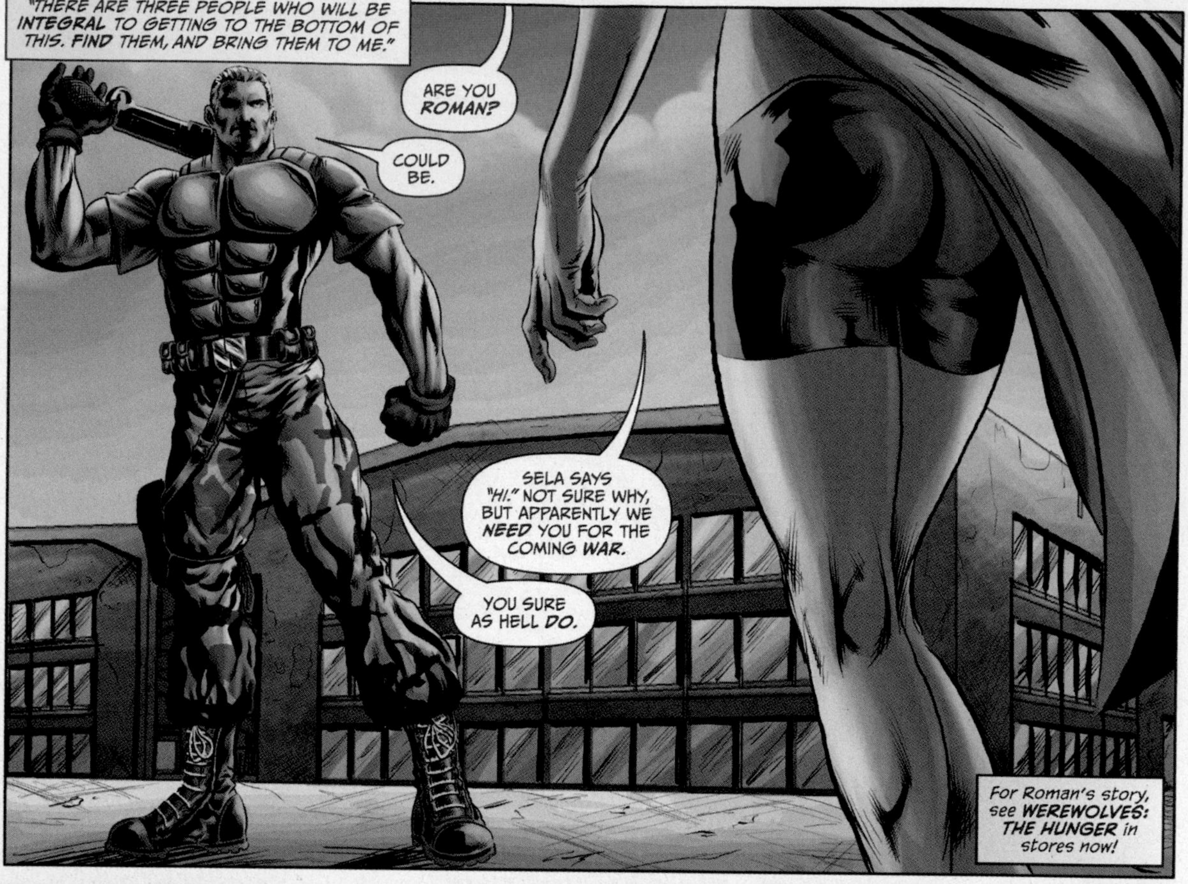
"THERE ARE THREE PEOPLE WHO WILL BE INTEGRAL TO GETTING TO THE BOTTOM OF THIS. FIND THEM, AND BRING THEM TO ME."
ARE YOU ROMAN?
COULD BE.
SELA SAYS "HI." NOT SURE WHY, BUT APPARENTLY WE NEED YOU FOR THE COMING WAR.
YOU SURE AS HELL DO.
For Roman's story, see WEREWOLVES: THE HUNGER in stores now!

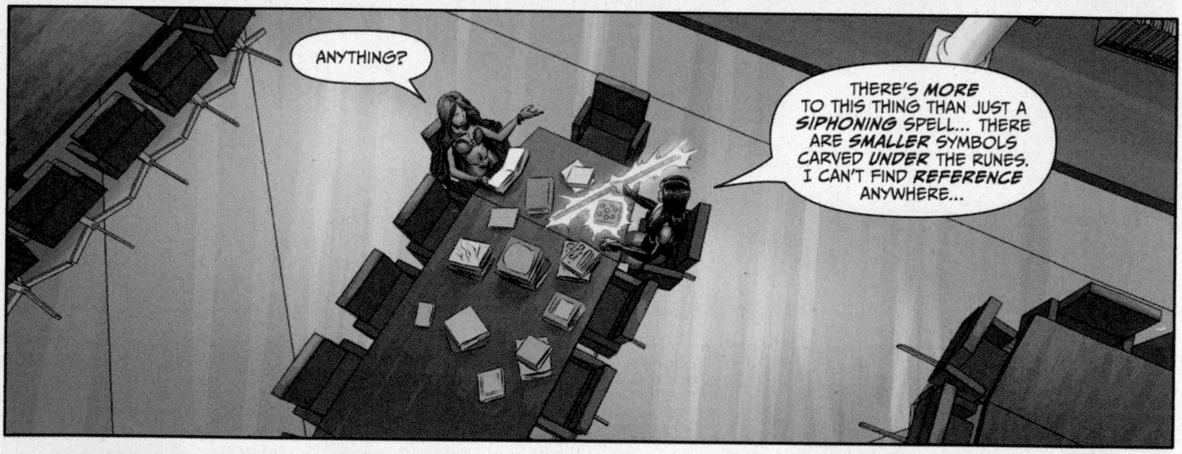
ANYTHING?
THERE'S MORE TO THIS THING THAN JUST A SIPHONING SPELL... THERE ARE SMALLER SYMBOLS CARVED UNDER THE RUNES. I CAN'T FIND REFERENCE ANYWHERE...

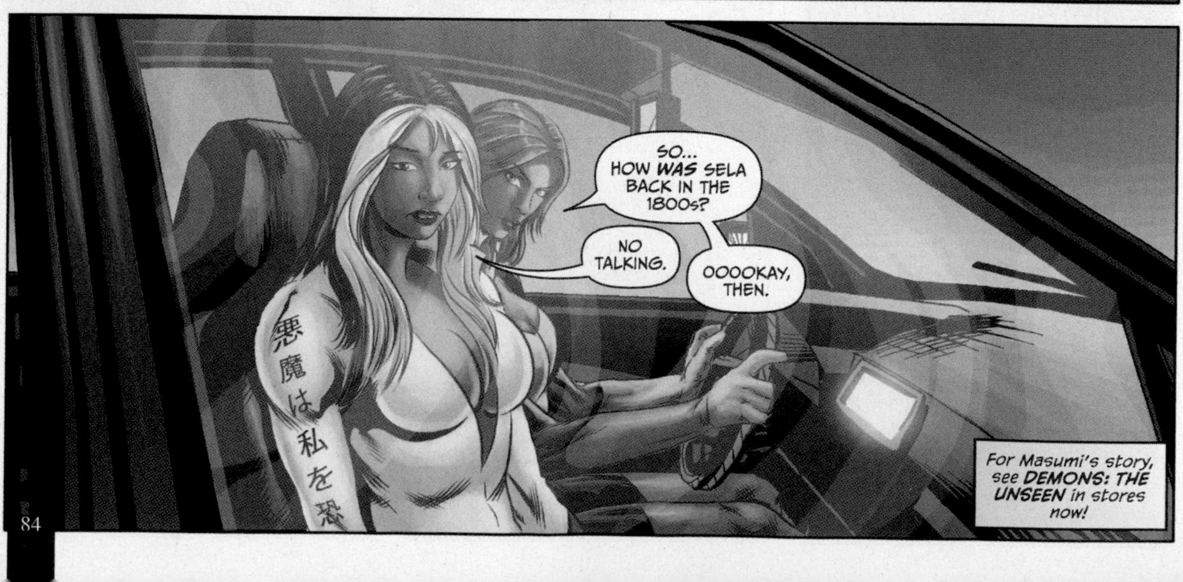
SO... HOW WAS SELA BACK IN THE 1800s?
NO TALKING.
OOOOKAY, THEN.
悪魔は私を恐
For Masumi's story, see DEMONS: THE UNSEEN in stores now!

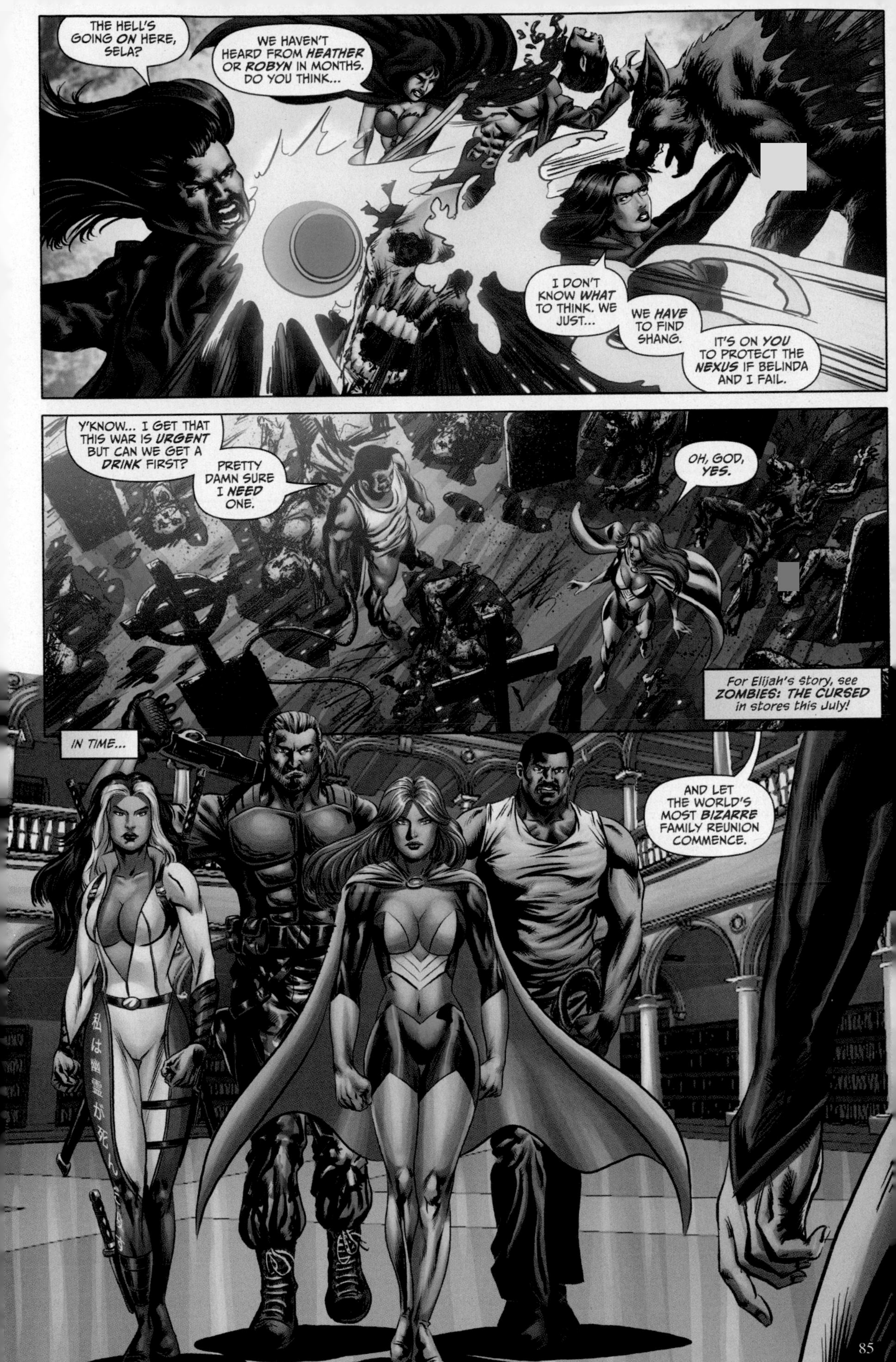
THE HELL'S GOING ON HERE, SELA?
WE HAVEN'T HEARD FROM HEATHER OR ROBYN IN MONTHS. DO YOU THINK...
I DON'T KNOW WHAT TO THINK. WE JUST...
WE HAVE TO FIND SHANG.
IT'S ON YOU TO PROTECT THE NEXUS IF BELINDA AND I FAIL.
Y'KNOW... I GET THAT THIS WAR IS URGENT BUT CAN WE GET A DRINK FIRST?
PRETTY DAMN SURE I NEED ONE.
OH, GOD, YES.
For Elijah's story, see ZOMBIES: THE CURSED in stores this July!
IN TIME...
AND LET THE WORLD'S MOST BIZARRE FAMILY REUNION COMMENCE.

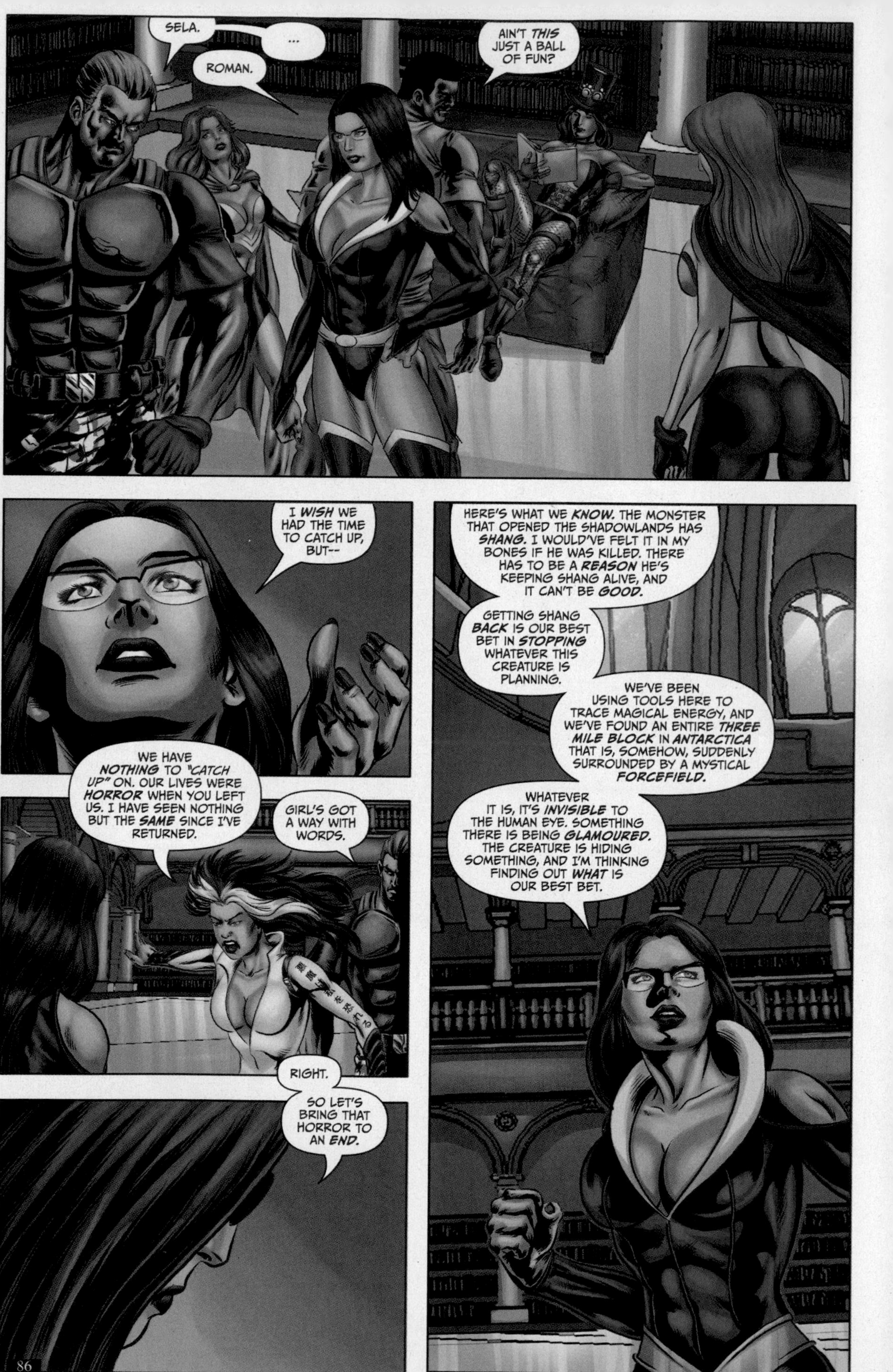
SELA.
...
ROMAN.
AIN'T THIS JUST A BALL OF FUN?
I WISH WE HAD THE TIME TO CATCH UP, BUT--
WE HAVE NOTHING TO "CATCH UP" ON. OUR LIVES WERE HORROR WHEN YOU LEFT US. I HAVE SEEN NOTHING BUT THE SAME SINCE I'VE RETURNED.
GIRL'S GOT A WAY WITH WORDS.
RIGHT.
SO LET'S BRING THAT HORROR TO AN END.
HERE'S WHAT WE KNOW. THE MONSTER THAT OPENED THE SHADOWLANDS HAS SHANG. I WOULD'VE FELT IT IN MY BONES IF HE WAS KILLED. THERE HAS TO BE A REASON HE'S KEEPING SHANG ALIVE, AND IT CAN'T BE GOOD.
GETTING SHANG BACK IS OUR BEST BET IN STOPPING WHATEVER THIS CREATURE IS PLANNING.
WE'VE BEEN USING TOOLS HERE TO TRACE MAGICAL ENERGY, AND WE'VE FOUND AN ENTIRE THREE MILE BLOCK IN ANTARCTICA THAT IS, SOMEHOW, SUDDENLY SURROUNDED BY A MYSTICAL FORCEFIELD.
WHATEVER IT IS, IT'S INVISIBLE TO THE HUMAN EYE. SOMETHING THERE IS BEING GLAMOURED. THE CREATURE IS HIDING SOMETHING, AND I'M THINKING FINDING OUT WHAT IS OUR BEST BET.

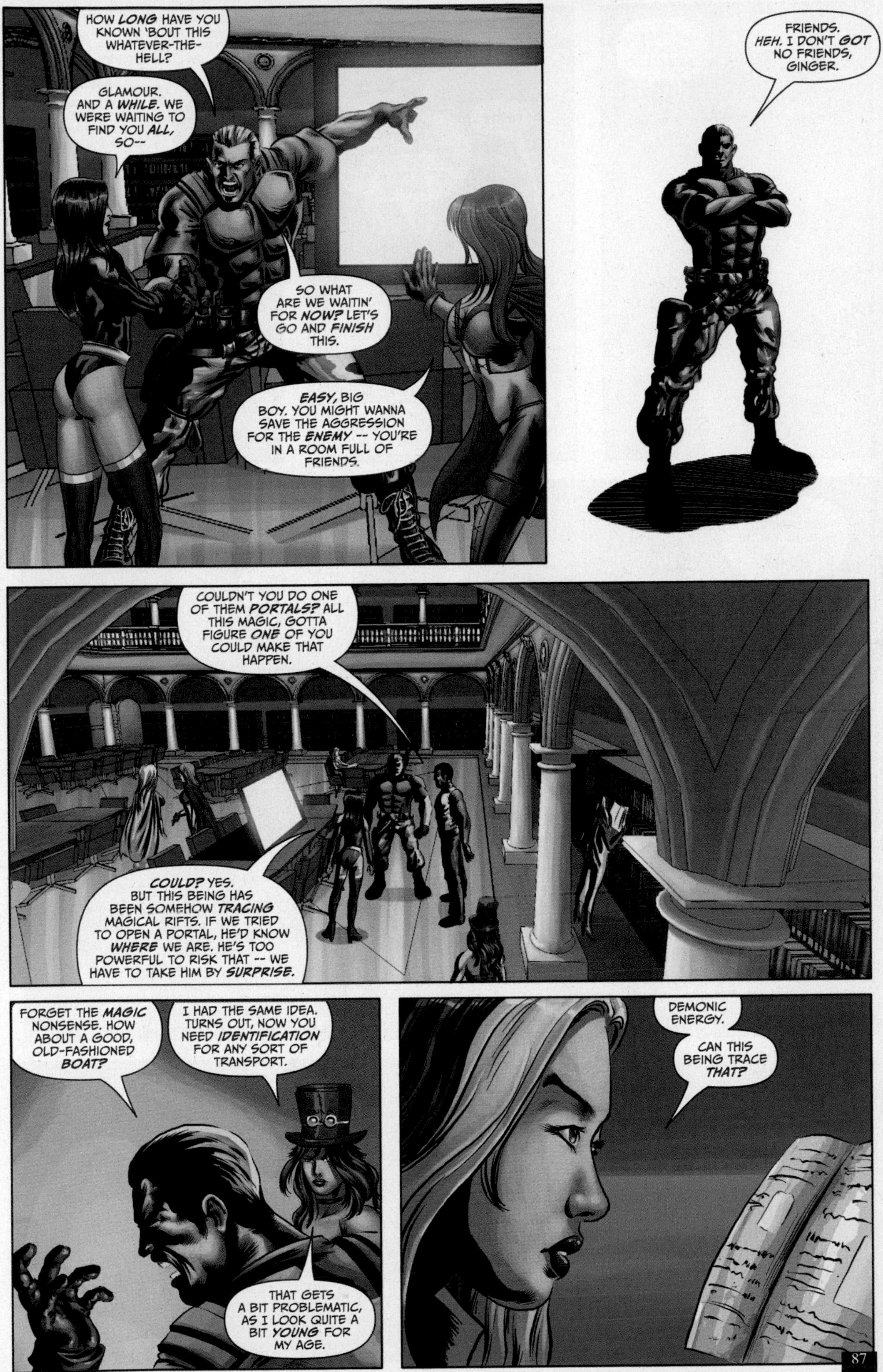
HOW LONG HAVE YOU KNOWN 'BOUT THIS WHATEVER-THE-HELL?
GLAMOUR. AND A WHILE. WE WERE WAITING TO FIND YOU ALL, SO--
SO WHAT ARE WE WAITIN' FOR NOW? LET'S GO AND FINISH THIS.
EASY, BIG BOY. YOU MIGHT WANNA SAVE THE AGGRESSION FOR THE ENEMY -- YOU'RE IN A ROOM FULL OF FRIENDS.
FRIENDS. HEH. I DON'T GOT NO FRIENDS, GINGER.
COULDN'T YOU DO ONE OF THEM PORTALS? ALL THIS MAGIC, GOTTA FIGURE ONE OF YOU COULD MAKE THAT HAPPEN.
COULD? YES. BUT THIS BEING HAS BEEN SOMEHOW TRACING MAGICAL RIFTS. IF WE TRIED TO OPEN A PORTAL, HE'D KNOW WHERE WE ARE. HE'S TOO POWERFUL TO RISK THAT -- WE HAVE TO TAKE HIM BY SURPRISE.
FORGET THE MAGIC NONSENSE. HOW ABOUT A GOOD, OLD-FASHIONED BOAT?
I HAD THE SAME IDEA. TURNS OUT, NOW YOU NEED IDENTIFICATION FOR ANY SORT OF TRANSPORT.
THAT GETS A BIT PROBLEMATIC, AS I LOOK QUITE A BIT YOUNG FOR MY AGE.
DEMONIC ENERGY.
CAN THIS BEING TRACE THAT?

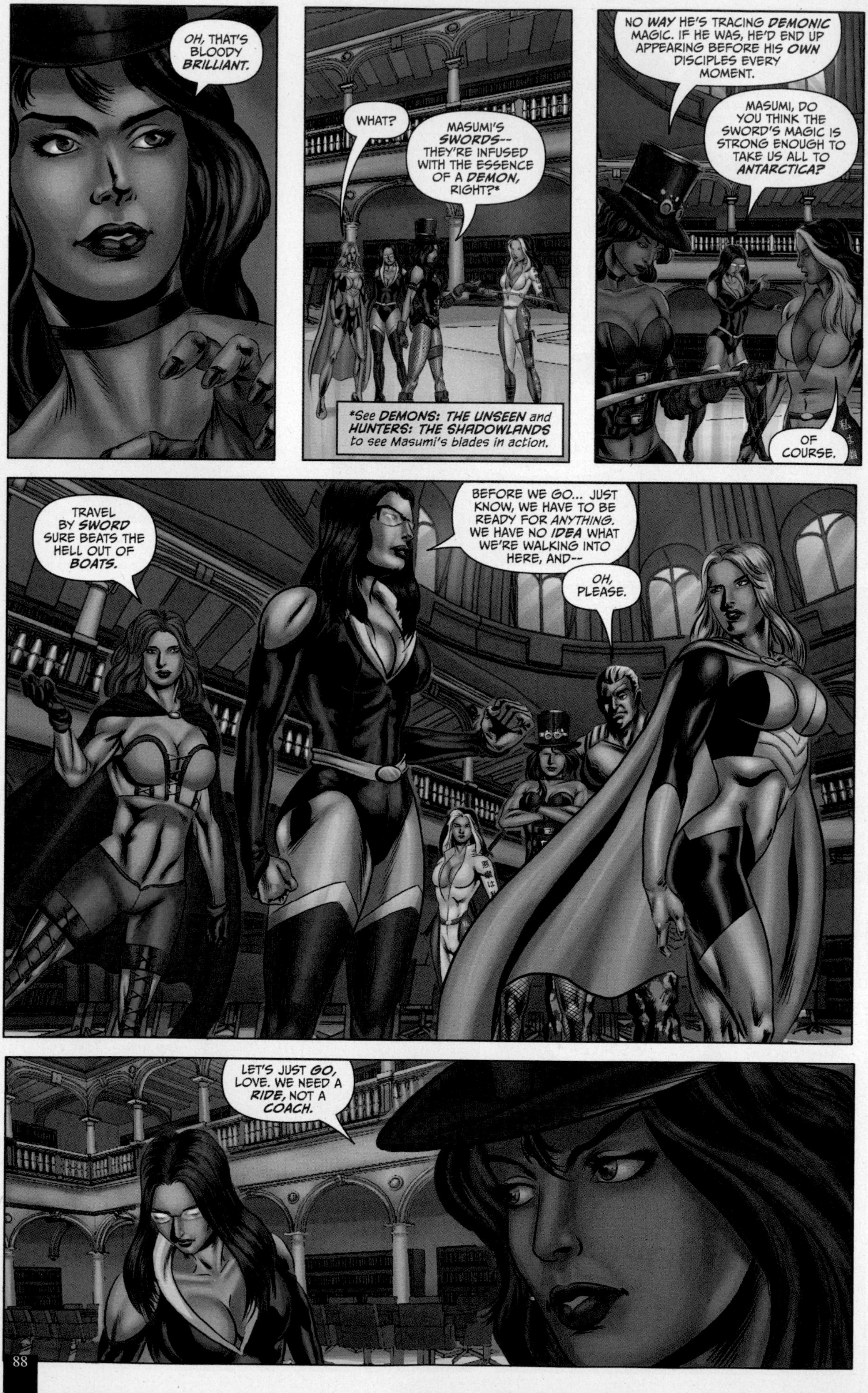
OH, THAT'S BLOODY BRILLIANT.
WHAT?
MASUMI'S SWORDS-- THEY'RE INFUSED WITH THE ESSENCE OF A DEMON, RIGHT?*
*See DEMONS: THE UNSEEN and HUNTERS: THE SHADOWLANDS to see Masumi's blades in action.
NO WAY HE'S TRACING DEMONIC MAGIC. IF HE WAS, HE'D END UP APPEARING BEFORE HIS OWN DISCIPLES EVERY MOMENT.
MASUMI, DO YOU THINK THE SWORD'S MAGIC IS STRONG ENOUGH TO TAKE US ALL TO ANTARCTICA?
OF COURSE.
TRAVEL BY SWORD SURE BEATS THE HELL OUT OF BOATS.
BEFORE WE GO... JUST KNOW, WE HAVE TO BE READY FOR ANYTHING. WE HAVE NO IDEA WHAT WE'RE WALKING INTO HERE, AND--
OH, PLEASE.
LET'S JUST GO, LOVE. WE NEED A RIDE, NOT A COACH.

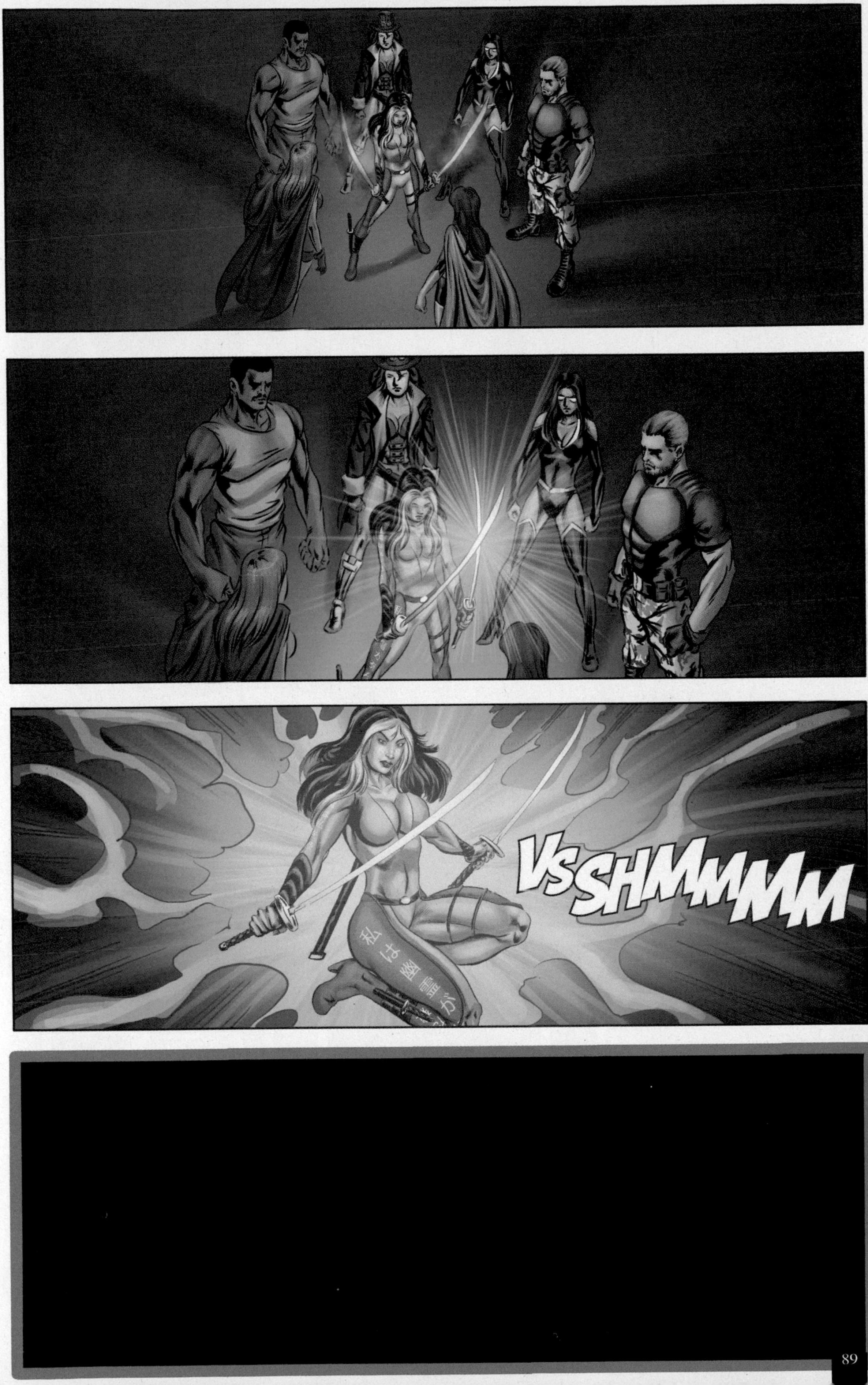
私は幽霊が
VSSHMMMMM

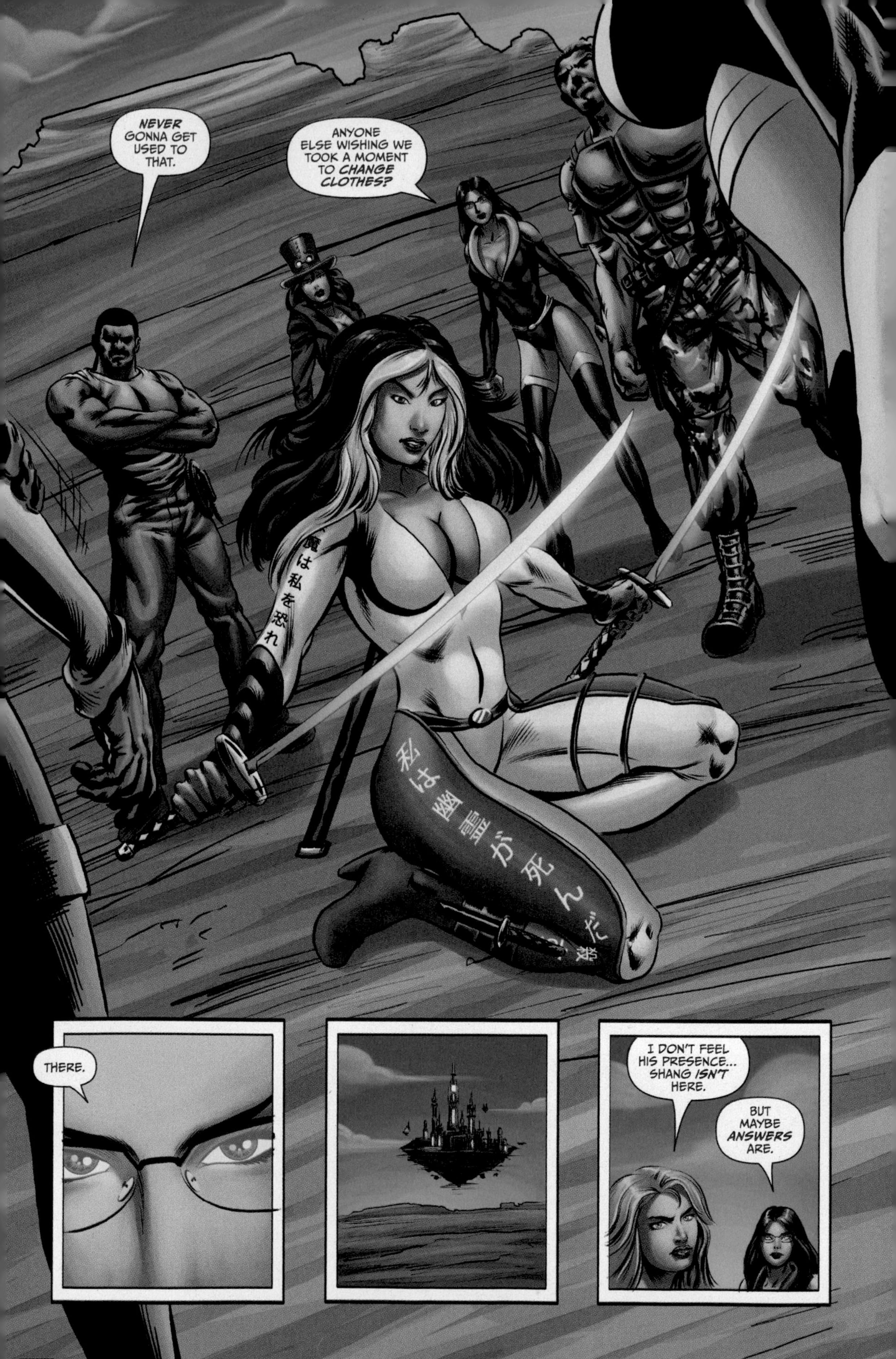
NEVER GONNA GET USED TO THAT.
ANYONE ELSE WISHING WE TOOK A MOMENT TO CHANGE CLOTHES?
魔は私を恐れ
THERE.
I DON'T FEEL HIS PRESENCE... SHANG ISN'T HERE.
BUT MAYBE ANSWERS ARE.

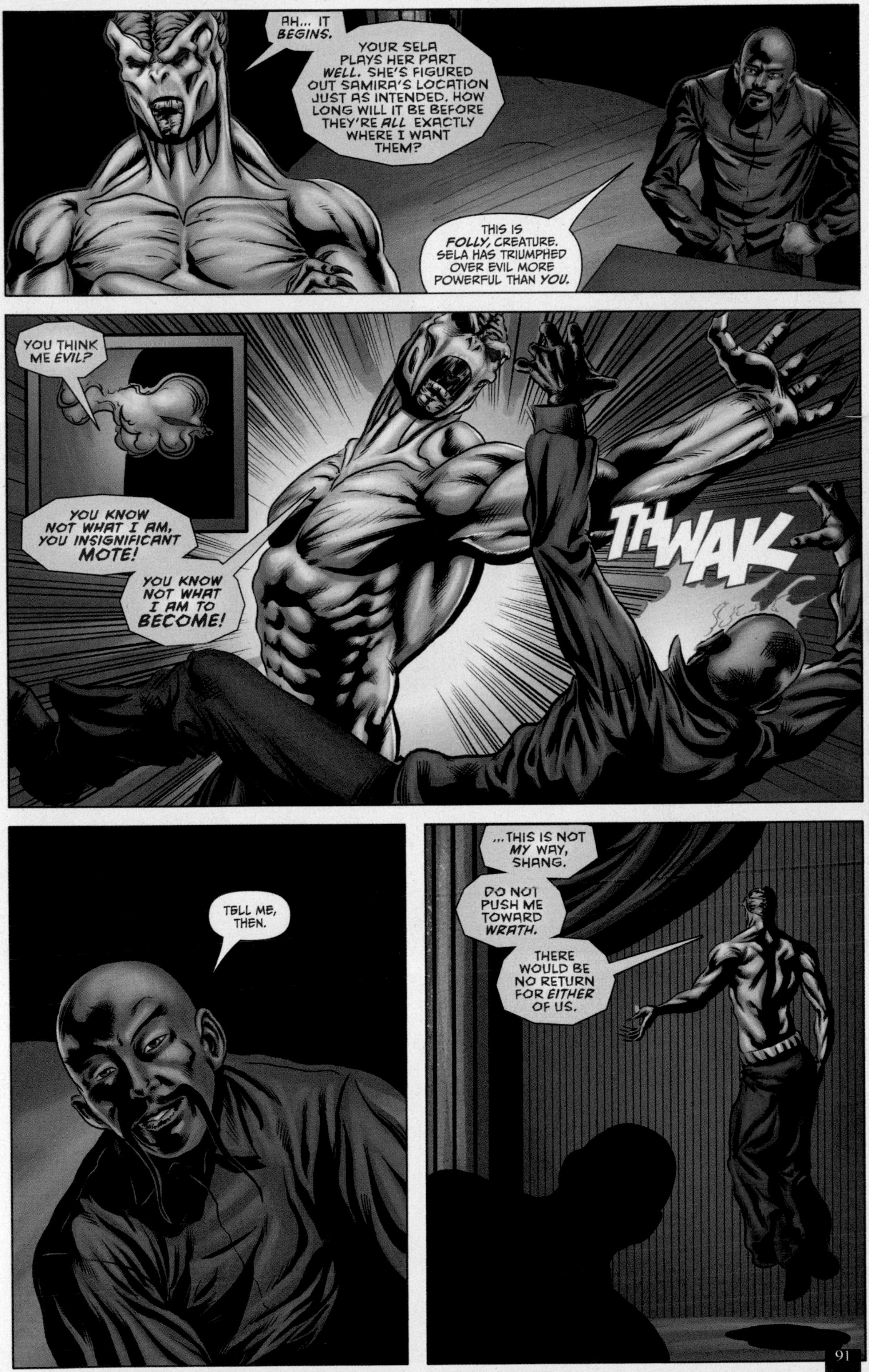
AH... IT BEGINS.
YOUR SELA PLAYS HER PART WELL. SHE'S FIGURED OUT SAMIRA'S LOCATION JUST AS INTENDED. HOW LONG WILL IT BE BEFORE THEY'RE ALL EXACTLY WHERE I WANT THEM?
THIS IS FOLLY, CREATURE. SELA HAS TRIUMPHED OVER EVIL MORE POWERFUL THAN YOU.
YOU THINK ME EVIL?
YOU KNOW NOT WHAT I AM, YOU INSIGNIFICANT MOTE!
YOU KNOW NOT WHAT I AM TO BECOME!
THWAK
TELL ME, THEN.
...THIS IS NOT MY WAY, SHANG.
DO NOT PUSH ME TOWARD WRATH.
THERE WOULD BE NO RETURN FOR EITHER OF US.

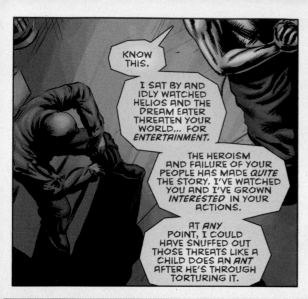

KNOW THIS.

I SAT BY AND IDLY WATCHED HELIOS AND THE DREAM EATER THREATEN YOUR WORLD... FOR *ENTERTAINMENT.*

THE HEROISM AND FAILURE OF YOUR PEOPLE HAS MADE *QUITE* THE STORY. I'VE WATCHED YOU AND I'VE GROWN *INTERESTED* IN YOUR ACTIONS.

AT *ANY* POINT, I COULD HAVE SNUFFED OUT THOSE THREATS LIKE A CHILD DOES AN *ANT* AFTER HE'S THROUGH TORTURING IT.

I'VE KEPT YOUR WORLD *SAFE.*

YOU'VE DONE QUITE THE JOB.

YOU COULDN'T *BEGIN* TO UNDERSTAND THE GAME I PLAY.

THAT IS YOUR FIRST MISTAKE, CREATURE... YOU KEEP REFERRING TO IT AS A *GAME.*

FOR A WISE MAN, SHANG, YOU KNOW SO *LITTLE.*

YOU DON'T EVEN KNOW *WHAT* BROUGHT YOU BACK FROM THE BOWELS OF DEATH. YOU DON'T KNOW WHAT *POWER* YOU'VE TAPPED INTO.

AND THAT'S WHY I WILL *WIN.*

YOUR MOVE.

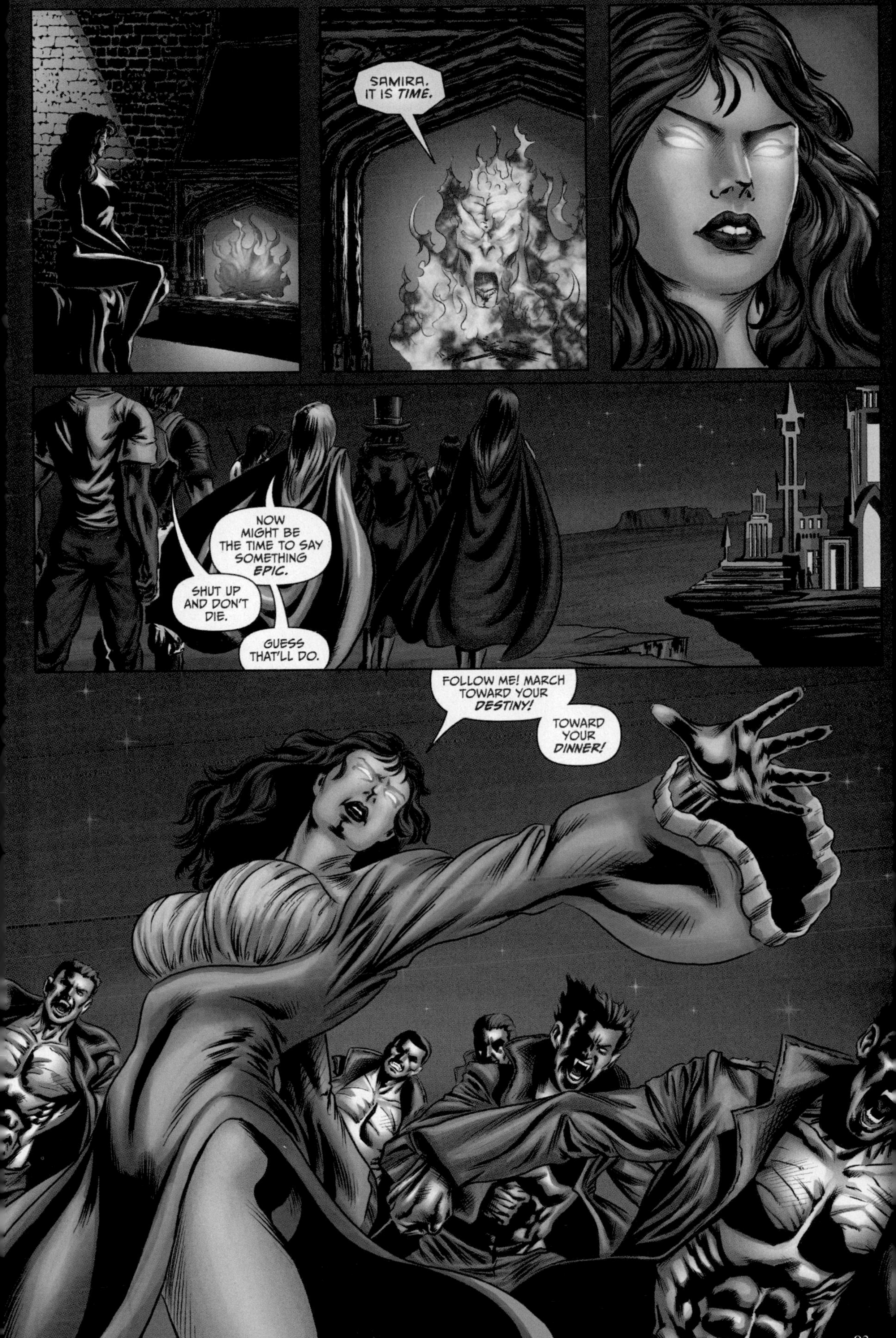
SAMIRA. IT IS TIME.
NOW MIGHT BE THE TIME TO SAY SOMETHING EPIC.
SHUT UP AND DON'T DIE.
GUESS THAT'LL DO.
FOLLOW ME! MARCH TOWARD YOUR DESTINY!
TOWARD YOUR DINNER!

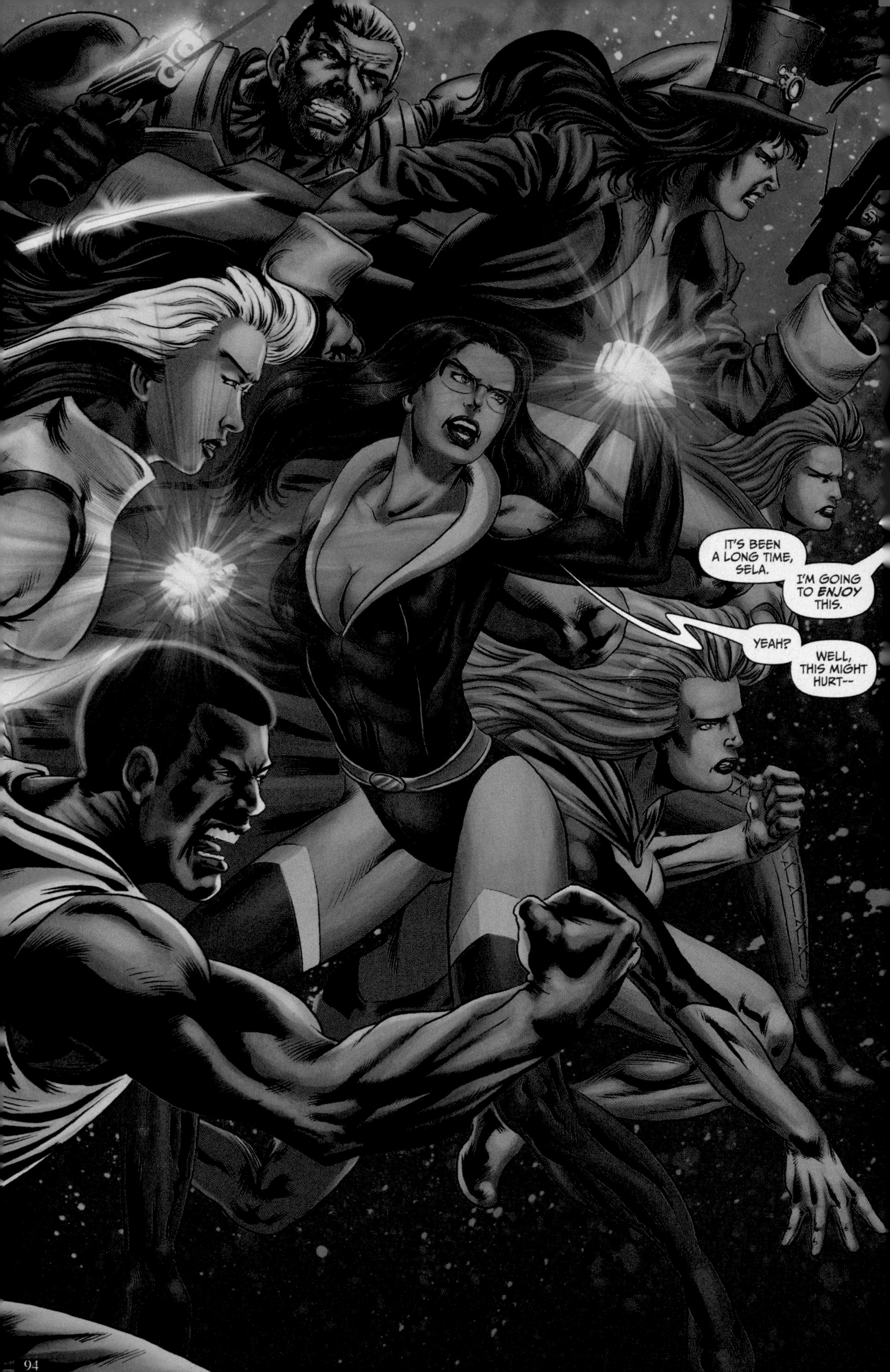
IT'S BEEN A LONG TIME, SELA.
I'M GOING TO ENJOY THIS.
YEAH?
WELL, THIS MIGHT HURT--

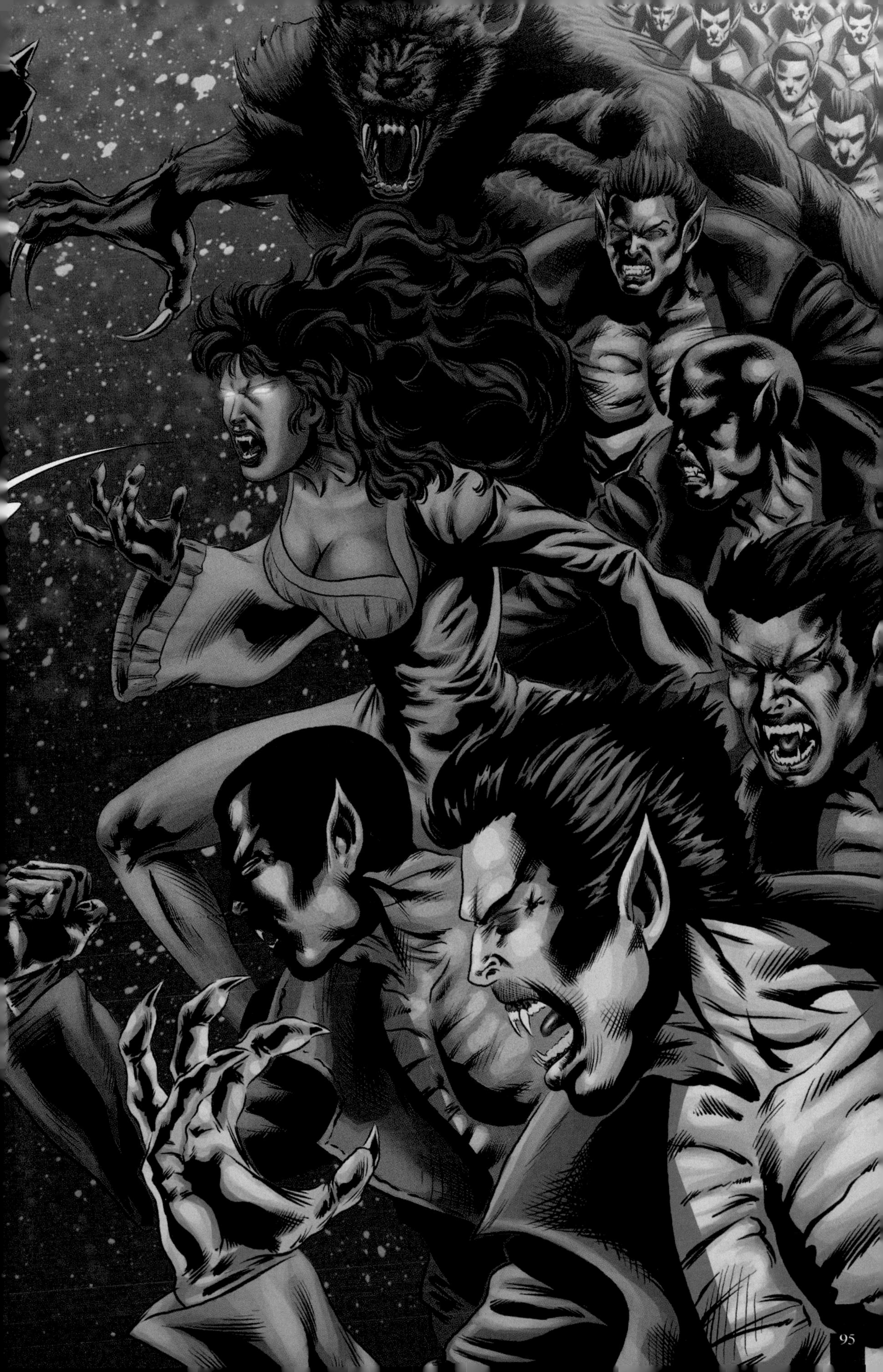

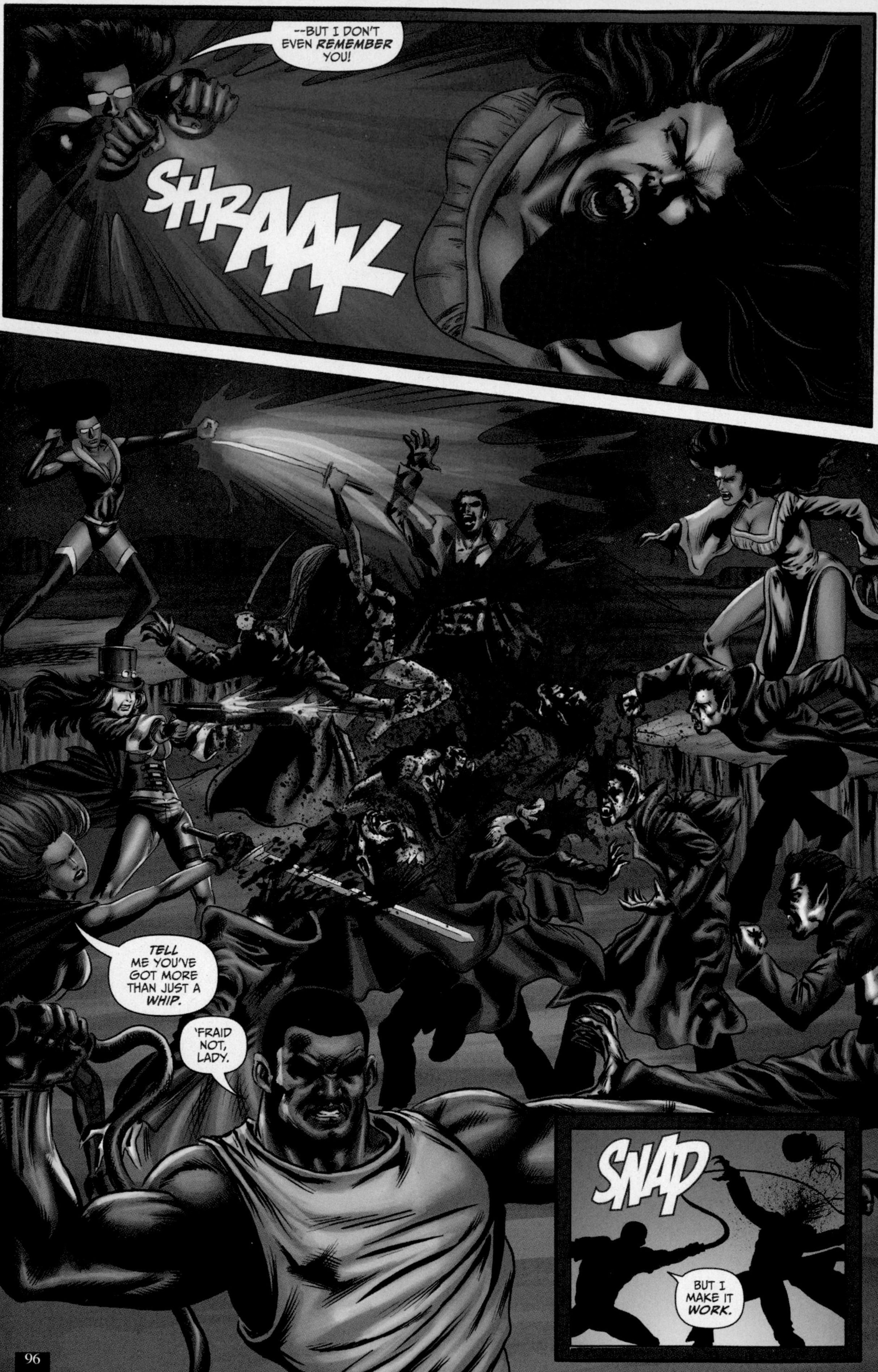
--BUT I DON'T EVEN *REMEMBER* YOU!
SHRAAAK
TELL ME YOU'VE GOT MORE THAN JUST A *WHIP*.
'FRAID NOT, LADY.
SNAP
BUT I MAKE IT *WORK*.

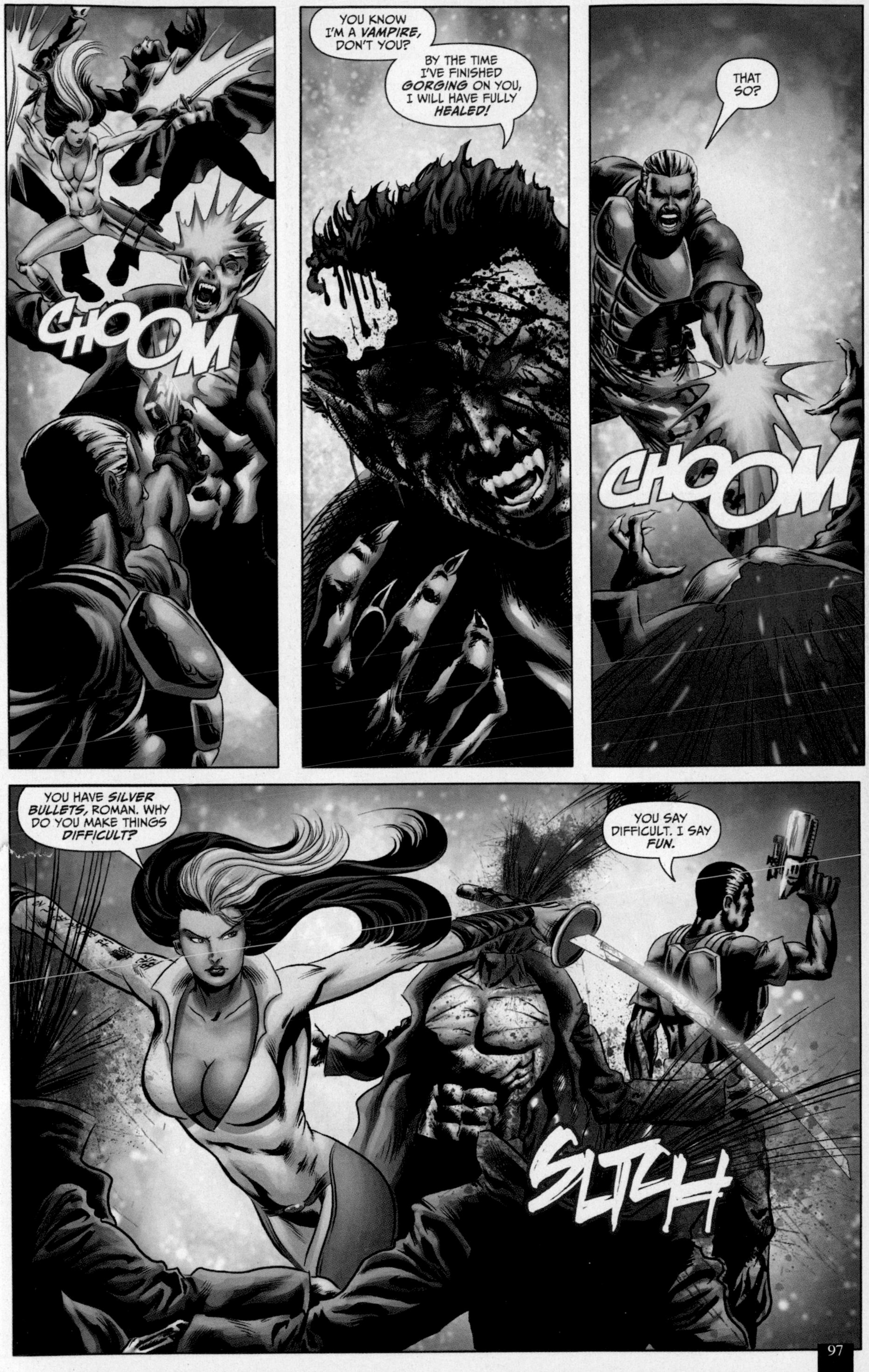
CHOOM
YOU KNOW I'M A VAMPIRE, DON'T YOU?
BY THE TIME I'VE FINISHED GORGING ON YOU, I WILL HAVE FULLY HEALED!
THAT SO?
CHOOM
YOU HAVE SILVER BULLETS, ROMAN. WHY DO YOU MAKE THINGS DIFFICULT?
YOU SAY DIFFICULT. I SAY FUN.
SLTCH

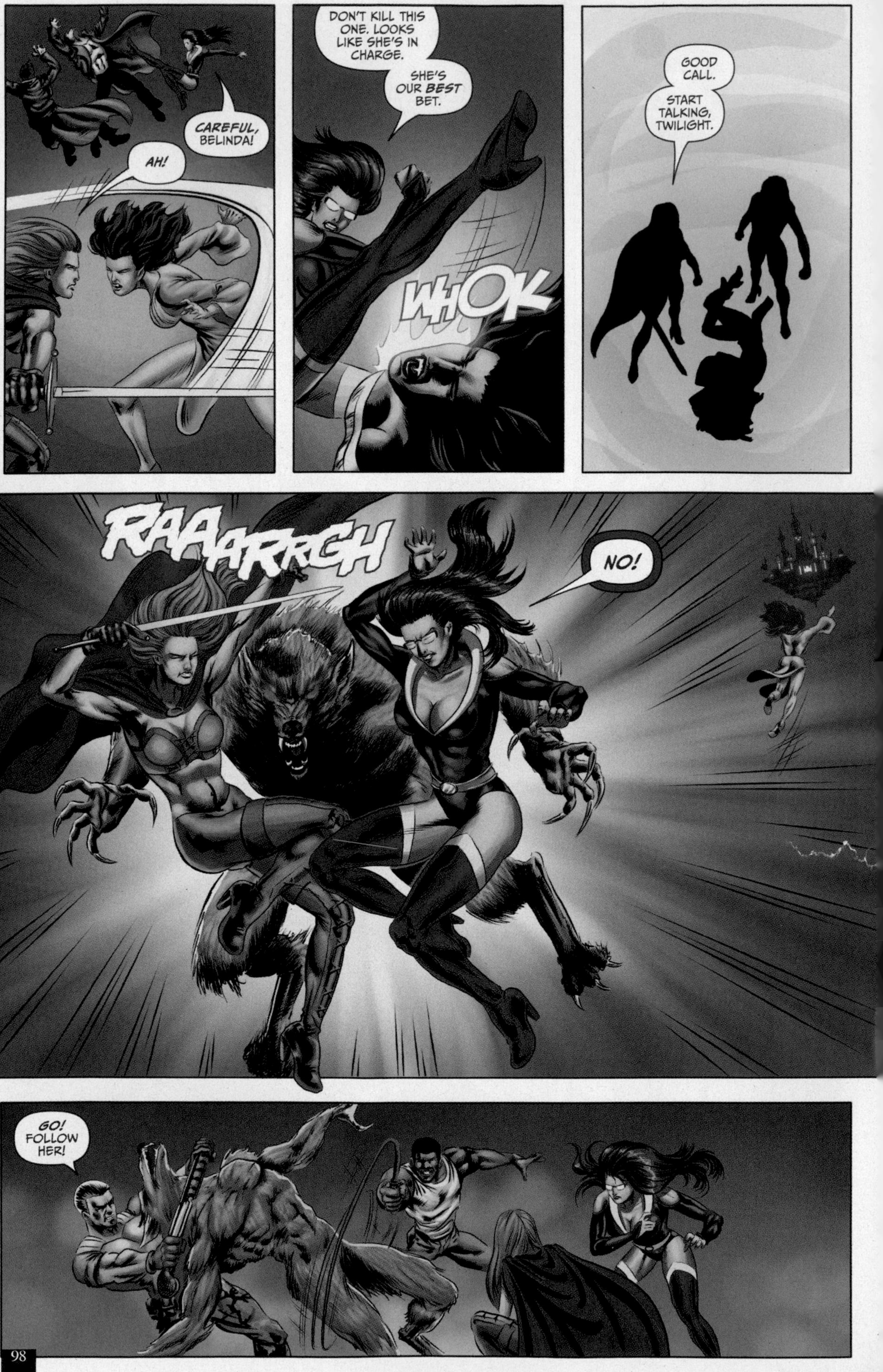
CAREFUL, BELINDA!
AH!
DON'T KILL THIS ONE. LOOKS LIKE SHE'S IN CHARGE.
SHE'S OUR BEST BET.
WHOK
GOOD CALL.
START TALKING, TWILIGHT.
RAAARRRGH
NO!
GO! FOLLOW HER!

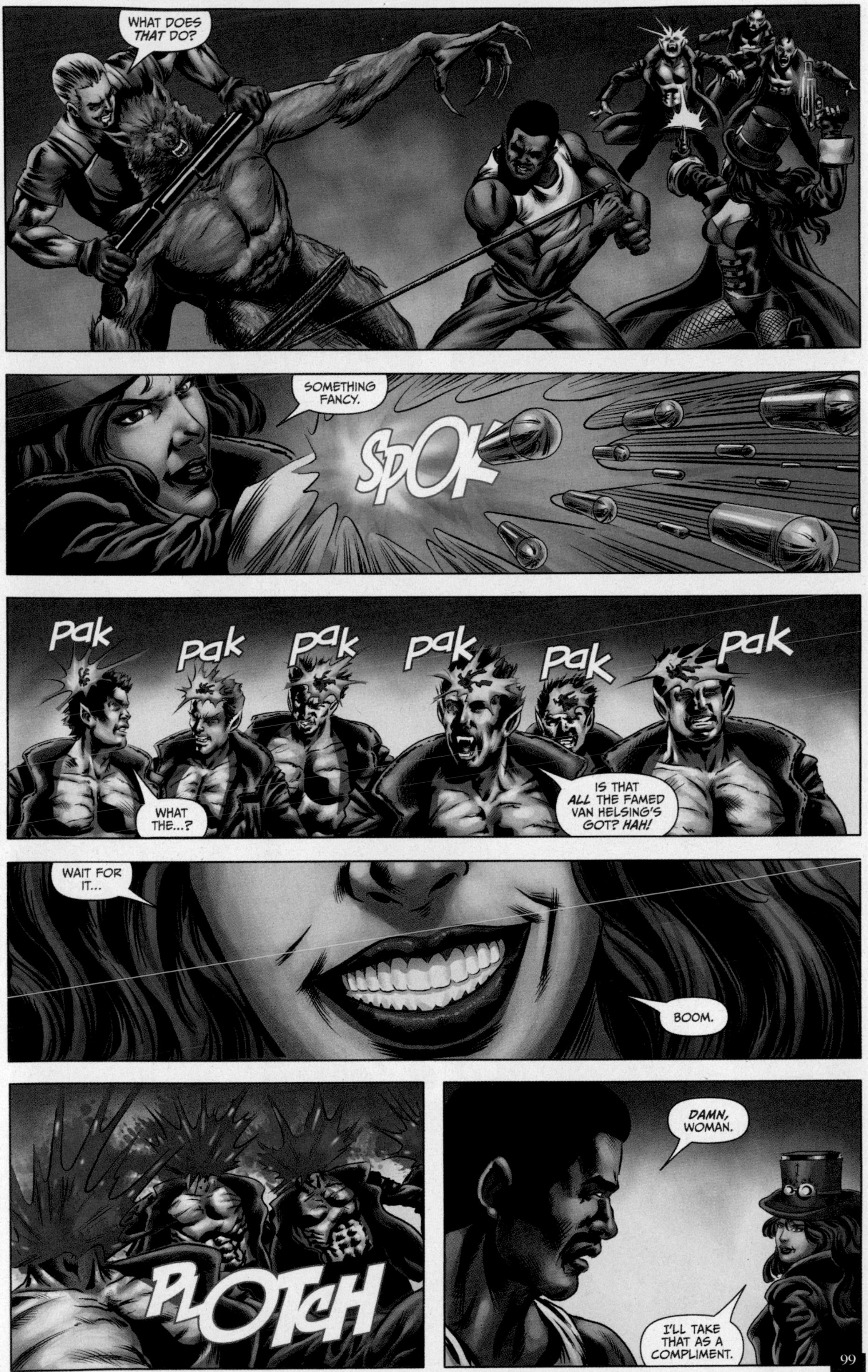
WHAT DOES THAT DO?
SOMETHING FANCY.
SPOK
PAK
PAK
PAK
PAK
PAK
PAK
WHAT THE...?
IS THAT ALL THE FAMED VAN HELSING'S GOT? HAH!
WAIT FOR IT...
BOOM.
PLOTCH
DAMN, WOMAN.
I'LL TAKE THAT AS A COMPLIMENT.

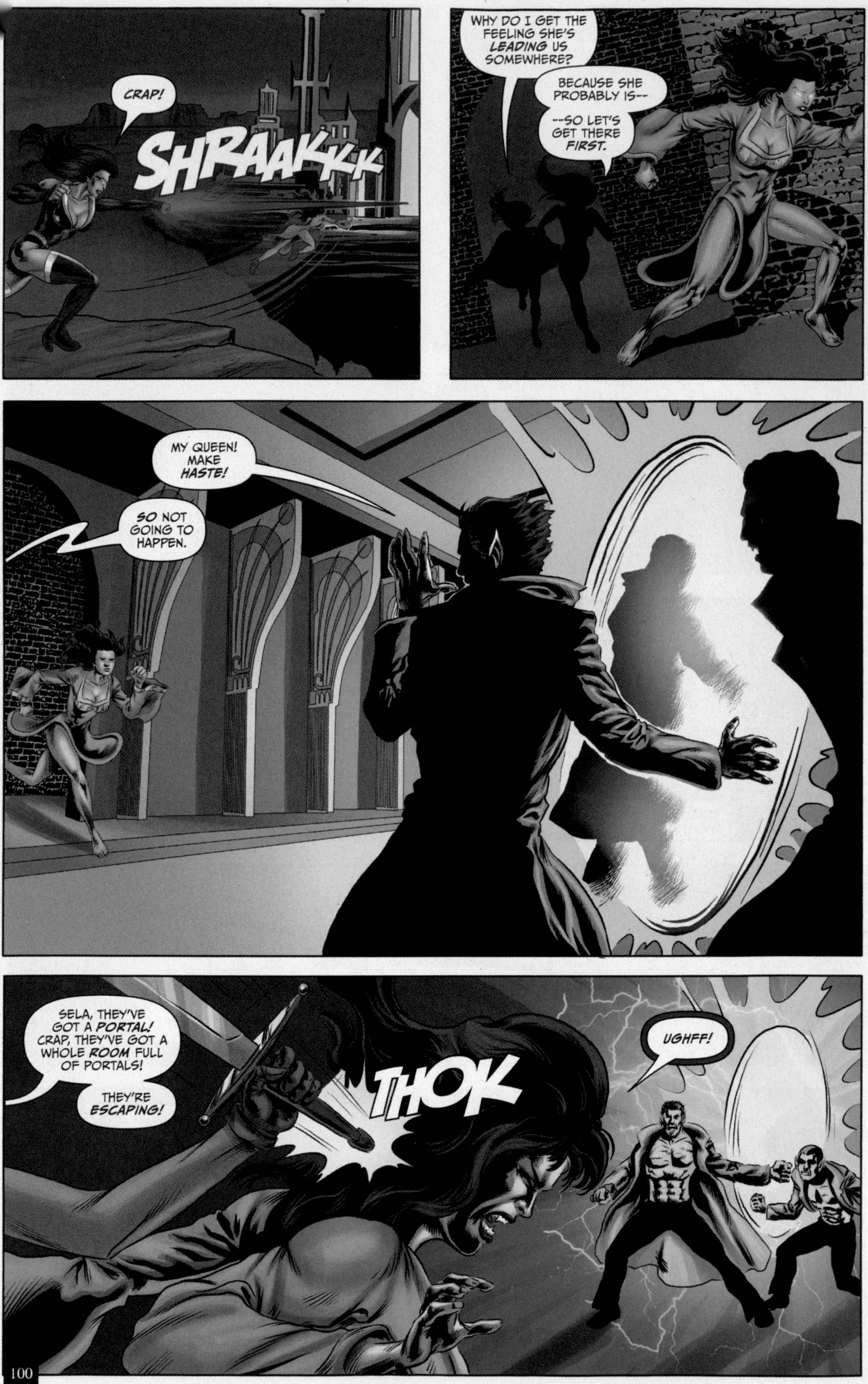
CRAP!
SHRAAKKK
WHY DO I GET THE FEELING SHE'S *LEADING* US SOMEWHERE?
BECAUSE SHE PROBABLY IS--
--SO LET'S GET THERE *FIRST*.
MY QUEEN! MAKE *HASTE!*
SO NOT GOING TO HAPPEN.
SELA, THEY'VE GOT A *PORTAL!* CRAP, THEY'VE GOT A WHOLE *ROOM* FULL OF PORTALS!
THEY'RE *ESCAPING!*
THOK
UGHFF!

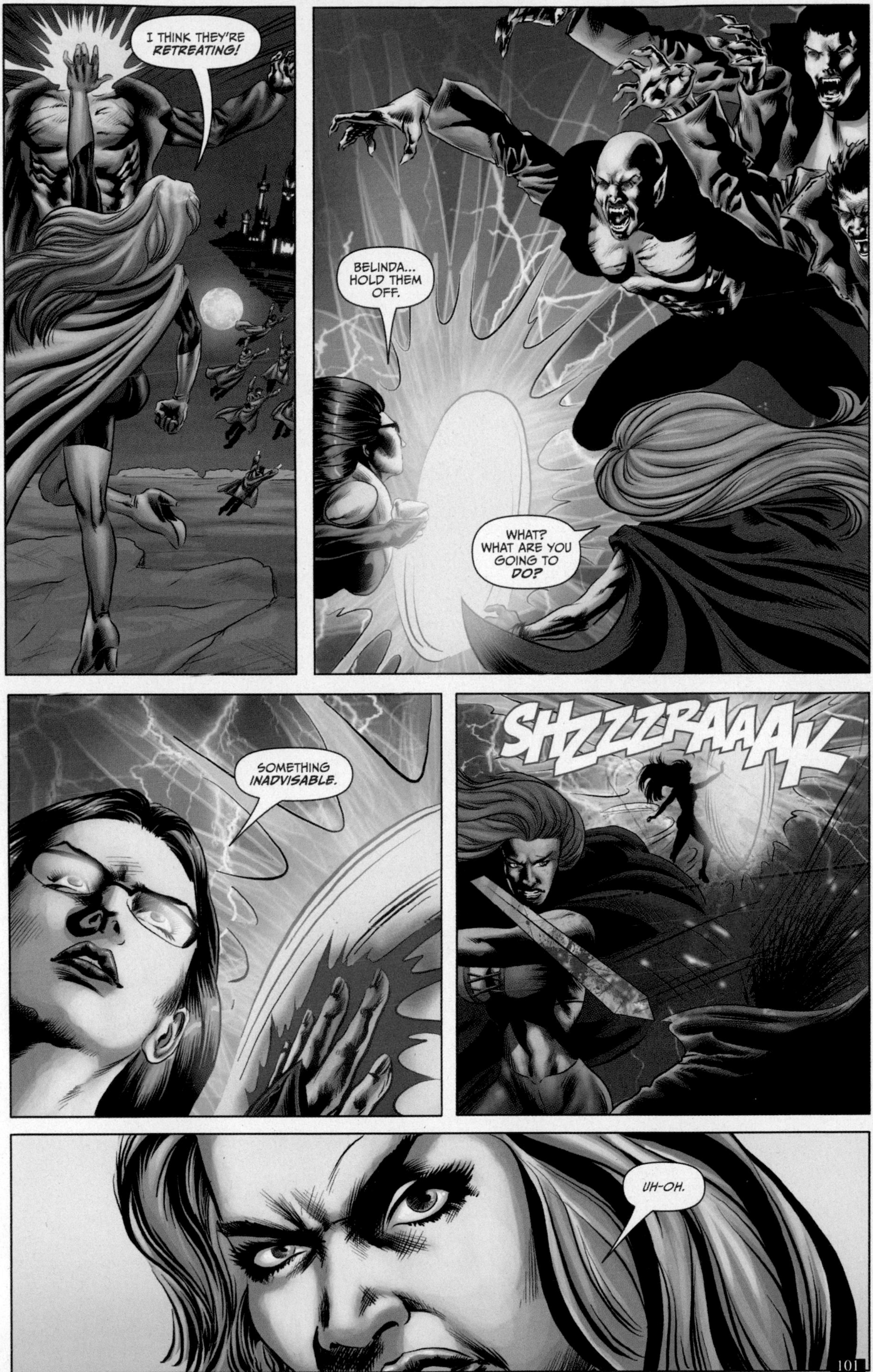
I THINK THEY'RE *RETREATING!*
BELINDA... HOLD THEM OFF.
WHAT? WHAT ARE YOU GOING TO *DO?*
SOMETHING *INADVISABLE.*
SHZZZRAAAK
UH-OH.

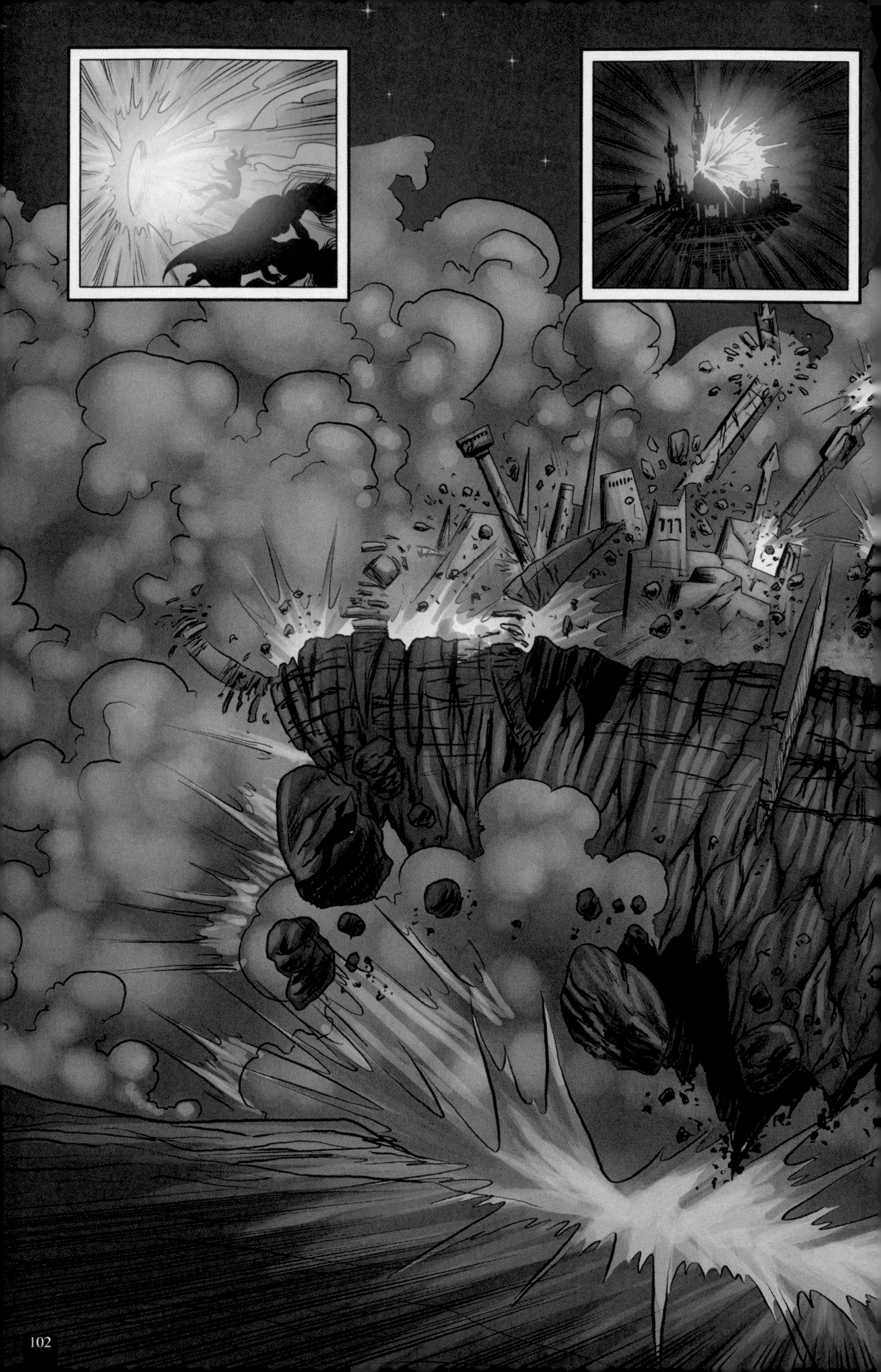

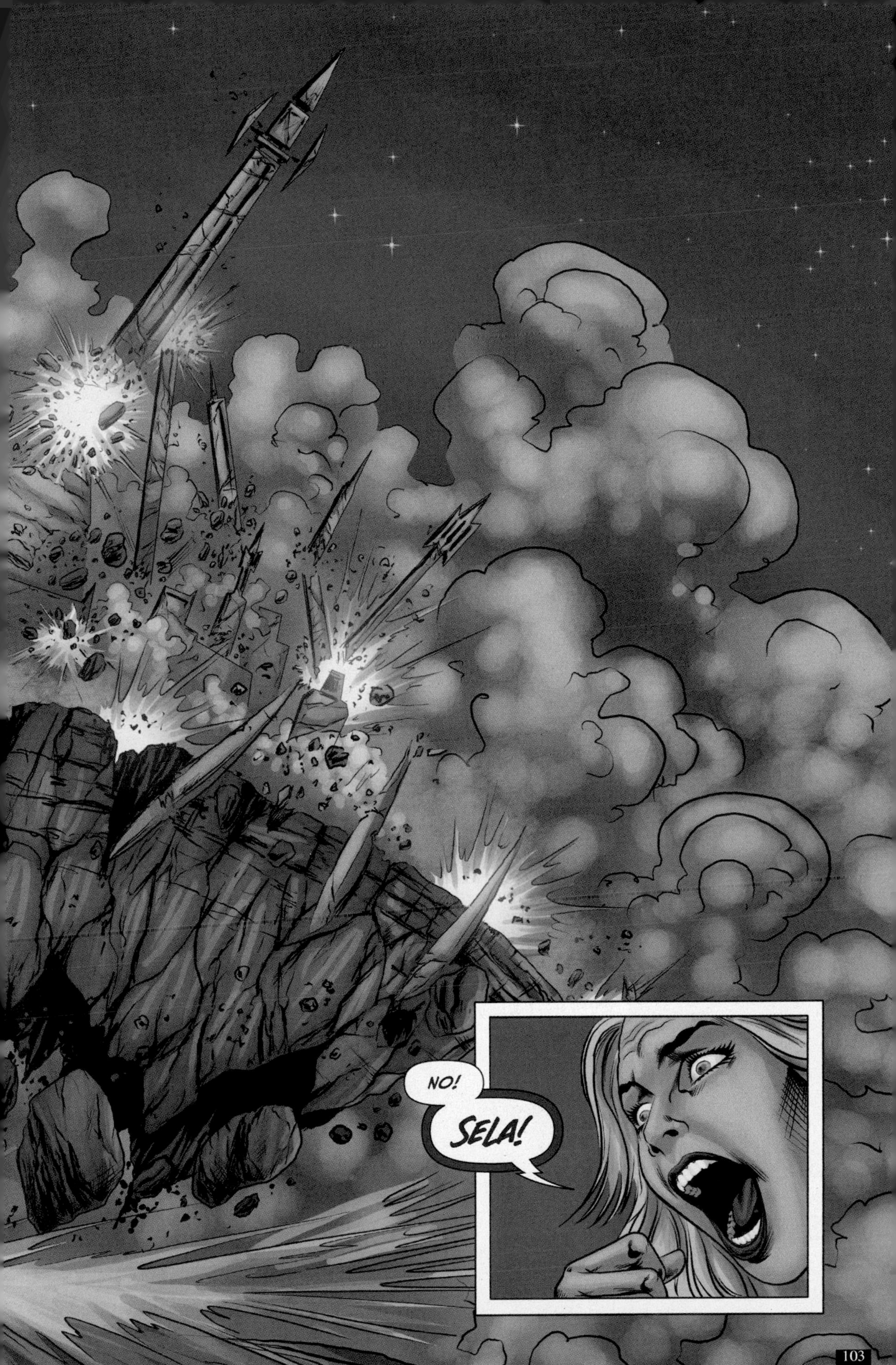
NO!
SELA!

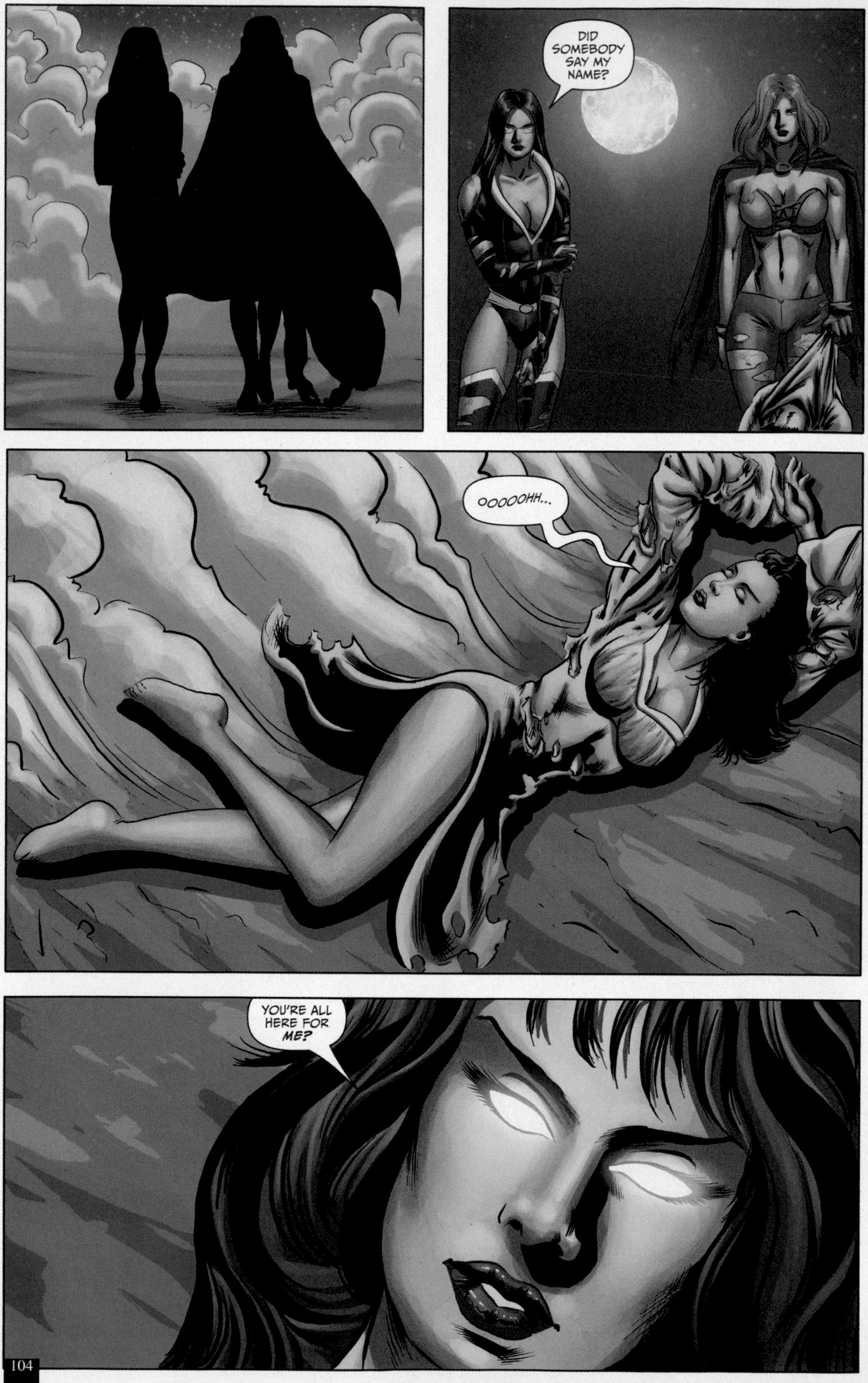
DID SOMEBODY SAY MY NAME?
OOOOOHH...
YOU'RE ALL HERE FOR *ME?*

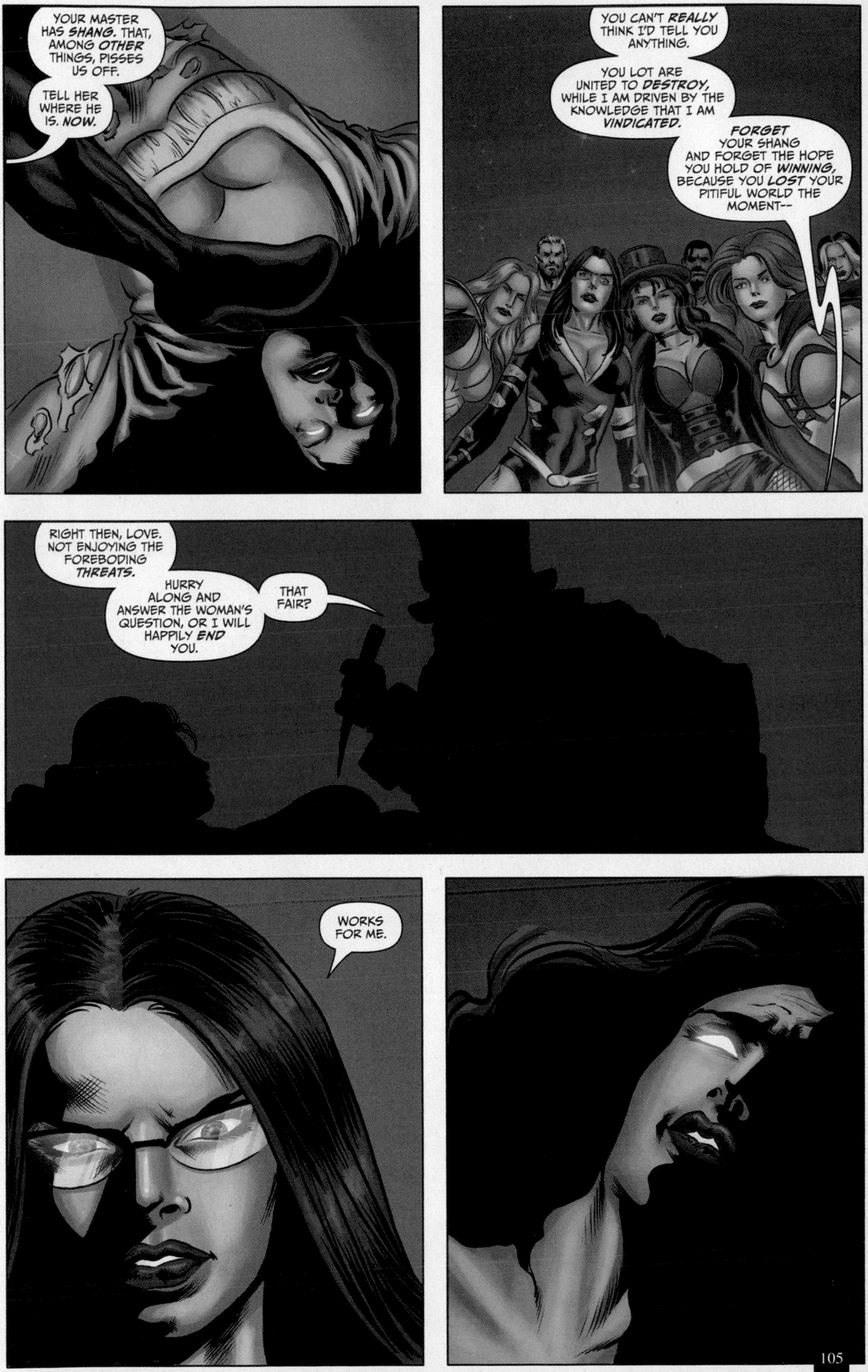
YOUR MASTER HAS SHANG. THAT, AMONG OTHER THINGS, PISSES US OFF.
TELL HER WHERE HE IS. NOW.
YOU CAN'T REALLY THINK I'D TELL YOU ANYTHING.
YOU LOT ARE UNITED TO DESTROY, WHILE I AM DRIVEN BY THE KNOWLEDGE THAT I AM VINDICATED.
FORGET YOUR SHANG AND FORGET THE HOPE YOU HOLD OF WINNING, BECAUSE YOU LOST YOUR PITIFUL WORLD THE MOMENT--
RIGHT THEN, LOVE. NOT ENJOYING THE FOREBODING THREATS.
HURRY ALONG AND ANSWER THE WOMAN'S QUESTION, OR I WILL HAPPILY END YOU.
THAT FAIR?
WORKS FOR ME.

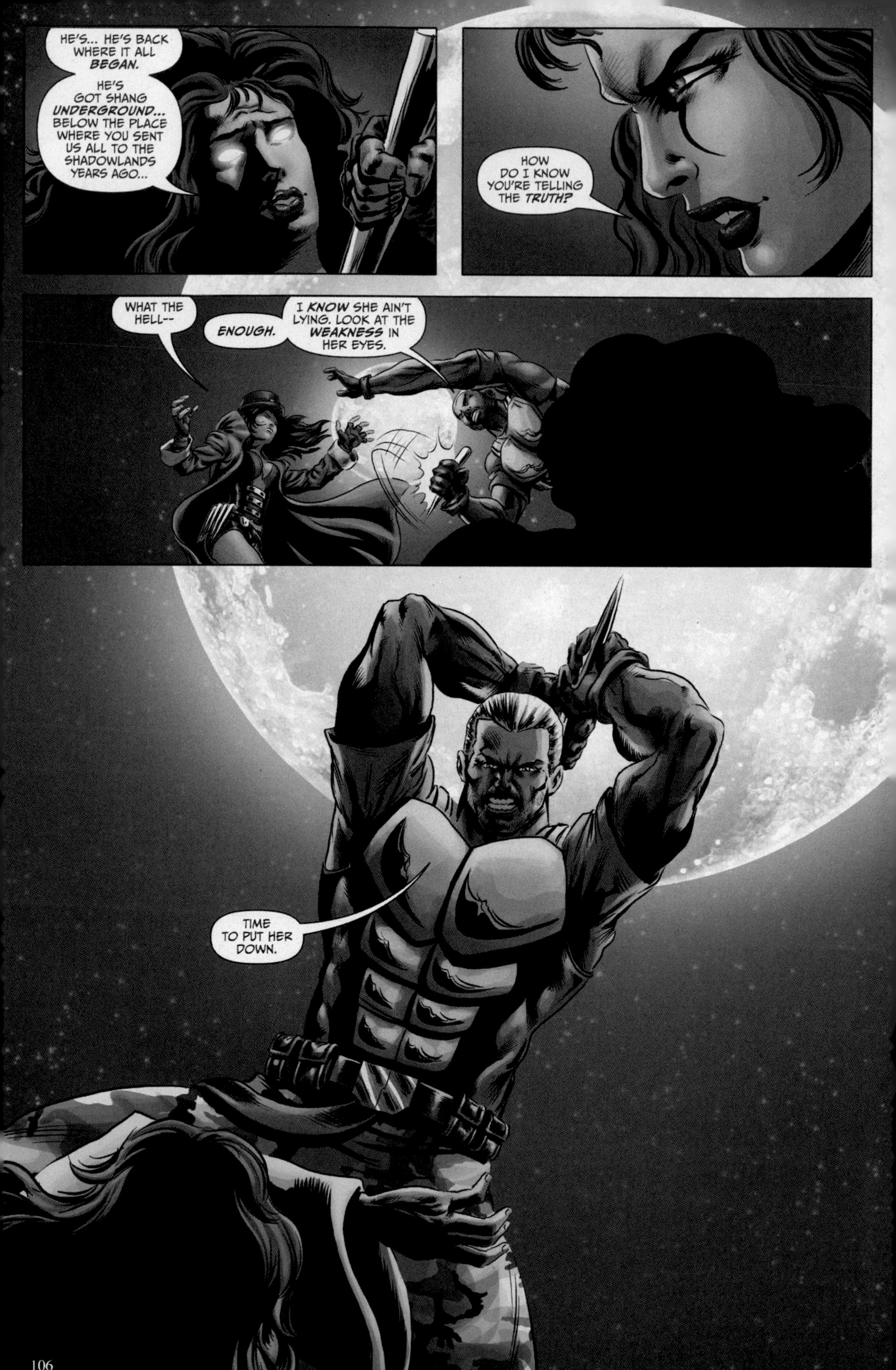
HE'S... HE'S BACK WHERE IT ALL BEGAN.
HE'S GOT SHANG UNDERGROUND... BELOW THE PLACE WHERE YOU SENT US ALL TO THE SHADOWLANDS YEARS AGO...
HOW DO I KNOW YOU'RE TELLING THE TRUTH?
WHAT THE HELL--
ENOUGH.
I KNOW SHE AIN'T LYING. LOOK AT THE WEAKNESS IN HER EYES.
TIME TO PUT HER DOWN.

SPAK

IDIOT!

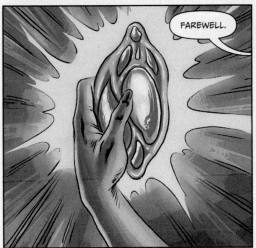

FAREWELL.

NO!

WHAT THE HELL WERE YOU THINKING?

SMAK

HEH... YOU'LL WISH YOU DIDN'T DO THAT, GINGER.

BELINDA! WHAT'S WRONG WITH YOU?

HE LET HER GET AWAY!

WE DO NOT FIGHT EACH OTHER.

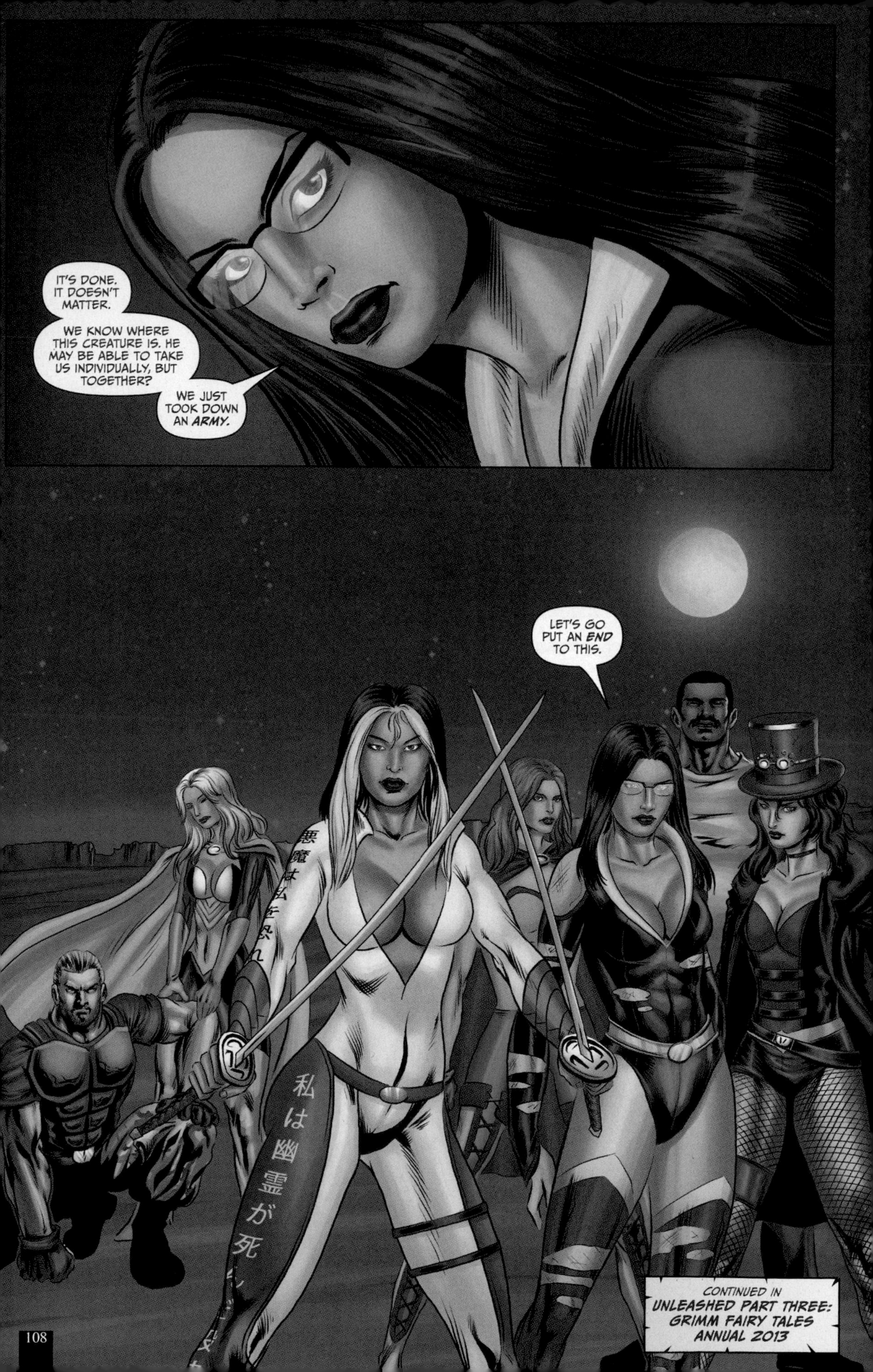
IT'S DONE. IT DOESN'T MATTER.
WE KNOW WHERE THIS CREATURE IS. HE MAY BE ABLE TO TAKE US INDIVIDUALLY, BUT TOGETHER?
WE JUST TOOK DOWN AN ***ARMY.***
LET'S GO PUT AN ***END*** TO THIS.
悪魔は私を恐れ
私は幽霊が死
CONTINUED IN
UNLEASHED PART THREE: GRIMM FAIRY TALES ANNUAL 2013

Grimm Fairy Tales

UNLEASHED

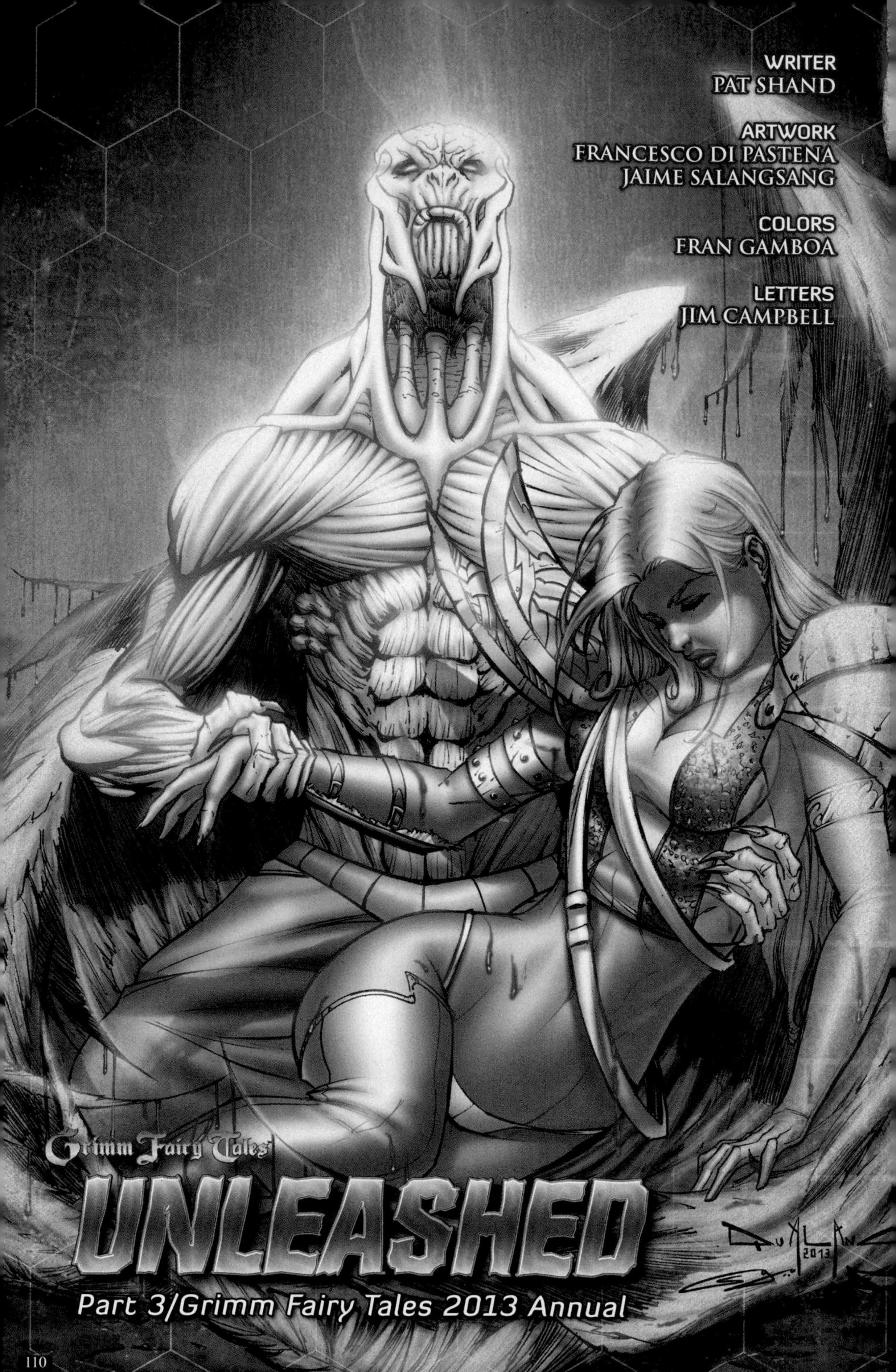
WRITER
PAT SHAND
ARTWORK
FRANCESCO DI PASTENA
JAIME SALANGSANG
COLORS
FRAN GAMBOA
LETTERS
JIM CAMPBELL
Grimm Fairy Tales
UNLEASHED
Part 3/Grimm Fairy Tales 2013 Annual

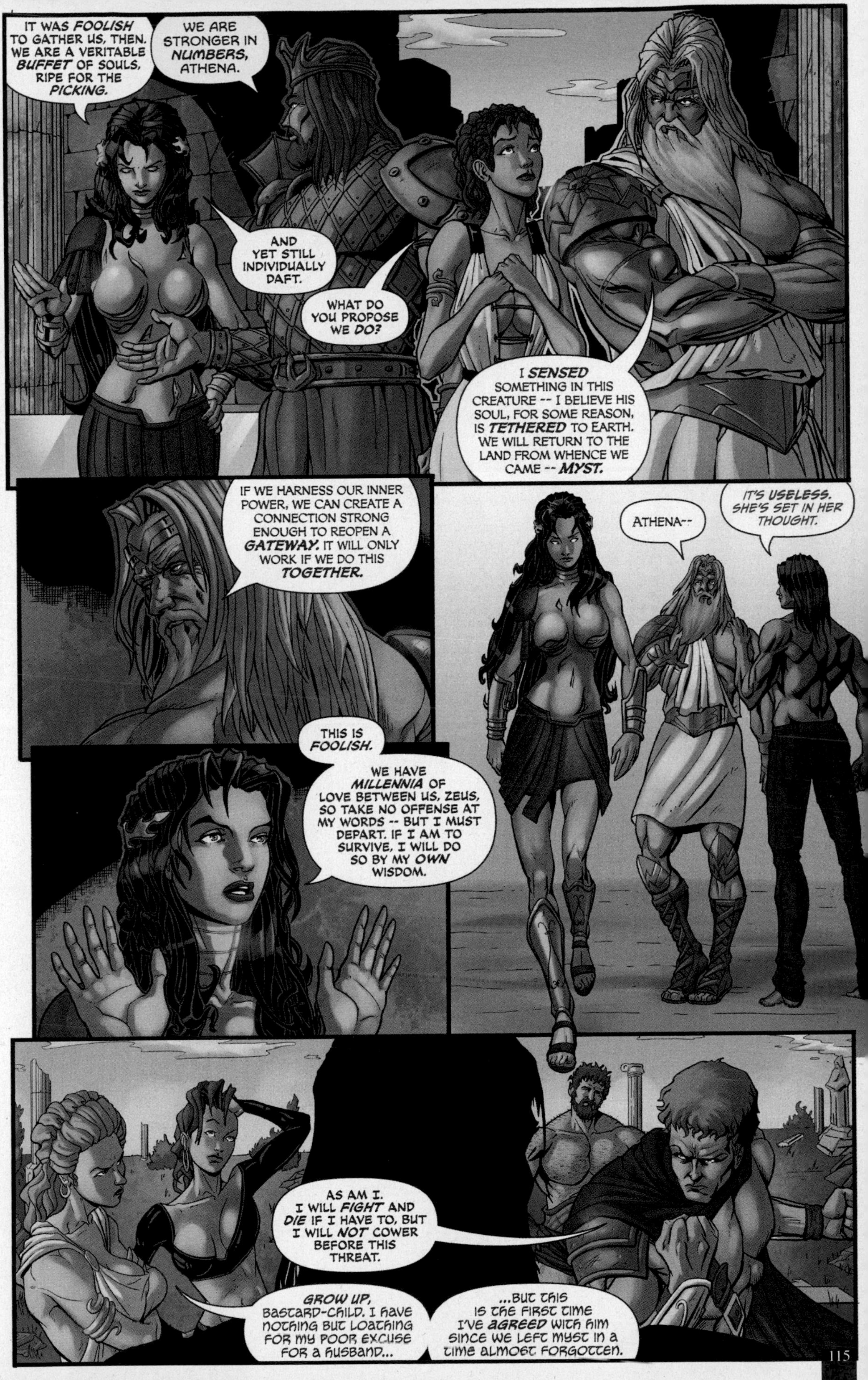

IT WAS *FOOLISH* TO GATHER US, THEN. WE ARE A VERITABLE *BUFFET* OF SOULS, RIPE FOR THE *PICKING*.
WE ARE STRONGER IN *NUMBERS*, ATHENA.
AND YET STILL INDIVIDUALLY DAFT.
WHAT DO YOU PROPOSE WE *DO?*
I *SENSED* SOMETHING IN THIS CREATURE -- I BELIEVE HIS SOUL, FOR SOME REASON, IS *TETHERED* TO EARTH. WE WILL RETURN TO THE LAND FROM WHENCE WE CAME -- *MYST*.
IF WE HARNESS OUR INNER POWER, WE CAN CREATE A CONNECTION STRONG ENOUGH TO REOPEN A *GATEWAY*. IT WILL ONLY WORK IF WE DO THIS *TOGETHER*.
THIS IS *FOOLISH*.
WE HAVE *MILLENNIA* OF LOVE BETWEEN US, ZEUS, SO TAKE NO OFFENSE AT MY WORDS -- BUT I MUST DEPART. IF I AM TO SURVIVE, I WILL DO SO BY MY *OWN* WISDOM.
ATHENA--
IT'S USELESS. SHE'S SET IN HER THOUGHT.
AS AM I. I WILL *FIGHT* AND *DIE* IF I HAVE TO, BUT I WILL *NOT* COWER BEFORE THIS THREAT.
GROW UP, BASTARD-CHILD. I HAVE NOTHING BUT LOATHING FOR MY POOR EXCUSE FOR A HUSBAND...
...BUT THIS IS THE FIRST TIME I'VE *AGREED* WITH HIM SINCE WE LEFT MYST IN A TIME ALMOST FORGOTTEN.

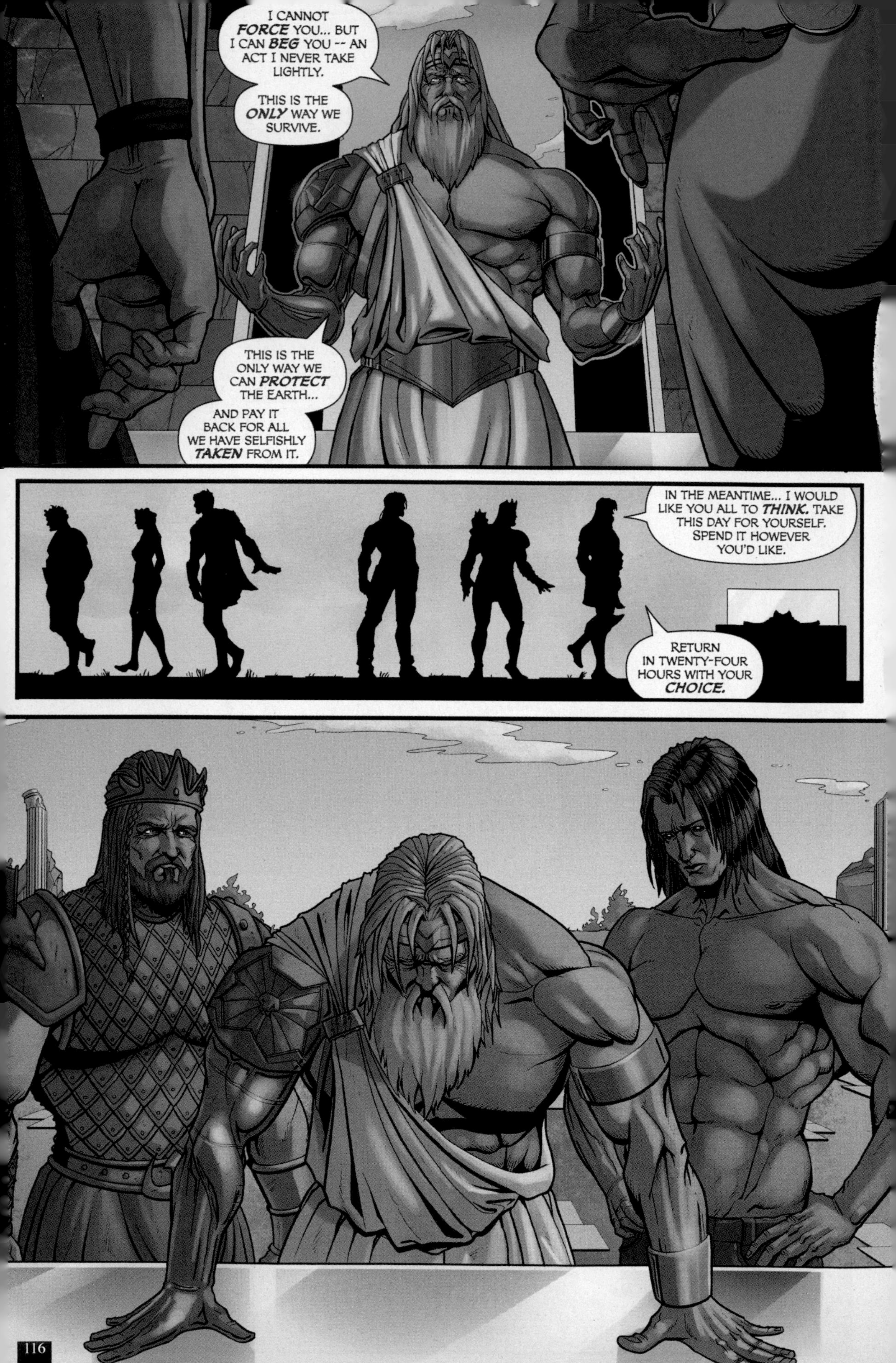
I CANNOT FORCE YOU... BUT I CAN BEG YOU -- AN ACT I NEVER TAKE LIGHTLY.
THIS IS THE ONLY WAY WE SURVIVE.
THIS IS THE ONLY WAY WE CAN PROTECT THE EARTH...
AND PAY IT BACK FOR ALL WE HAVE SELFISHLY TAKEN FROM IT.
IN THE MEANTIME... I WOULD LIKE YOU ALL TO THINK. TAKE THIS DAY FOR YOURSELF. SPEND IT HOWEVER YOU'D LIKE.
RETURN IN TWENTY-FOUR HOURS WITH YOUR CHOICE.

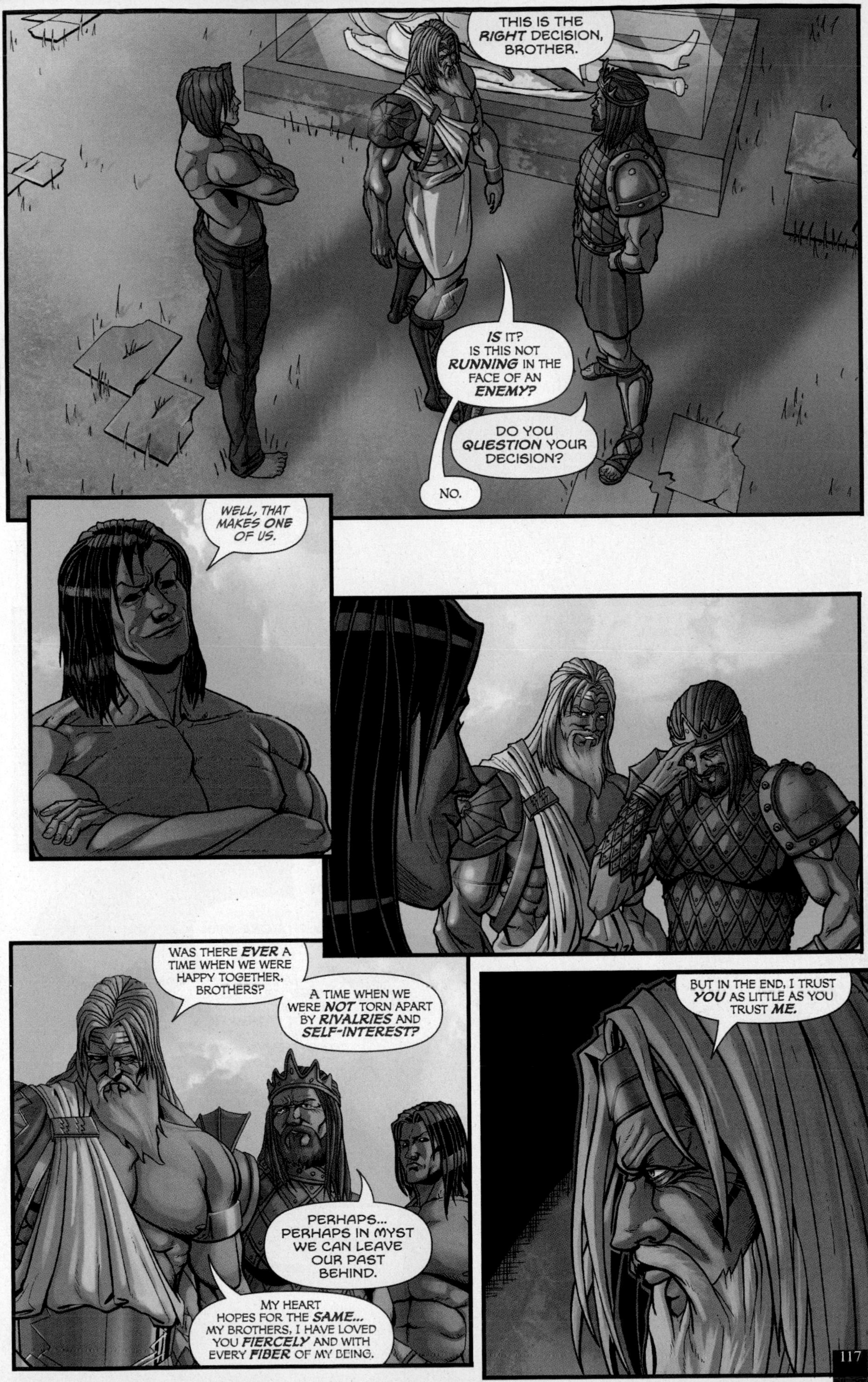
THIS IS THE RIGHT DECISION, BROTHER.
IS IT? IS THIS NOT RUNNING IN THE FACE OF AN ENEMY?
DO YOU QUESTION YOUR DECISION?
NO.
WELL, THAT MAKES ONE OF US.
WAS THERE EVER A TIME WHEN WE WERE HAPPY TOGETHER, BROTHERS?
A TIME WHEN WE WERE NOT TORN APART BY RIVALRIES AND SELF-INTEREST?
PERHAPS... PERHAPS IN MYST WE CAN LEAVE OUR PAST BEHIND.
MY HEART HOPES FOR THE SAME... MY BROTHERS, I HAVE LOVED YOU FIERCELY AND WITH EVERY FIBER OF MY BEING.
BUT IN THE END, I TRUST YOU AS LITTLE AS YOU TRUST ME.

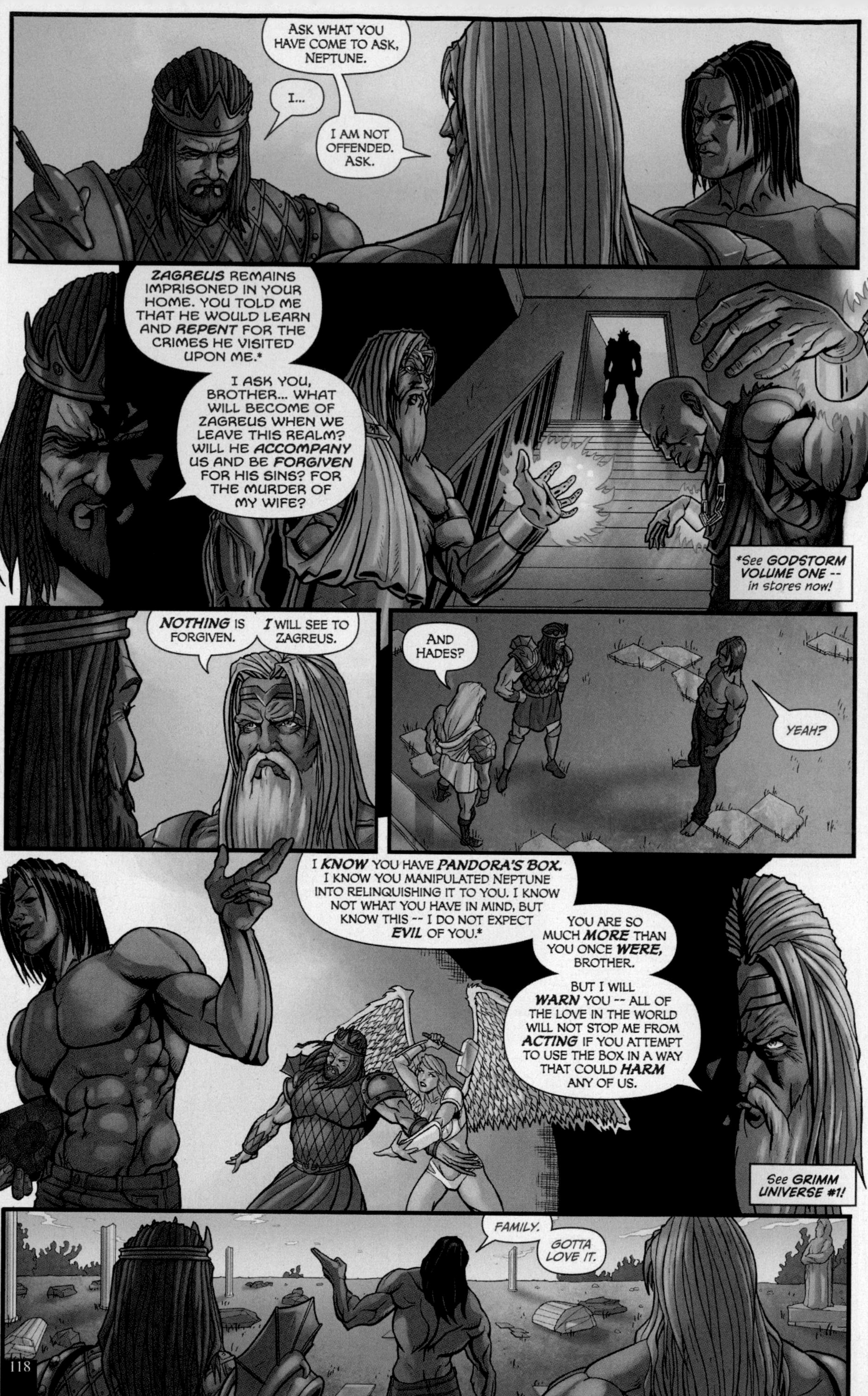
ASK WHAT YOU HAVE COME TO ASK, NEPTUNE.
I...
I AM NOT OFFENDED. ASK.
ZAGREUS REMAINS IMPRISONED IN YOUR HOME. YOU TOLD ME THAT HE WOULD LEARN AND REPENT FOR THE CRIMES HE VISITED UPON ME.*
I ASK YOU, BROTHER... WHAT WILL BECOME OF ZAGREUS WHEN WE LEAVE THIS REALM? WILL HE ACCOMPANY US AND BE FORGIVEN FOR HIS SINS? FOR THE MURDER OF MY WIFE?
*See GODSTORM VOLUME ONE -- in stores now!
NOTHING IS FORGIVEN.
I WILL SEE TO ZAGREUS.
AND HADES?
YEAH?
I KNOW YOU HAVE PANDORA'S BOX. I KNOW YOU MANIPULATED NEPTUNE INTO RELINQUISHING IT TO YOU. I KNOW NOT WHAT YOU HAVE IN MIND, BUT KNOW THIS -- I DO NOT EXPECT EVIL OF YOU.*
YOU ARE SO MUCH MORE THAN YOU ONCE WERE, BROTHER.
BUT I WILL WARN YOU -- ALL OF THE LOVE IN THE WORLD WILL NOT STOP ME FROM ACTING IF YOU ATTEMPT TO USE THE BOX IN A WAY THAT COULD HARM ANY OF US.
See GRIMM UNIVERSE #1!
FAMILY.
GOTTA LOVE IT.

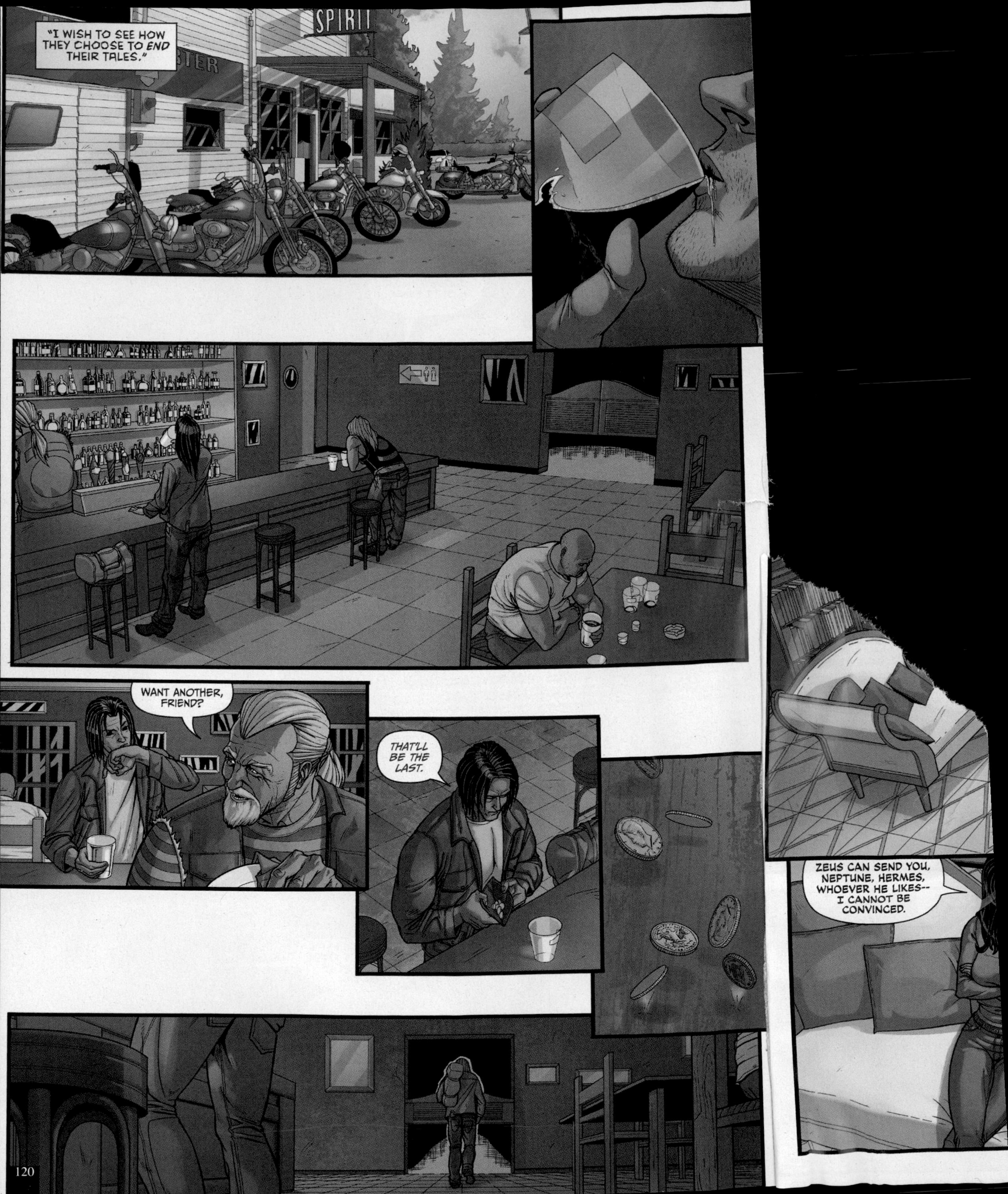
"I WISH TO SEE HOW THEY CHOOSE TO *END* THEIR TALES."
SPIRIT
WANT ANOTHER, FRIEND?
THAT'LL BE THE LAST.
ZEUS CAN SEND YOU, NEPTUNE, HERMES, WHOEVER HE LIKES-- I CANNOT BE CONVINCED.

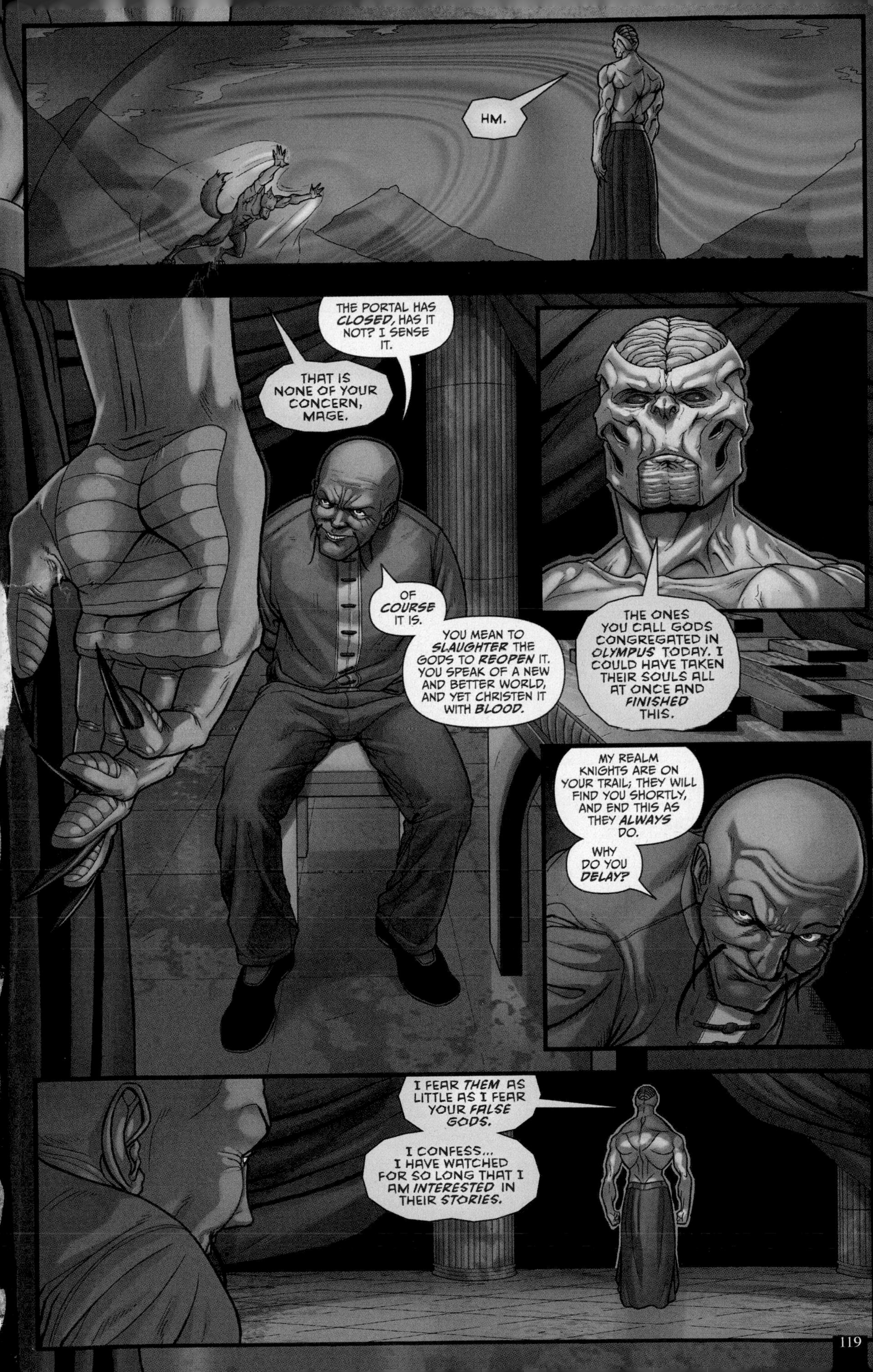
HM.
THE PORTAL HAS CLOSED, HAS IT NOT? I SENSE IT.
THAT IS NONE OF YOUR CONCERN, MAGE.
OF COURSE IT IS.
YOU MEAN TO SLAUGHTER THE GODS TO REOPEN IT. YOU SPEAK OF A NEW AND BETTER WORLD, AND YET CHRISTEN IT WITH BLOOD.
THE ONES YOU CALL GODS CONGREGATED IN OLYMPUS TODAY. I COULD HAVE TAKEN THEIR SOULS ALL AT ONCE AND FINISHED THIS.
MY REALM KNIGHTS ARE ON YOUR TRAIL; THEY WILL FIND YOU SHORTLY, AND END THIS AS THEY ALWAYS DO.
WHY DO YOU DELAY?
I FEAR THEM AS LITTLE AS I FEAR YOUR FALSE GODS.
I CONFESS... I HAVE WATCHED FOR SO LONG THAT I AM INTERESTED IN THEIR STORIES.

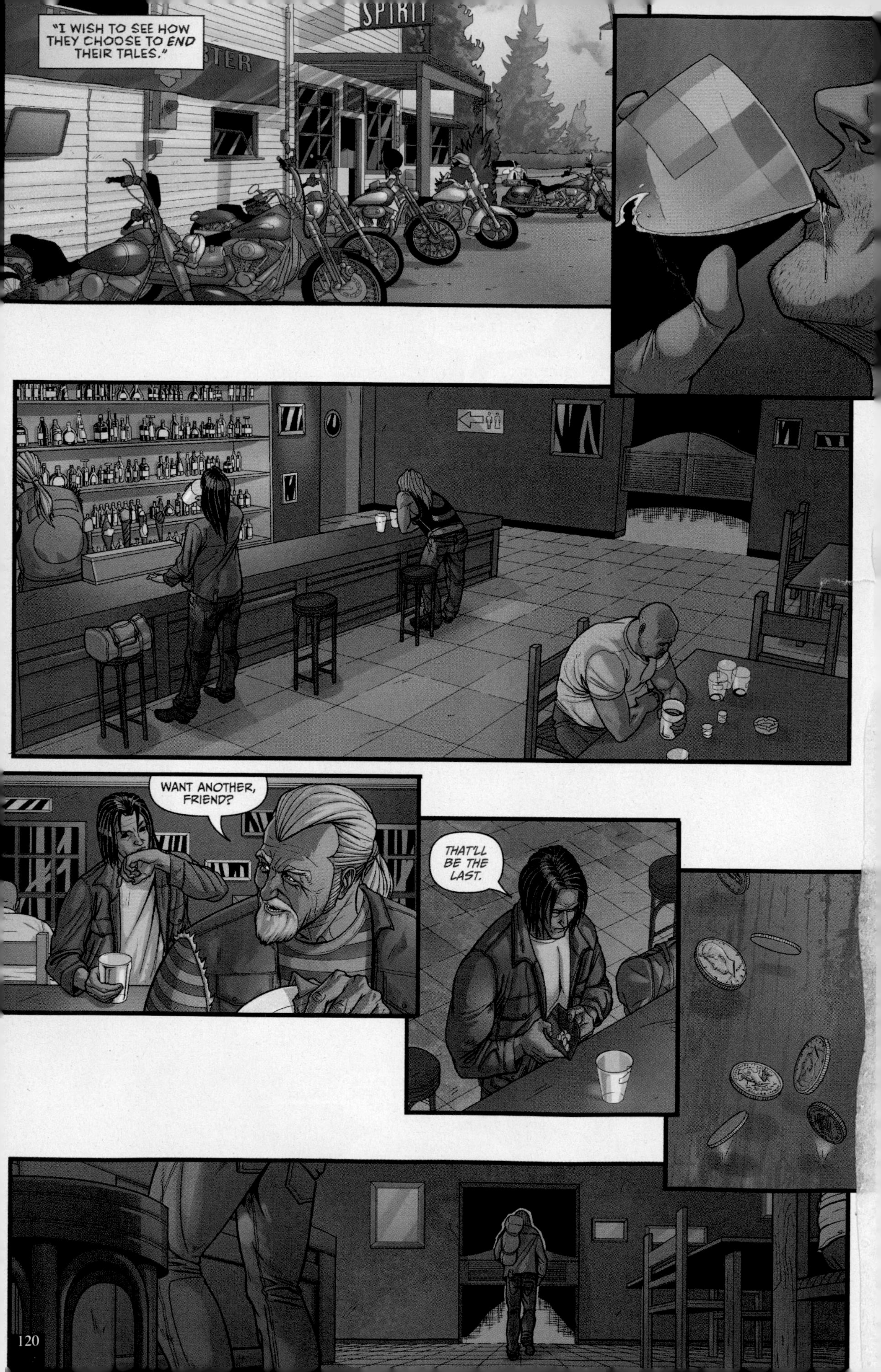

"I WISH TO SEE HOW THEY CHOOSE TO END THEIR TALES."
SPIRIT
WANT ANOTHER, FRIEND?
THAT'LL BE THE LAST.

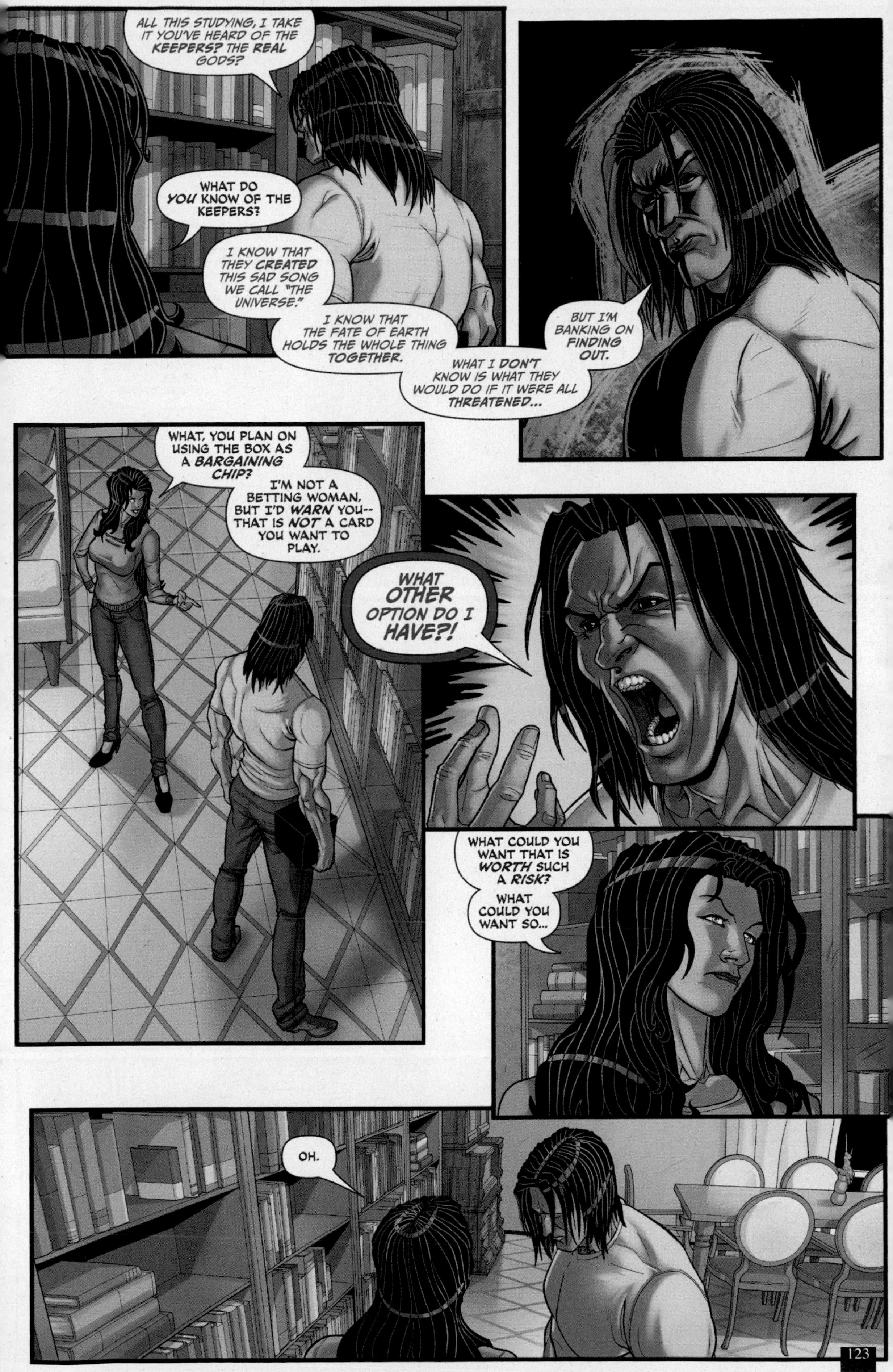

ALL THIS STUDYING, I TAKE IT YOU'VE HEARD OF THE KEEPERS? THE REAL GODS?
WHAT DO YOU KNOW OF THE KEEPERS?
I KNOW THAT THEY CREATED THIS SAD SONG WE CALL "THE UNIVERSE."
I KNOW THAT THE FATE OF EARTH HOLDS THE WHOLE THING TOGETHER.
WHAT I DON'T KNOW IS WHAT THEY WOULD DO IF IT WERE ALL THREATENED...
BUT I'M BANKING ON FINDING OUT.
WHAT, YOU PLAN ON USING THE BOX AS A BARGAINING CHIP?
I'M NOT A BETTING WOMAN, BUT I'D WARN YOU-- THAT IS NOT A CARD YOU WANT TO PLAY.
WHAT OTHER OPTION DO I HAVE?!
WHAT COULD YOU WANT THAT IS WORTH SUCH A RISK?
WHAT COULD YOU WANT SO...
OH.

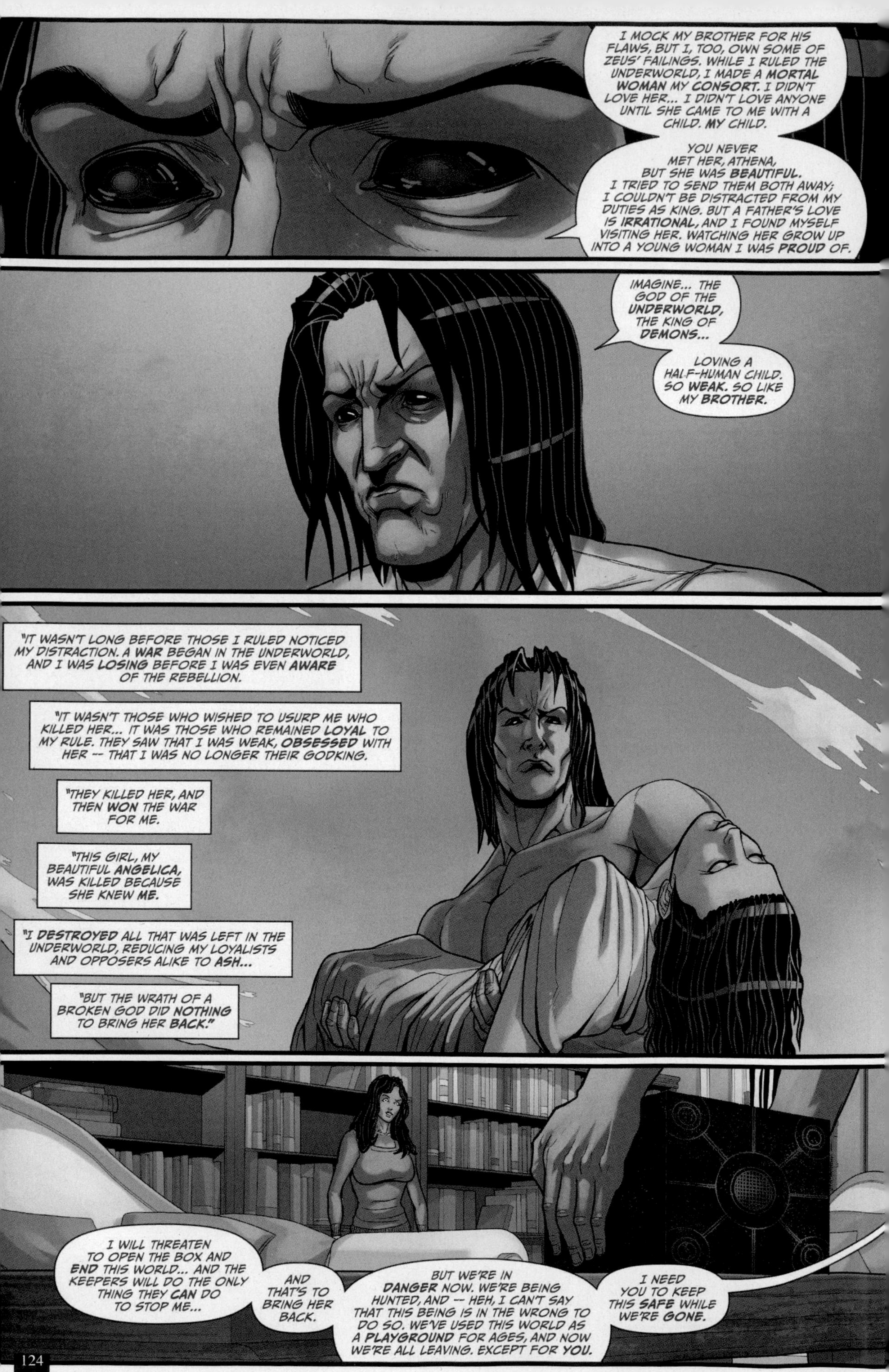
I MOCK MY BROTHER FOR HIS FLAWS, BUT I, TOO, OWN SOME OF ZEUS' FAILINGS. WHILE I RULED THE UNDERWORLD, I MADE A MORTAL WOMAN MY CONSORT. I DIDN'T LOVE HER... I DIDN'T LOVE ANYONE UNTIL SHE CAME TO ME WITH A CHILD. MY CHILD.
YOU NEVER MET HER, ATHENA, BUT SHE WAS BEAUTIFUL. I TRIED TO SEND THEM BOTH AWAY; I COULDN'T BE DISTRACTED FROM MY DUTIES AS KING. BUT A FATHER'S LOVE IS IRRATIONAL, AND I FOUND MYSELF VISITING HER. WATCHING HER GROW UP INTO A YOUNG WOMAN I WAS PROUD OF.
IMAGINE... THE GOD OF THE UNDERWORLD, THE KING OF DEMONS...
LOVING A HALF-HUMAN CHILD. SO WEAK. SO LIKE MY BROTHER.
"IT WASN'T LONG BEFORE THOSE I RULED NOTICED MY DISTRACTION. A WAR BEGAN IN THE UNDERWORLD, AND I WAS LOSING BEFORE I WAS EVEN AWARE OF THE REBELLION.
"IT WASN'T THOSE WHO WISHED TO USURP ME WHO KILLED HER... IT WAS THOSE WHO REMAINED LOYAL TO MY RULE. THEY SAW THAT I WAS WEAK, OBSESSED WITH HER -- THAT I WAS NO LONGER THEIR GODKING.
"THEY KILLED HER, AND THEN WON THE WAR FOR ME.
"THIS GIRL, MY BEAUTIFUL ANGELICA, WAS KILLED BECAUSE SHE KNEW ME.
"I DESTROYED ALL THAT WAS LEFT IN THE UNDERWORLD, REDUCING MY LOYALISTS AND OPPOSERS ALIKE TO ASH...
"BUT THE WRATH OF A BROKEN GOD DID NOTHING TO BRING HER BACK."
I WILL THREATEN TO OPEN THE BOX AND END THIS WORLD... AND THE KEEPERS WILL DO THE ONLY THING THEY CAN DO TO STOP ME...
AND THAT'S TO BRING HER BACK.
BUT WE'RE IN DANGER NOW. WE'RE BEING HUNTED, AND -- HEH, I CAN'T SAY THAT THIS BEING IS IN THE WRONG TO DO SO. WE'VE USED THIS WORLD AS A PLAYGROUND FOR AGES, AND NOW WE'RE ALL LEAVING. EXCEPT FOR YOU.
I NEED YOU TO KEEP THIS SAFE WHILE WE'RE GONE.

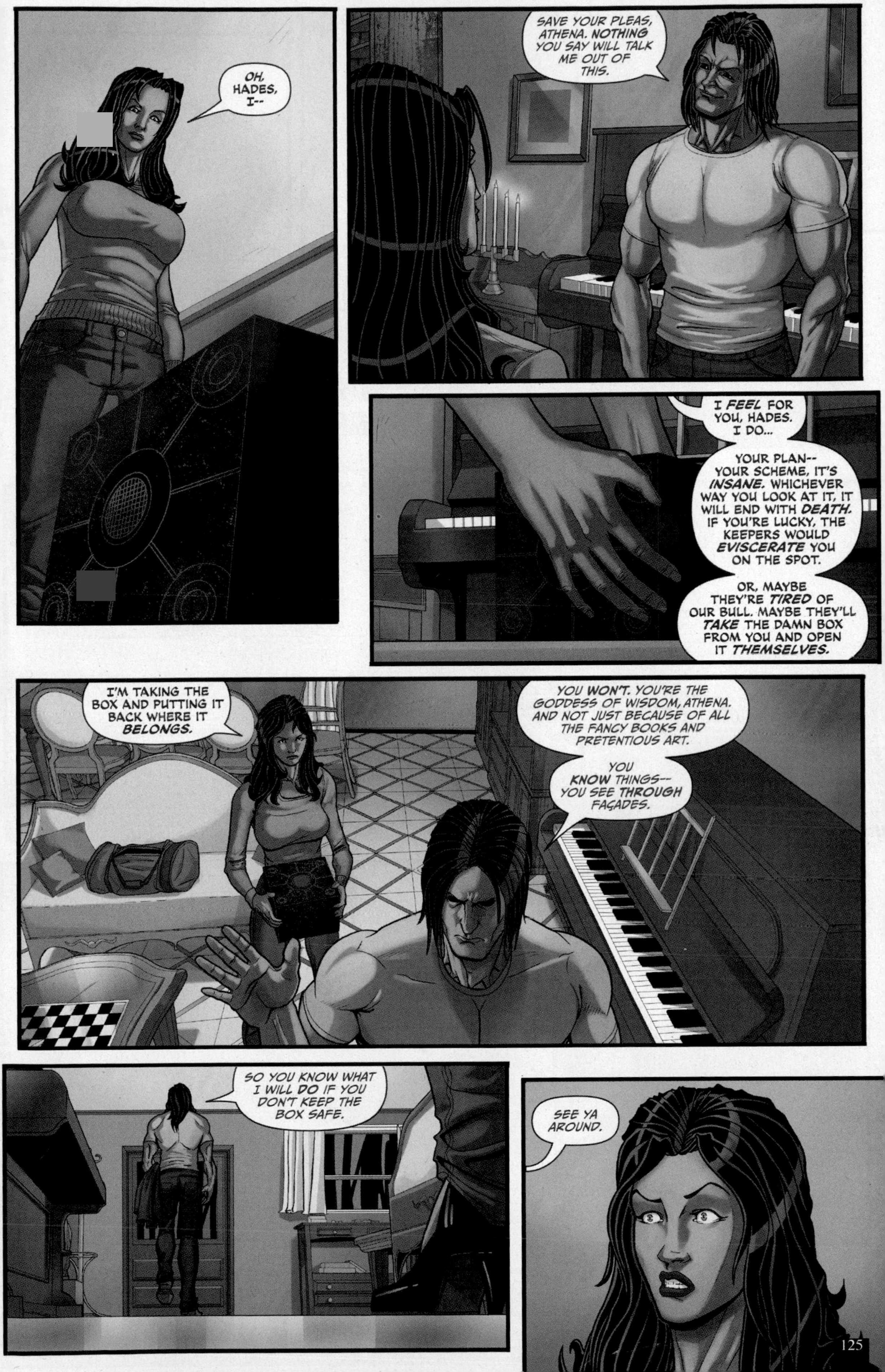
OH, HADES, I--
SAVE YOUR PLEAS, ATHENA. NOTHING YOU SAY WILL TALK ME OUT OF THIS.
I FEEL FOR YOU, HADES. I DO...
YOUR PLAN-- YOUR SCHEME, IT'S INSANE. WHICHEVER WAY YOU LOOK AT IT, IT WILL END WITH DEATH. IF YOU'RE LUCKY, THE KEEPERS WOULD EVISCERATE YOU ON THE SPOT.
OR, MAYBE THEY'RE TIRED OF OUR BULL. MAYBE THEY'LL TAKE THE DAMN BOX FROM YOU AND OPEN IT THEMSELVES.
I'M TAKING THE BOX AND PUTTING IT BACK WHERE IT BELONGS.
YOU WON'T. YOU'RE THE GODDESS OF WISDOM, ATHENA. AND NOT JUST BECAUSE OF ALL THE FANCY BOOKS AND PRETENTIOUS ART.
YOU KNOW THINGS-- YOU SEE THROUGH FAÇADES.
SO YOU KNOW WHAT I WILL DO IF YOU DON'T KEEP THE BOX SAFE.
SEE YA AROUND.

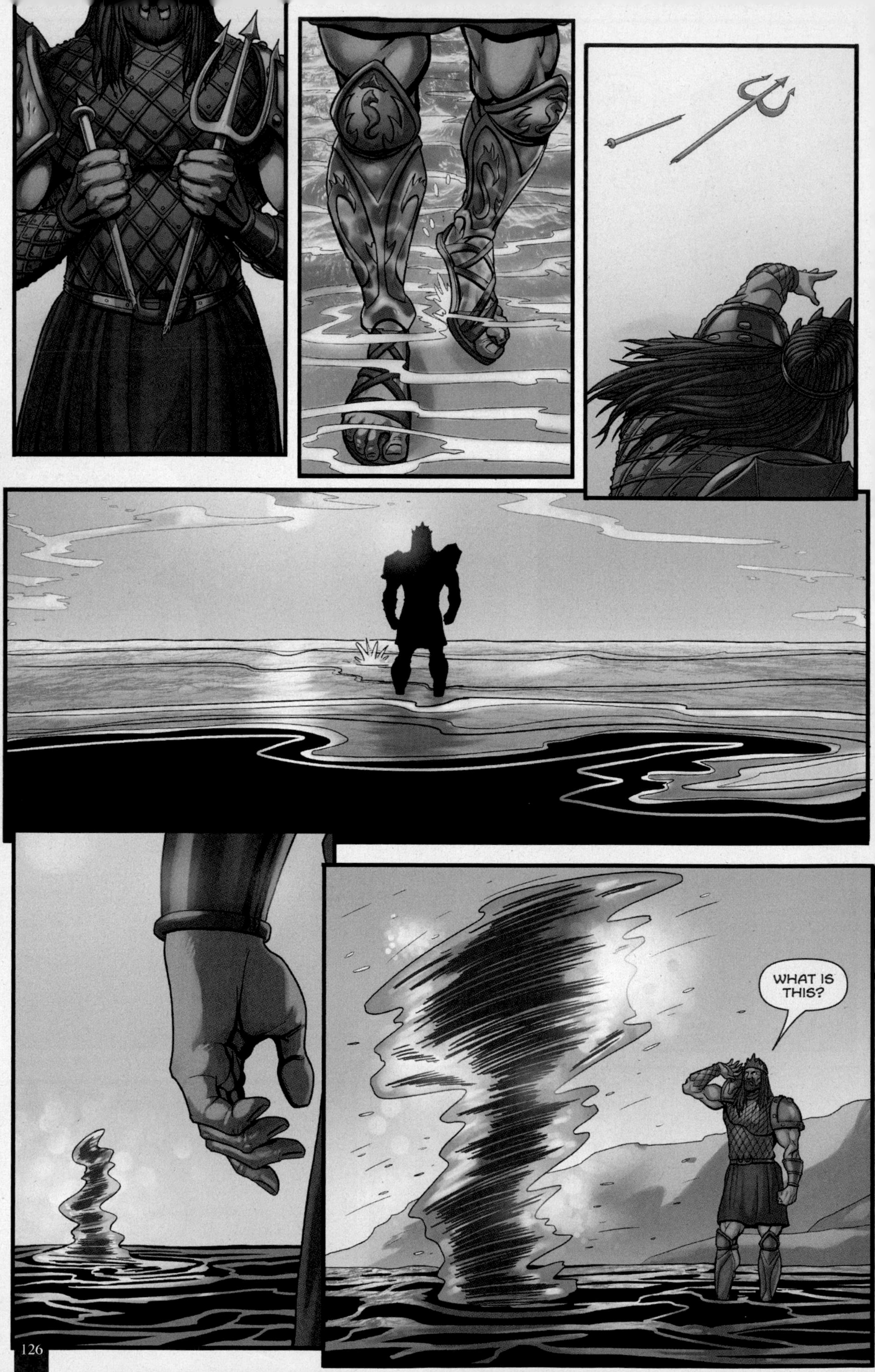
WHAT IS THIS?

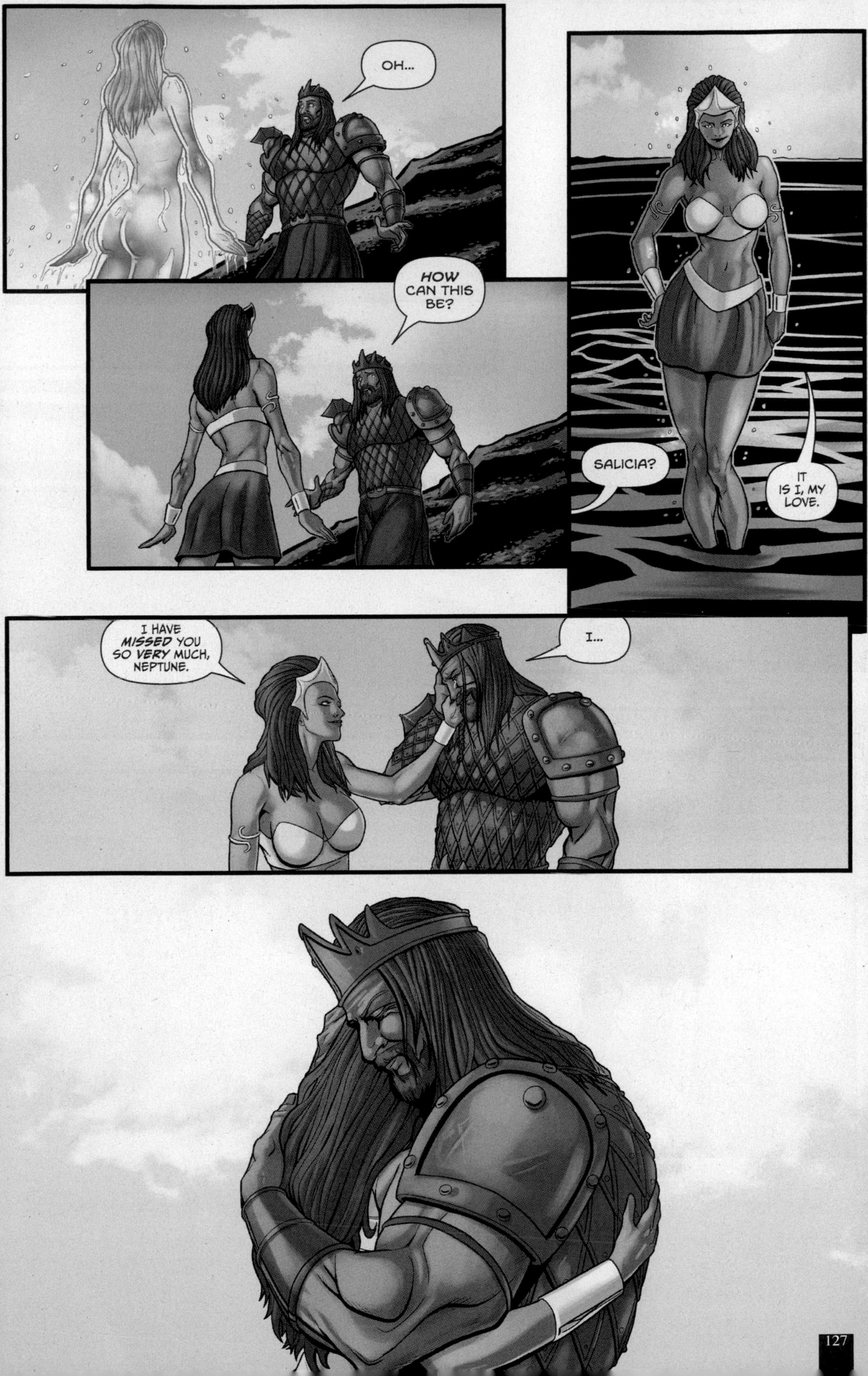
OH...
HOW CAN THIS BE?
SALICIA?
IT IS I, MY LOVE.
I HAVE MISSED YOU SO VERY MUCH, NEPTUNE.
I...

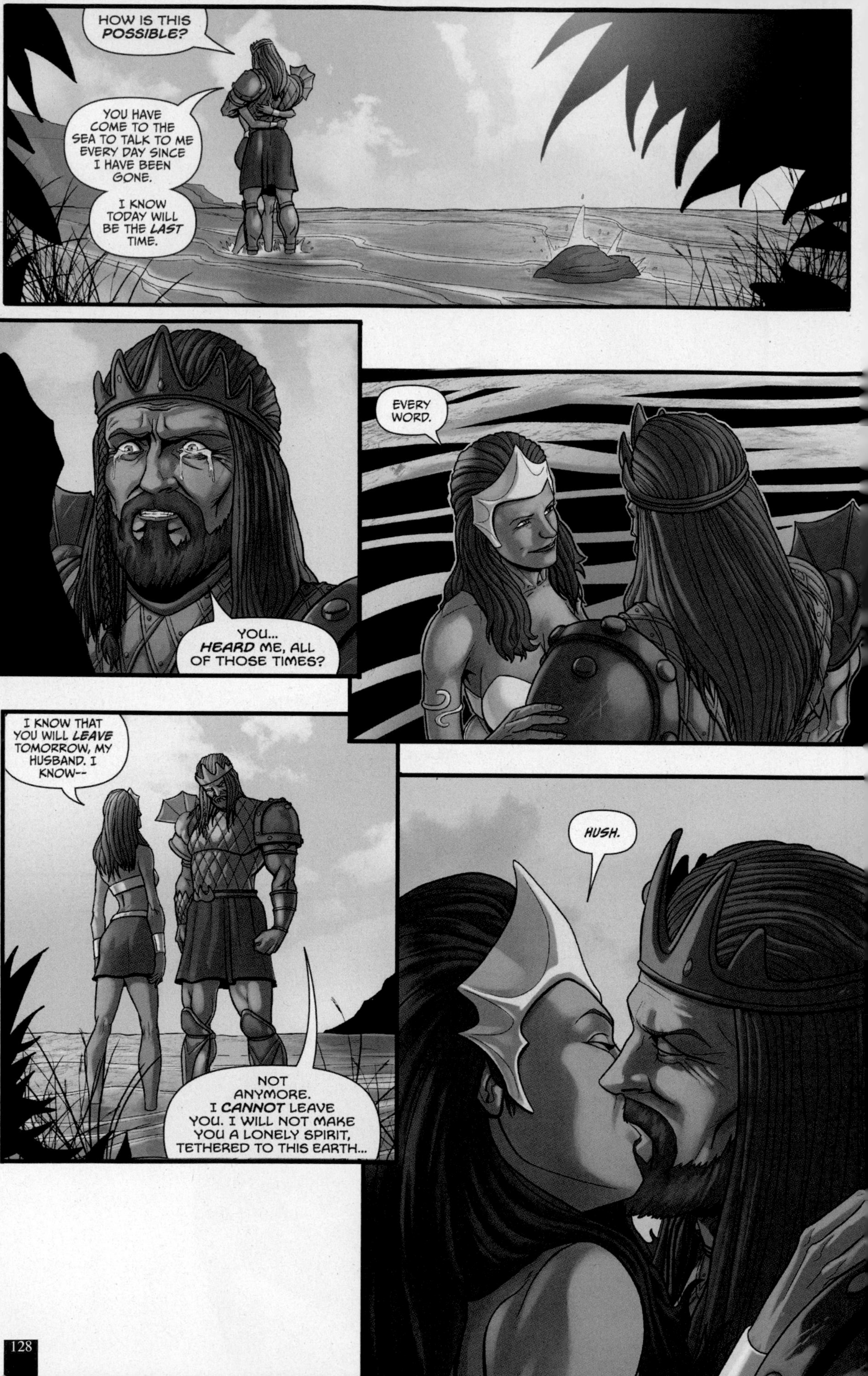
HOW IS THIS POSSIBLE?
YOU HAVE COME TO THE SEA TO TALK TO ME EVERY DAY SINCE I HAVE BEEN GONE.
I KNOW TODAY WILL BE THE LAST TIME.
YOU... HEARD ME, ALL OF THOSE TIMES?
EVERY WORD.
I KNOW THAT YOU WILL LEAVE TOMORROW, MY HUSBAND. I KNOW--
NOT ANYMORE. I CANNOT LEAVE YOU. I WILL NOT MAKE YOU A LONELY SPIRIT, TETHERED TO THIS EARTH...
HUSH.

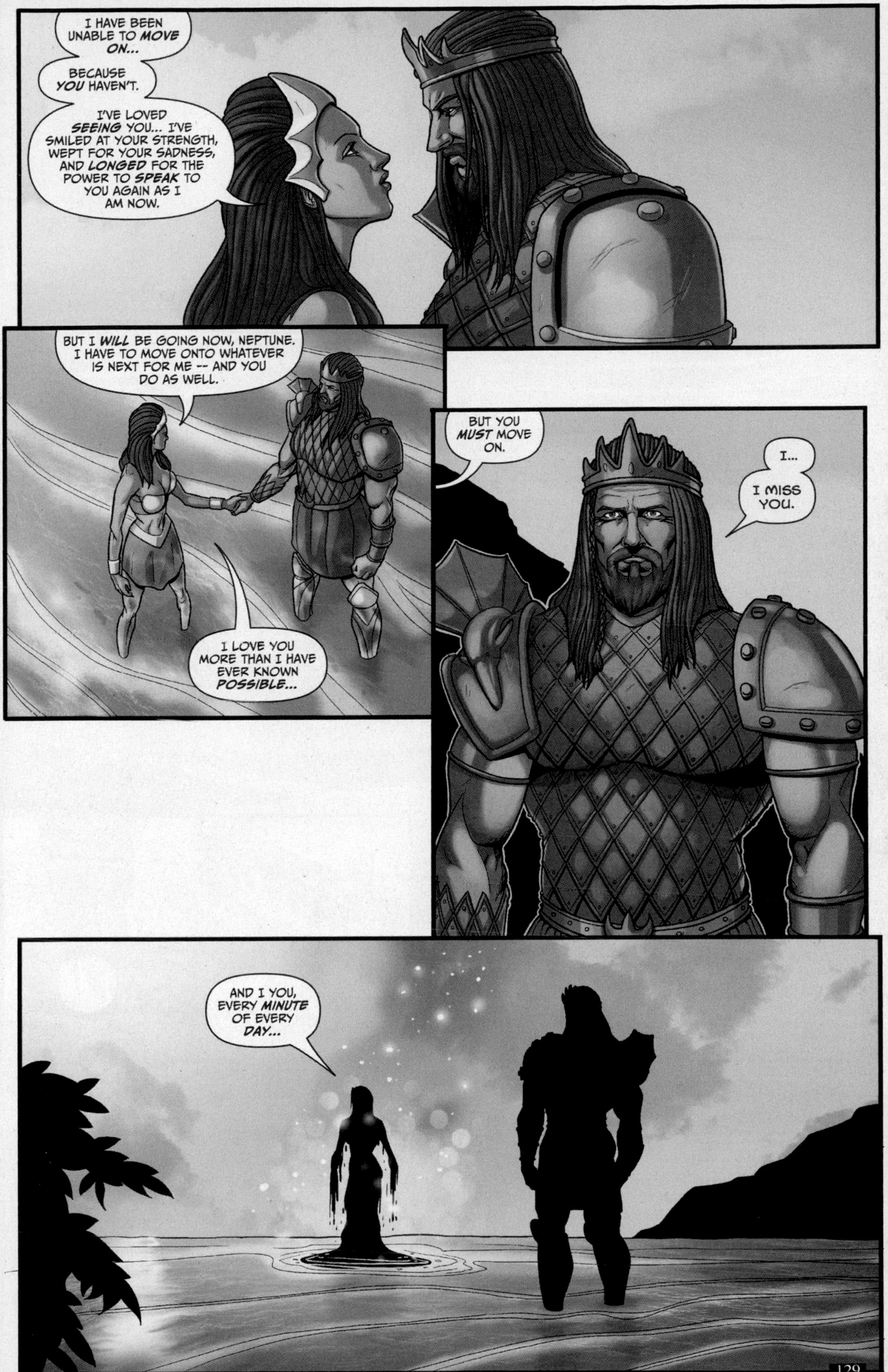
I HAVE BEEN UNABLE TO MOVE ON...
BECAUSE YOU HAVEN'T.
I'VE LOVED SEEING YOU... I'VE SMILED AT YOUR STRENGTH, WEPT FOR YOUR SADNESS, AND LONGED FOR THE POWER TO SPEAK TO YOU AGAIN AS I AM NOW.
BUT I WILL BE GOING NOW, NEPTUNE. I HAVE TO MOVE ONTO WHATEVER IS NEXT FOR ME -- AND YOU DO AS WELL.
I LOVE YOU MORE THAN I HAVE EVER KNOWN POSSIBLE...
BUT YOU MUST MOVE ON.
I...
I MISS YOU.
AND I YOU, EVERY MINUTE OF EVERY DAY...

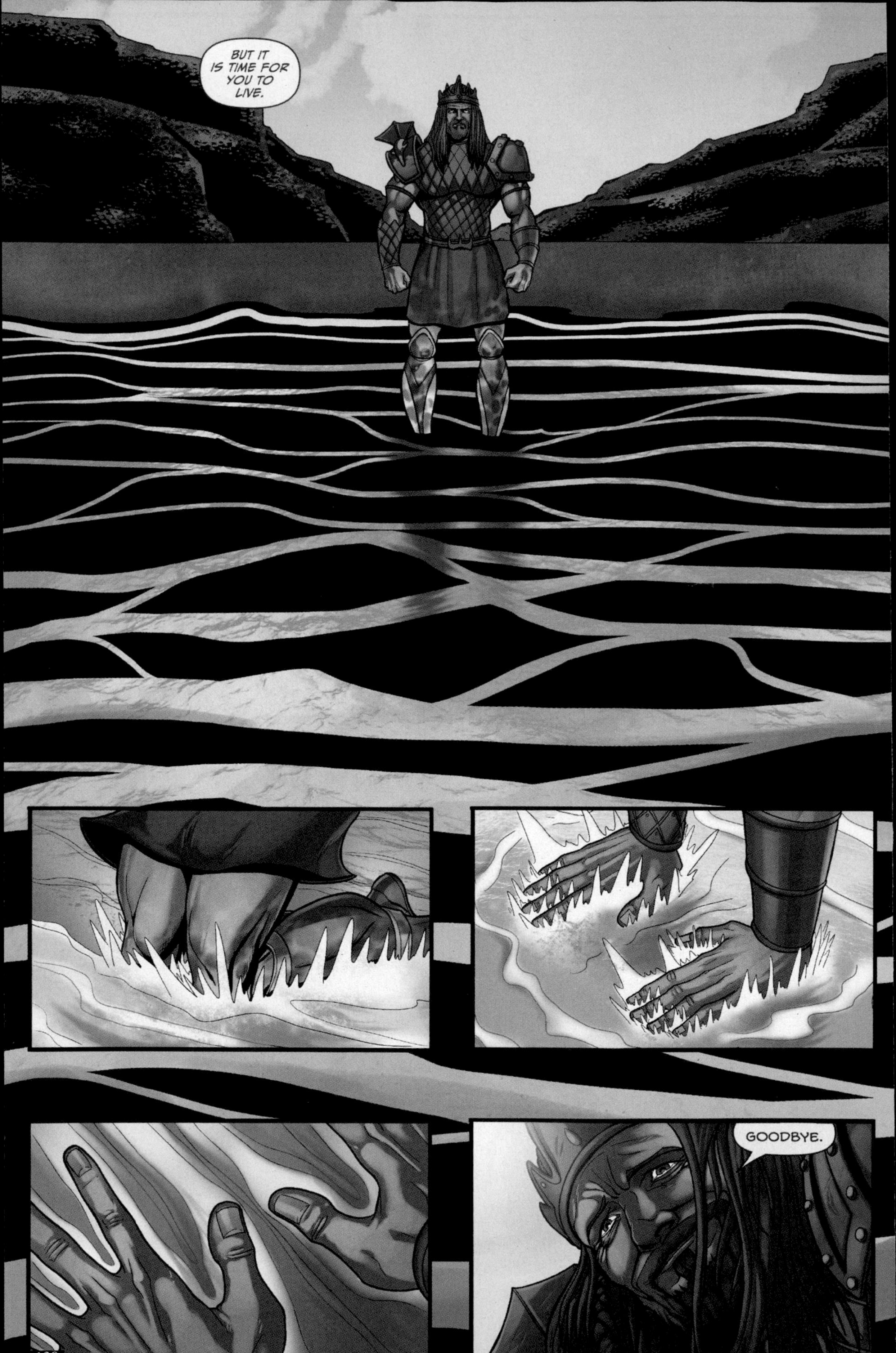
BUT IT IS TIME FOR YOU TO LIVE.
GOODBYE.

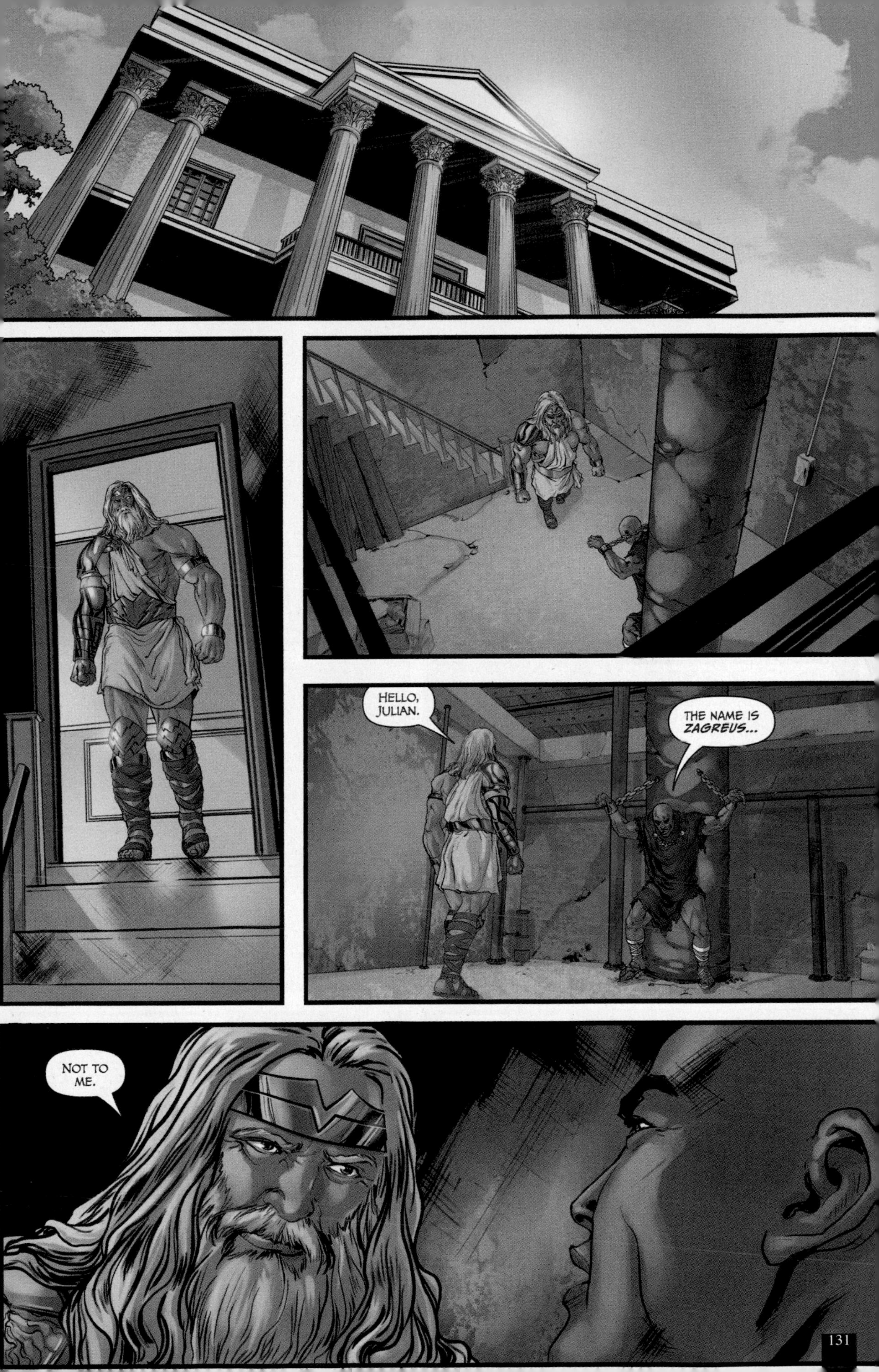
HELLO, JULIAN.
THE NAME IS ZAGREUS...
NOT TO ME.

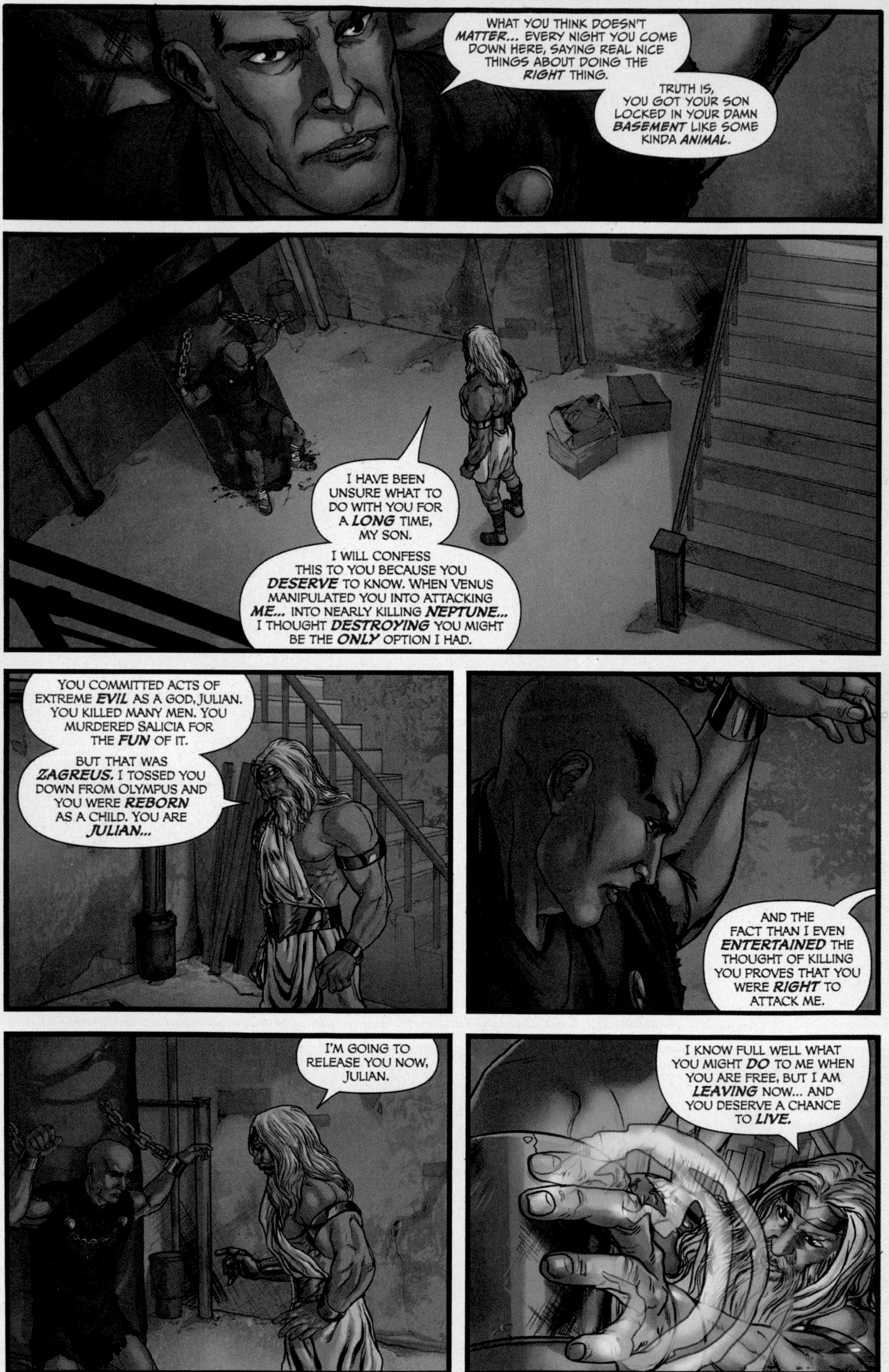
WHAT YOU THINK DOESN'T MATTER... EVERY NIGHT YOU COME DOWN HERE, SAYING REAL NICE THINGS ABOUT DOING THE RIGHT THING.
TRUTH IS, YOU GOT YOUR SON LOCKED IN YOUR DAMN BASEMENT LIKE SOME KINDA ANIMAL.
I HAVE BEEN UNSURE WHAT TO DO WITH YOU FOR A LONG TIME, MY SON.
I WILL CONFESS THIS TO YOU BECAUSE YOU DESERVE TO KNOW. WHEN VENUS MANIPULATED YOU INTO ATTACKING ME... INTO NEARLY KILLING NEPTUNE... I THOUGHT DESTROYING YOU MIGHT BE THE ONLY OPTION I HAD.
YOU COMMITTED ACTS OF EXTREME EVIL AS A GOD, JULIAN. YOU KILLED MANY MEN. YOU MURDERED SALICIA FOR THE FUN OF IT.
BUT THAT WAS ZAGREUS. I TOSSED YOU DOWN FROM OLYMPUS AND YOU WERE REBORN AS A CHILD. YOU ARE JULIAN...
AND THE FACT THAN I EVEN ENTERTAINED THE THOUGHT OF KILLING YOU PROVES THAT YOU WERE RIGHT TO ATTACK ME.
I'M GOING TO RELEASE YOU NOW, JULIAN.
I KNOW FULL WELL WHAT YOU MIGHT DO TO ME WHEN YOU ARE FREE, BUT I AM LEAVING NOW... AND YOU DESERVE A CHANCE TO LIVE.

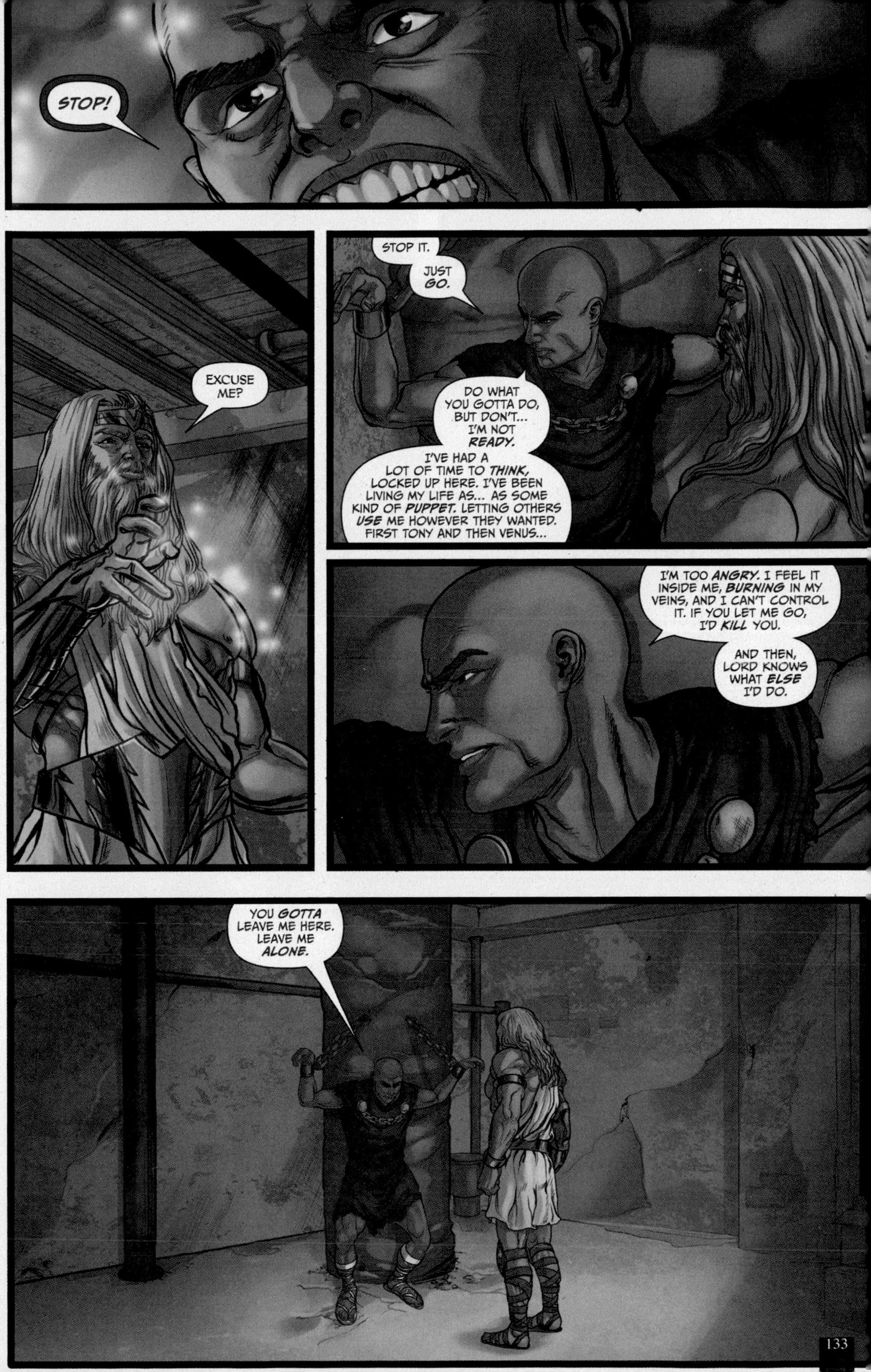
STOP!
EXCUSE ME?
STOP IT.
JUST GO.
DO WHAT YOU GOTTA DO, BUT DON'T... I'M NOT READY.
I'VE HAD A LOT OF TIME TO THINK, LOCKED UP HERE. I'VE BEEN LIVING MY LIFE AS... AS SOME KIND OF PUPPET. LETTING OTHERS USE ME HOWEVER THEY WANTED. FIRST TONY AND THEN VENUS...
I'M TOO ANGRY. I FEEL IT INSIDE ME, BURNING IN MY VEINS, AND I CAN'T CONTROL IT. IF YOU LET ME GO, I'D KILL YOU.
AND THEN, LORD KNOWS WHAT ELSE I'D DO.
YOU GOTTA LEAVE ME HERE. LEAVE ME ALONE.

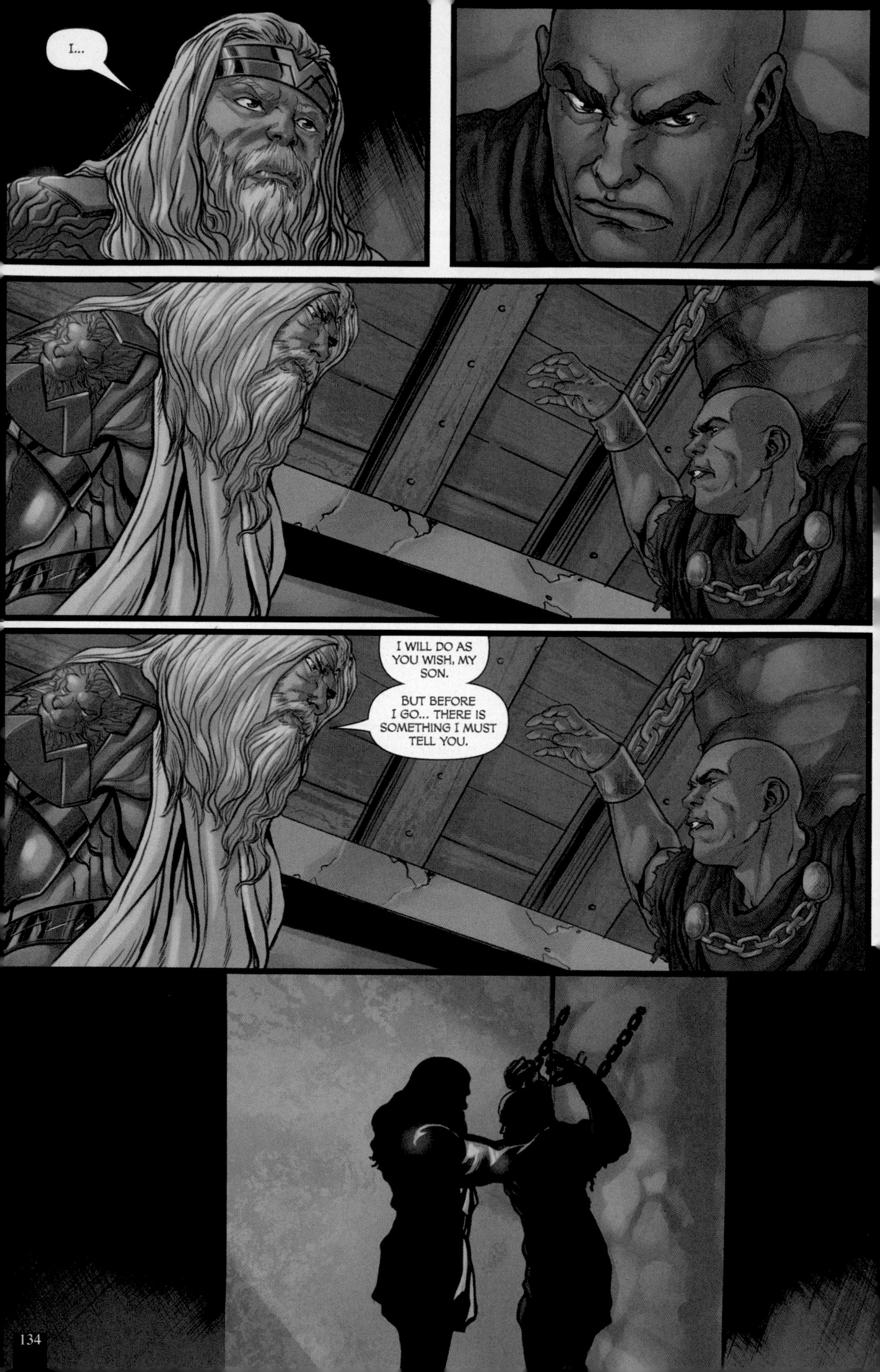
I...
I WILL DO AS YOU WISH, MY SON.
BUT BEFORE I GO... THERE IS SOMETHING I MUST TELL YOU.

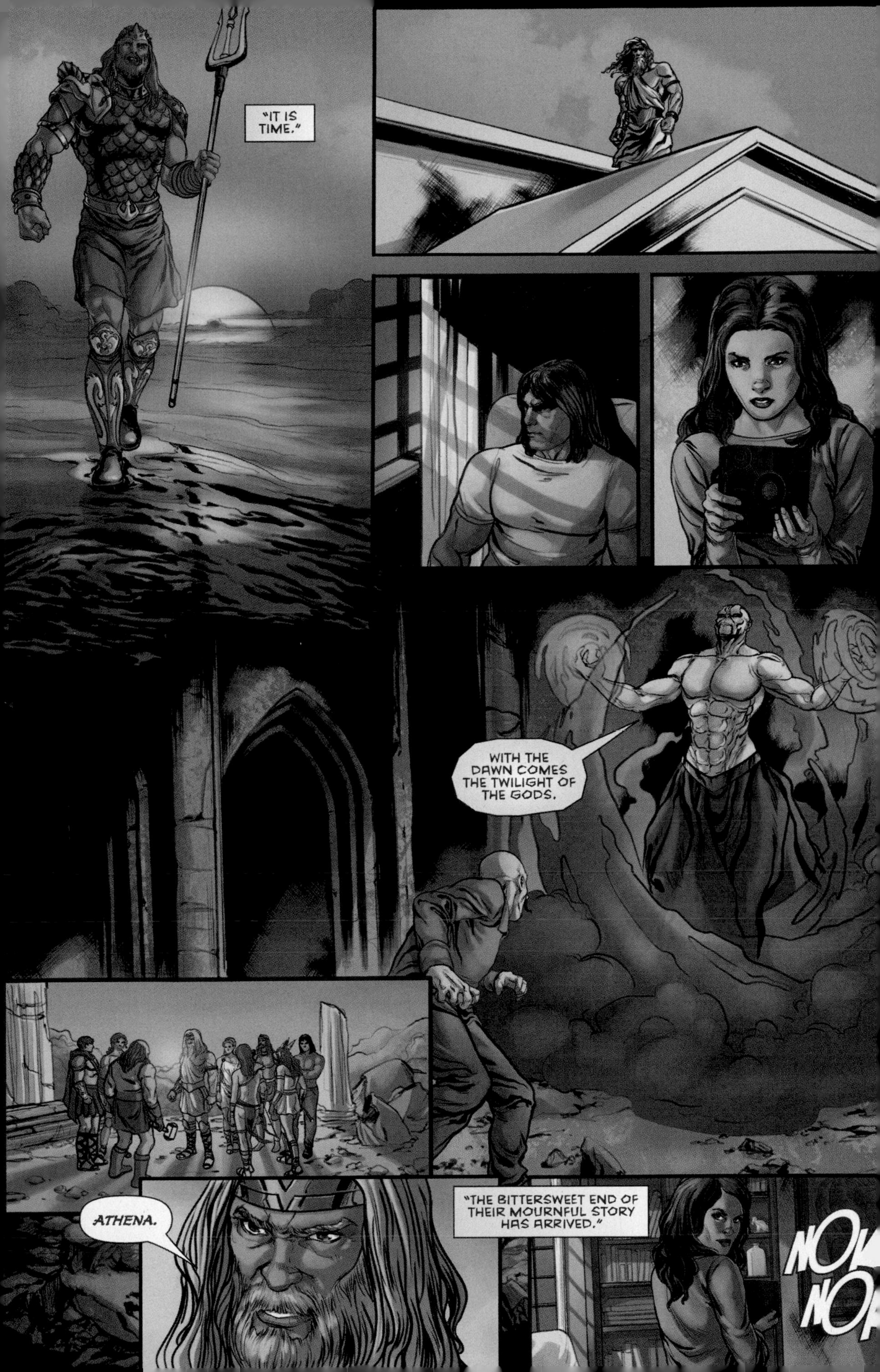
"IT IS TIME."
WITH THE DAWN COMES THE TWILIGHT OF THE GODS.
ATHENA.
"THE BITTERSWEET END OF THEIR MOURNFUL STORY HAS ARRIVED."

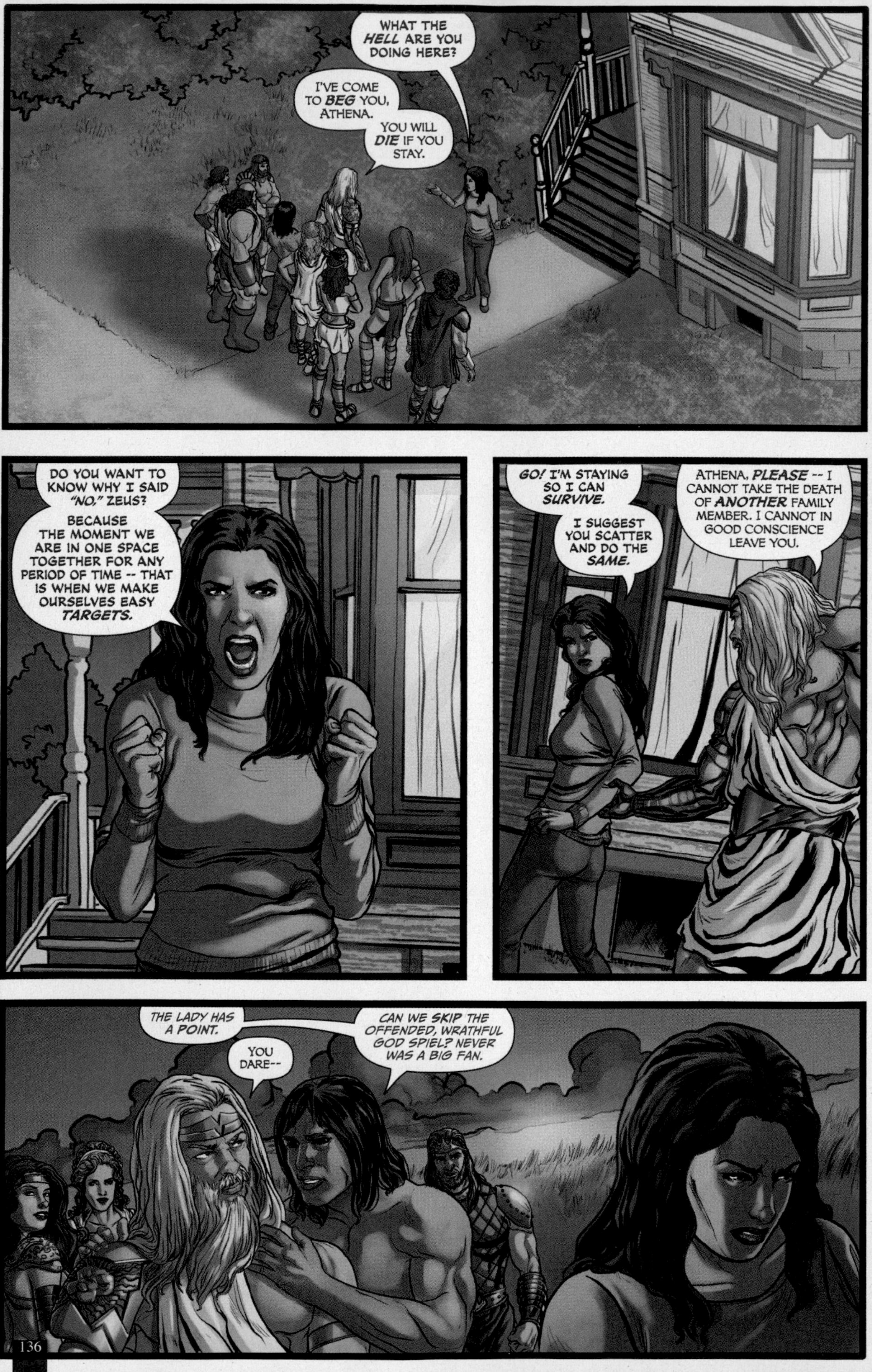
WHAT THE HELL ARE YOU DOING HERE?
I'VE COME TO BEG YOU, ATHENA.
YOU WILL DIE IF YOU STAY.
DO YOU WANT TO KNOW WHY I SAID "NO," ZEUS?
BECAUSE THE MOMENT WE ARE IN ONE SPACE TOGETHER FOR ANY PERIOD OF TIME -- THAT IS WHEN WE MAKE OURSELVES EASY TARGETS.
ATHENA, PLEASE -- I CANNOT TAKE THE DEATH OF ANOTHER FAMILY MEMBER. I CANNOT IN GOOD CONSCIENCE LEAVE YOU.
GO! I'M STAYING SO I CAN SURVIVE.
I SUGGEST YOU SCATTER AND DO THE SAME.
THE LADY HAS A POINT.
YOU DARE--
CAN WE SKIP THE OFFENDED, WRATHFUL GOD SPIEL? NEVER WAS A BIG FAN.

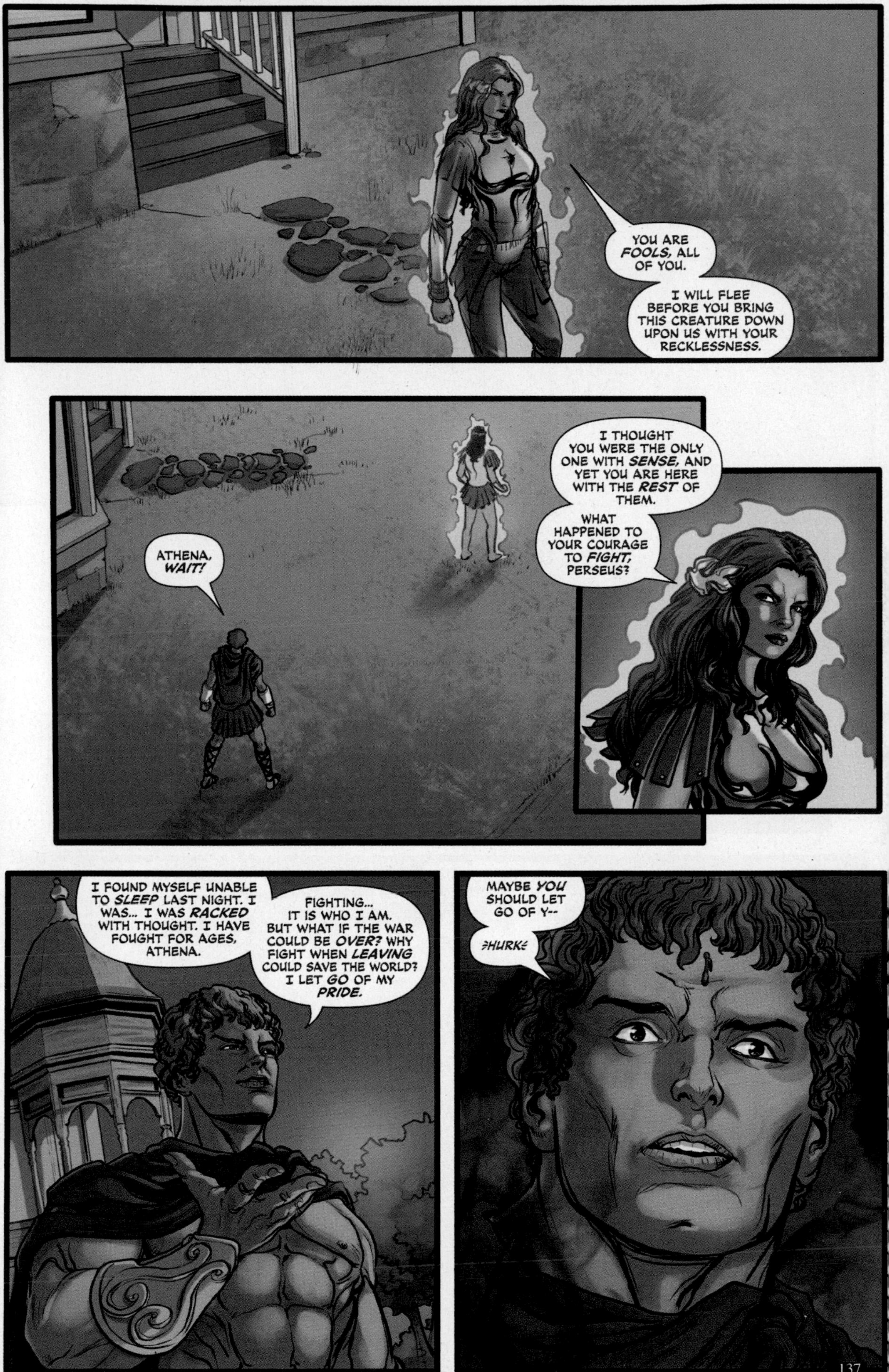
YOU ARE *FOOLS,* ALL OF YOU.
I WILL FLEE BEFORE YOU BRING THIS CREATURE DOWN UPON US WITH YOUR RECKLESSNESS.
ATHENA, *WAIT!*
I THOUGHT YOU WERE THE ONLY ONE WITH *SENSE,* AND YET YOU ARE HERE WITH THE *REST* OF THEM.
WHAT HAPPENED TO YOUR COURAGE TO *FIGHT,* PERSEUS?
I FOUND MYSELF UNABLE TO *SLEEP* LAST NIGHT. I WAS... I WAS *RACKED* WITH THOUGHT. I HAVE FOUGHT FOR AGES, ATHENA.
FIGHTING... IT IS WHO I AM. BUT WHAT IF THE WAR COULD BE *OVER?* WHY FIGHT WHEN *LEAVING* COULD SAVE THE WORLD? I LET *GO* OF MY *PRIDE.*
MAYBE *YOU* SHOULD LET GO OF Y--
HURK

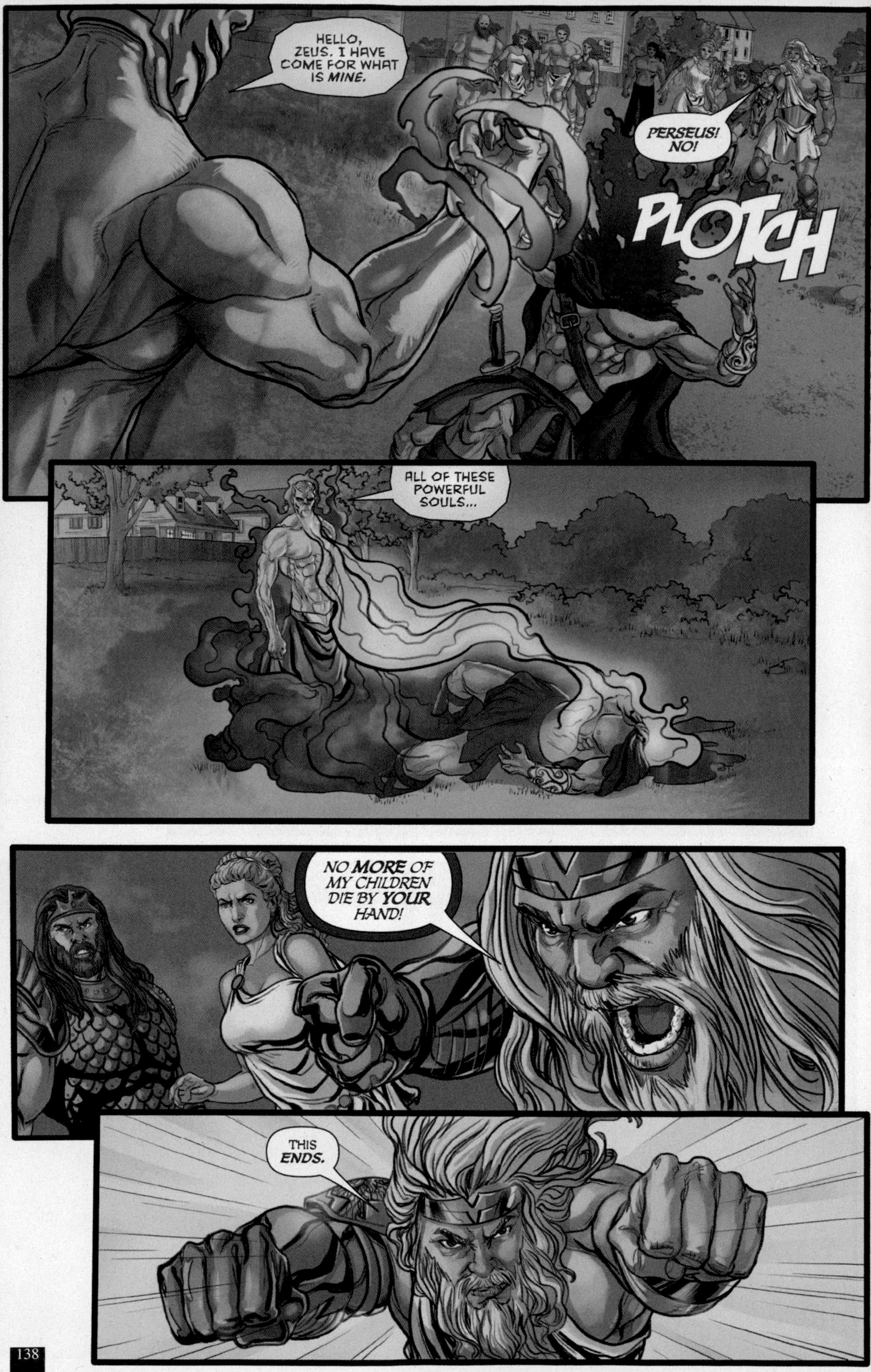
HELLO, ZEUS. I HAVE COME FOR WHAT IS *MINE.*
PERSEUS! NO!
PLOTCH
ALL OF THESE POWERFUL SOULS...
*NO **MORE** OF MY CHILDREN DIE BY **YOUR** HAND!*
THIS **ENDS.**

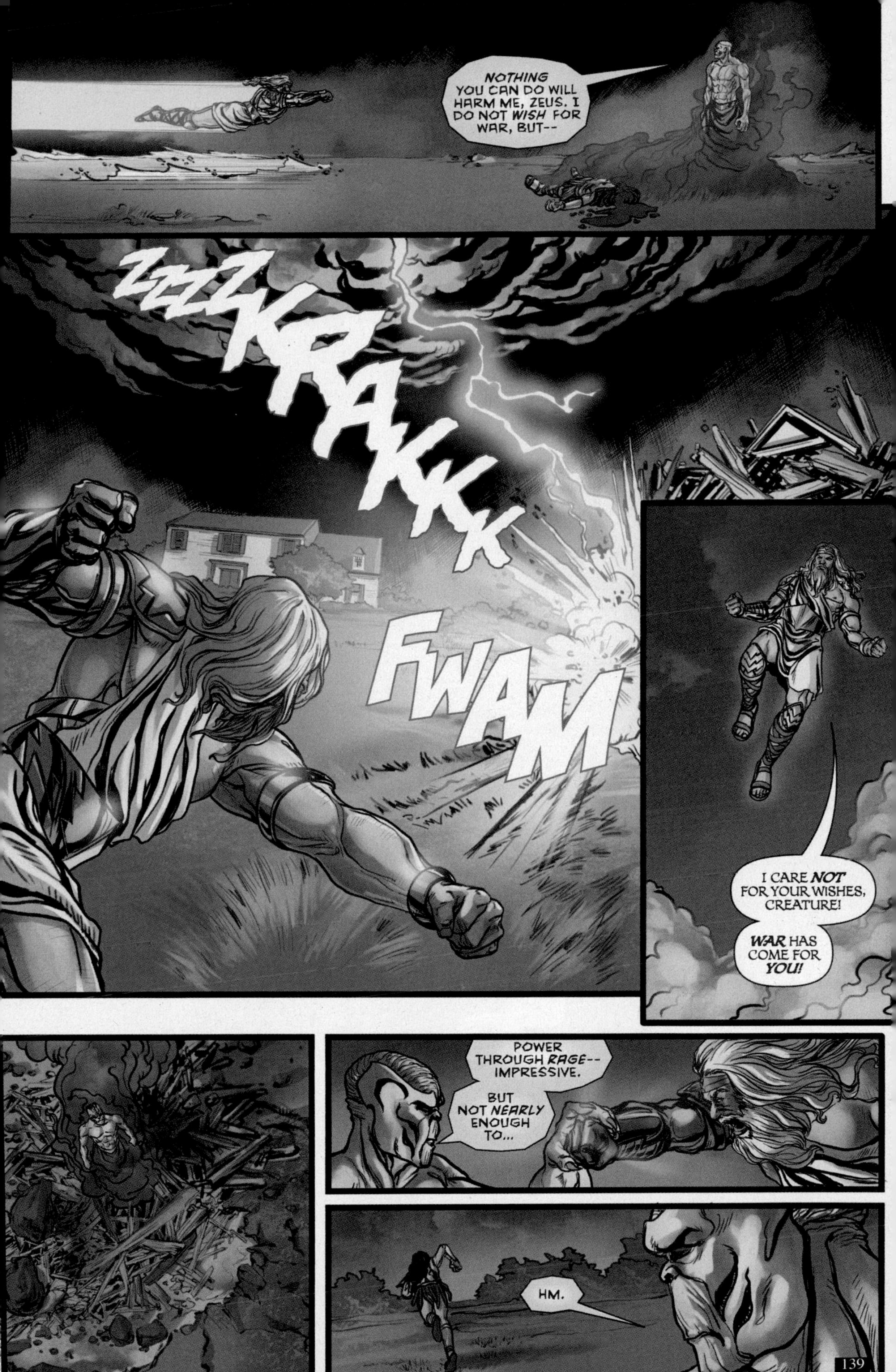
NOTHING YOU CAN DO WILL HARM ME, ZEUS. I DO NOT WISH FOR WAR, BUT--
ZZZZKRAKKKK
FWAM
I CARE NOT FOR YOUR WISHES, CREATURE!
WAR HAS COME FOR YOU!
POWER THROUGH RAGE-- IMPRESSIVE.
BUT NOT NEARLY ENOUGH TO...
HM.

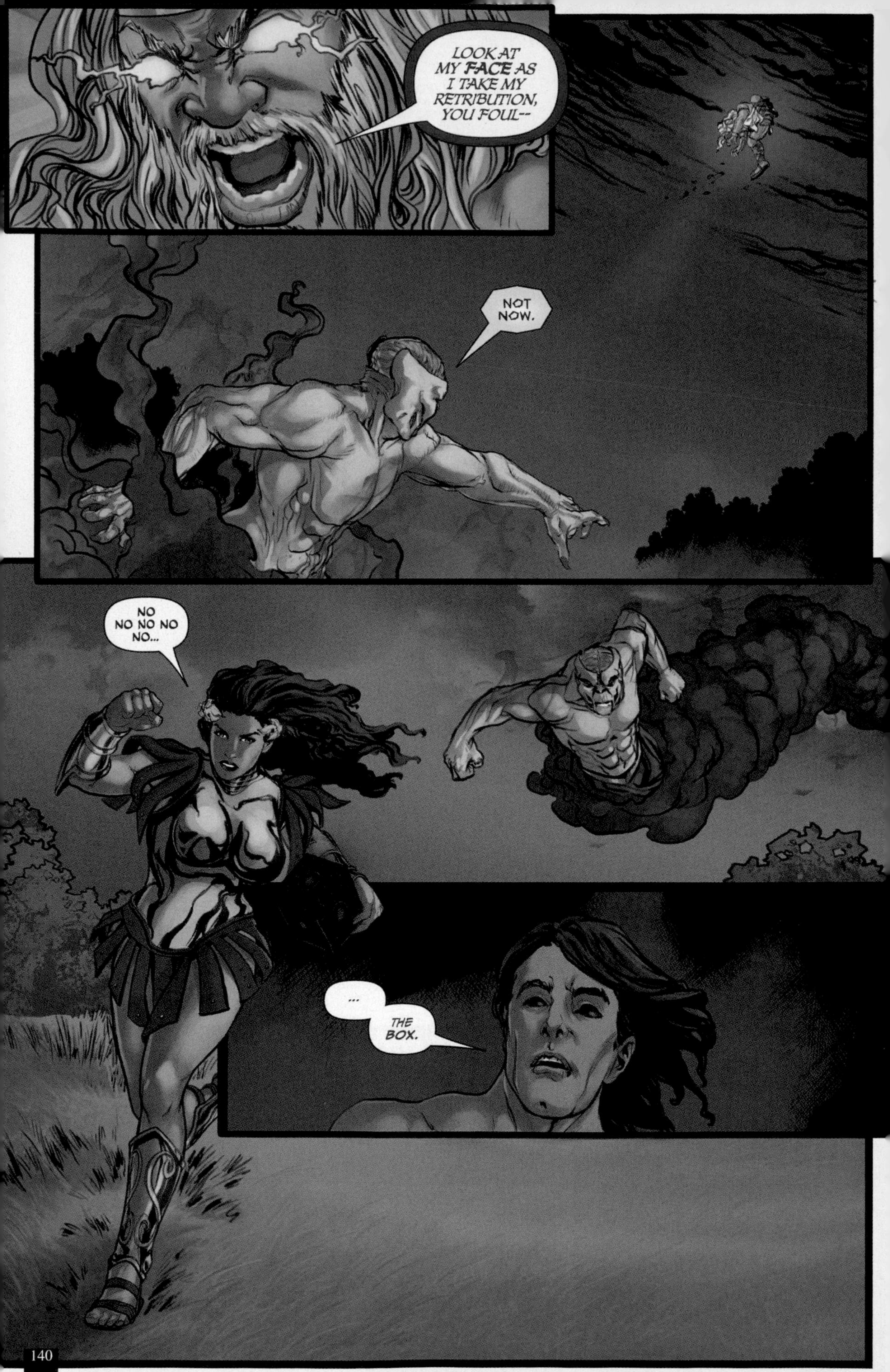
LOOK AT MY FACE AS I TAKE MY RETRIBUTION, YOU FOUL--
NOT NOW.
NO NO NO NO NO...
...
THE BOX.

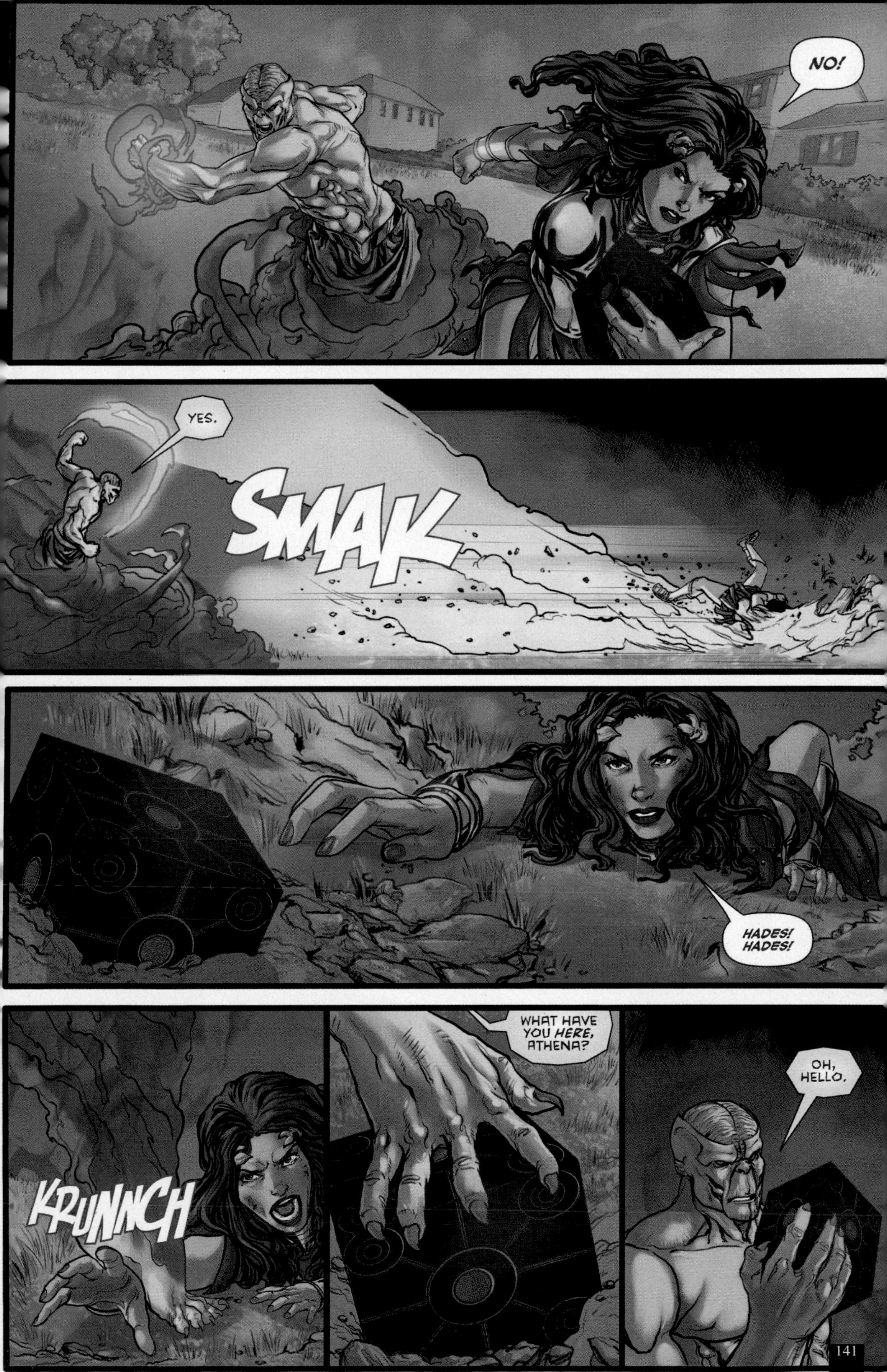
NO!
YES.
SMAK
HADES! HADES!
KRUNNCH
WHAT HAVE YOU HERE, ATHENA?
OH, HELLO.

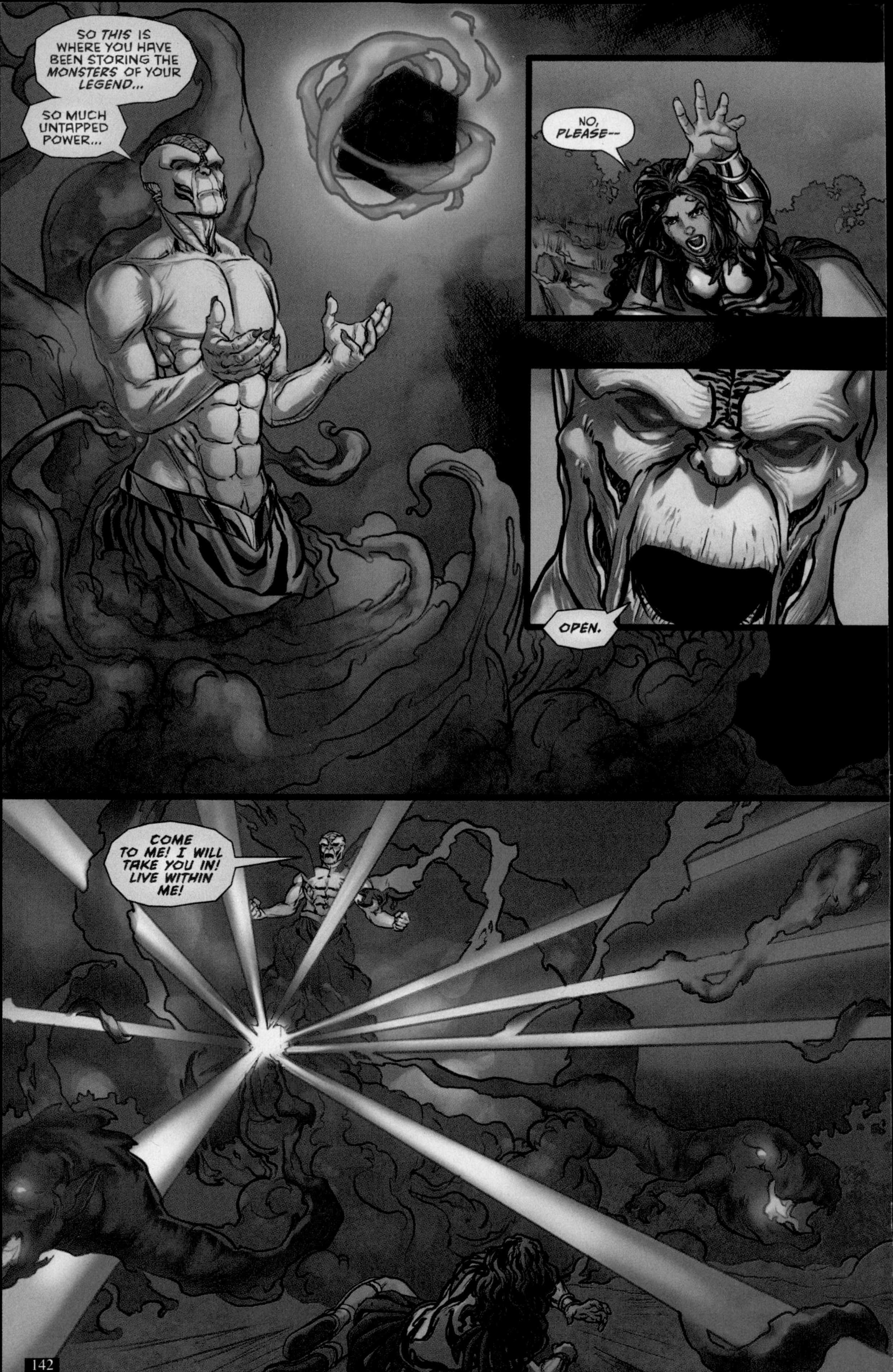
SO THIS IS WHERE YOU HAVE BEEN STORING THE MONSTERS OF YOUR LEGEND...
SO MUCH UNTAPPED POWER...
NO, PLEASE--
OPEN.
COME TO ME! I WILL TAKE YOU IN! LIVE WITHIN ME!

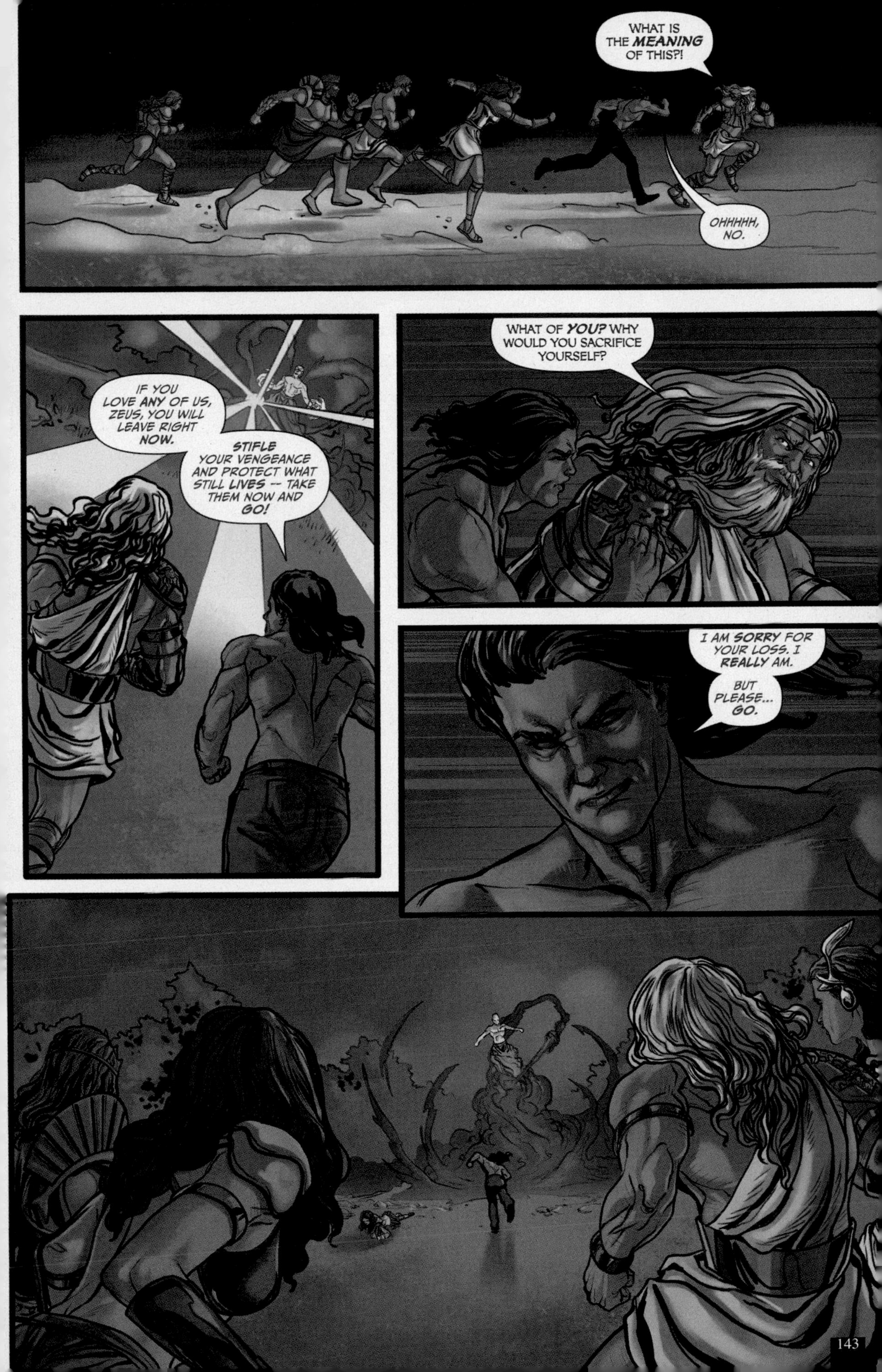
WHAT IS THE MEANING OF THIS?!
OHHHHH, NO.
IF YOU LOVE ANY OF US, ZEUS, YOU WILL LEAVE RIGHT NOW.
STIFLE YOUR VENGEANCE AND PROTECT WHAT STILL LIVES -- TAKE THEM NOW AND GO!
WHAT OF YOU? WHY WOULD YOU SACRIFICE YOURSELF?
I AM SORRY FOR YOUR LOSS. I REALLY AM.
BUT PLEASE... GO.

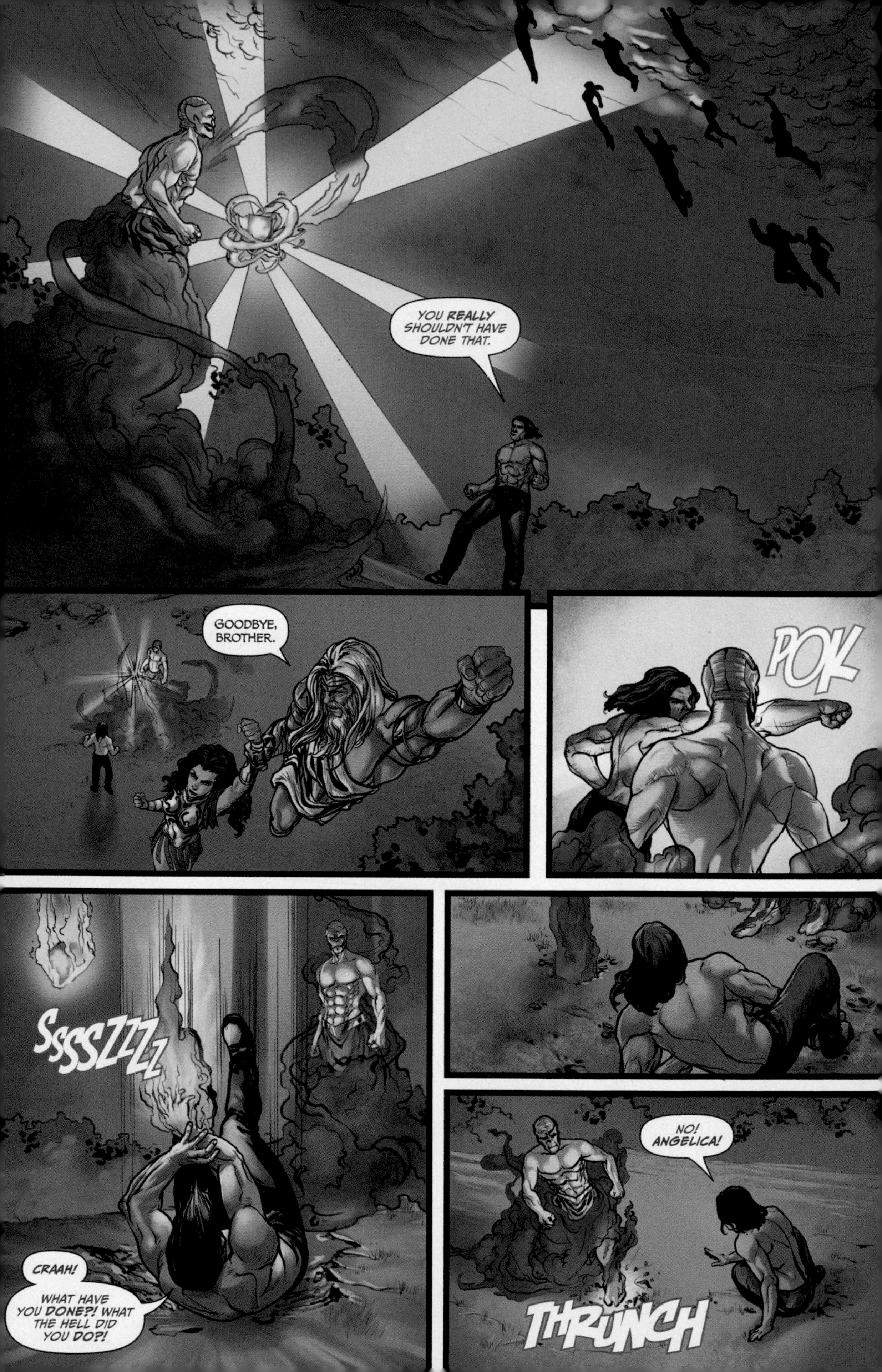
YOU REALLY SHOULDN'T HAVE DONE THAT.
GOODBYE, BROTHER.
POK
SSSSZZZZ
CRAAH!
WHAT HAVE YOU DONE?! WHAT THE HELL DID YOU DO?!
NO! ANGELICA!
THRUNCH

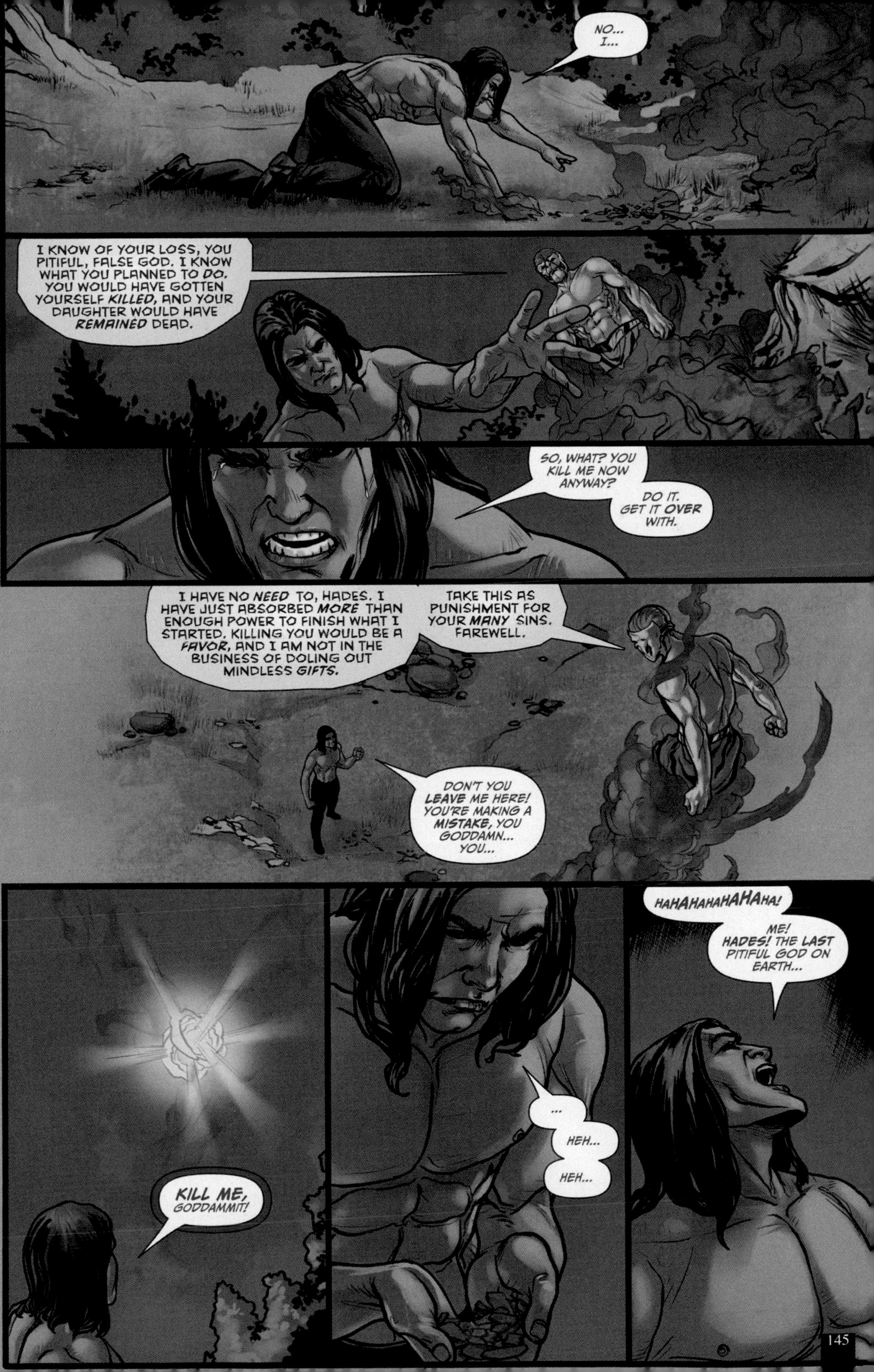
NO... I...
I KNOW OF YOUR LOSS, YOU PITIFUL, FALSE GOD. I KNOW WHAT YOU PLANNED TO DO. YOU WOULD HAVE GOTTEN YOURSELF KILLED, AND YOUR DAUGHTER WOULD HAVE REMAINED DEAD.
SO, WHAT? YOU KILL ME NOW ANYWAY?
DO IT. GET IT OVER WITH.
I HAVE NO NEED TO, HADES. I HAVE JUST ABSORBED MORE THAN ENOUGH POWER TO FINISH WHAT I STARTED. KILLING YOU WOULD BE A FAVOR, AND I AM NOT IN THE BUSINESS OF DOLING OUT MINDLESS GIFTS.
TAKE THIS AS PUNISHMENT FOR YOUR MANY SINS. FAREWELL.
DON'T YOU LEAVE ME HERE! YOU'RE MAKING A MISTAKE, YOU GODDAMN... YOU...
KILL ME, GODDAMMIT!
...
HEH...
HEH...
HAHAHAHAHAHAHAHA!
ME! HADES! THE LAST PITIFUL GOD ON EARTH...

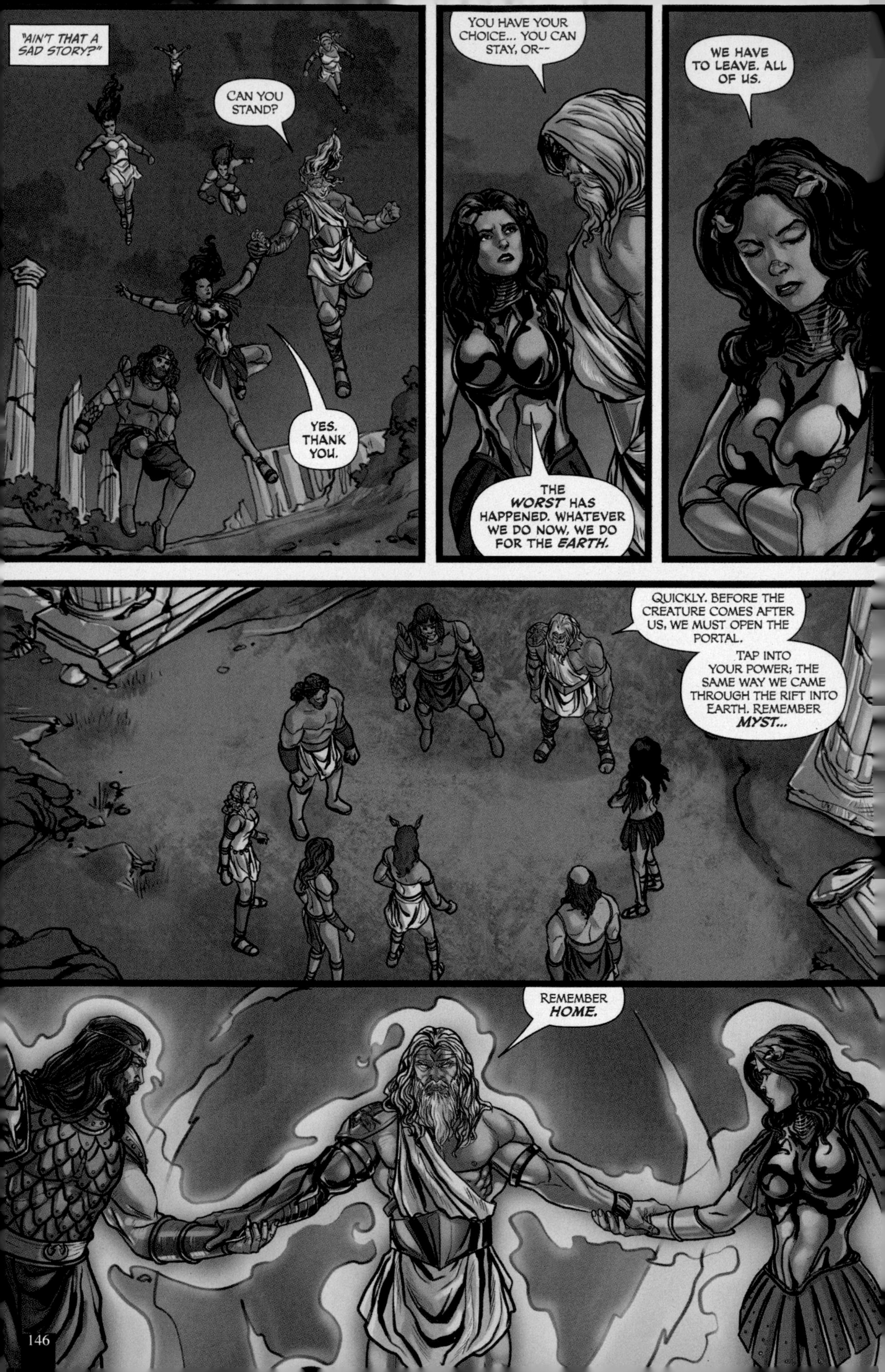
"AIN'T THAT A SAD STORY?"
CAN YOU STAND?
YES. THANK YOU.
YOU HAVE YOUR CHOICE... YOU CAN STAY, OR--
THE WORST HAS HAPPENED. WHATEVER WE DO NOW, WE DO FOR THE EARTH.
WE HAVE TO LEAVE. ALL OF US.
QUICKLY. BEFORE THE CREATURE COMES AFTER US, WE MUST OPEN THE PORTAL.
TAP INTO YOUR POWER; THE SAME WAY WE CAME THROUGH THE RIFT INTO EARTH. REMEMBER MYST...
REMEMBER HOME.

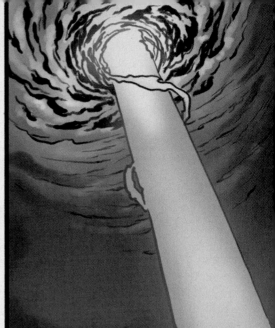

I watch the world disappear under my feet. I have loved and lost, and this... this feels like the **end** as much as it does a new beginning.

I quietly say **good night** to the world I have come to know, and with it my son and daughter...

I cannot fathom the depth of the loss that bears down on me.

And yet... after centuries, despite war and death and insurmountable odds, I stand with the remains of my family. And I am **proud.**

I WISH TO THINK OF THIS AS A GLORIOUS RETURN... BUT WE HAVE LOST SO MUCH, ZEUS. LEAVING THE EARTH FEELS LIKE ONE LOSS TOO MANY.

WE **WILL** RETURN, MY BROTHER.

AND UNTIL THEN? WHAT WILL WE BECOME?

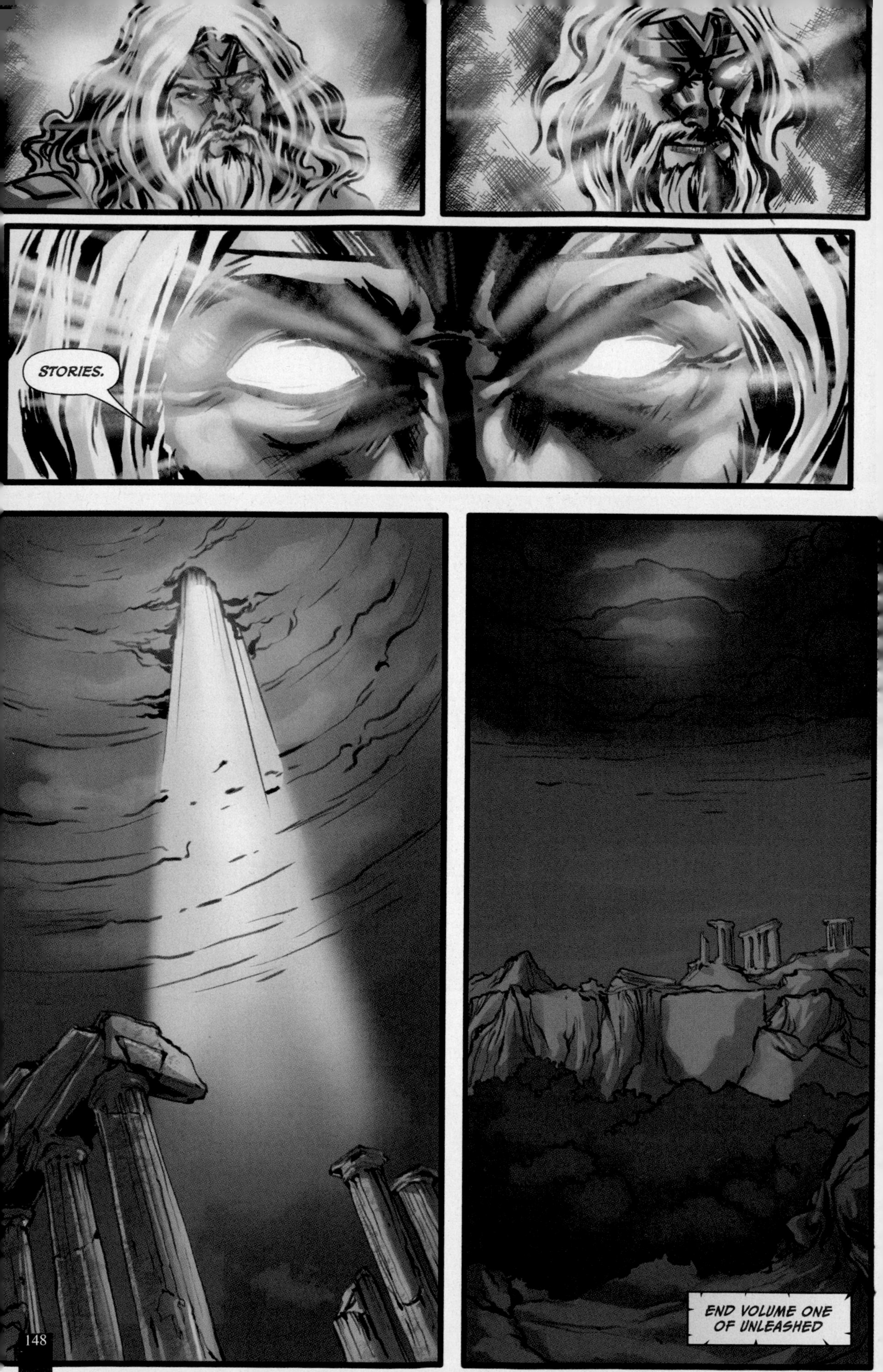
STORIES.
END VOLUME ONE OF UNLEASHED

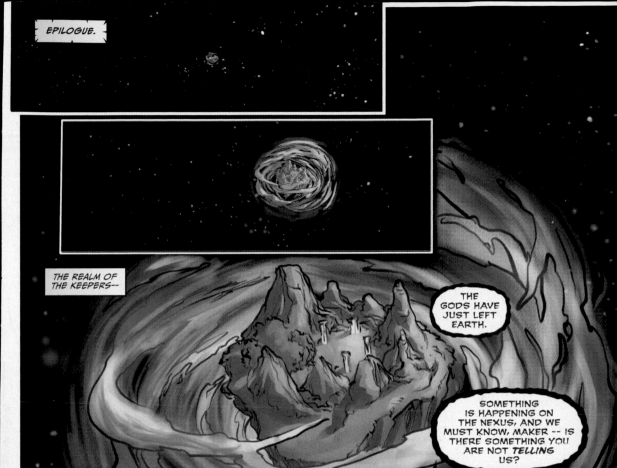

THE REALM OF THE KEEPERS--

THE GODS HAVE JUST LEFT EARTH.

SOMETHING IS HAPPENING ON THE NEXUS, AND WE MUST KNOW, MAKER -- IS THERE SOMETHING YOU ARE NOT *TELLING* US?

LOVE
Formerly Alice Liddle

CORRUPTION

THE INNOCENT

YOU BID US *WAIT*, BUT WE SEE NO CHANGE IN THE SITUATION.

IT IS NOT PERMITTED FOR ONE KEEPER TO WITHHOLD INFORMATION FROM ANOTHER...

HATE
Formerly Venus, the goddess of love.

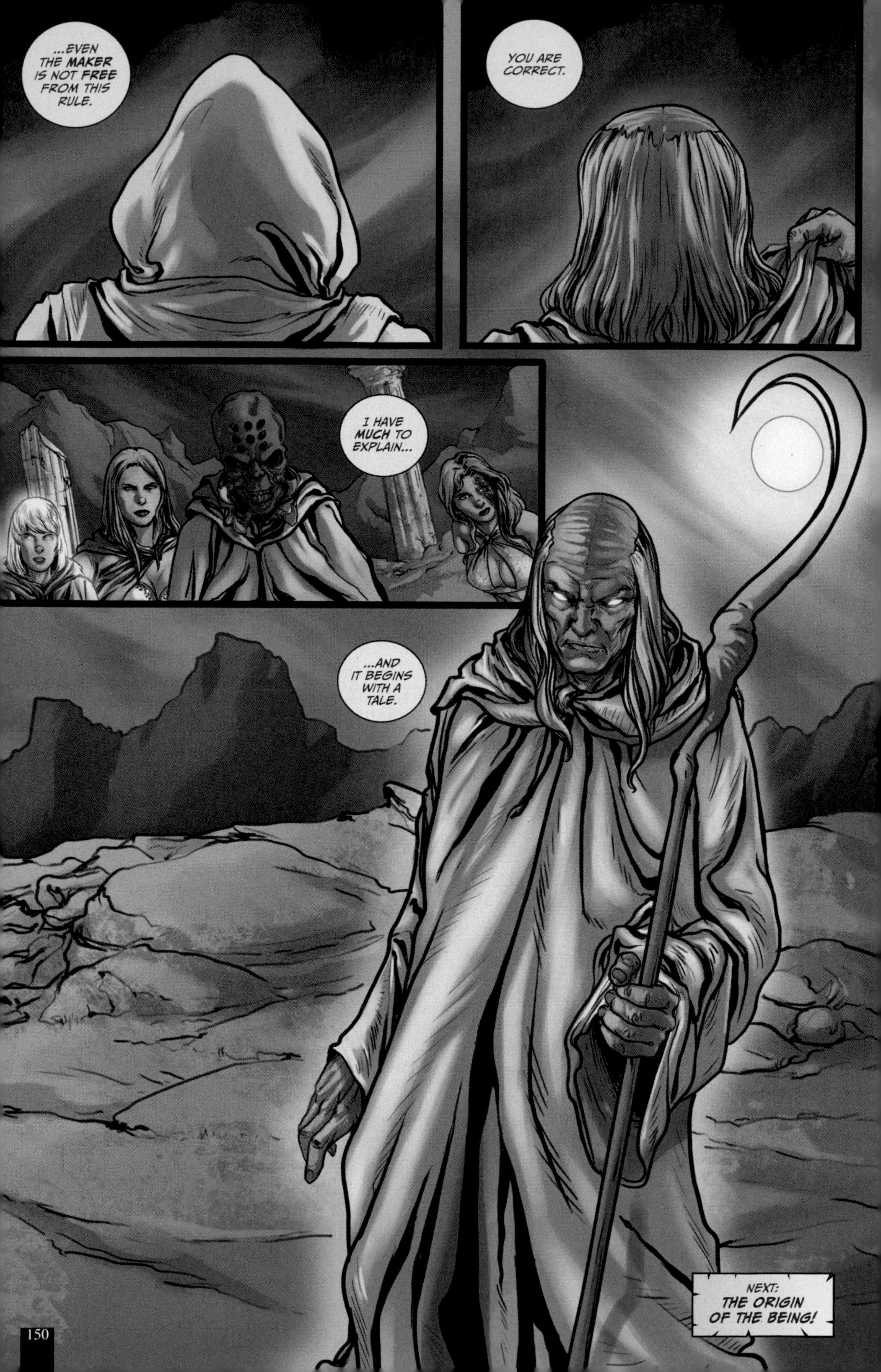
...EVEN THE **MAKER** IS NOT FREE FROM THIS RULE.
YOU ARE CORRECT.
I HAVE **MUCH** TO EXPLAIN...
...AND IT BEGINS WITH A TALE.
NEXT: **THE ORIGIN OF THE BEING!**

Grimm Fairy Tales
UNLEASHED

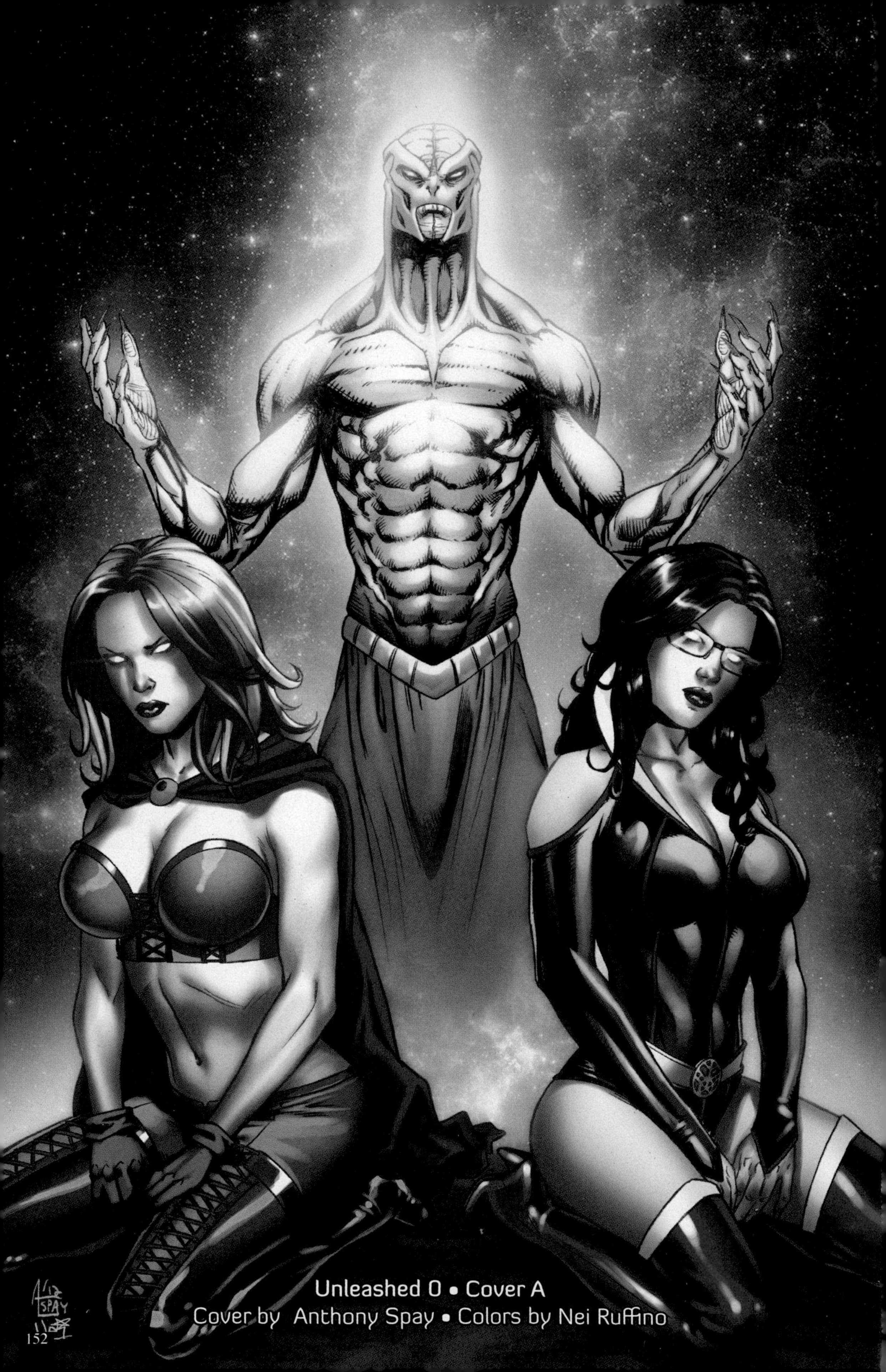

Unleashed 0 • Cover A
Cover by Anthony Spay • Colors by Nei Ruffino

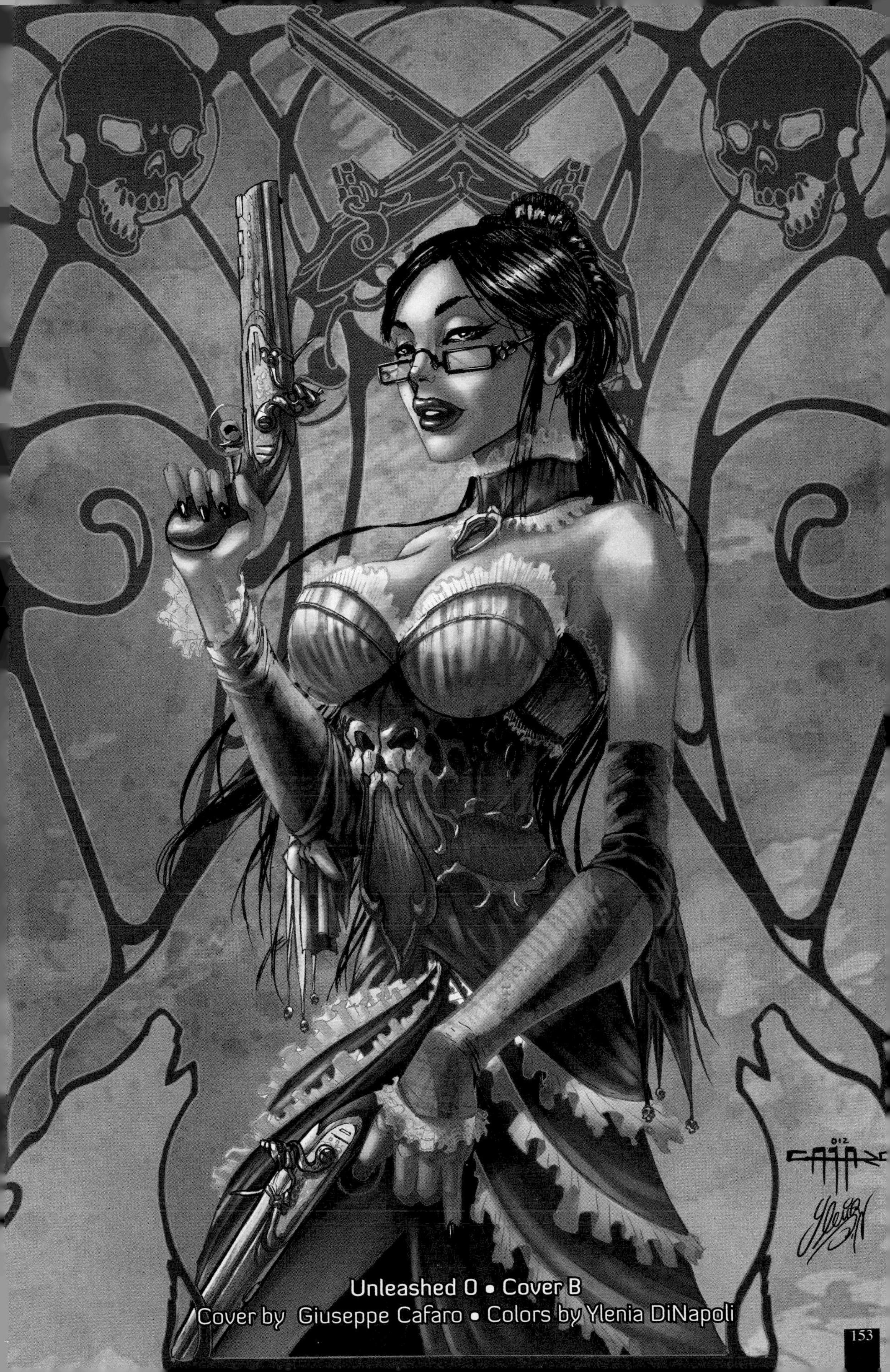

Unleashed 0 • Cover B
Cover by Giuseppe Cafaro • Colors by Ylenia DiNapoli

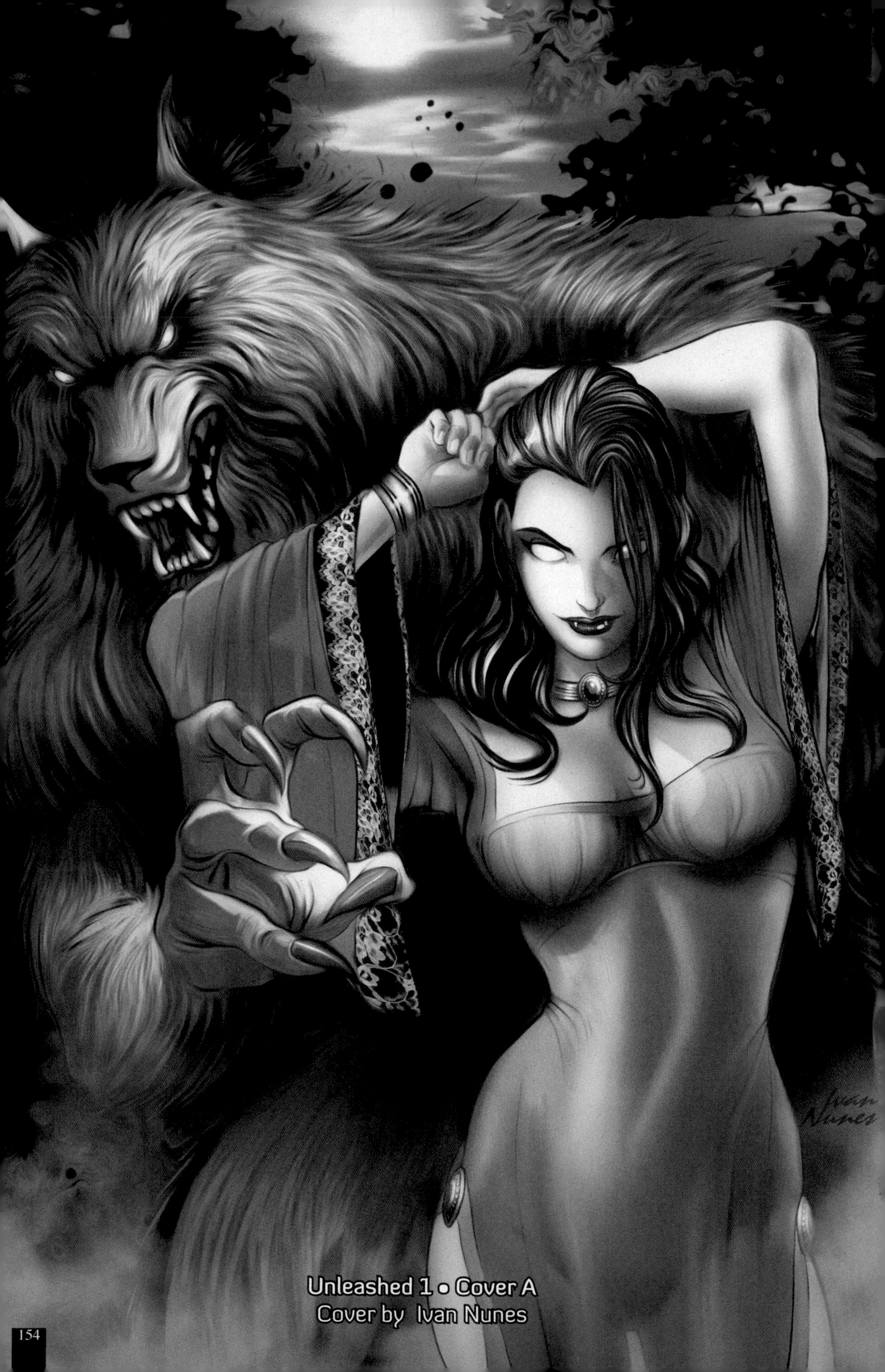
Ivan Nunes
Unleashed 1 • Cover A
Cover by Ivan Nunes

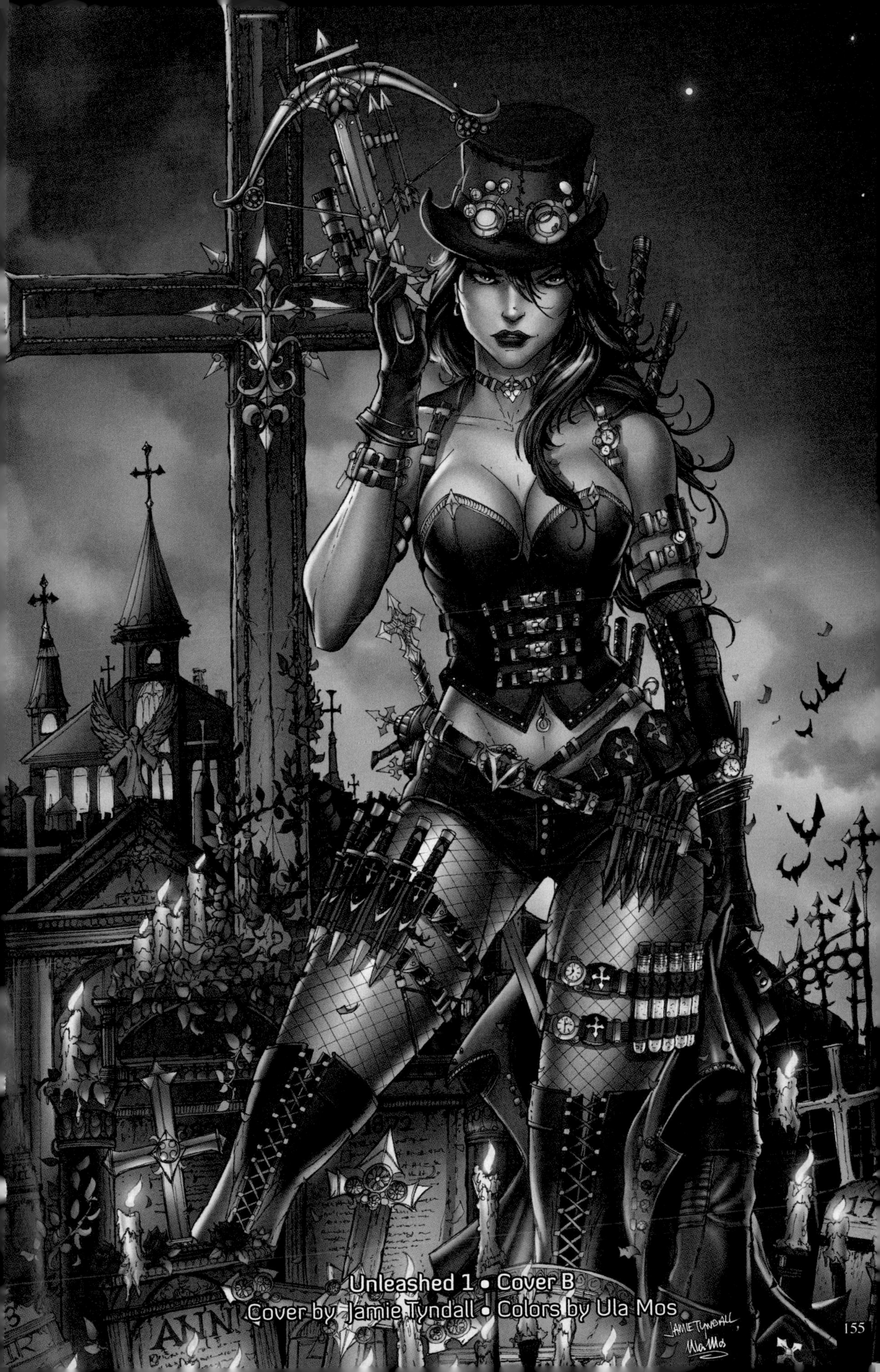

Unleashed 1 • Cover B
Cover by Jamie Tyndall • Colors by Ula Mos

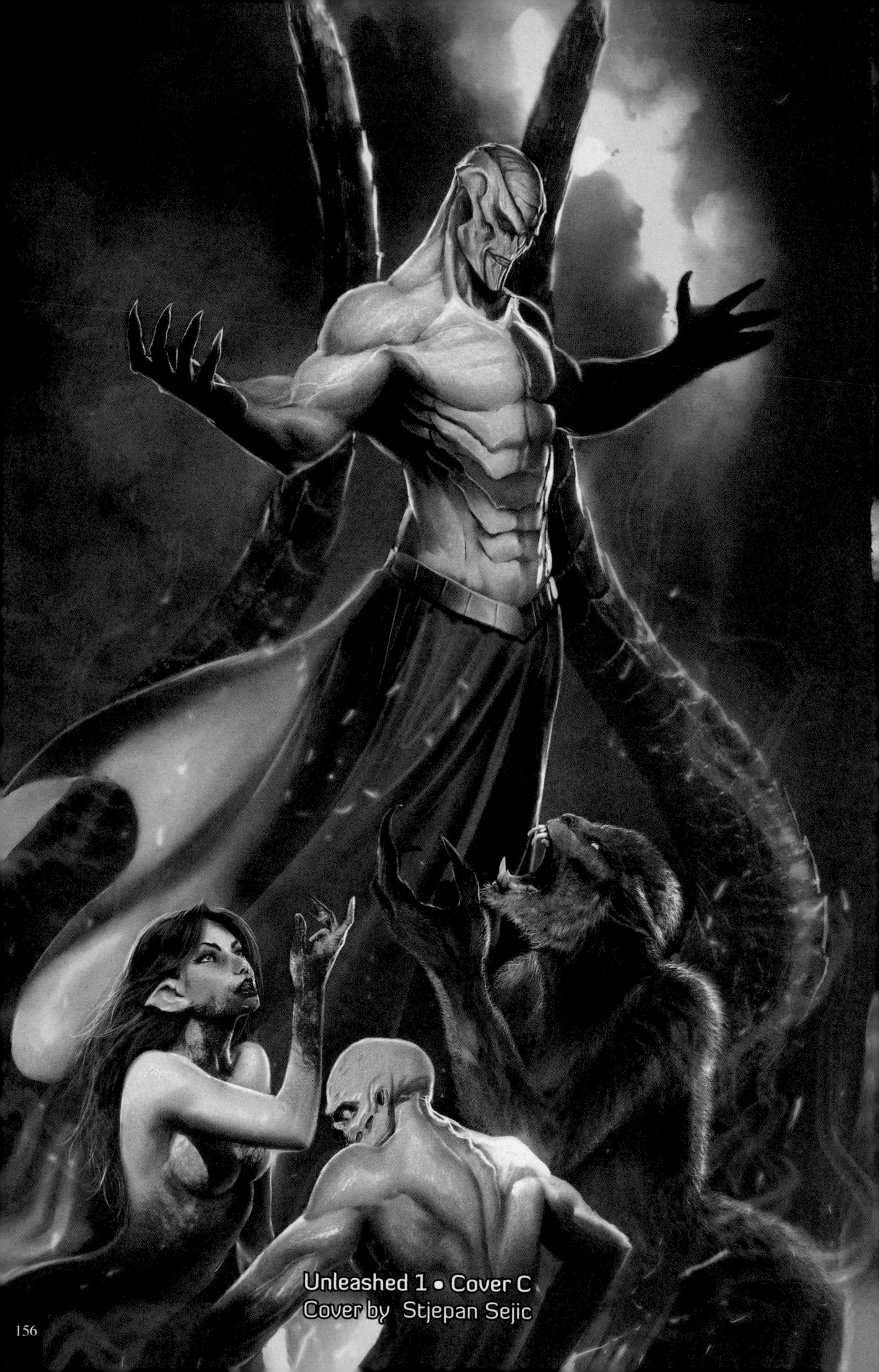
Unleashed 1 • Cover C
Cover by Stjepan Sejic

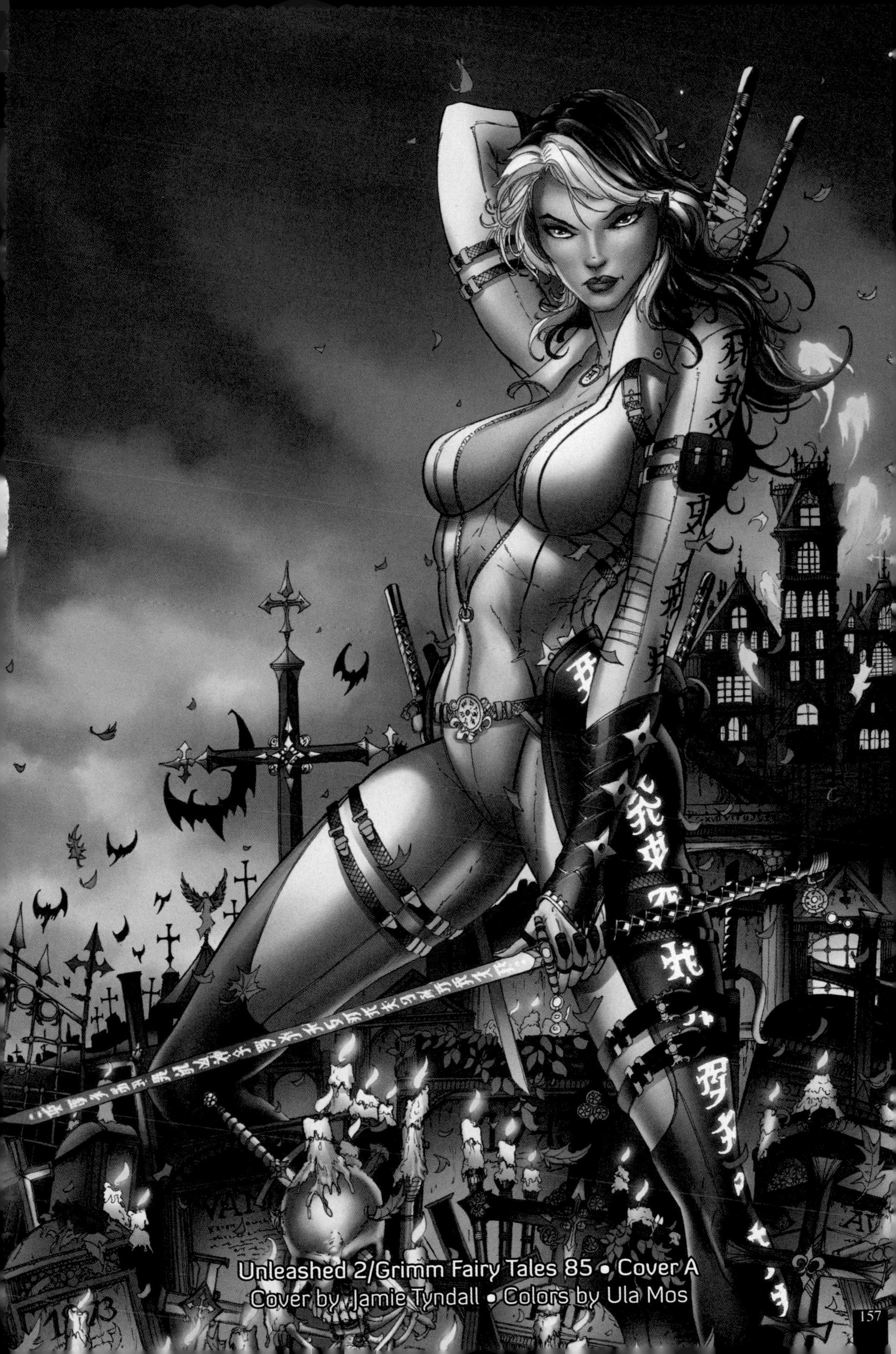

Unleashed 2/Grimm Fairy Tales 85 • Cover A
Cover by Jamie Tyndall • Colors by Ula Mos

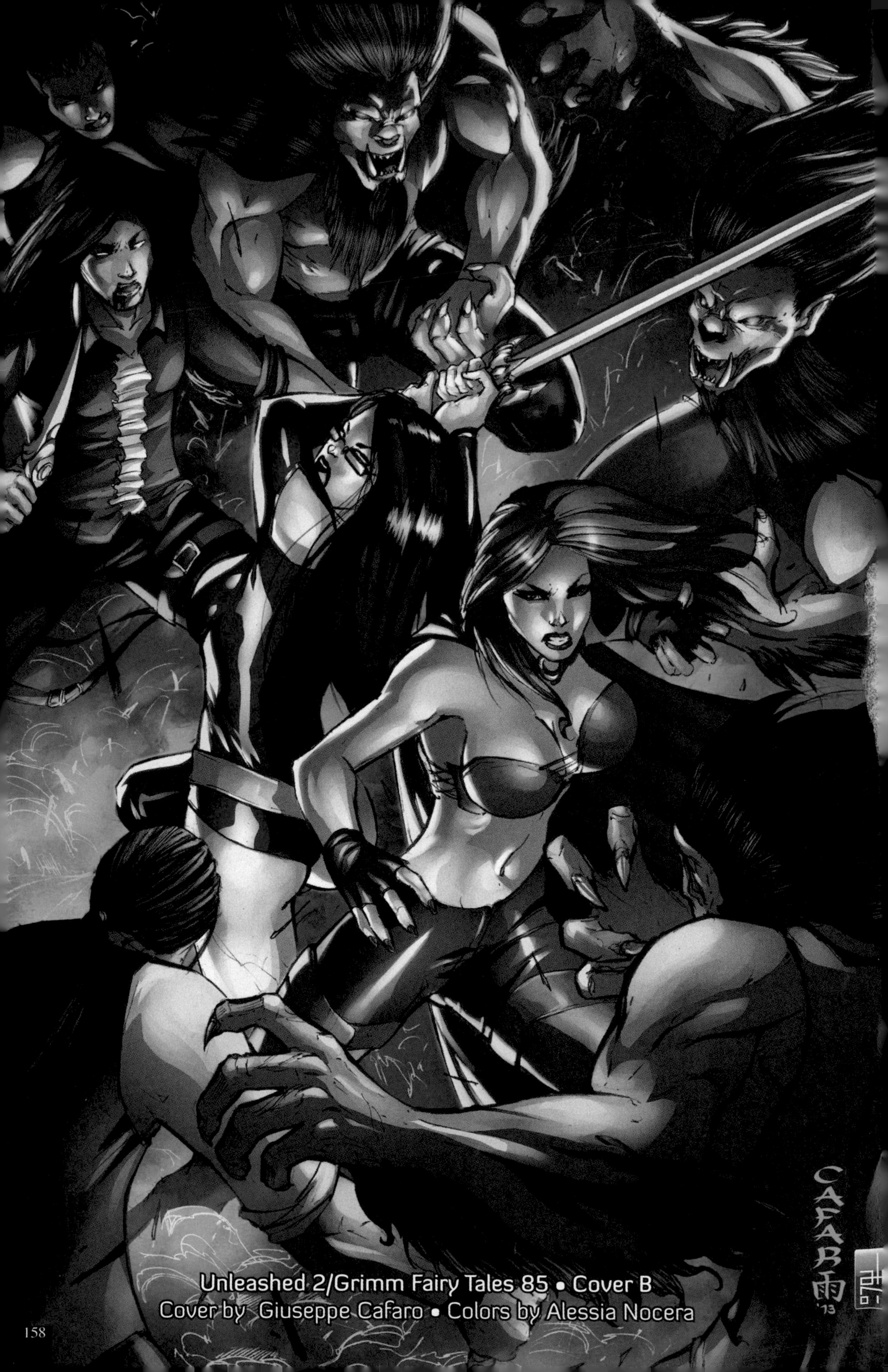
CAFARO
'13

Unleashed 2/Grimm Fairy Tales 85 • Cover B
Cover by Giuseppe Cafaro • Colors by Alessia Nocera

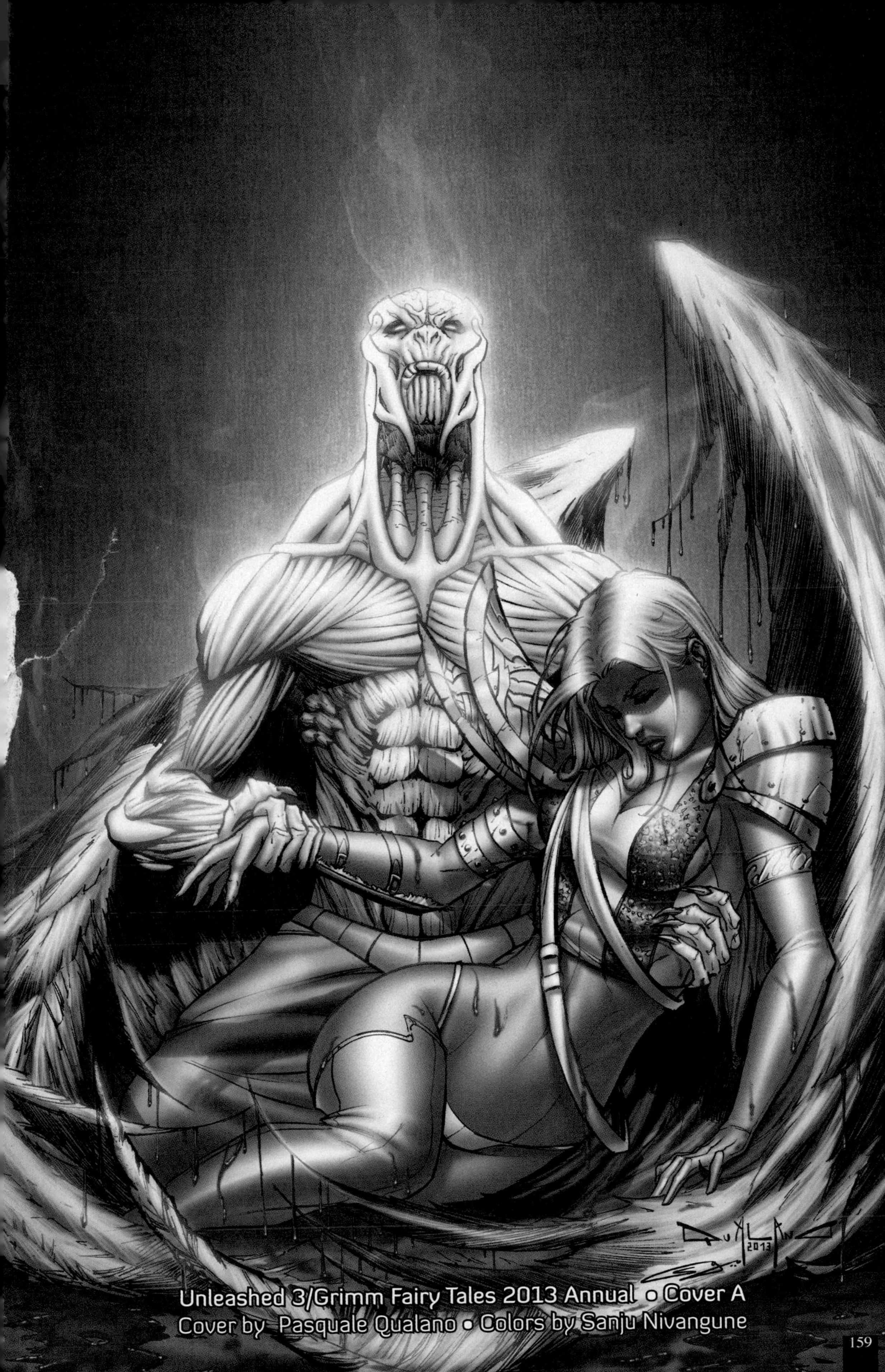

Unleashed 3/Grimm Fairy Tales 2013 Annual • Cover A
Cover by Pasquale Qualano • Colors by Sanju Nivangune

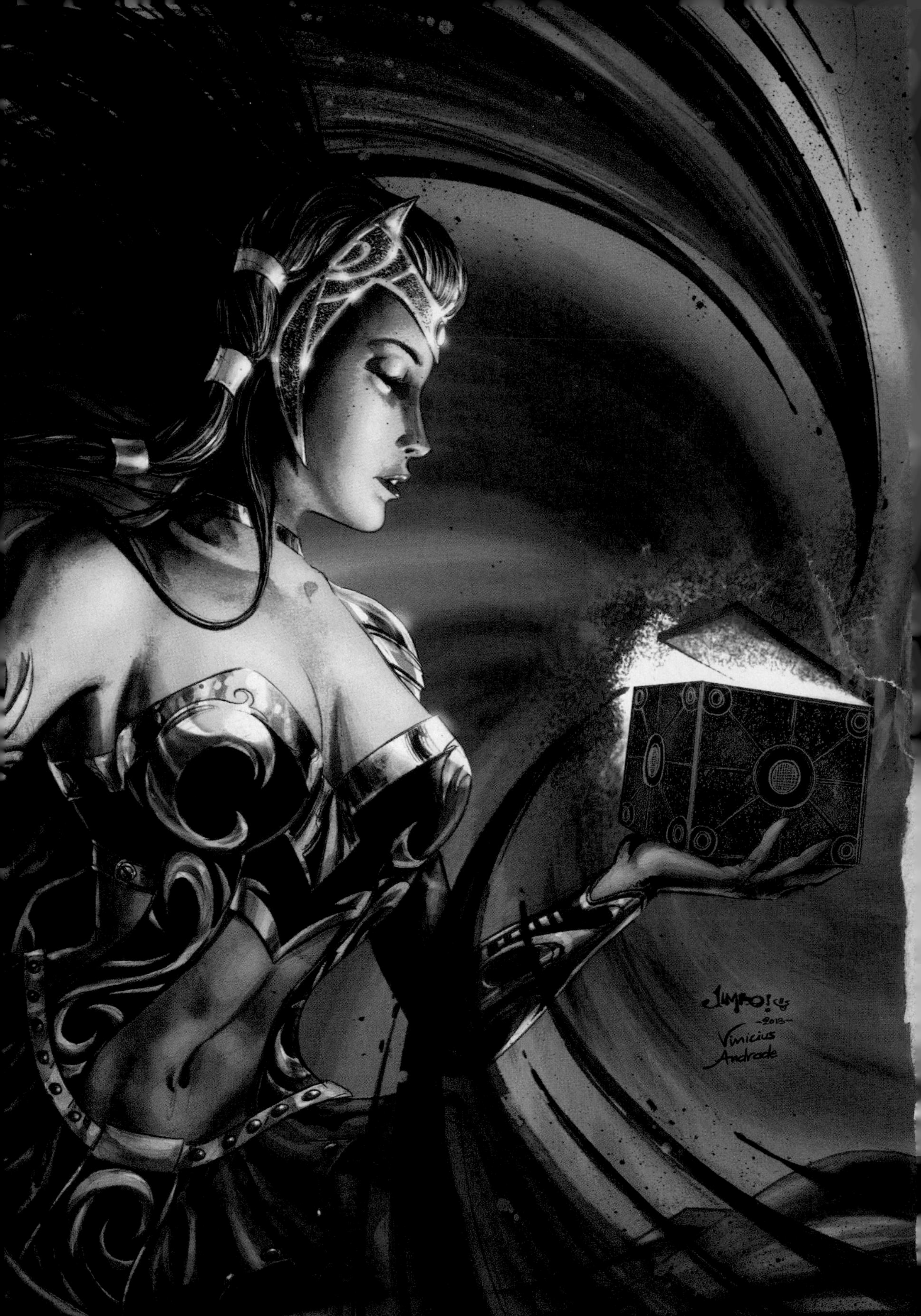
JIMBO!
2013
Vinicius Andrade

Unleashed 3/Grimm Fairy Tales 2013 Annual • Cover B
Cover by Jimbo Salgado • Colors by Vinicius Andrade

Grimm Fairy Tales
UNLEASHED

Hunters

Before Sela began using fairy tales to help people make important decisions, she fought alongside four monster hunters. These are their stories.

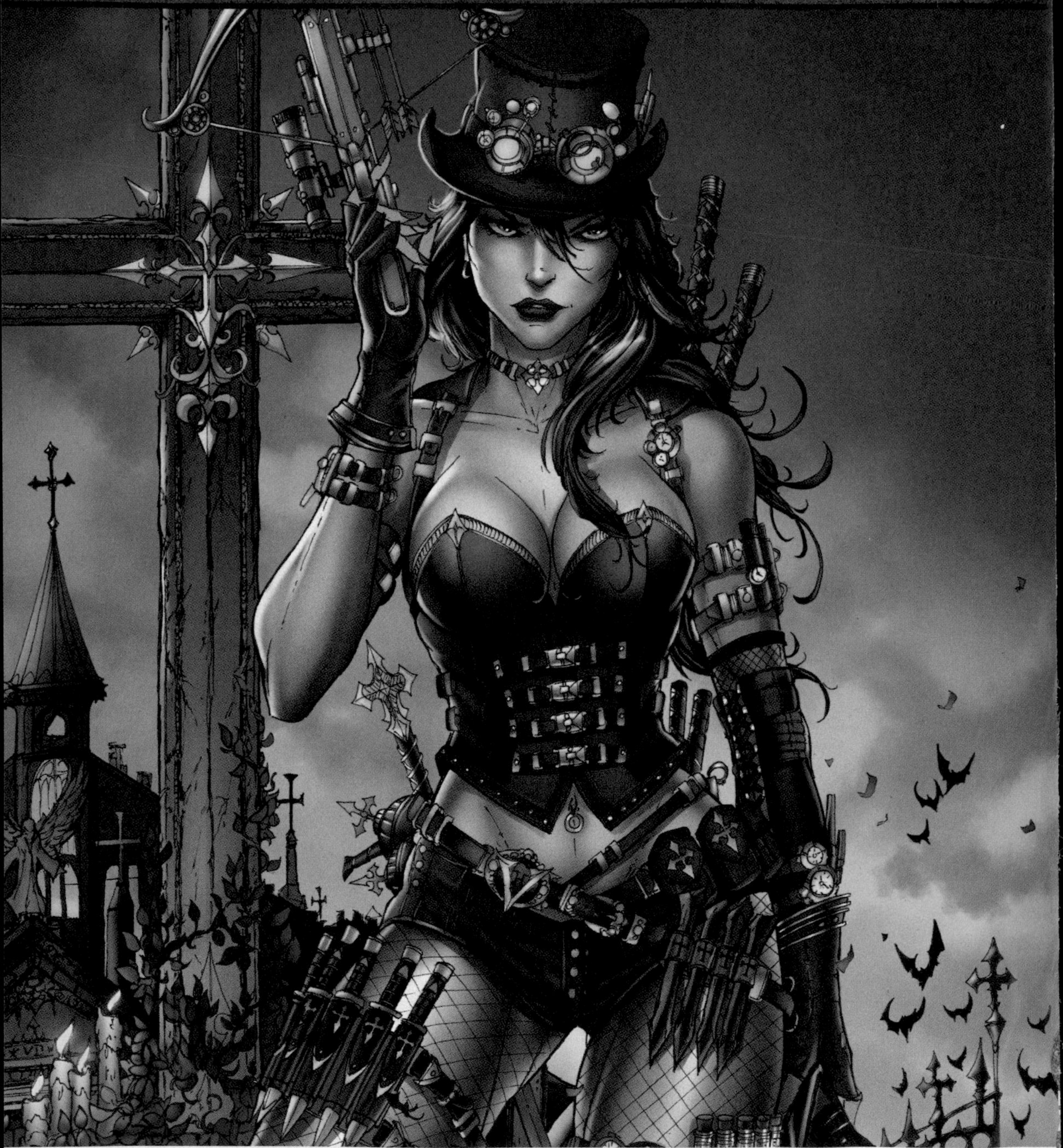

Liesel Van Helsing

Daughter of the famed vampire hunter Abraham Van Helsing, Liesel is the best there is. Possessing an even more innovative mind than her father, Helsing is known for her steam-powered inventions and contraptions that she uses to hunt and vanquish vampires and other supernatural threats. Liesel is one of Sela's most trusted friends, and with the impending struggle ahead, the two will likely find themselves fighting side by side.

Roman

Roman is a werewolf hunter... and he's damn good at it. He's also a bit of a loner and a man of few words — but when he does speak, it's usually to throw insults at those around him. In Roman's world, there's no such thing as compromise. While some find his tactics extreme and risky, others would call them necessary. The way Roman looks at it, sometimes in order to beat a monster, you must become one.

Masumi

Descending from a long line of assassins, Masumi was raised as a weapon. She has a deep knowledge of witchcraft and demonic lore. Simply put, she possesses the state of mind it takes to be a warrior. Masumi has seen everyone that she has loved perish in their war against demons, so she is careful to not allow herself to get too close to others. Aside from her immense skill in martial arts and witchcraft, Masumi's swords are also a great asset. Both of her blades are imbued with the essence of a powerful demon, which allows her to teleport, open portals, and understand demonic languages.

Elijah

Sold into slavery as a child, Elijah spent most of his life never knowing freedom. Even after he escaped the cane fields and his sadistic master, he found himself caught in the middle of a battle between the hunters and hordes of horrific creatures. Though it is unknown why he chose to fight by their sides instead of fleeing, Elijah was banished to the Shadowlands with the rest of the group. He became comrades with the Helsing, Masumi, Sela and Roman, but they would never know the truth of his history and how it weighs on him. Elijah has quickly learned to channel his anger into a weapon to use against the armies of undead that are rising up all over the world.

Falsebloods and Highborns

Highborns are powerful beings from the Realms of Power (Myst, Neverland, Wonderland, and Oz), and Falsebloods are those born with both human and Highborn blood. Many of them are embroiled in a war for control of Earth – the Nexus.

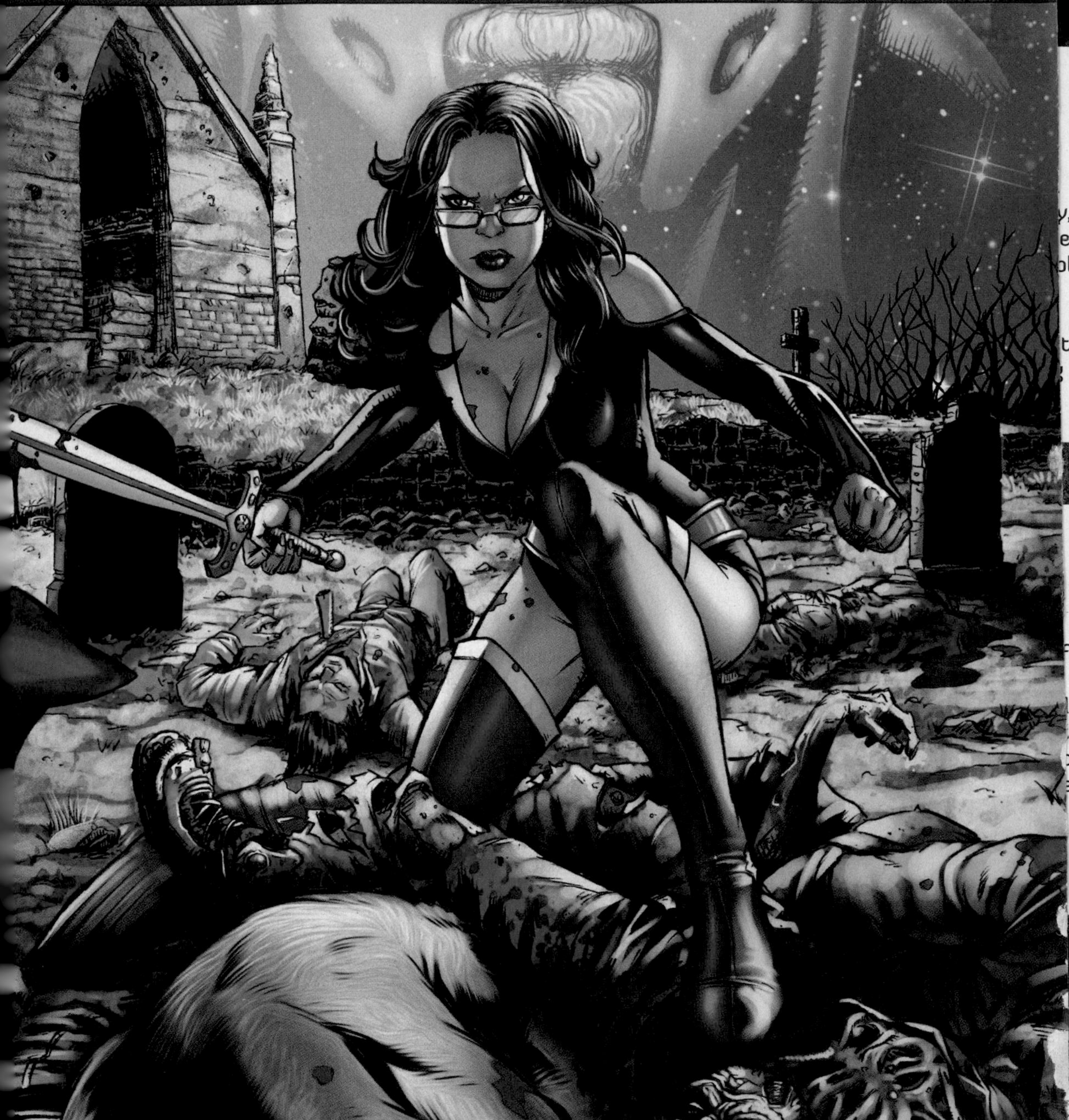

Sela Mathers

Sela Mathers, a powerful Falseblood, is the Guardian of the Earth. After years of using fairy tales to teach life lessons to people on the cusp of making immoral choices, Sela has taken a more active role in the wars between the Realms. She has fought against the Dark One, the Dream Eater, and other creatures of unfathomable power. Sela is extremely skilled and well-equipped to take on any enemy who stands against her, but nothing will prepare her for the Being and his horrific plan.

Belinda

After years of manipulation, Belinda freed herself from the grasp of the Dark One's power and mind games. Though her life was defined by poor choices and wicked acts, she selflessly sacrificed her life for the greater good in the battle against the Dream Eater. Now mysteriously resurrected, Belinda will join her former arch-nemesis, Sela Mathers, and attempt to atone for her past. But how can someone who is responsible for so many deaths and evil acts hope to achieve redemption?

Samantha Darren

When Sela was trapped in the Realm of Myst, Samantha became the new Guardian of the Earth. Though Sela has returned to Earth, Samantha continues to fight and act as the Guardian of the Nexus. However, a recent string of failures has led Samantha to question herself. While Sela and Belinda will take an active role in hunting the Being, it is up to Samantha to gather the Hunters and lead the resistance against the droves of monsters that threaten the Nexus... but is she up to the challenge?

Ilys

Stolen from her real mother, Sela, at birth, Ilys was raised by the evil VENUS, the goddess of beauty and deception. Raised to think that Sela is nothing more than a threat to her safety, Ilys lived in ignorance to Venus' wicked scheme. With Venus murdered by the Being, Ilys is left motherless — and her hatred of Sela continues to fester as she is unwillingly mixed up in the battle between good and evil.

Grimm Fairy Tales
UNLEASHED